Praise for Robert Creeley

"In over thirty years of publication Creeley has never sounded like anyone but himself—a rare achievement, and one which is possible only to an authentic voice, a voice constantly discovering the exact words it has need for."
—Denise Levertov

"Following the tradition of the classical storyteller, Creeley weaves an unending skein of relationships. . . . All are sensitive, deeply felt and minutely observed expositions of complex human emotions, with a fair amount of ribaldry and sexual revelry."—*Publishers Weekly*

"Genuine prose poetry."—M. L. Rosenthal, *New York Times*

"Creeley turns from continuity, structure, and plot as we know it toward 'that intimate, familiar, localizing, detailing, speculative, emotional, unending talking.' Indeed, talk is the fuel his fiction runs on and love is the spark that starts the machine; the driving's all stop and go, the road signs are ambiguous."
—*Library Journal*

SELECTED BOOKS BY ROBERT CREELEY

POETRY

Collected Poems: 1945-1975
Echoes
En Famille: A Poem
Just in Time: Poems 1984-1994
Life & Death
Memory Gardens
Selected Poems
So There: Poems 1976-1983
Windows

FICTION

Collected Prose

ESSAYS

Collected Essays

ROBERT CREELEY
Collected Prose

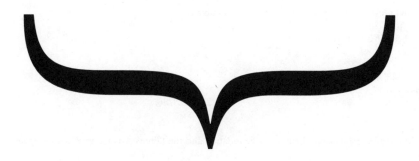

Introduction by the Author

Dalkey Archive Press

Originally published by Marion Boyars Inc., 1984
First paperback edition published by University of California, 1985
First Dalkey Archive edition, 2001

Sources

pp. 256-57 "Now if you are sitting opposite me . . . different from one's relationship to a person." Quoted from *The Divided Self,* by R. D. Laing (London: Penguin Books, 1965): 21.

p. 257 "The I, the I . . . Not the I . . ." Quoted from *Notebooks, 1914-1917,* by Ludwig Wittgenstein, trans. by G. E. M. Anscombe (New York: Harper & Row, 1969): 80.

Library of Congress Cataloging-in-Publication Data

Creeley, Robert, 1926-
  [Prose works]
  Collected prose / Robert Creeley.– 1st Dalkey Archive ed.
     p. cm.
  ISBN 1-56478-303-0 (acid-free paper)
   I. Title.

PS3505.R43 A15 2001
818'.5408–dc21
                                2001028786

Partially funded by grants from the Lannan Foundation and the Illinois Arts Council, a state agency.

Dalkey Archive Press books are published by the Center for Book Culture, a nonprofit organization with offices in Chicago and Normal, Illinois.

www.centerforbookculture.org

Contents

Introduction

INITIALLY I had thought that my work as a writer would be
primarily in prose and so *The Gold Diggers*, published by my
wife then and myself as The Divers Press in 1954, is the first
book of my own imagination despite three small collections
of poems preceding it. More to the point, however, is the fact
that I could never separate a writer's work into comfortable
categories and so was much irritated that Lawrence's
extraordinary poems were overlooked by the very people who
so approved his novels and stories—a circumstance much
magnified in the case of either Hardy or Melville. There was
a sense that if one did the one thing, one couldn't do the other.
And yet it was all a compact of words, surely—and I could
not believe that the literary form, so to speak, could so
determine the resources of maker or materials. In short, I
presumed a writer was a writer all the time, no matter the
instance necessity or choice had fixed upon.

Therefore I wish there were much more in this book than
there is. I always felt I was momently to write at least a
various *War and Peace* if not a purposeful one. I love Céline's
work and always have—likewise Stendhal, Dostoyevsky, and
increasingly Turgenev, of all people, e.g., that brilliantly
wandering two-part (in Constance Garnett's translation)
story, which begins with one small landowner's befriending of
another who's gone bankrupt and ends with a remarkable
grey horse, etc., etc. It is the story teller in that sense Walter
Benjamin has defined him in his essay of that name, which

I value—that intimate, familiar, localizing, detailing, speculative, emotional, unending talking that has given my life a way of thinking of itself in the very fact and feeling of existence. God knows one wants no end to that ever.

Most happy would be a reading and a reader who recognize that there is forever this need, to my own mind a very human one. It hardly matters that stories or poems are the particular issue, or say that they are all apiece. That blessed person is and has always been my reassurance and delight. For him and for her I have written.

Robert Creeley

Wilmington, N.C.
August 8, 1983

THE GOLD DIGGERS

For my Mother

HAD I lived some years ago, I think I would have been a moralist, i.e., one who lays down, so to speak, rules of behavior with no small amount of self-satisfaction. But the writer isn't allowed that function anymore, or no man can take the job on very happily, being aware (as he must be) of what precisely that will make him.

So there is left this other area, still the short story or really the tale, and all that can be made of it. Whereas the novel is a continuum, of necessity, chapter to chapter, the story can escape some of that obligation, and function exactly in terms of whatever emotion best can serve it.

The story has no time finally. Or it hasn't here. Its shape, if form can be so thought of, is a sphere, an egg of obdurate kind. The only possible reason for its existence is that it has, in itself, the fact of reality and the pressure. There, in short, is its form — no matter how random and broken that will seem. The old assumptions of beginning and end — those very neat assertions — have fallen way completely in a place where the only actuality is life, the only end (never realised) death, and the only value, what love one can manage.

It is impossible to think otherwise, or at least I have found it so. I begin where I can, and end when I see the whole thing returning. Perhaps that is an obsession. These people, and what happens to them here, have never been completely my decision — because if you once say something, it will lead you to say more than you had meant to.

As the man responsible, I wanted to say what I thought was true, and make that the fact. It has led me to impossible things at times. I was not obliged, certainly, to say anything, but that argument never made sense to me.

Bañalbufar, Mallorca
1954

The Unsuccessful Husband

Such a day of peace it was, so calm and quiet, with the haze at the window, beginning, and from there going far out over the fields to the river beyond, a morning haze, such as the sun soon burns and has done with. Yet all through that day there was quiet and the haze of calm. It was not the first of many such days. None followed. But it became the reminder of something somewhat better than what one had, the stasis of peace, which, once found, can always remind one and even be found again. Such a day, a peaceful day, so calm and quiet, one is never done with no matter how long . . .

We were married fifteen years ago, at a quiet ceremony attended by a very few people, close friends, and following the ceremony we travelled to a place where I had not been since my childhood but where, as it were, I had always lived or at least wanted to. My wife was then a very pretty woman, a quiet face with a smile of destructive calm, and a figure which, at the very least, provoked one to thoughts not at all in keeping with a usual intention. I cannot say how it was but it was simply that she could not be won, not in the usual manner. Although I do not remember it as deliberate, still I can see now that it was a matter of giving in the old sense such as I had believed no longer to exist. Nothing so much suggested it as when, after we had eaten and had spent what was left of the evening reading, perhaps, with some time of quiet conversation, she would at last turn to me with an air of permission and would then rise and set about the task of going to bed. What I had expected was not necessarily something more, but certainly something

different, and when on that first night I was so permitted, I saw
that nothing again would ever be as I intended it, or ever what
I had hoped for.

I am not a successful man in any sense of the word and if my
wife has permitted me in her own way, the rest of the world has
allowed me to live in another. I have never been openly molest-
ed, not with intention of the sort I might imagine for myself.
I have often thought that an open attack might be fairer for all
concerned but I can see now that I was only thinking of myself.
Others seemed not to care that much and I suppose that they
had every right not to. I have annoyed them but, after all, I
have never essentially disturbed their lives. Let live, they say,
and they know what they are doing.

The fact of my failure can be seen in many instances but it
is not so much this fact as the other of my not having been a
success. Because, after all, I haven't failed if it was my own
intention not to be successful, although to anyone else it might
seem that way. I will allow that I am not successful, but I
confess it is more difficult to admit of my failure. I agree to the
compromise but must reserve the choice for myself.

When it was that I first gave evidence of my intention to be
an unsuccessful man, I do not remember. In any event it was
a long time ago, and quite probably not long after our marriage.
Before that time I was not quite so sure as I am now of the
fact that it is at all costs necessary to oppose oneself to the
determinations of one's destroyers. I had not then thought that
my wife would be in some sense their general. But it turned out
so and soon after I began the task of opposition on whatever
level they should choose. Though I have never been successful,
even in this, I have the eventual satisfaction of a life so empty
that even they will be hard put to it for praise.

At the time of our marriage my wife had a small sum of
money with which we intended to make our start. This sum she
put at my disposal, to use in whatever way I thought best. She
had given me this sum or rather she had given me a check on
her bank for the amount and told me that it was now mine to
do with as I pleased. So, taking the check, I set out toward the
business district of the town and when I had come to the first
bank, I went in and deposited the check in her name. And there
it has been ever since.

This gesture, which was to be sure very much a gesture,

began the understanding between my wife and myself which
was never obscured in all our years of living together, which did
in fact survive those years more gracefully than we ourselves. It
was an altogether simple act, half-understood and at best angry,
but it served us better than any of the more deliberate ones that
followed. Nothing made it quite so plain to each of us where
the other stood, and there never was a better reminder.

I would often say to my wife who was not so well controlled
that she could forbear mention of the money at all times, that
when I had at last made my fortune, this money we would use
to make a wonderful time for ourselves, spending it on a trip to
the Bahamas or some such nonsensical place. On such occasions
she would smile and laugh a little but the success of my wit had
really more to do with the fact of my certainty that even should
I have had those tickets in my hand at that very moment, she
would have laughed just as delightfully and would not have
moved one inch from her chair. The surety with which we grew
to deal with one another was actually what delighted us and we
always knew exactly what to say. If it had not been for the
money to begin with, it would not have been so easy and this
first gesture of mine served as model for many more. Still, if my
gesture seemed the first, and the money the source of all our
understanding, as time passed I began to understand my wife
a little more acutely than at first, and also to see that if it was
I who had put the money to such good use, it was nevertheless
she who had had the good sense to give it to me.

In past years I have often had called to my attention the
constant infidelities of husbands and wives which marked them
much more than they would have, had they been confined to
the flesh only. Because the flesh is at best flesh, and would look
as poor as any hanging in a butcher's window. But these whom
I have watched were dealing primarily with other values, with
lives in a more total sense, and they could only be condemned
for their lack of understanding. Their bickering was constant,
never-ending, and the wives waited only for the moment when
their husbands would return from their various jobs so that it
could all begin again. And I suspect that even the husbands
hurried a little faster on their way home from work, to get at it
and to miss as little as they possibly could. For myself, perhaps
a month or two would pass before either my wife or myself was
aware of our differences. Perhaps they were not even differences

but rather our unholy similarities, our understandings. We were not thought to be unhappy, to be fighting all of the time, and to tell the truth we weren't. But I suspect that each of us was sure that there was, after all, something better, though we had long since given up trying to think about it. It was the suggestion of this which reminded us, which gave us all our pleasure.

Yet we did live together in a way in which few people do nowadays. We dealt with one another constantly and were never put off, never refused, unless it were a condition of our understanding that was in question. We knew one another as well as anyone ever knew another and, if it had not been for our loathing, we should have been happy.

Other people, although I don't for a moment believe that what they say is true, at least claim a continuity in their lives, a going up or a coming down. The rise or fall which they maintain is their way of saying that they have lived and even those who stay in the middle suppose that they narrowly missed worse or very nearly achieved better. For me this doesn't apply, and I find it very hard to believe that it does even for others. If I say that I got to know my wife better during the time we lived together, what I intend to say is that after a time I knew her whereas before that time I did not. Neither of us lived for much more than ourselves, one another, though not in the usual sense. God knows we lived long enough, both of us, though I can't say we grew older or younger or that we grew at all. If one lives at all, one lives for the kind of thing that my wife and I lived for, understanding, the security of knowledge. One certainly does not live to grow old.

But now for my purposes it is necessary to suppose a continuity although none comes readily to hand. What my wife said a year ago is no more to the point than what she said on our wedding night. There is nothing to suggest that we have lived in between. No, for both of us it was like going past some beautiful spot, stopping to look, and then never leaving, always looking to see more and more and more. We never tired of one another and we spent our lives in such looking, though at times we might wish to be gone. But still we stayed where we were.

Taken only as years our life seems very uneventful. After our marriage we settled in the town where we spent the days of our honeymoon, an acquiescence on the part of my wife which I was then still too confused to understand. Now I see that it was for her purposes, not mine, that we settled there for it was intended that I should fail on home-ground, so to speak. It was to be the place of my failure or at least the place of my giving proof. But my failure was never what they intended or, because they so deliberately intended it, it was not really mine. I was an unsuccessful man, to be sure, but the failure was all theirs. Had they intended my success, it would have been something else again but, as it was, the failure belonged to them.

I can remember the occasions of the first trials quite well just as I can remember almost all of my relations with my wife. A friend would sponsor me, set me up in business, and then quite quietly I would fail. It was always the same, always followed by the half-expressed reproaches from the friend. They could never say that I did not try because I did, but what they forgot was my own intelligence which made each of my efforts consistently contributive to my ruin. It was a way I had about which they really knew nothing. My wife knew, though perhaps, not as well as I, but it was for her own purposes that she never said anything and always expressed her confidence in me with the same sure tone, just as if nothing had happened. If at first I was tempted to tell her why I so often failed, I soon saw that she knew quite well without my telling, and it was better for all concerned to keep silent.

Such conduct on my part was never very simple and I always envied my wife her own part. She was never obliged to come and go as I was, never forced into tedious misrepresentations, never compelled to show failure if not actually to fail. On some evenings I came home as tired as any honest man, no matter what I had been up to, but never was there anything more than what I had left in the morning. Gently my wife would question me about the day's work and I would answer that it had gone well and that I was sure that soon everything would be all right. It was our particular joke, this question, and it never failed to bring a smile from my wife. But it was never quite so simple for me because there were those evenings when I wished that my own work had gone for something more than jokes whose humor was not always so apparent.

It was wrong of me to worry and I did worry quite often during the middle of our life together. At that time it became more difficult than I had thought possible for me to keep my own attitude free of the suggestion of failure directed at me from every side. My wife's friends came frequently to call during that time, and when I came in from work I found them there with my wife, waiting no less than she to see how my day had gone. Perhaps my wife agreed after awhile to the more private engagement I had intended because after some time had passed, her friends were no longer there when I came in, and once again it was only my wife I had to face. To me this seemed fairer and, moreover, it was she whom they had chosen.

It was wrong of me to worry because, as we went on, I began to see that I had very nearly won, at least so far as my wife was concerned. Perhaps it was that her questions concerning the business I so carefully guided into failure seemed more genuine, more tired. My own answers were never more cheerful, more full of hope, and I told her each day that perhaps tomorrow would see the final victory and, I would add with a smile, the long-promised trip to the Bahamas. I don't know if it was wrong to take advantage of her growing weakness but I was sure that if it had been I who had been first to give in, she would have been no less kind. There was little chance to do more than I had always done, those things upon which we had so long ago agreed, and I am even inclined to think that my wife would never have respected a response to her own weakness. And I wonder even now if her weakness, so persuasive in its own way, was not, after all, just another trick.

In any event the time after that was a great deal easier for me because I could begin to relax though not too much at first. I had lived with my wife too long to realise the infinite resources at her disposal and I could suspect with some justice that at any time, a time when I should least suspect it, she would again attack and my long-built defences would fall in ruins. In consequence I was careful, very careful, at first, and then I did relax a little but she gave no sign that she noticed it, my relaxing, until at last I was almost sure that what I did no longer concerned her and my time of trial was at an end.

One evening I came home as usual with much the same news and when I came into the house, I called to her but she did not answer. It did not surprise me very much because she had begun to show signs of deafness and although I was not altogether convinced that it was not her last attempt to defeat me, it did seem that she could not hear as well as she once had. Calling again, I went into the room where she spent most of her time

and there she was, sitting in her chair. But I could see immediately from the slack position of her hands, fallen beyond the
arms of her chair, that she was not well and then, when I came
closer, I saw that she was dead.

The next day I have already spoken of, such a calm and
peaceful day, and I spent the greater part of it arranging for
her funeral. Needless to say, I had only to express a few brief
wishes and the rest of the matter was taken out of my hands.
The day of her funeral passed without event and I found myself
watching her go into the ground without much feeling of any
kind. I knew that her part in it was over, and my own very
nearly so. In any event it was something to think about.

Mr. Blue

I DON'T want to give you only the grotesqueness, not only what it then seemed. It is useless enough to remember but to remember only what is unpleasant seems particularly foolish. I suspect that you have troubles of your own, and, since you have, why bother you with more. Mine against yours. That seems a waste of time. But perhaps mine are also yours. And if that's so, you'll find me a sympathetic listener.

A few nights ago I wrote down some of this, thinking, trying to think, of what had happened. What had really happened like they say. It seemed, then, that some such effort might get me closer to an understanding of the thing than I was. So much that was not directly related had got in and I thought a little noting of what was basic to the problem might be in order. That is, I wanted to analyze it, to try to see where things stood. I'm not at all sure that it got to anything, this attempt, because I'm not very good at it. But you can look for yourselves.

(1) That dwarfs, gnomes, midgets are, by the fact of their SIZE, intense;
(2) that dwarfs, gnomes, midgets cause people LARGER than themselves to appear wispy, insubstantial, cardboard;
(3) that all SIZE tends towards BIG but in the case of dwarfs, gnomes, midgets.

But perhaps best to begin at the beginning. And, to begin, there are two things that you must know. The first of these is that I am, myself, a tall man, somewhat muscular though not unpleasantly so. I have brown hair and brown eyes though that is not altogether to the point here. What you should remember is that I am a big man, as it happens, one of the biggest in the town.

My wife is also large. This is the second. But she is not so much large as large-boned. A big frame. I sound as though I were selling her, but I'm not. I mean, I don't want to sound like that, as though I were trying to impress you that way. It is just that that I don't want to do. That is, make you think that I am defending her or whatever it is that I may sound like to you. In short, she is an attractive woman and I don't think I am the only one who would find her so. She has, like myself, brown hair but it is softer, very soft, and she wears it long, almost to her waist, in heavy braids. But it is like her eyes, I mean, there is that lightness in it, the way it brushes against her back when she is walking. It makes me feel rather blundering, heavy, to look at her. It seems to me my step jars the house when I walk through a room where she is. We have been married five years.

Five years doesn't seem, in itself, a very long time. So much goes so quickly, so many things that I can think of now that then, when they were happening, I could hardly take hold of. And where she comes into it, those things that had to do with her, I find I missed, perhaps a lot that I should have held to. At least I should have tried. But like it or not, it's done with. Little good to think of it now.

I did try, though, to do what I could. She never seemed unhappy, and doesn't even now. Perhaps upset when the baby was sick, but, generally speaking, she's a level woman, calm, good-sense.

But perhaps that's where I'm wrong, that I have that assumption, that I think I know what she is like. Strange that a man shouldn't know his wife, but I suppose it could be so, that even having her around him for five years, short as they are, he could still be strange to her and she to him. I think I know, I think I know about what she'd do if this or that happened, if I were to say this to her, or something about something, or what people usually talk about. It's not pleasant doubting your own knowing, since that seems all you have. If you lose that, or take it as somehow wrong, the whole thing goes to pieces. Not much use trying to hold it together after that.

Still I can't take seriously what's happened. I can't but still I do. I wish it were different, that in some way, I were out of it, shaken but at least out. But here I am. The same place.

It was raining, a bad night for anything. Not hard, but enough to soak you if you were out in it for very long. We thought it would probably be closed but when we got there, all the lights were going and I could see some people up in the Ferris wheel, probably wet to the skin. Still they looked as if they were having fun and some of their shouts reached us as we went through the gate and into the main grounds. It was fairly late, about ten or so, another reason why I had thought it would be closed. Another day and the whole works would be gone and that's why she had insisted.

I feel, usually, uncomfortable in such places. I don't like the crowds, at least not the noise of them. They never seem to stop, always jumping, moving, and the noise. Any one of them, alone, or two or three, that's fine. As it happened, we went by a number of our friends, who yelled at us, fine night, or some such thing. I can't remember exactly what the words were. But I didn't like them, or didn't like them then, with that around them, the noise, and their excitement.

No reason, perhaps, to think she knew where she was going. I didn't. I think we followed only the general movement of the people, where they were going. It was packed and very difficult to go anywhere but where you were pushed. So we were landed in front of the tent without much choice and stood, listening to the barker, to see what might be happening.

I can say, and this is part of it, that I didn't want to go in. For several reasons. The main one is that I don't like freaks, I don't like to look at them or to be near them. They seem to have a particular feeling around them, which is against me, altogether. A good many times I've seen others staring, without the slightest embarrassment, at some hunchback, or some man with a deformity that puts him apart from the rest. I don't see how they can do it, how they can look without any reaction but curiosity. For myself, I want only to get away.

But this time she decided. It seemed that not very much could be inside the tent. They had advertised a midget, a knife-thrower, a man with some snakes, and one or two other things.

Nothing like the large circuses and none of the more horrible things such might offer. So I got the tickets and we followed a few of the others in.

They were just finishing a performance. It was so packed at the front, that we stood at the back, waiting until the first crowd was ready to leave. I felt tired myself. It must have been close to eleven at that point. It seemed an effort there was no reason for. But she enjoyed it, looked all around at everyone, smiled at those she knew, waved to some, kept talking to me, and I would say something or other to hide my own feeling. Perhaps I should have been straight with her, told her I was tired, and ducked out. It would have saved it, or at least got me free. But I kept standing there, with her, waiting for the show to finish and another to start.

It did soon, the first crowd moving out, and our own coming up to take its place. The man on the platform had got down at the end and now we waited for him to come back and the new show to begin. There was talking around us, sounding a little nervous the way most will at those times when something is being waited for, though what one can't say with exactness. At this point, I was almost as expectant as the others. Nothing else to be, perhaps. In any event, I had got over my other feeling.

The first act was a cowboy with a lariat, rope tricks. Not much but he was good with it, could make it spin all kinds of loops, shrinking them, making them grow right while we watched him. It was good fun, I thought, not much but enough. At the end he started stamping with one foot and at the same time, he slipped his loop off and on it, brought it up around both feet at the end, jumping and grinning. I think there may have been some music with it, something for the beat, but it doesn't matter. The man told us he was deaf, couldn't hear a thing. There didn't seem to be much point in telling us that but I guess we're apt to like that adding of what we don't expect.

We enjoyed it, the both of us. It's not often that we can get out, like that, to see anything. And after the first I forgot about being tired and liked it as much as she did. The next act was the knife-thrower. He could put them all in a circle no bigger than my hand, eight of them, so that they shivered there with a force which surprised me, and each time one hit, she gripped my arm, and I laughed at her nervousness, but it was a funny thing, even so.

Then came the snake act, which wasn't up to the others, or simply that dullness in it, the snakes much the same, doped, I expect, though perhaps I was wrong to think so. Then sort of a juggling act, a man with a number of colored balls and odd-shaped sticks, which he set into a strange kind of movement, tossing them, one after the other, until he must have had ten, somehow, going and all this with an intentness that made us almost clap then, as they did move, through his hands. Altogether a wonder it seemed, his precision, and how it kept him away from us, even though some stood no more than a few feet away. Until at last he stopped them one by one, and then, the last, smiled at us, and we all gave him a good hand.

It's here that I leave, or as I go back to it, this time, or this way, that is, now that I make my way out, through the rest of them, my hand on her arm with just that much pressure to guide her, or that is my intention. Perhaps the lights that make my eyes ache, begin to, or simply, that it's now, this point, that I am happy, that it's ourselves, the two of us, have come to some sort of feel of it, that makes us so. Just that I am, now, running, that it is just that I do.

What she had been doing, or going to that, it was a cigarette she asked me for, and I reached into my pocket for them, had got out the pack, and given her one, and then lit a match for her. She bent a little, got it lit, then looked back to the platform where the juggler had been.

But the trick, that it's him who's there, the midget, as such he is named, but the size, it's that which hits me, at first, that he isn't small, or looking, he must be five feet, or perhaps a little smaller. Four feet. But not small.

The eyes, catch, get me so into it, that they are so, void, in the head, shaded, the shades like changing shadows, colors, coming in to want, to want to be filled. Seem huge. He looks at all of us, moves over us so, to bite, to have some thing to be there, to bite.

But nothing, certainly, to make of it more or more than what I could see, would be, that is, the barker introduced him and we stood, as we had, in that group in front of him, the boards which made the platform, that roughness, and the poles on which the lights were strung, the wire sagging between them. That is, what is it had come in, as this was, to be not or to make it not as it had been, if it were, as it was, the same place, which I couldn't say or put my finger on, then, but waited like any of the rest.

I could see the muscle of his arm, where the sleeve had been pulled up, rolled, above it, and with his movement, that slightness of tension made him lift it, slightly, from time to time, the muscle tightened and it looked hard, big, below the roll of the sleeve. As my own would. He was smiling, the face somewhat broad, well-shaped, the smile somewhat dreamy, or like sleep, that vagueness, which couldn't be understood.

The barker had laughed, the pitch of it rolled out, on us, and I wondered if he was as drunk as he looked. He was calling the midget, cute, saying, a cute little fellow. He made a joke of it, looking at the women and laughing. Saying, who would like to take him home. There was laughing, they liked the joke, and he carried it further, sensing their tolerance, and played it up. It was the joke he seemed intent on making us remember, the cuteness, the idea of the women.

Taking the cigarettes out of my pocket, the pack crumpled, I held it out to her, but she was intent on what was before us, and I expect that I was myself, and only did what I did, took them out, to somehow break it, to make it break down. It seemed that, that is, that gesture or an act, an action, so meant to serve double, to be a break, but what was it, that is, more than the taking, just that, of the cigarettes, which I didn't want to smoke, had even just put one out. I looked, then, around me at the rest of them and they were looking at him, the midget, and I couldn't see one that noticed I looked, or gave the least sign.

The midget stood still, beside the barker, who staggered a little, under the lights, moved from one side to the other, his face to us, that drunkenness. He was still on the joke, fumbling, and it wore down on us, that weight of it, kept at us, and I wanted to get out. There seemed breaks, lengths of silence, hung there, made the other, the midget, the whole of it, in his own silence, which he kept as a distance around him, that the eyes made actual.

I would have gone, or as I think, I should have in spite of it, simply slipped out, when the others weren't looking, just left and waited for her outside. I can't see that she would have been hurt. That is, I would think, or think I would have that right to, that it would make no difference to her, that is, that she would understand my going, seeing that it had begun to tire me, even became painful to stay. I think of it so, being such, that no difference could be in it, since she was enjoying it, or so it seemed.

I tried to, but the people around pressed too tight, pushed me from the back, all forward to the one on the platform in front of us. Not the barker, I knew that much, but the other, who pulled them, kept them all, because the barker had somehow fallen altogether to pieces, had just the joke he hung on to, and that was played out. But then he switched it, perhaps feeling it had, and turned to the midget, and said, but you should have some say in this. Which one would you like.

The midget turned, then seemed to pull himself out of it, the distance, out of nothing, the eyes pulled in, to focus, to grow, somehow, smaller, larger. The eyes went over us, the voice, when it came, was breath, a breathing but way back in, wire, tight, taut, the scream and I couldn't hear it, saw only his finger move to point at her, beside me, and wanted to say, he's looking at you, but she was turned away from me, as though laughing, but struck, hit. I looked, a flash, sideways, as it then happened. Looked, he looked at me, cut, the hate jagged, and I had gone, then, into it and that was almost that. But she said, then, she had seen him, earlier, that same day, as he was standing by a store, near the door, I think, as it had opened, and she, there, across the street, saw him motion, the gesture, then, a dance, shuffle, the feet crooked, and the arms, as now, loose, and it was before, as before, but not because of this that made it or I thought, so made it, was it, or it was that thing I hung to, when, the show over, they motioned us out, and I pushed a way for her out through the crowd.

A Death

Vestida con mantos negros
piensa que el mundo es chiquito
y el corazón es inmenso. . .

LORCA

AHEAD OF THEM the path went round the trees, and into a clearing of stones, which had rolled from the higher points of the hill to make a sort of flat and broken plateau above the sea. Again, the children went in front, with Amos carrying the basket in one hand, and the other two crowding in back of him. She puffed at the cigarette for the last time, and dropped it, to step on it, and asked them all, how much farther it all was.

She was not a very pretty woman. Amos was six years old, and her one son. The facts sorted themselves like much too brief messages, not trivially but too quickly. She wanted to say something to the man now beside her, who was her brother, and his wife walked beside him on thick legs, wide and heavy at the ankles. Beginning to say it, she heard the children cry out, and there was Amos standing in the sun with the stone in his hand, in front her, and then he threw it.

But that, at least, was not enough to bother them. James bound the wound, as he said, expertly, and soon the little girl had forgotten it, and ran once more after the others. The sun picked them out, in the shadows, and in and out they ran, around the rocks, and behind them, crouching, then waving the sticks again, and the parents sat in a small three-cornered circle watching them and then looking at one another.

In her own head she now resolved, or arranged, a pattern of hostility, a final war against them, but that was her love for Amos. Or if he cried, that was too much. Or if he did not cry, but hit her, as he would and did, she would rather it were in their own room at the hotel, and not here in front of the others. He is a very nervous child, she said, his father makes no gesture of love to him. Or of affection.

So they pitied her. What was it like, they thought. What ever could it be like, in the heathen country of New Zealand. James said, he'll get over it. He laughed. His wife smiled at her, and she felt the edge of it coming in like the sharpness intended, to cut at her politely and to wound her. So she got up, and said she would take a little walk, calling Amos, and the two of them left and went down the hill to the sea.

As they grew smaller, the wife smiled again. James was uneasy, and their own children bored and impatient. He began to pile small stones, one very carefully on another, to build a small house. He made a door and two little windows, with small sticks for supports, and then the little boy kicked at it, and it fell to pieces.

In New Zealand, he said, but his wife would not listen to him. She took the children in her arms, one against each leg, and smiled again at him. He was the man she knew, and she would hear nothing at all to the contrary.

Closer to the sea the rock became sharper, and lifted into big, over-hanging bunches. A few pine trees grew somehow out of them, but these were very stunted, and low. The water was very lovely and very clear. One saw to the bottom. The fish moved out from the shallows, and seeing people come, disappeared altogether.

Amos was a fisherman. He had his own little pole, with a little reel on it, and would sit hours by the water without bothering her at all. Sometimes her husband came too. The first fish Amos ever caught, after many days and even years of fishing, was one which her husband had put on the hook for him, without him any the wiser. In a way it was sad that that had been the first, but after that he caught some actually.

Looking at Amos, she now wondered what she would change, if she could. His eyes were blue, almost shut in the intensity of their color. Perhaps he would be a great man in spite of them. His hair had bleached almost white, and under it the darker

tawny color came through. But his arms were very thin and
stick-like, and his chest corded with little muscles. He was like
a goat, an obscenely precocious goat, who had no use for people.

Taking off their clothes, she put them in a pile, and then put
a stone on top of it. Amos giggled. She had forgotten the bathing-
suits, and they were in the basket, high up on the hill with the
others. Even so she slipped into the water quietly, and calling
softly to Amos, drew him in after her.

Above them, James fumbled in his embarrassment. His wife
smiled again, and watching him, thought only of his remarkable
innocence. It was pleasant that it should be so. He was very
unmarked, and untouched by so many things. His sister might
well be a photograph, she thought, which he wished to be proper
and in focus. Otherwise she was a nuisance, as, for example,
she paddled away down there, with the boy, and seemed almost
completely foreign. James coughed, he wanted not quite to see.
The bodies went under the water, to leave the heads free, then
they too ducked under.

Still watching him, his wife said, what do you think of it,
James. As she had said, three days earlier, to a young man on
the beach with them, do you see how he treats me?

But what was so simple about it. Make me happy, she said.
Don't please think of her. James was very much in the middle
and began to know it. He knew love was not multiple, or could
not be here divided. He said, be patient with her. He let it all
rest on kindness.

The water around them changed all that, on their bodies,
very much on their bodies. Amos jumped up, shrieking, and she
loved him more than she admitted. Look, she said. The small
fish darted out, past their white feet, and then back again to
the darker places. But Amos had seen them. It was lovely.

Then she left him, swimming out and free of it. The water
was buoyant, so that she hardly swam but floated, lifted out on
the wash of the waves as they fell back. Beneath her the colors
changed from the green to blue, and then a darker blue, and
then black. She dove and felt the tips of her fingers touch bottom,
and on her hands the weeds were very light and brushed them
gently.

Far away she thought that the house was now gone. Her
husband loved no one anymore. At last they were also free of
him. He sat in a chair in the yard which he had made. There

was no car. The street was long, and at the end there was a
tram-stop. People spoke English but he answered them, *no se*.
He was a Greek with rings in his ears, and his hands were folded
in his lap.

So one could change it as he might. She held to that, and
here the water helped her, taking her as she was. One saves all
one's life, against the one instant it is all real, and all enough.
Why, she said, tell me now otherwise! Tell me nothing.

If it is obscene, she said. Her husband's mother was obscene.
Of her own husband she had known nothing, she had not even
known his body. And when at last he grew sick, to die, she took
off his clothes for the first time, and saw the body for the first
time, dying.

Gulls flapped off the rocks behind her. Amos slapped at the
water with a stick he had found. The quiet grew over all of
them.

But what was to be done with James. His wife thought she
knew, and yet he was strangely moved. The children were
happy, they played behind them with the toys they had brought
in the basket. So she attacked him directly, and asked him, what
was it. He said he did not know.

Is it your sister, she said, and looked down, and away, to the
form still clear to them, a white odd shape on the top of the
sea. He answered that he did not think it was. She said, you
must see the difficulties. He was not sure that he did.

But, corruption, she would have insisted if she had dared to.
The small knotted boy giggled at them, he caught at his mother's
skirt and giggled. She had neither sympathy nor time for that
horror. She has had a difficult life, he said. And what is
difficulty. He lifted the skirt, giggling at her own children, he
said to them, look. It was not possible to be kind.

To that James agreed, and yet it was still possible. The
children played happily in back of them. The little boy threw
the ball to the little girl. She missed it, and ran off to bring it
back.

What do you think, his wife said. But a small boat now came
into view, and he pointed at it, and they watched it crawl out
past the rocks to their left, and then begin to come down the
coast.

Hearing the sound of the motor. Amos looked up, and out.
There it was, very white, with a little line of exhaust trailing

the back. His mother was also out there, and he thought of it. He wanted the boat to take him away, perhaps to put him into the front somewhere, but he would never have the courage to go. He felt for a stone under the water, and found one close to his toes, and then threw it out as far as he could at the boat.

It missed the boat, but fell beside her, splashing her face. It was usual, and yet she looked back at him, in anger, to see him squatted there in the water, and, she thought, shivering. She wondered if the man, standing upright in the boat, could see her. He had seen the stone. His hand was on the tiller, his other let him lean back a little, braced against the boat's side. He was not tall, but he was strong-looking, his chest heavy. Now he did look, at first at the boy, and then coming closer, looked down and saw her as she took a stroke to swim back.

At that even James was angry. They had all expected it. She had only done what she would, but his wife was now right beyond all question. They watched the two figures collect themselves. The boat was no longer visible. Slowly they came up the hill again, and now it was impossible for James to swim, or for his wife, or children.

You know, his wife said, what this will mean. For the last minutes she wanted to be clearly fair. James watched his sister coming towards them, and saw her smiling. Was it to be a simple thing? She was not ashamed. Amos dragged at her hand, she pulled him along almost without realising it.

Such a lovely swim, she said. The water was so lovely, and refreshing. And the boat, the wife asked. But did she really say it. Her own children were safe behind her and never again would she really let them go. Amos giggled, he pulled at his mother's skirt, raising it, and James saw the tight thigh, and the brown, close flesh.

Did you see the boat, his wife said. She knew it was her brother's wife. She knew her own husband was dead. She saw the faces all in front of her, and if she cried out at them, she was still in love with everything.

Three Fate Tales

1

I PUT IT this way. That I am, say, myself, that this, or this feel, you can't have, or from that man or this, me, you can't take it. And what I would do, with any of this, is beyond you, and mine. But for this time, yours too.

I haven't always lived here. I used to live in the city, in the middle of it, straight, tall buildings, some of it, but where I was they were cramped, squat, four stories. There was a trolley-line ran down the middle of the street. Noise. Each day the iceman came, under the windows. I could hear him shout. I even waited for him to shout.

Thinking of that time, as it comes here, here and now, I think of the other, somewhat different. I say time. I say time, to mean place.

Let me put it another way. What have we got but this, which is myself, yourself. Or that word, self. You figure there's more, some way to make it more, but what you keep is the means, the ways. Make them the end. And that's the end of it, what might have been more.

But nothing more strange, taken or not, than just that, the self which is single. And I make it such, so call it, because it is so. I only call it what it is.

One day, any day, there could be these people, or make them three people, this man and this woman and this little girl. They live in the next place to mine. I see them go down the steps, out on to the street, there, the three of them. I don't say, look for yourselves, see them, or what you may take as enough to convince you. They are there. That is the fact of it.

The days are long, as it happens, hot. The sun in the city is a hard thing, up, inaccessible, hangs over the hardness of the city, out of it. Hot. I hate it but that is, again, my own business.

The woman sits there by herself, in the place with just the girl. They work out the day the best they can. Make the time pass. I know there are at least a hundred and one things anyone can do, to get through these days. Hold to, the actions, the little things done. I have my own things. I get up, eat breakfast, sit around, read, look out the window. There are these ways.

They wait, the two of them, in the place next to mine. The noises come through. The little girl has a ball. It bounces on the floor. Its noise is exact. The woman calls her for her dinner, she complains, doesn't want to come. There is some sharpness in the voices. I listen. I hear all that I want to hear of it.

Then, as it happens, there is this one day, again, one day out of the number, fifty, twenty-five.

The chair slides across the floor. I hear the girl push it.

There is no other sound. Just what comes comes up from the street, what I have grown used to, the trolley, and the cars, the people, below me, out the window, down. This is what I am sure of, what is down there, that I can speak of without looking, seeing any of it. It is the one pattern which cannot be broken because it is the general, the collection. The numbers.

It is still quiet. But then out, it goes by me, and down. Stops. But I can't do anything, sit only for a moment, and then, jump, and look out, see there, down, the girl and the people already around her. Nothing of the woman until her head is just opposite mine, the mouth wide, scream, and someone I see the face of below, looks up and calls to her. It's all right. She isn't hurt. A miracle.

It's all right, or right is what they have said, that it's all right, but myself, I can't find their answers or even what they answer, to say it's all right. To her, or myself, or anyone, or even looking straight down at it, after it happens, what happens?

It isn't known. I make that sense of it, that it isn't known, any of it. This woman or this girl or what has happened, and how I would have it, or my hand there. To feel. To be felt.

Which they want, or I want, more than the seeing. Any day of
the week this could happen, to any, this girl, to others, me, you.
I suppose it is something, even, done with. As it turned out.
Past, and even complete. I am left with it, made different,
because of it. Or, am I? We are back to that.

2

I take it another way, since in this or in what is around is,
perhaps, some of it, that such can come to interest, or finds, so,
some place in the attention. Let me begin.

There is an old woman who lives in the country and she is
very old indeed. Her husband, somewhat younger than herself,
has grown tired of waiting but being an honest man, he cannot
bring himself to the act of deciding just how old she should be
before she is ready to die. It is to be thought that this old
woman's days are inaccessible, even to herself, and though she
is certainly alive, for the most part she is dead because she
cannot remember anything and when she talks, her words slide
into one another and the sentence breaks down before it is even
half begun. It is a practice of her husband, a rather cruel one,
to have the old woman do the week's shopping, so that each
Saturday she arrives in the village and totters from store to
store, usually led by some old friend of the family who has
happened to be standing on the street corner at the time when
she is let down from her husband's car. Often the job is divided
so that one begins it and then another goes on with it while a
third appears at the end to guide her to the car where her
husband sits waiting. And behind them comes the clerk carrying
the groceries. It is a common sight each Saturday.

This is, it can be supposed, one of the old woman's horrors,
but her joy, which is equally distinct, has to do with something
which for others would be even more horrible. In the cemetery
where she is, once dead, to be buried, her stone is already set
in place and her name with all but the final date has been
carefully cut into it. She is often taken to the cemetery to see
her stone, perhaps with a certain willingness on the part of her

husband who may think that if she sees it often enough, this place where she is to be laid to rest, she will hurry up the process of getting there once and for all. For some years she worried about the possible annoyance her choice of a final resting place might cause another member of the family but when with reluctant decision, she made her choice known to the family, she was overjoyed to find this doubtful one quite approved.

In any event this old woman seems to be doing it all by herself, so that when it does come time to bury her, one would not be too surprised, should the knotted old hands reach up and, pushing the shovels aside, pull the dirt over all by themselves, for at least that's one way to think of it.

3

I think we deal with other wisdoms, all more real than our own, which is to say, I think we have to do with others. Sometimes, sitting in a chair by the window, I see a man go by on foot and I wonder at the precision with which each foot advances, so controlled and so sure. I would hope that if the man and I were to trade places, he might think the same of me going by but I am not at all sure that he would.

I think it is always a question of where we have come from and where we are going. I think they are important in just that order and I think there is little else to think about. Of course, we are ourselves. It would be foolish for us to believe those who tell us different. But to know exactly, to know each time and all the time, about that I am not so sure.

After all, what do we have to do with that is not ourselves? What can exist that we are not part of or that we do not in some sense *allow* to exist. This is an old story but a true one. The world is my representation. So it is, all of it. And what is more, this world belongs to us.

But the order is important, the grasp of the keys and the lay of the land, so to speak. One must know these. Like the man with the car I see each morning, racing its motor, tearing down the road over bumps and stones, what does he know about his own possession? Certainly not enough to make actual use of it, not the use of understanding. This, then, should be criticised, such misuse, and avoided at all costs.

But it is true that everything becomes our own. It's what things are for. We see them and they are ours. It's as simple as that.

The story I have to tell has to do with familiar objects in familiar relations. Unlike the others, it does not suppose a stretching of the usual context. It has to do with a usual reality.

I am in the habit of feeding our cat each night before I go to bed after I have put coal on the fires. This is my usual procedure and one I rarely vary. Both the cat and I are at home in it. When it comes time, if the cat is indoors, she will be sitting by her dish, waiting for me to put food in it. If she is outside, I have only to open the door and there she is, waiting to be let in and fed.

On the night of which I am speaking, or at least now I am speaking of it, I had let the cat out earlier and so when it came time to feed her, I went to the door and opened it but the cat was not in sight. But do not take this as something altogether unusual. I am not such an automaton that I cannot vary my movements at all. It is often the case that I am a few minutes late with the cat's food. And the cat, too, has her differences.

I opened the door but the cat was not to be seen, so I called to her, once, then twice, but she did not come.

On that night there was a full moon. It was very bright outside, almost like day but still very different. The tall pines at the edge of the field beside our house cast their long shadows over the snow and each object in the field itself that was big enough to have a shadow had its own. But though it seemed very light and the shadows black and distinct, still there were no sharp details such as are to be seen when a bright sun is shining.

I stood for some minutes, looking out over the fields, and then, because she made a sudden, brief movement, I saw the cat not too far from where I was standing, crouched, her own shadow black and irregular on the snow. I called again to her but she gave no notice, so I walked over to where she was, thinking to pick her up and bring her into the house. When I came to her, however, I saw that she had a mouse and although it's no pleasant sight to watch a cat and a mouse together, one, in fact, which I remember always with unpleasantness, my wife and I have decided that since we have the cat in order to catch the mice which bothered us previously, we have to put up with the unpleasantness, even though it's difficult. So it was that I started to walk away from her in order to let her finish the mouse but as I did so, I was caught by the strange sight of their shadows, the mouse's, though smaller, very distinct and the cat's, like some horrible shadow trying to erase it. I stood there, absorbed, completely caught, until suddenly the mouse's shadow was gone, but no, it appeared again, coming towards me uncertainly, jerkily, until I saw that what it wanted was to hide in my own shadow, which I now saw to be there, just as their own, long and black on the snow. It came towards me, the mouse, and then just as quickly as I had seen it, I lost sight of it again. So again I started back to the house but as I did so, I felt something wriggling on my sleeve and with a sudden brush of my hand, I threw it back on the snow. Only then, because the cat jumped on what I had knocked from my sleeve, did I know it was the mouse.

I don't think that story much more than unpleasant but still it has the point of all I believe. For these things, so powerful in themselves, in their own way, are there to be looked at, I expect, and with more than the eyes. It's a case of making them ours the best way we can. I can remember that as it happened, then, even as it was happening, a good many things occurred to me, each with its relation, and if these things did, as they did, lessen that first impact of horror, they also made it my own.

There are other stories, some with more purpose, and one, perhaps, bears hearing here, tacked on though it is. In any event, it's short. After that snow and before the next, I went out, as usual, to do the chores, and found one afternoon, patches of blood on the snow. And seeing them there, I guessed that the cat had cut her foot and was able to find her and dress the wound before there was chance for it to become infected.

A short time after, it did snow and the patches were covered and I forgot about them. It stayed cold for a week and then it turned warm and the snow began to melt. And going out again I saw the patches of blood on the snow and without thinking twice, I went off to find the cat, supposing she had cut another foot. But finding her, I found, as well, that none of her feet were cut and then saw it was the melting of the snow had caused the old patches to come back. I expect that all this might suggest is that a reality, before it becomes our own, is often tricky and can be easily mistaken.

The Party

OF UNCLEANLINESS, he was saying, there are, one must come to think, a good many kinds. Or more, put it, than dirt on the hands.

The wind shifted, slightly, pulling them down the lake and in towards the dock which he saw now as a line, black, on the water, lying out and on it.

Not one, he said, not one sense would give you the whole of it, and I expect that continues what's wanted.

But they sat quiet, anyhow, the woman at the far end, slumped there, and the length of her very nearly flat on the canoe's bottom. The man kept upright, the paddle still in his hands, but he held it loosely, letting it slap the water, lightly, as the waves lifted to reach it.

Nothing important, she said. Nothing to worry about, and what about tonight? We forgot that.

He began to paddle again, but slowly, and looked back at her reluctantly, almost asleep.

That doesn't please you, she said. You seem determined not to enjoy yourself.

Not that, he answered, and it had taken him, at that, some way beyond where he had been.

Not so simply, he said. You make it too easy.

But why easy, she answered. I don't see that it's not easy, any of it. These people will hardly care to attack you personally. They are all much too busy.

Looking down at her, he found her laughing at him, and smiled himself.

You are all so very serious, she said, all of you. What is it makes you think the world is so intent on you at whatever age you are.

Because I don't know, she added, just how old you are. But you look young. You look very young.

He whistled, a little song, and looked back towards the dock which they now came to, bumping against it, and he reached out to steady them, and then pulled the canoe alongside for her to get out.

Easy, she said. Don't jerk it.

He watched her swing out, a foot on the dock, then pull herself up, and clear, to wait for him.

Help me pull it up, she said. It might break loose.

He got out and helped her lift it, and then pushed to roll it over, on the dock, easing it down gently, when her hands were clear.

There, she said, now it will be safe.

He followed her back along the dock, crossing at the end, another, and then up a path to where her car sat, shaded, by the trees. She opened the door for him, and reaching in, spread a towel on the seat, then crossed round to the other side. Sliding under the wheel, she leaned over and caught him with one hand, pulling him to her, to kiss him.

For your sullenness, she said, although you hardly deserve it.

He pushed free and watched her start the car.

Sometime you will have to answer me, she said. Sometime there will be nothing else for you to do.

They moved off quickly, along the road, and coming to another, swung in, grating, and up to the house, and stopped there and got out.

Leaving her, he went to his room, took off his bathing-suit and dropped it on the floor. To his right a mirror hung, on the wall, and he turned to look at himself, the whiteness, and then dressed quickly, and left the room.

Here, she called.

The voice echoed a little, finding him, and he followed it out to where she was sitting, waiting for him.

There's not too much time, she said. Would you like a drink before we go?

He nodded and she got up, and went out. Returning, she

came to him and put the glass on the small table by his hand.
Then she went back to her own chair and sat down.

Thanks, he said, and picked up the glass from where she had
put it.

But nothing at all! Very happy to do it.

He smiled, then drank, and put the glass back.

This is a very comfortable room, he said. Very airy, very nice
and big.

She nodded, quiet, and looked round at the walls, the high
ceiling, then back at him.

He wanted it this way, she said. He did most of it himself.

He looked away, turning, and settled on a picture which was
across from him, a small one of some trees and a house.

His favorite room, she said. This and the shack were all he
cared about.

A damn shame, he said, to have just got it, and then to have
to lose it.

She didn't answer, and looked, instead, out the window, her
head somewhat bent, and loose, and he watched her, quietly,
letting the time pass.

It makes me feel rather dirty, he said, rather stupid, if that's
how to say it.

It's not you.

But it must be me a little, he said. That I walk in on it.

You don't. There's nothing to worry about.

She had got up and now looked at her wrist, the little band
there, of some bright metal, and then at him, saying, it's very
late.

He followed her out and into the car, and starting it, she
drove off quickly, hurrying because of the lateness. Some cars
were already there and they pulled in behind them, and stopped.

It won't be bad, she said, or it won't be if you'll try to help
a little.

He shrugged and went after her up the path, waiting behind
while she knocked, lightly, on the door. Abruptly it opened and
he saw a woman smiling at both of them, reaching, to pull them
in. He let them talk, standing back, and then went in after them.

You're the last, the woman said, but that's an honor?

Yes, she said, and they went in, closely, following the woman,
laughing, and he saw them all sitting in a ring about the room,

the chairs all back against the wall, and going to one near the door, he sat down.

Mr. Briggs, they said, and all laughed, is a strange young man!

But he had not heard them, and only sat, placid, and again waited for a drink, thinking it enough that there should be one for him. It came soon and taking it, he thanked the woman and lifted the glass to his mouth.

Cheers!

He sat back, more relaxed, and nodding to the man beside him, said, very fine, and smiled.

There's not much hope for them, the other answered, if they won't make an attempt to see both sides.

No, he said, I can't see that they will find any other way out of it.

But it doesn't matter, she asked. Who could care about such a thing.

The sandwiches went by him, and reaching out, he caught one, smiling, and put it into his mouth.

The truth, the other said, is what rarely seems to be considered.

But they had not heard either, and one woman now stood up, and looked at all of them, saying, to John. Wherever he is. They drank in silence. A windy void, which he felt himself, lifting the glass, and drinking, then, with all of them. It was love, she said, a very true love.

From the next room the children's voices came, clearly, and they were crying, wailing, he thought, with a very specific injury. Getting up, he said, I'll go, not thinking, and had gone through the door before anyone had noticed him.

But, seeing him, they cried louder, screaming and the woman was there behind him, and motioned him out.

But no, she said, it's no use. You bad children, go to sleep!

Bewildered, he looked down at her, beside the bed, and younger than she who he had come with, he thought, but she will not allow me, she will not understand.

We'd better go back, she said. They'll go to sleep by themselves.

In the other room they had got up, and stood only to wait for her, to say, goodnight, apologetically, and left. She watched them go, blankly, and he stood beside her, trying, as he thought, to help.

My party, she said. There's no reason to leave.

It's late, someone answered. It's been very fine.

The room cleared, slowly, the doorway crowded but at last empty, and they sat, the three of them, on the couch, looking after the others. In the room behind them the crying continued and softened, finally, to die out.

They're all asleep, he said, and turned, but could not see her face.

Does it matter, he said. I mean, does it matter in any way you can think of?

But the woman had got up, and the other now raised herself, to lean over, and seeing him, laughed, and sank back.

You make it sound momentous, she said. You really prefer disasters.

She smiled at him quickly, lifting again, but he had turned his head and she could not see him.

Anyhow, it was a good party, she said then, turning to the younger woman. There was certainly nothing wrong with it.

The Lover

OUTSIDE, beneath the window on the grass which grew in an uneven covering, the earth coming through in patches where the grass had worn thin, the cats were playing. The sun was as high as the noon would find it and yet the air had an edge of chill in it and the sky was a yellow-blue, the chill, and hardness. It was summer but they were north, so far north that even the summer was part of it, cold and not the open warmth of the south which they had grown used to a year ago, that they had travelled in with the cats as unwelcome retainers, servants of their love. They had need for an audience.

At noon the glasses and sandwiches sat on the table, and they before them, and they both ate without haste, or eagerness, but more as occasion, usual, for which there was custom. Still, looking at them, together, it was to catch some of the reason for them being together. There seemed to be a reason. She was short and he was tall and both were somewhat dark with brown hair, eyes, rather oval, long faces, and then their bodies, having some sense of strength in them, and one thought that they would look better without the clothes than with them. There was too much awkwardness and constraint, although one might have been mistaken.

Too much subtlety, he was thinking, altogether, to want much to eat today. He said, I've been reading about this new book here. It says, that *his unwavering growth is continuing*, that he *has been achieving universal recognition as a master craftsman of the very first order.*

Taking another sandwich, he said, what has happened to my generation? Tell me. Where are those that stood with me?

And she answered, looking up above his head through the window, to the peak of the barn : Isadore, shot in a raid, 1938; Leo, serving 2 years for addiction, 1944; Sarah, teaches dancing in New York, 1948 – those are the ones that matter. When will they call me, he said, when shall I resume my command?

But she was clearing the table and then she had gone into the kitchen, leaving him on the chair, still sitting, and he looked at the door and then turned to look out of the window and saw there the black and white cat, with a mouse, while the other, the grey cat, sat some distance away, watching.

Poetically, he was an instance of despair, one more, as he would put it, in the noon's sun. He could plan himself out of books or without them, what he could do but couldn't then get to it or come to do it. He thought of Sarah as a body, before him, which he would put out hands to touch, or fingers to move over. That would be a body, he thought, love. Was she one of those mentioned? She was. She is dancing in New York, although where wasn't mentioned. Would she dance well? He thought, I guess she would. I guess that would be love, another instance, dancing or not. But the others, that would be more subtle.

He spent that afternoon cleaning out a henhouse, moving the caked litter in a basket to the truck, then taking it when he had got the house cleaned to the dump at the edge of the woods. It wasn't hard work so much as dusty, and his nose was blocked with the dust and he coughed now and then. But it had to be done, he thought, but will they remember it five years from now.

And then it was evening and he could sit down again, at the table, and eat his supper. He ate it fast and with appetite, and she was pleased. After they had finished, he went into the other room, she before him, and sat down again in the chairs some feet apart. He took up the book he had been reading in the morning, opened it, then shut it and put it back. His wife had one of her own which she had begun to read.

I think I'll go to New York, he said, and then waited. She went on with her reading. I think I'll leave tonight. She put the book down and looked at him, but annoyed and even hurt, and this surprised him. Go ahead, she said, but there isn't any money. I'll walk, he said, I'll run, I'll fly. Go ahead, she said. But why get angry, he said, why take it that way? What is here to keep me? And why won't you come? I don't like New York, she said.

It was there he could stop, he thought, right there. To hell with it. Women with bodies but each different and each with incomparable differences and each with exciting differences. But I'm a lover, he thought, good god, this is my vocation. You fat, stinking hag!

Around the edge of the chair one of the cats came and pushed against his foot, rubbing itself on his leg, and purring. He put down his hand and stroked its back, slowly, so that his fingers could feel the fur very soft and even and almost like oil, very thin, on the fur. The cat purred and arched its back, then tired of being stroked and moved over to where his wife sat and jumped up to her lap, landing on the book and covering it. Annoyed, she pushed it down.

Outside, down in the field, there was a mist coming up from the river which he could still see in what light was left. It softened the outlines of the trees, covering them, and what he could now see of them was not the trees, but the mist covering the trees.

A softness of the world.

Sentimental and odious.

But what could he put against it, he thought, that it hadn't got to and covered? A softness of the world. A vacuum, an impenetrable emptiness. Two years ago he had been in New York with Leo and Sarah. They had stayed at Leo's apartment. Leo wanted Sarah. It was what he wanted, her, that is, but still the idea of having some one, that being what he had mentioned later. I was so alone, he said, having no one to sleep with. So what did you do. He didn't know, he thought, then or now, not much in any event. I've never done much of anything. But Leo said, you slept with her. Which was right, but that was up to her, and he could think of her in the bed, after, when he had got up to go back to his own, saying, she said, stay with me, don't go back, and he felt her face because he was obliged to see what she was up to and found there that she was crying, the tears coming down over her face, and he stayed where he was. And when Leo asked, he told him. How old, he thought,

23, 24, and still I can't keep my mouth shut? And old men talk too much?

He saw her moving in her chair and he sat up, quickly and straight, in his own. You've been asleep, she said. But he couldn't think that he had been, or remember, and answered, no, that would be too easy and too right. I haven't been asleep. I watched you, she said, and you fell asleep. She was smiling and why should she have to smile. What did you dream about, she asked, and smiled. Women, he said, nothing but women. Nice ones, she asked. You don't know them, he said, and tried to remember what he had dreamt about, but couldn't. But he thought, was I asleep, and, where am I now?

Whose room with such impossible furniture is this? The cat lay in a corner of the room, the one that he had stroked, curled on a blanket that lay there, the other close to it. So where am I, he thought, is it still 1938? What year is it if it isn't 1938?

He said to her, I don't do anything but think, do I? She had got up and was going out to the kitchen to feed the cats. She hadn't heard him. He tried again. I don't do a goddamn thing, but think, do I? She was in the kitchen and he wondered if she heard but didn't answer because she didn't want to. Why don't I work, he shouted, why don't I get a job? Good Christ, who do I think I am? Sitting around here all day doing nothing? Look at other people. They work. They have jobs. They support their wives. Why don't I?

It was very quiet in the house, he thought, and now that he had stopped shouting, he could hear her in the kitchen, getting the cats' food. No noise from the night came into the room and looking out, all he could see was the black and the quiet. Nothing moved. Stop thinking about it. Get out of it. Let go. But the women are there, he thought, all of them, one, two, three, four, five. Were there that many? No, he thought, there weren't. But there could be, there might be even more. As a possibility he could add a half a dozen, to begin with, that he knew of and could, perhaps, someday add. That would be a beginning. But what compels me here?

How about some music, he called to her. She was still in the kitchen, feeding the cats. Some big wide chords? He waited and then she answered, don't you want to go to bed? No, he said, I'm not tired. Let's have some music. He got up and went over to the phonograph. Reaching down to a rack below it, he pulled

out an album, very worn and patched on the sides with tape.
He took out three records, put them on the spindle, joggled
them a little to make sure they would drop down one at a time,
and then turned on the phonograph. In a minute the sounds
came out, loud, deep, and fast. He moved out to the middle of
the room, stood there, listening, and then let his arms swing out
in lazy circles, easy, and murmured to himself the sounds of the
music. When it had finished, he turned around to find her
standing in the doorway, smiling again, and watching him. You
look like Buddy, she said, but not very much. That's one you
forgot, he answered, what about him? Where is he? He's in
Mexico, she said, but you know that. He looked at her in the
doorway and wondered. I know it, he said, but do you know it?
Do you know what it means to me, for example? I think so, she
said. No, you don't, he said, I do but you don't. Wait a minute.
He walked over to a table and took a letter from a small pile
on one side. Listen to this. He unfolded the paper and read, *que
nunca olvidate* . . ., he says here, *Your lad que nunca olvidate* . . . He
had trouble pronouncing the Spanish and she asked him to spell
out the words. What does this mean, he said. It means, which
nothing will obliviate. Nothing, he said, how does he get that
way? What does he know about it down there in Mexico? Don't
you like him, she said. But he turned and folding the letter
again, put it back on the table with the others. I like him, he
said, very much.

She had gone over to the door and opening it, she looked at
him, to see if he was going to come, but he went back to a chair
and sat down and said that he would read for a little while.
Take a bath, I'll be up soon. I haven't much to read. Then she
was upstairs, moving around, turning the water on in the tub,
and no other sounds but these. He took up the book again,
opened it, but couldn't read it, and closing it, put it back on
the table. Too often, he thought, I've done that. Too goddamn
often these days. But thought then that what he would like
would be no more than something obscene, of the sort that he
could remember having got hold of as a boy, in school, but this
was usual. But for a grown man, he thought, is it still usual?

Upstairs, he found her still in the tub, stretched out, and
almost asleep. He had left the door open as he came in and she
complained of the cold draft from the hall, but he left it open
long enough to annoy her and wake her up. Or perhaps no more

than to annoy her. He didn't know. Then he closed it and stood waiting for her to get out of the tub, but she stayed where she was and he looked at her there, in the dirty water, grey, so that he couldn't see her under it but only what was above, her breasts, head and knees. My wife, he said, look at you, you big, common thing. Get up or you'll go to sleep. She smiled and then slowly started to get up and the water slopped against the sides. He didn't wait but went out, closing the door behind him, and into their bedroom, and there undressed, and putting on his pyjamas, got into bed.

Another book on the table, he thought, and there it was. Books everywhere, he thought, nothing but books. It was another he'd been reading with a torn match-book in it to mark the place where he had stopped. He reached down to his pants which lay where he had dropped them on the floor, took out a package of cigarettes and a lighter. He lit one of the cigarettes and then put the pack and the lighter on the table beside the bed.

Then she was in the room and looking up at her, he saw she'd let her hair down and had put on lipstick, so that her mouth looked bigger. Just like those books, he thought, and she said, I'm all clean, do you like me? She got into the bed and rolled over against him and began to stroke him with her hand, her hair falling over his chest, and he said, look, what do you think I can do, what do you think I'm good for. But he was getting excited, himself, and he reached over and with his hands, took hold of her.

But who is it, he was thinking, that I would want if it wasn't her? But would this be important now? He wondered. He wondered if it were, then, those projected images of other, those other, women he was dealing with, then, in the bed with her, on top and around her, and over her. Or if it were himself, or where was he in it. Like some kind of impotent shell, useless to protect, he thought of the day and the sun and the lack of warmth, the north, being that climate he had no business in, too cold and hard, around him and over, on top, and talk, damn you, talk, he thought, say something, that makes sense, that won't leave me always alone, here or there, or nowhere I have chosen for myself, as I am now, here or there, but nowhere I would be. And the cats, he thought. The shell. The need for necessity, to have dependents. She liked them, she fed them. They were hers. And it was useless not to be angry anymore because he was and expected he would be, for a long time, that it would continue to be her that he didn't want or like or didn't want to have close to him, and always busy, he thought. Always busy. And could, then, scream, get away from me, you common thing! But she had rolled off and away, or he had, and lay there thinking, what was I thinking of.

In the Summer

I AM NOT saying that it was ever to the point or that a purpose could be so neatly and unopposedly defined. Or that twenty-one or so years ago, on that day, or on this, he was then, or is now, there or here, that we could know him and see him to be what he is. I don't much care for that. I had my own time to do, a number of things to do. I had heard, then, that the growing-up of anything could become an involved and crippling process. I could see the sun each day, coming up, and then each night, going down. I gave my time to that.

She said: do you really believe that, do you really see things that way.

Of course, it isn't so neat, he said. He was being somewhat difficult, he thought, to allow her to speak of things which didn't have to do with her, but her hands, in his own, were chafed, and rough, and his own, moving over them, in a kind of tired realisation that they were not what they might be, said, here's a little warmth, take it.

No, I couldn't have to do with him, then, because I was afraid of him, of having him come too close to me, or to himself, for that matter. I knew then what I was, what gave me pleasure, or how I should best set about getting it. It was no sin, to know that. I got up early in the morning, each day, to get that jump on everyone else. They didn't see that I did, but just the same I did.

So is love, in itself, a kind of inverse plunging, which I cannot say more about, or much more, than that.

She said: why love, what has that got to with this, what you were saying about him.

And withdrew, a little, her hand from his hold which was to say to him, that she had become suspicious and was now thinking of something else. But he drank what beer he had left in his glass and took that occasion for speech, finishing.

Like that, he said, that I was then thinking of it, the beer. That was what I had in mind. And I could love that too, I expect. One thinks of hot days and it's not so hard then.

She said: but not the same way.

The same way, he said, no different. And that is what was wrong then. Wanting to give. That is itself a sin. There is no other sin that I can think of that is worse. And I should damn it more thoroughly, than I could myself, for considering it or any one thing. That I haven't the time for, now or then.

The question would be always the same in love, and is: can it be taken. How can I best take hold of it, in what multiple ways, and all of these with the obscenity of blindness. Since it will never be what I take.

She said: this is all the same, I know all this, and the kind who say it.

And he could not himself have made such a thorough round comment, as she had made, for which he didn't so much as remember, later, that she had said it but forgot then, in himself, that she was even there, or that he again had her hand, the fingers of which he went over, one by one, counting, making sure.

What summer is more beautiful, he began, and then began again. What summer is more beautiful than the one I can tell you about. Let us think of it as all orchards and that kind of smell, a freshness there, which one couldn't lose hold of if one wanted. From the house, between the single row of maples that stretched down over the slight hill to the field below, it was always to be going somewhere far from the house though I could be called to it by even the slightest of voices, to come back for whatever it was they wanted. And close to the top of this hill I had my coops, for my pigeons, and they were all different colors, different shapes. On the windy days I would let them out, with the clouds, and they would go up, very high, except for those who could not quite get there or loop in long fast circles, but would hang in the air, to wait for the others to come round or back, and then would start off, as leaders, only to be left again, and to wait. These were my fantails, which were awkward, strutting birds, with wide spread tails. Mine were white and one spring I had a very nice one but he wasn't banded and so he was never worth very much to anyone but myself. But that is another tragedy, and not this one.

We spent that summer at home and when my mother's vacation came, we didn't go anywhere, to the beach or up to the mountains, but stayed there in the town. I expect that I was a little sorry then, but not too much. I had any number of birds that year and could not be got very far from them, except to see someone else's, which got me about at least a little, here and there, to see the other boys of my age, or the men who had not got beyond this time in their own lives and whose garages or houses still sprouted with flycoops and a variety of pens. It was something to do.

He had left the first part of that summer, to go to a camp, a caddy-camp, some distance away, at a big hotel, in the mountains, which his father thought would be good for him, to learn to take it, and to make a little money. He was somewhat stronger than myself, a year older, so in that way he went, without thinking much of myself or that it was strange that I didn't go too. Another year I was to have gone, he said. I would go, as it had then been agreed. But for myself, I missed him very much, the first part, and would get cards from him, these not very often, and painfully written, as a fifteen-year-old boy will write to one a year younger than himself, in a way that neither can understand, being fragments thrown off from the very force of his living. I wrote to him much the same things as we had been doing when he was at home, that such and such had come or gone, these all on the only postcards I could get, of the town-hall, looking very grey and shoddy against the hard geometry of the square with the surrounding and enclosing stones. It was not wrong, then, to consider myself, in spite of the summer's warmth, and what I had to do with it, still abject and though I could not then have thought so, pathetic.

Sometimes I would go down to the barn which his father had moved and built again, by himself, though we boys gave what help we could, to be doing something during the fall he put it up. And there it was, then, and maybe now, what tribute he could put into so much wood, for his son, that he could move and put up again with his own hands, to put the pony in, which he couldn't afford, yet would have. I was allowed to ride the pony that summer, now and then, when he was around but he fed it while his son was away, and would let no one else do very much for it. So for most of the day it was staked out, like a cow, under the apple trees for shade though not so near to any of them that it would eat the apples and get sick.

The barn wasn't too big, just room enough for a good-sized box stall and what hay the pony ate during the winter, and a place for harness and saddle. And he hadn't finished it off altogether, being in a hurry as he was to get it done, so the pony could come, and only himself to do it. So a good number of the boards were nailed with only a single nail in the corners where the pony wouldn't go, though where the stall was and the way out to the main door he had fixed with two-by-eights, double-planked, which the pony would never break through.

A year before the boy and myself had hit upon one board in particular, soon after the pony came, when we were down in the barn, most of the time, that we lifted and put things under, pushing them far back, as far as we could reach, cigarettes and what else we had.

And reaching under there, then, that summer, I could get hold of the corner of the magazine and pull it out, without tearing the page I had got hold of, slowly, dragging it, and then the book, with the back off and the pages mildewed from having been under there so long. And on the first page could see the woman under the slightness of the slip, with its fine line of cloth covering only that much of the breasts which would have been in itself enough for the hand of a fourteen-year old. And where the cloth moved down the body against the flesh, to the leg, and there stopped, to end in a kind of torn edge, against the flesh, which I knew almost by heart, and then to the face, with the look of kind, that kind of, dismay, which then explained the man with his own face, in the picture, across from her, but coming closer, with his hands stretched out and wanting, about to, tear off the slip.

Or the book, which I can, perhaps, still quote, being those pages which I have no right to forget, or not quite so quickly, since it was there written, that '. . . she did not at first understand what he expected of her. But he came closer and then she knew that he was about to . . .' As I myself was.

At least this much we had stored against a time when we should know more of it, that those pages should themselves secure us, that we should then know, all. But not enough then, to see what we were cheated of. Those times I came alone, that summer, to the barn, perhaps, what was I looking for, and here I am very near tears, or much closer than you may think, to look at me. That I should somehow have expected his own words to have been there, on the edge of the page, which would have been meant for me.

What embarrasses here is not altogether what you think but is that which will always be more sad than embarrassing. I am not sure that I speak now, even for myself, that I have not become the fact of much more than I intend. But I do speak of myself, nonetheless.

With the end of summer or towards the end of summer, since it had not quite come but only that slight feel of the days somewhat faint and beginning to go into another kind of color and tone, with that time I began to look for him to come home again, from the camp. Later I read of those fair lovers who lay, without sleep and all cares, on those no harder beds than love's own caring, but then I could not invoke them. That much you must understand. I had no idea of what part I should have in anything, much less in this. So he came home one day towards the first of September, with his father in their car, and drove into the yard opposite ours which was where he lived then, in a small white house, Cape Cod, as they call them, to which his father had added some dormer windows and inside, rooms, so that there would be places for them all. I could see them getting out of the car and then the bags and boxes coming out of the back, with all his things, and then I expect I wanted to go over and help, but didn't, and instead went down to the barn, since I knew he would come there, soon, to see the pony, if it was all right after the summer and his being away from it.

She said: he came.

He came, he said, but it wasn't sad. There was nothing there or in that that got me, then, and it wasn't until later that I got what I should have got there. It had been strong enough apparently to carry the summer with it, all that fine weather, into the colors of the fall, the cold, and then all that winter, sometimes in his house, sometimes in mine.

She said: what had you expected from any of it, being fourteen as you were, or any age, for that matter, what was it you wanted to get out of something like that, that you knew you couldn't, and didn't, later, much want, but just then wanted, as though you knew that later it would have to come to me, this kind of thing, to ask me what I thought and did I understand, as if there, in any of it, was what I was supposed to understand.

I don't know, he said, since then or there I haven't been for sometime. Sometimes it is just that I can't remember any of it or have like a kind of fog that which I felt then, to wonder about, and to put against, even, what I have now.

She said: you haven't anything, even with him here, it's yourself you care about, and want, that you can hurt both of us, or I don't care about him, if it's what you want me to do, that I shouldn't care.

The Seance

SOMEWHAT COLDER, the wind came in at the door, and with a quick turn, shifted and moved down the hall. There, they were sitting, waiting, at the table, backs to the fire, the shadows of them on the wall, against it, big black shapes there which, because they were talking, they didn't see.

A ghost story. An involution back into what was, he said to the other, remember? I give it to you straight, listen.

You see the face, say, that face there. What is it gets on it, I mean, the fact of it coming over & thru, now, as you are looking. Or, how it dies, perhaps, or softens, the thing gone relaxed, like a dying. My hands are cold. I move them a little, flex & wind the fingers together. The coldness. Or rub them, perhaps, one with the other, chafe the skin a little. A charm against what harms them. The coldness. Not so much to laugh at this, or to be laughing, as to see, simply, what it is I am about.

Perhaps, then, in some ways something, something different. Someone is moving. The chair, itself, edges a little, & grates, the legs of it, against the floor. Listen. Unmistakable sound. The slight shifting. The slight noise in the ear. Enough to prove it. Something there. Well, someone. A person, like they say. Man, woman, or child. Who is cold? Not so much cold, as there. That is itself a character.

But even with that, it is still not there, or better, it is away from where we are. Where I am. Or put it simply. I am alone.

To move from this to that. That shift, from here to there where the weather is softer, warmer, & the sun already grows big against the edge of the hills, where the eye hangs, to look at the sun, against it. Strikes out. The trees, green but soft green in the rising fog which the rising wind pushes. He said, never a morning without the slight wind. Clears this fog, cuts thru & lifts it, clears sight.

So good to be stretching. Out, lifts over the edge of the bed, one leg, looks down at the foot, then gets up. Stretches. Through the window, the sun works clear & up, moves higher, & the air is warm.

Lucy sings in the garden, two hours before him, gropes for the weeds, is mad. Tra-las, echoing song. Lifts high as the sun these symptoms of the desperate sound. Weeds, where they grow, catch to her flowers & crowd. She, meticulous, takes each, one by one, carefully, & pulls, lightly, works them loose. The flowers. Color & the morning sun.

Not much more than that, he was saying, I was thinking, again. My head feels thick as a bag of barley. Thick? Well, barley not so much that as slippery. That too, in my head. What was it you wanted to know about – let's get clear on that. At this point it's hard to think straight. I'm in a hurry.

Colder & colder. He rubs his hands more frequently, puts them to his mouth & blows on them, thru. The warm breath. Is uncomfortable & the fire burns out. But flickers. The shadows even more.

The sun, higher & higher. The day burns out. Along. And she is still in the garden, still pulls at the weeds. Which move thru her hands. Counters, Lucy, green, Louise, green. Lionel, green. Lilacs, purple. Purple. Moves her hands with exactness, picks & pulls.

Behind her, thru a chink in the wall, he is watching. Takes after a time, a small pebble & throws it, tosses it, at her. It hits her back & bounces, lightly, down. She shakes & keeps working. He takes another pebble, & throws it, she shakes & keeps working. Another. Throws. She keeps working. Another, larger, throws, harder, another, larger, throws & harder another. She keeps working.

The whistle, far-off, a kind of long screech. All over, they stop. Put down the tools & move in long lines, past the tools & out. A digression.

But the wind shifts, again, comes down the hall, and finds him. Close to the fire, what's left, he puts his hands out to catch what heat is left. Cold, very cold. No moon but out on the fields the weather. Light light. He rubs his hands.

The Grace

FROM SOMEWHERE else he could hear it, but the crying at least had stopped, and turning, he saw her at the door, shutting it quietly, and putting a finger to her lips.

Quiet, she said, and came in, then, to sit down in the chair opposite him, sinking down there and letting her legs go out, slack, in front of her. Behind him he had put the candle and it burned, flickering, but a light, and as soft as any he might hope for.

Otherwise, there was a moon, and this rose, very gently, somewhere back of the house. The road looked a liquid, or water there, translucent. He felt it as pleasant, perhaps, but was too tired to get up and at her suggestion, that they might walk, said, no, and slumped back.

There is no time, he said, but knew she had another sense of it. Something, he said, makes a mess of it.

She got up to light another candle and put it on the table behind him, but bitterly, he thought, and watched her sit down again.

We can hope for another place, he added. This is just for the time-being. Call it a vacation, or anything like that.

But the house, or the rooms, something bothered, and she had little peace, accepting nothing of it, and moving with a kind of rigidness through it all. Now she got up again, impatient, and lighting the stove, began to heat water for the dishes.

Can I help, he said, when she looked at him, but she turned away again, and he relaxed.

Outside it grew light, or seemed to, almost like day, but

whiter, again that translucence, and he wondered if out there one might not be another thing altogether, even though it should seem otherwise. To the west were some small lights, single, each a small brightness, and separate from the rest. He imagined gaiety, or even singing, the tables of some place packed and people altogether without malice. He thought it might be like that, and felt, too, the moon was the sign.

She had cleared the table, taking the dishes to the sink, to put them at the side, and then filled the sink with the water she had heated. Meticulous, in some sense, she washed them one by one, to put them down again, again at the side, until they were done. Then left them there, to dry by themselves.

Sitting down, she looked up at him, and waiting, she reached over to pick up her knitting, and then began, the needles very bright, and quick, in her hands.

But he had started, and spoke, now, of what he had thought himself to have forgotten, a picnic so long ago it seemed inconsequential, though he could not have said, then, why. Somewhere his grandmother had carried out the lemonade, or he remembered it, in a bright tin pitcher, to place it on the long table, under the trees.

It should be like that, he said. What do we give of that, or what do we try to. Tell me one thing we do that is as nice as that.

She hadn't answered, but anyhow he assumed her attention, and wanted to make it clear.

A fine old lady, he said, I mean, really. She knew what work was, though I suppose she minded, certainly. That it couldn't have been very pleasant for her.

I don't suppose it was, she said, and looked at him.

Or that other, the one the old man told us about, his mother, who died by the window there, took three drags on her pipe and then slipped out. How about that!

She laughed, herself, and found it simpler, the time less persistent, and had gone back again, with him, and sat in the old room, as she supposed the old lady had, lifeless, and in the dark.

That was in our house, she said. In the living-room, by the back window. He said she used to knit there too, in the moonlight.

One would like to go back, he had said. One would rather not move away ever, or go anywhere but where one was.

Even so, the moon rose, higher, and now came clear through the door they had left open, and came across the floor very softly, to touch the back of his chair. He grew quiet, sinking down, and pushed out his legs, reaching her, one foot against her own.

From somewhere above the boy cried, whimpering, and putting down the knitting, she got up, to cross to the stairs, and then he heard her go up, the crying continuing, and growing louder. He started to get up himself, but sat down, annoyed, and wondered what the matter was, calling to her, to hear her answer, nothing.

Echoes, he thought. But the crying grew less, then stopped, and soon she was back, and sat down again across from him.

He was frightened, she said, and seeing him angry, added, he isn't settled yet.

The anger went, and left him lost in some other thought, of the house, and where they had been, call it, in another place.

He must miss it, he said. But there it is, I mean, one moves anyhow? And stopped, to say, isn't it? Isn't that what has to happen?

I don't know, he said, insistent. I don't know why it is so much place with them. Not that I don't get it, that is, don't get what moving does to a kid, but what else? We've been here close to two months.

She let him go on, and sat only there, silent, and not with any malice. Hard to believe it otherwise, or he wondered, then, if it could be otherwise. Something he thought of as impenetrable, but getting up, he asked her to come out, saying he felt like a walk now, if she still wanted to.

She followed after him, and they started off down the road, past the other houses, close and then off through the fields, the moon there very much a whiteness and lying on the ground with grace. He said he could not really believe it. That it was, then, a world so very close to their own.

But it is here, he insisted, and took her arm to hold it. It has to be?

They went on, following the edge of the field, the ground rough and uneven under their feet. Now and again she stumbled, and he held her up, and at last they sat down there on the grass, and lay back.

Straight up, above them, the moon was beginning to slip, and sink down, but shone with a fierceness, and made them seem bluish to each other, hands looking pale and unreal.

She had raised herself, a little, then leaned on him, over, and her hands took his own, lightly, as she kissed him. But he had not stopped, or only for that instant, and looked up at the distance above him, saying, he didn't know, and felt the ground hard under both of them.

It's all right, she said, and moved to stroke him, hoping to help, to ease it. One knows that it will be.

He rested, and felt her fingers very careful, finding him with a certain gentleness, or that sure. He said, thanks, and laughed a little, lifting to take hold of her, but they heard the faint crying, from the house, coming after them, and got up.

She went ahead, running, and he called to her to be careful, then saw her reach the road. From somewhere another sound, a cry, rising, to die out. He tripped and fell down, sprawling, and got up again, rubbing his knee.

Coming in, he found it quiet, and she was sitting in the chair by his own. He looked towards the stairs, but she shook her head, and told him the boy was asleep, so he sat down himself, going loose, hopeless, in the chair.

What the hell does it, he said, what starts it off?

But she shrugged, and he saw she had the knitting, and watched the needles begin, easily, moving in and out.

What a night, he said. What a goddamn miserable night.

It seemed nothing, and he grew restless, watching her, intent, and could say nothing, to break it. Getting up again, he asked her if she were tired, and so she put down the knitting, to follow him, blowing out the candle beside her, while he took the other from the table to carry up with them. But there was light enough, from outside, and so he blew it out, to leave it again on the table.

Upstairs, he felt the room deeper, or open, the light making a wideness, and breaking against the sides, pushing, to make a space. He could not know that she saw it, but hoped, and undressing, quietly, laid his clothes on the chair, and got into the bed. He looked back to see she had finished, and then felt her slide in against him, to sink back, on the bed, then turn.

A place, she said, but didn't, and put her hands on him, again gently, and he put his arms around her, still hoping. The room was very light, and the whiteness now altogether actual, seeming even a drift, of some wave, in, to make the room a space, of an intention, or where one might come to live.

Waiting, he went back against the pillow, easily, but somewhere he heard the scream, behind him, and asked if she would want him to go quietly, and being more, he thought, that I can do something, perhaps, which she might wish me to. But she got up, and went into the other bedroom, opening the door then, so that he heard the sounds very close to him, a pain there, and continuing. Quiet again, she came back, but again it started, the boy calling, and she went back.

All right, he called, asking, and she answered, soon, and he lay back, tired, and a little lost. The moon seemed to sink, a crest reached and lost, and he watched it, catching the edge against the window, to try to hold it, but felt it pass.

She came in, standing at the door, and waited to see if the boy would now sleep, but he didn't, calling to her, and she went back.

What's the matter, he said, but she didn't hear. What's the matter, and she answered, again, soon, and he fell back again, to wait there, the night going deep, and on, he said, it must be late.

Then she got into the bed, and lay down, coming to him, then, but nothing, he thought, and heard it, the cry, and got up himself to run to the door, pulling at it, and yelled, what, seeing the boy sitting straight in the bed, staring, and crying, screaming, the sound driving in on him as he came.

What, he yelled, what, what, what, and got hold of the boy, by one arm, dragging him clear of the blanket, then bringing his own hand back, hard, to slap him, the head jerking back, and down. But useless, the screaming now louder, and he felt it useless, picking the boy up, to cradle him, holding him, and walking beside the bed's length, the moon still against them, a light, a light, he said, and went back to the other room to find her waiting with the candle.

Jardou

. . .und leise tönen im Rohr die dunkeln
  Flöten des Herbstes . . .

TRAKL

CLEARING, the wind left, and the sky was very light, and walking along behind them, he sang, but softly, saying, you want to pick all the olives, but I will pick them all. And sang, again, feeling very good, the sky now altogether clear, and from behind the high house in front of them a single white light climbing down and falling all over them in one heap.

But she was in a hurry, and had the boy's hand in her own, to hold it, pulling, as they went on. We are late, she said, and looking back, found him still there behind them, and waited until he had come up to them, to take his hand too. Opening the gate, he went in and they went in after him.

I love you, he said, and stopped to shout, hello, and heard it echo around the building to be answered from the field, another shout, and they started, calling, the boy running in front of them.

He had expected some diligence, to put it that way, or some aspect of determination. But he now saw them almost finished, the mother by the furthest trees, reaching up and pulling off the olives. There was no hurry, he thought, and saw the trees were very old, the branches filled with the fine leaves, fluted, and still wet from the rain. He waved again, to the husband by himself, in the wet grass, and listening, heard the first sounds of their speech not understood, but it was, she said, *le jardin des olives*.

He listened, then went to the mother saying, hello, again, not caring that she would not know it. I love you, he said, but to the other, coming up now to join them, and she made a face back, laughing, the woman standing still nervous, her skirt held out to catch the olives which he began to toss down. Straining, he raked them clear, then dropped them to her, not looking, and saw the olives above him he could not quite reach.

Those, he said, and pointed at them, and his wife explained, the speech wavering, breathy, and she said, he thought, even things he could not understand. Bringing the chair, they both held it firm, and he got up on it, quite safe. Stretching, he picked more, leaning back to get them, and found himself among the higher branches. He picked what were left to give them to the woman, and shook the branches. Getting down, he looked at her, then felt the chair give and put out his hand and touched her, quickly, then stood on the ground.

Once there, they all sat down, and he lay back against the tree's trunk not caring about the wet. The father still sat past them, over to the side, and watched the children. They did not think to bother him at first, then called, and getting up, he came to sit with them.

They grew quite content, under the trees, the father stretched out by the women, an old hat pulled down to the back of his head, nearly reaching the ears. His hair fell very straight beyond it, curling slightly at the neck.

But he was not, even so, unformidable. There was a very precise weight present. The younger man might not have budged it, he thought, but thought then of the woman, and looking, saw her dress almost worn out, and pulled tight about the shoulders.

I love you, he said, and echoed it in invariable silences saying, each time, I love you, but never feeling very much.

Shall we begin again, his wife said, and translated it, to them, so that they both stood up, waiting, but the father was not very interested.

You are not concerned, he said, but could not think of the right words, and his wife repeated it, to the man, smiling, and he shrugged in answer.

I had thought to pick olives, he said then, to his wife, and grew angry. This doesn't seem very close?

And laughed. One didn't care. And got the chair and brought it to another tree, placing it under the high branches, and then climbed up on it, to stand there. Following, both women took hold, so that he might have been their own, held there, in some attitude of attention.

Still the children ran by them, shouting, and played, very happy, the boy tagging after them to join in. Above them all, he looked down, thinking to pronounce any spell, perhaps, saying that it could be that way, but they waited, and he went back to picking.

He gave it, now, all care, parting the leaves with his fingers, and trying to find all those which might be left. It was difficult because the colors were too similar, and hiding in all shadows, it seemed there might be one more. But, below him, they pointed, and following their hands he saw the olives, and picked them, dropping them down.

All done, he said, but asked, and looking down, saw them pointing, and he reached out, to get it, then tossed it down to them.

Are you done, she said, and he got down off the chair, falling down beside them, then took the bag from the woman, smiling, to look at it.

Back of them, the father came back, and stood in a tangle of brush, and lifted a camera, holding it steady, to point, the hands very quiet. But the children would not hold still, and all crammed together until the father shouted at them, something, and they stopped and grouped themselves nicely, the grass brushing against their legs. He took the picture, then bent to wind the film, and went off to the house to leave them, there, by the trees.

Let go, the children would have run off but the mother held them, pulling down the youngest to sit on her lap, and he saw the cloth pull tight, watching, and called to his own boy to come.

Sitting him on his knee, he stroked the hair, the boy chafing, but held quiet there and let him do it. He would have spoken, but couldn't, and looking to his wife, wanted to push, then, at her, to explain, but did not know what he wished explained.

The woman watched, even so, intently and smiling, he

thought, or perhaps she smiled. Behind her, the other children stood all looking at him, and he wished to say something, but knew no words to.

She spoke to his wife, and listening, he heard them wander into sounds so very distant he could think of nothing they might mean, and said, stop it, and hearing him, his wife stopped, to smile, and getting up, he pointed again to the trees.

Some left, he said, but the women still sat and looked after him, and would not come. Behind him, their voices grew alien, and broke too far away to make him listen, so that he walked to the field's edge and turned to see no one but the children, still running among the trees. He watched, then brought them to him, calling, then sent them up into the trees for no reason, and they brushed past him, climbing up into the branches.

Waving, he tossed up twigs, and old bark, and looked for more in the trampled grass, then threw what he found up to see it fall, past the children, to the ground. One, now above him, sang, and he looked up to see her there, braced tight against the crotch of the limbs, and white along the ankles, and up the legs, to the skirt, and waved to her, crying out.

But she said, come, and turning, he saw them there now behind him, and nodding, he took the bag they had given her, and put it into his pocket.

The Boat

No ONE was moving but for William, and they paid him little attention. He came, now, down through the trees, and behind them, very carefully, to a huge rock that overlooked the water. The boat was too far out to see who was in it, but the sails looked beautiful, tight out and driving the boat through the water in a series of chopped lunges. He climbed up on the rock, took a stick he found there, and leaning out, dabbled it in the water. He wrote his own name three times, then his wife's, then those of their three children.

Way off up the field Mrs. Peter had talked of the weather, and she repeated herself, endlessly. The heat came, the sun rising very high and white in the sky, and beyond the field the trees in the orchard looked wilted and dull. She cried. Her face grew very tiny and alone, and with a sense of relief the other man, her friend, bent over quietly with a white handkerchief, and dabbed at her eyes. He implored her to have reason, the conversation had been so tiring, and if they were to be together, ultimately, they must have the necessary courage. But she cried again, until her face was wet, and he held the handkerchief on her cheeks, rubbing them, hopelessly involved to be sure, but some small part of him seemed heroic and manly, and that was the part she looked to.

William, on the rock, knew nothing much more than the heat, and if the sun got any higher, he said, he would lose his mind entirely. The trees rustled slightly, the wind went past them with a murmur, but it was a hot wind, and William crawled down lower on the rock to wet his face in the water. And feeling it cool, he quickly took off his clothes and left them there, and jumped in.

All this the children were aware of, and in the boat they prepared to attack him, not sullenly, but as quickly as he had thought to go into the water like that, they as well saw him and wanted to surprise him by bearing down on him with the boat. They tacked, and the boat shuddered. For a minute the smallest boy's legs were covered with the foam, and he shouted to them all to look. But coming off, the boat righted itself, and again they watched William who swam beyond them.

Hence, in a vague way, it was all, Mrs. Peter said, a question of the heat. William could not hear her, he would not have heard her in any circumstances, but to her friend, recovered, the comment was apt and sensible. Weather as an inexhaustible subject, or he answered her, that this as well they would have to consider, and above all its effects on William's nerves. The right time would be precisely the time when, at an impasse with everything, and with, particularly, the heat, he should no longer give much of a damn about anything, and if he did treasure her, or anything, even so would give it all up quietly enough.

Supposition, she said, was not accurate. The wind blew. But to be in love was to be something, and if heat were elemental, they were likewise of nature's force.

It was a ridiculous time for anything. She couldn't really say that she loved him, and had to think quickly, which one. Her friend looked at her, her eyes were a little red but the face was not for him. He took her hand, because he wanted something, and she let the pressure come, then relax, and squeezed back a little and smiling, wondered again what would become of them.

William was not the question, she knew, or at least she thought it, and then kissed the other man, in almost trite fashion, saying it is very like it always is. And, do I now think what I think because I think other people have thought it. For this there was no reply, the kiss being remote, and very near insult. The speech, anyhow a question, which the friend wanted to answer, but could not. He dressed in a loose shirt, worn outside of his pants, and with a check-like design. The pants were brown, something like khaki. He had black hair, and a small clipped beard on the end of his chin. To be romantic was to be insular in one's concern for others, and in love he acted as though he were looking in a mirror.

Against all that, viciously, the boat went on and in it the children hung one to the rudder, and one to the jib lines, while the
third kept hold of the rope for the boom, and sighted William for
the one sitting behind him. They were almost there. William's
head showed itself a little off to the right, and with a sudden
push, the rudder went over, and they were on top of him.

At that moment he saw them, and why he hadn't before, or
heard them, he had no time to think of, but dove, the boat's
bottom hitting his head. He went down and down, and in spite
of it, thought of them all up there, on the surface. The boat had
gone over, the water again grew light, and from his mouth a
very thin line of little bubbles. Time passed, the weeds shone
blue and green in the depth, the mud felt cool and close on his
body. Then he gave a push with his feet and felt them sink in,
then lift, and then he swam up, and broke the water with a kind
of gasped cry.

They were on the shore, and called out to him, and he
answered by a wave of his hand and swam to them, slowly,
feeling his head ache but had no resentment. The three children
were there, the boat was now anchored and the sails rolled up,
and tied. The rudder had been taken off, and lay across the
back of the boat, drying. At the top of the mast a small red flag
flapped in the breeze and the boat lifted and dropped in the
ground-swell.

It was very lovely, he thought, but even more, this immediate
solicitation, and pulling himself out of the water, he let himself
fall into their hands, and be carried all the long distance to the
house, as the friend took the bulk of the load by holding him
under the arm-pits, gently, and lifting him very carefully so as
not to joggle his head. He swore at the children, and they came
behind him, somewhat afraid. He made no conditions, the sound
of his own voice was ugly, or seemed ugly, to him. When he
had been lowered to the sofa, he wanted to cry, and let them
see it. But their faces were too far away, and he found himself
asleep.

He dreamt of three tigers, in a forest. Their bodies were
striped as he had expected. Their faces were long, with, on each
one, a red tongue lolling out over white teeth. He gave a banana
to each one of them. They ate the bananas, and put the skins
to one side, whereupon he grew frightened, shifted his position,
and began to snore.

Mrs. Peter continued with the business in hand, and she had no doubt that it was, despite the difficulties, an act that could be transacted as elaborately and as completely as the buying of potatoes. In the garden, she drew up a chair, close to the friend whom the matter of the boat had frightened. He felt himself now an outsider, or, more simply, unable to recover his own place with quite the same manipulation. To quiet him, she took off her sun-hat and began to fan herself, then fanned him, so that the moving air lifted the collar of his shirt, which he had left unbuttoned to the middle of his chest, and blew it against his beard.

Now, she said, that there is quiet, now we can settle all of this. He raised himself to listen, and to say what he himself would have to. She said, do you love me. To that, certainly, he replied, yes. They kissed.

But, she said, being married and all, does it matter to you that another man has had my love. And that was not a fair question. The woman who loves is beyond it, she does not see anything more than what she does have, just there and then, in front of her nose. He said, if it does not matter to you, it does not matter to me.

It was enough, and might have been for anyone else, but not for her. She wanted to go away, a long voyage, or anything to get away from him, and from both of them. Well, she said, I love you, but you don't love me. For my own part I think we are not so much in love as I had thought, but, seeing that we have no reason to hurry, take a walk to the beach, and in an hour I will come and join you.

Once he was gone, she went back into the house to look at William. He lay with an arm down over the edge of the sofa, and she could see the place where the boat had hit him. The bruise began at the edge of his hair, back of his ear, then went into the hair itself. It all looked swollen and painful. But she was not sure that she loved him.

If she whistled, or cried out, one of the two might come. Otherwise, she then thought, I have three children. Who would have killed their father this morning, and not even meant to do it.

So it was impossible not to think about life, or the sense of the kind of life she herself might find possible. The room came in, a picture of her own father, or someone, hung at an odd

angle over the cold fireplace. There was no fire and yet she
screamed. But did not scream. In the emptiness she saw William
coming toward her, carrying an oar. He was about to found a
city.

As an alternative she left the room, and went out again into
the garden. The remains of their lunch were still there, and,
over the plates, she saw a swarm of flies. Looking past them,
she saw a briefcase, on the seat of a chair, with gold initials just
over the lock. She went over, and picked it up, and tried to open
it, but could not, and threw it back in the chair in anger. It was
the life of a dead man, not to have kindness, and openness, in
each person met or dealt with. To have secrets was finally to
have desires, and if she could not satisfy them, to keep them
like that was dishonest. She picked up the briefcase again and
threw it into a bed of yellow flowers. What she gave was open,
and all air, she thought. But for them it was the careful locking
up of each particular, because they thought they were men.

The children used another way of things, and taking in the
friend, now they played with him, and soon he was exhausted,
panting after them, foolishly, up and down the beach. He had
taken off his shirt, but they ran too fast, and if he caught one,
another suddenly pelted him with a handful of sand, and, in
trying to see which had done it, he lost hold of the one he had
had, and found his eyes full of sand and tears.

He wanted her to come very badly, he saw their future life
together floating over his head, and, as the wind might take it,
blown away from him. He indulged in this metaphor, and was
like a man lost in himself completely. If he wanted her, then,
he thought, it must be that they leave together right away. To
have the children, he said, and a stone hit him, and a small
spot of blood appeared on the inner side of his ankle.

Mrs. Peter watched all this, and again was powerless. But
coming down, she told the children to stop, and from their own
audacity, which they felt they had perhaps taken too far, they
stopped, and ran down the beach and out of sight. Then she
said, love me, very simply. And, as she asked it, he brushed off
his pants, and came to her, and then led her back to the field,
where they lay down. I want you to be for me, she said, but she
hated him. As his hands touched her, she felt cold finally, and
thanked him for that.

The Gold Diggers

WEST OF the mountains, the land rides out on a flat and open plain and continues for more miles than any one man ever knows of. The light is high, it comes from the farthest point of the sun. If you put a man here, already you find him lonely. If you put two, then what happens is not so much what either one man decides on, but what happens to them no matter.

For both of these reasons they built the shed in the shadow of one tree, which was the only one. To the back they put another slight covering for the machine, that is, the machine which dug for the gold. Sometimes it covered an acre a day, and on others, meeting with less, over twice that area. Their car stood back of it all under a thin canvas. In one of the rooms of the shed there was another machine which gave them electricity, and it ran on the same gasoline which they had provided for the other, at the first, making a cache of fifty large drums of it, at the far end of the site. That much was all safe, and because it had been regulated at the beginning, it now went on without significant interruption.

Only this night one of the men sat by himself on a chair leaning against the tree. He had pushed back with his feet, and the chair lifted, and rested against the tree's trunk. The car was gone, and had left two days before, making a dust cloud far out over the dry ground to the east, and at last leaving him there, as now, sitting on the chair and watching. He said he could drink, and did drink, and left a single bottle, empty, on the ground. It was unpleasant. He sang to himself, and his voice rose out into the air, and against the sun he sang one thing that he could remember, which he called a lament. But he knew this loneliness.

Toward seven or eight the car came back, and at first he saw the small cloud of dust, which might have been made by some incredible stray horse, although there were none. It came closer and closer, and as it did he felt himself aching, and beginning to cry a little not much caring. The car came finally into the yard, and slurred past his chair to stop back of the shed. For a few minutes the doors stayed shut, and from behind the dusty windshield he could see the other man watching him. He tried to smile, but the skin of his face felt too cracked, so that he called out, in protest, and let himself wait for the other man to answer.

Getting out of the car, the man spoke, and motioned him to come over. Now he could smile a little, and saw the packages in the back of the car, piled up as high as the window. Reaching in, he took an armful and followed after the other man into the shed. He watched while the other man put his load down, by the table, but not on it. Then he put his own down.

There was nothing to say but he looked at him, knowing the face so exactly he could see the eyes pushed back into the narrow and quiescent head. He tried to say something, of the sitting there, but the other began to talk now, and they sat down together, facing, while the other paused to open one of the boxes, taking out two small bars of chocolate, and ripped the papers off both, first the shiny and smooth label one, and then the silver under it. He listened.

At first there was only a sort of low and discontinuous obscenity, the phrases marking out a street of the city he could not remember. He knew it was late. There was a bar open, on the corner. The other man went in and sat down there. There were women.

One of them came up to him. He saw her head nodding under a high light, and some of it fell off the hair, glancing down to the glass in his hands. She was smiling at him or trying to also, and her hand had come forward enough to find his own. Speaking to her, his mouth was like the substance of his whole body, and twisted itself to answer. The low phrases continued, marking again and again each act of the meeting.

In her room she went completely into him, against his own will tearing at him, so that he left her, he thought, unconscious.

The obscenities were now actual, they surrounded him. He thought of each thing, and could not even say who he was, or whether this had happened to him, or had not. When he made supper, because the other man was too tired and hardly ate it, he went in a daze, and even the food which the other had brought was almost something he could not taste.

The next day the sun cleared early, and getting out the machine, he oiled it. It looked black, and squat, on the ground. It moved like a tractor, and was long and low. The earth broke under it, shovelled into the front opening, and then ground down and down and down into small, and sortable, fragments. In a hopper at the back the gold itself slowly collected, in a half pure state. To some extent a man could become rich, insofar as the nature of the place allowed him that, and let the gold come up without difficulty. Here they found it uncertain, and some days travelled mile after mile without much of anything.

Because of practice he rode it easily, and without concentration. Before him the land spread flat. The mark of the other days was on his right, and there the land looked chewed and broken. In front of him it was utterly smooth, showing only a trace of rock, here and there, as something too far under him to be important perhaps came up to declare itself. But the gold was there. To that extent it was a job he had chosen for himself, although he had not known then what it would be. But that sort of argument he had the same contempt for he would show against any alternative, to the chosen thing, and had not as yet needed it.

Riding high, he set the steering wheel against his knees, and held it loosely with his hands. He kept his eyes low, clear of the glare of light from the horizon. Under him the machine moved along, carrying him straight forward.

So it went on. He didn't forget anything, but lumped it, now, altogether. He thought the light killed the woman, or the idea of her. He didn't know whether his companion was lying. Perhaps he was. There was no way to prove it. The machine grated on rock, then lifted and slid off, to dig in again ahead of it, and continue. He never looked back because he thought he would not be able to bear it, like a cut on his hand when the blood came too fast. Now he rode it, or drove it, regardless.

Then he stopped. He got down from the seat, swinging clear of the treads with a push of one hand and landed hard on the ground. For a moment he crouched there, leaning against the machine, and then looked around the back of it to the shed. But for the car again, there was nothing different. The tree was there. The shed stood over from it only a short distance, and the door was shut. He couldn't see anyone, and thinking to call, stopped himself, and got back on the machine.

But it was a persistent thought. Somewhere in the screaming, still under him, the sound alone enough to kill out any other, even so there was something else. He would have driven a tractor the same way, and could see no difference possible. He made as straight a furrow as he could, and at the end, let it rear on the turn, to settle again to the run back. Forcing it only a little, he judged he could make it in an hour, and settled himself back to watching the shed reappear, at first a small and indeterminate blur, then larger, until at last he saw it almost clearly, and the tree again beside it.

When he came in, the other man started to talk to him. He told him more of the trip, with the car, and took each mile as it had come, the rabbits shying in front of the lights at night, then the flat emptiness of the day, until, at last, he saw the first towns coming up to him, and then the city. But it was not really possible to believe it. Together they knew everything, and nothing, because one false thing and none of it was true. He thought, he didn't even like the other man, and was with him because he needed him, but not in a way that he might. He poured out the water, carefully, and got the bottle the other had brought from the cupboard and put it on the table beside the plates. Drink, he said, damn you. You have all the fun.

You want to know a real woman, the other said, some real thing. Because that's why I stay here at all. To earn money.

He didn't answer him. He put the rest of the things on the table, and pulled up his own chair to sit down. A real woman, the other man said. One with real hair, and real legs, and real eyes. Real, he said.

But the plates were clean, the food left, unavoidably, dried, and hardened, on the tin. The other man got up and pushing them all together, he picked them up and carried them off to the bucket. He sat down beside it, and poured some water into another tin, and sloshed it over the dishes.

There was nothing to say. He watched the other man's hands, he saw them take the dishes, rubbing them. The water poured over them, back to the tin, then repeated, until the other man got up, and wiped them all with his hand, shaking them, and put them beside the tin on a shelf to dry. It was time to go.

Once again on the machine, the sun came down, clearing his head, he thought. The noise came again. It started as the motor started, then ground deeper into the final sound of the machine moving, and the earth lifting into it. He whistled, and high above the sound could hear the thin, sighing noise. Now he rode the machine, letting it take him, like a horse. Perhaps the gold rattled into the box. The lumps were as big as his fist, he scooped them up, and let them fall through his fingers. Somewhere the whole noise was constant, and became a continuity through which he rode the afternoon.

So he drove carefully. Now and again a ragged patch of mesquite, or some bush, passed him, or else he struck it head on, eating it up. Far ahead sometimes the sun glinted on rock, and as he came up to it, he eased the machine, then hit it. There was the lifting motion, and then they went on. Time after time the plain blurred, and to his eyes it was an ocean, or a place without any disturbance at all. The sun flattened it, it pressed hard in, and down, and forced the nature of the ground itself out.

Then, turning, he saw the woman, not really as even he knew, but there she was even so. He felt embarrassed by the noise, and the nature of the work he was doing. He wished the dust might be not so thick, or the roar so heavy he could not even speak to her. He had no hat that he could rightly raise for her, since the cap he did wear seemed impossible to him to lift. All of it was impossible, he saw her float for a moment, clear of the ground, then she was gone completely. He let the idea stay inside of him. He thought he would never speak of it. He let the roar come back, and drove ahead, sighting the shed, and watched the tree grow larger beside it.

But that night he spoke of it. It was night in the shed now. They ate. The other man got out the bottle and they drank, and he sat there listening to the other man talk again. There were other things to be said. The pictures came, faded, and came back. The woman was all alone. It was an echo coming again and again, back, and in the words of the other, with no intention, continuing until he spoke at last himself, telling all of it, of her being there, and then not there, and finally fell down himself, crying and crying, until the other pulled at him, to make him stop.

You should stop, the other man said. There's no good in that, you wait a minute.

He heard nothing but the sound of the other moving away from him, back to a corner of the room. He waited. His eyes were wet but he made no move to rub them. He lay still forward on the table, keeping his head covered with his hands. Behind him the sounds shifted to a rattling of some paper, something unrolling, and then again he heard the man walking across the room to him. The hand pulled at his shoulder, lifting him, and light hit his face, while the other said, look, pushing it at him, the odor incredible but certain, and again the light fell off the silk and the hair into his eyes.

He went forward, grabbing at the cloth. The other man fell down still holding it, and then sat, on the floor. He kicked at him, and the other fell over completely and rolled flat on the floor, then quiet. The room was quiet. He bent over and picked up the table, and lifting it as high as he could, he let go.

The Suitor

Let them say 'tis grossly done,
so it be fairly done, no matter . . .

THE MERRY WIVES
OF WINDSOR

STAGGERING back along what he took to be the path, he thought, long roads are happy roads, and continued. Somewhere inside the shape now looming beside him, like they say, was also the woman he loved, or had taken himself to, as she had apparently also taken him to. Not to mention her mother, amiable woman, who at least allowed him bedspace. There was a kind of gaiety about it all, and since the party was over – it was about four in the morning – he felt he might well be the last one so possessed.

Kate, he called, through the door, and fell through it because the light stayed off, firmly off, and decidedly. But where was she, in the dark? He listened for sounds of breathing and heard, from somewhere in the blackness, a sough, a kind of sighing wheeze, which hardly bore him much confidence. So he waited, even held himself, quiet, and said, again, Kate?

Finally it answered him, to wit, the dull black form on the bed, now a little at least visible, as it raised itself on an elbow almost, he thought, god bless her, like his own mother, last seen waving to him across or obscured by the tailgate of a truck. But he would never run away from home again. What home he had, could have, there he stayed, forever.

But it was a short night. He heard them talking in the kitchen, through the open doors, of the living-room, and looked out from under the sheets. There was a large painting on the wall opposite him. The voices said, first we will take knives and cut little bits out of his knees, eyes, and toes, and then we will cover him all over with flour, and lard, and push him into this nice big oven, for which we have ordered one ton of coal. She said, he heard it, the coal has come. Will you? He nodded, and she backed out of the room, closing the door behind her.

It was part of the system. To eat is to work, he worked. He got up, dressed quickly in the same clothes he had already, he found, been already, partially, dressed in. He had never taken them off. But once in the air, he took stock of his surroundings. The house across the street had certainly moved in the night. It crowded close to the fence which, he supposed, was the only thing holding it back. In one of the windows a face pressed hard against the glass, looking. He turned and saw, then, a large pile of coal which had been dumped close to a bulkhead which he briefly opened, and began to shovel.

How much later he was never to know there was a rustle at the screen-door also by the bulkhead, and he saw, dimly, someone motioning to him. Come in, she said. He came in. Sitting down, he took up the cup of black coffee gratefully. Thank you, he said. He drank it, gulping a little, an odd but definite constriction in his throat which even the half-cooked egg, eaten later, failed to dislodge. There was no toast because the bread had not yet been got. She said. She looked at him. He looked at her.

Once again he began, this time singing, he did not know why, but soon there was standing close to him a small boy of about ten years, listening. What would you like to hear, he thought. There was certainly enough to tell. Sometimes he thought even of writing it all down, and of then putting it into a bottle, and of then throwing it out the window. Somehow it might arrive on a beach.

Otherwise there was not very much to hope for. The coal was shovelled, all of it, but then there was the bread to be got. He trotted down the road, down the hill, wondering if his buttocks joggled too preposterously. Love had no objections at least. But it also occurred to him, why should it. There were compensations. In the store he asked for one loaf Italian bread, and they gave it to him. Whereupon he handed them the folded dollar, and they returned him change.

This he gave back to them, not to them, but to the two women now in front of him. The bread he put on the table. There was never a clear demarcation between times. Sometimes, idiotically enough, he thought he was sitting in a chair. But if this were so, and if he had taken the bath sometime ago, being obviously dirty, why now should he be objected to? The water dripped from a crack in the ceiling over his head. The mother looked at him, greying hair, grey hair, he thought. She said, oh, you must have sloshed, in your bath. Blackly, he felt himself gripping the arms of the chair but it was an iron sling chair, or something. He sat precariously enough.

No, I did not, he said. How could he prove such a thing? Next time they would certainly think themselves entitled to watch. He sat on the toilet, gripping, dully, the fact that in order to flush it one must bend over, somehow, and turn the little tap handle underneath the seat so that the water could then fill the bowl. And hence, away! There had been that scene. Someone had wanted to brush her teeth. Take me away, he thought. He picked up a magazine and tried to remember how to read.

On page five she asked him if he were thirsty. It was five o'clock? After five o'clock one could drink, seriously. Up till then, beer and wine. She handed him the glass. On the glass, in adhesive tape, was the large, slightly frayed initial, *R*. For rest, he thought. Do you have my glass, the other said, the mother. Is your name ratface? How could he say it? It was too true. She took the glass, smiling, and another was handed to him. Ratface, he thought, ratface, ratface, ratface. I hate you, ratface. He thought.

But there was a scratching at the door, then another face. The face, he saw, of old Bill Bunch, lately hailed, at least frequently, by both mother and daughter as that lovely and impossible man. He was their next door neighbour, so that was helpful. Gossip had it that he could do very little, if anything. He fumbled, he tripped, one time when his son was sick (the ten year old of earlier acquaintance) and then his wife likewise, in the care of the former, and the man, Bill, sent to a hotel in the city to keep him out of the way or under cover, depending on the inference, anyhow he returned home, to help, and tripped walking up the steps and sprained both ankles. No one is safe, he thought, Bill smiled.

Fumbling, Bill took his drink, then faded back to the porch not yet in need of paint, and sat there, with all the security of a man who is an alcoholic and knows it. They would never let him forget it. Why he came here at all, who could say? The mother went after him.

So they were alone, there was a pause, then she turned on the phonograph. He winced. There was a scratching not unlike Bill's, then music, a man singing, screaming rather, a song. The singer was also interesting, like everything else. He was an ex-professor. He had lost his job at any rate. Perhaps to buy the record at all was legitimate charity. It was horrible.

Holding on to the glass, he looked at her. She sang to him, the same song. Along with the record. Let me take you away from all this, he said. It was a reasonable hope. He had shown her his letters. One possible employer wrote, *I should like very much to meet you if you are ever up this way.* Many men have started with less. Take him as anything they could get. That is, they had him. Sweep floors. Putty windows. Paint porches. Shovel coal. But the ton would last longer than that. He hoped. He looked at her. She looked at him.

Coming back in, the mother sat down again. Bill had been dismissed. Through the door, still swinging, he caught sight of an empty glass. How sad to be remembered! No one will do that for me, he thought. Cold wind, icy ground, put no wreathes, down here. Keep talking.

But the subjects were limited, at least now they were. They had heard most of his own stories, he had heard all of theirs. It was a deadlock. Ten more minutes, and they would all be dead. Or at least might be, except to keep drinking, also, and talk, the voices again becoming even last night's. So that to live was a very definite retrogression. Tomorrow will be yesterday, when you see the whites of their eyes, don't shoot.

A gun anyhow was what he wanted. A cool deliberate aim, to lift it, to hold it, pressed close against his shoulder. Here they come, he said. Pam, pam! You're stoned, George, said mother. Ok, he said, I give up.

The Musicians

HE WALKED out with her behind him. At least she stood there, still, hidden from the doorway but to the side, listening, as he went past her, and out into the hall. She was saying, he's there, although the hall was empty. If there was someone there, then he was not there now. He stopped to say, you see, and continued, no one. There is no one here at all. But she closed the door, hard, and left him standing, facing to the stairs.

So at this moment he saw the other man, like, as he thought, that now of course there he would be, to be alone with him. It was where he hadn't looked, above him, the stairs going up obliquely, to the roof, and now the man came down them and said, good morning. He answered, good morning, John. The sun was bright, what was it, eight or nine. One could go out, on the street, walk two blocks, go into some place, sit down, buy perhaps coffee, black perhaps, and a roll or whatnot, and that would be that and nothing more. But he had something else to do. Look, he said, John, come with me, that is, can't we get out of here? He thought, I knew you in school, one time I slept on top of you, with a mattress between us, which is love of a sort, is it not. His eyes filled, with tears. We're friends still, he said. You don't kill all that that easily? But caught himself, because how easy was it, to do it, anything, anytime, even with anyone.

Behind him the man walked down the stairs very quietly, his face down so that it could not be seen. This was simply protective. They went out, at the bottom of the stairs, the one in front of the other, expecting, at least the one in front did, to be there mowed down, a sudden abrupt barrage of machine-gun fire, cutting them precisely in half. The sun dropped past them, to the flat concrete of the courtyard. And tonight you will do the same thing, he thought, you. Getting up makes no difference whatsoever. To anyone. He walked across the courtyard and opened the door into the other half of the building. The hall was yellow, an ochre. They went along it, past the boxes for mail, and out into the street.

Here it was somewhat simpler. Forced, if there were anything, to happen, then a sidestep, or a push, could bring him past it, hidden against a doorway, or jammed into strangers who might, he thought, help him. This was a story of violence and murder. Three found dead, in a bed. Which, bitterly, the bed itself prevented, being not big enough. What would you like to eat, he said, and added, John, have you eaten? The man came up, then, and walked beside him. You know, he said, it wasn't easy. The man walked, beside him. How could it be easy, he said. Words poured into him, from everywhere. How, he said. Look, you know me.

As they went past the door of a cafe, the man made a sign, to go in, but would not go in himself. So he went in, and bought coffee, to go out, then some rolls, which he also thought indicated, and went out when he had them but he saw nothing of the man, and remembered he was to walk back, and up to the man's room, and they would eat, then.

He used this time to reconnoitre, which phrase he got, or had got, from the account of a British, he remembered, spy in Germany during the First World War. The man wrote, at length, of how he had managed to break over the line, between the two armies, and then by virtue of a straight face, hardly more, and a knowledge of the language, which was also given, he worked his way up and up, till at last he was actually in the very top group of the German Command itself. Work and work, keep at it, you too will be on top. An irony. But nonetheless where he both had been, he thought, and well might land again, helpless as he was to stand against it.

But, opening the door, he saw this plan was useless. The room in front of him scattered, fell into, many patterns. There was a picture of a long low car, an old one, tacked on the wall over a table. There were records, and beyond them, a small black phonograph. Simply enough, this was his friend. Well, he

said, do you want proof? Which photograph shall I show you.
Or, simply, the first, of a man, standing by himself in a street,
somewhere in Mexico City. Or rather he walked along the street
and because he did, or John did, his picture was taken, a small
card given him, which he, John, must have remembered later,
and he got the picture and he, John, sent it home. A fact. He
had seen it certainly. He had admired it. How nice to live in
Mexico! There was another, as well, a man sitting at a table,
in a long low room, a round one, which seemed unusual. On
the table there were some plates left over from eating. A girl, a
pretty girl, sat past him and had her head bowed. The picture
was large, the whole feel of it seemed to mean that someone had
both cared to take it, and, having taken it, cared also to print
it like this. So that it could be something not just a cheap
snapshot, however much that is all right too, but something also
better, more durable, simply more careful.

Are you hungry, he said. He put the food and the coffee on
the table, and then, unwrapping it, offered it to his friend. Where
shall I begin, he said. Perhaps I could tell you a story, too?
Let's put it, two men, ourselves, we live in a long black house,
like that one. He pointed to the car, on the wall. Every morning
at ten o'clock sharp we take it out of the place, wherever we
keep it, and we drive it, like hell, up and down, up and down.
We love it. We think there is nothing either greater or any damn
thing else. By god, we enjoy ourselves. Then one day, because
some idiot turns left on a street where there is a huge, huge sign
saying, do *not* turn left, that's it, the end of us. The goddamn
car so smashed, broken, disintegrated, that really we have
nothing at all left. So we go out and so on, maybe to a hospital,
where a beautiful nurse in a long black uniform, I think, sews
us up, good as new, and then we get another car.

Can't we get another car, he said. Can't we do it? The man
drank the coffee, lifting the cardboard cup very carefully. Are
you listening, John, he said. Can't you hear a goddamn thing I
am telling you? But then he sat back, and also drank his own
coffee, slowly. Look, he said, John. There are other ways than
this to tell it? He stopped. Are you listening to me? The man
smiled, and got up, and turning on the phonograph, put on a
record, and sat down.

At that the room became still, though there was the music, a
low quiet thing, perhaps a trumpet, he thought, if I can still

remember. You play the piano, don't you, he said. He thought.
A face, John's face, hair cut short, clipped. A man's funny odd
hands, on a piano, that is, on the keys of a piano. Even, if it
mattered, Boston, Mass. The end.

Play it for me, he said, *me*. He stopped. Did you ever hear
the one about there must have been three of them, people? He
said, there were three people, a man, a man, a woman. God
knows where they lived, a house? Ok. Not long and black this
time, this one is snow-white, has clapboards like in the movies,
roses, the works. Every morning not only the milkman comes,
he brings two dozen milks, the greatest, but also, mind you, at
least the plumber, the mailman, the electrician, the hairdresser,
the modista, the maestro who fixes the walls when they fall
down on your head because you will pound on them. Ok, he
said. What can I do more than that?

The man sat, watching. Behind them both, and through the
window, there was the upper side of the building opposite,
breaking off into a line of others, the roofs of them, even more
broken. Looking, he caught sight of a small crouched figure, on
the roof next to their own, above their heads, and it was her,
sitting there, with some kind of pyjamas on, with a bathrobe
over them, to cover her.

Look, he said. See this. The man got up and went over to the
window, then sat down again.

By god, he said. You know, John, I haven't really tried and
let me do that at least. He stopped again and coughed, and
added, what the hell do you like to drink, at which the man
bent over and pulled a bottle of sherry out from underneath the
bed, uncorked it, and handed it to him. He swallowed, quickly,
and handed it back.

It's never easy, he said, never. What should I say, that I
was walking down the street? When suddenly, and from out of
nowhere, comes a truck and hits me? That's love, John. Nothing
more, nothing less. You had a mother?

The man said, don't talk about my mother, saying it carefully,
so that he stopped, again, to listen to him. Because he did not
know John's mother, but wanted to, not for maudlin reasons,
but there it was, something unknown, and a pleasure. Why
don't we go to Mexico, he said. He watched the man carefully.
There's a bus, he said, it's not impossible?

Or work, he said. Look, I would like to work, I would like to do something outside. He made a movement of his hands, and there it was, perhaps a big hole in the ground, in which others sweated, but never himself. I would like to get out of this.

John, he said, for the last time, look. Nothing is easy. Because, he said, three things matter. That one eat, that one sleep, that one make it. Three finite actions, which can, I think, be accomplished?

The man got up, coming towards him, saying, to go, as he knew, and behind them, also she moved, on the roof, and seeing that, then it was ugly, unsimplified. Don't cry, he said. That doesn't help.

The Dress

MUCH WAS simple about Mary and Peter, and to describe them quickly, it was first of all two people, in a house into which not many others came. And three children, pushed into corners, and a friend or two who came to call. After ten years or so of living together, there were no very actual mementos, or none that either felt much disposition to recognise. There were no flags, and in fact few signs of even time except for the children, and a scar which traversed Mary from belly-button to bottom. Which both had *done*, but also for which Peter was in some sense guilty. Not her.

But, passing that, walking into the room, at this instant, saying something, Peter wanted one action, definite, to place them all in that place where time shall have no dominion. Louise, Mary's *present* friend, was a tall woman, dangling happy jiggly things hung from both ears with such weight that he was worried her ears might tear loose. The pain of speaking was in this way increased.

But. Now – for once he shook free of it, taking with him both Louise. And Mary. And through a small opening in the floor, pulled them down, into where *he* lived. Saying nothing, because there was nothing to say, *now* he led them through a tiny passage, obliging Louise in particular to crawl on all embarrassed fours, like the tiny and comfortable being she was. He snapped a whip. He turned on a light, and, in an instant, the cavern was flooded with a warm rich yellow searching glow. Peering into the two faces looking up at him, he saw, first dismay. Then, laughter.

And then, dismay. So back up they went, into the room, and sat there.

Mary's dress, half-finished, lay on the table, and this is what the two women had been talking about, planning, deciding, when he had, first, come in. It was question as to whether this material, as an added border, and so, design, would be the best, the most interesting, or, on the other hand, that. Two materials lay beside the half-finished dress, in long narrow strips, and on one there was a quiet, rich, oblique design of some warm grey and blue and red. And on the other, a more excited, flaring, intense design of green, yellow and blue. Louise asked him what he thought would look best, and Mary, by her listening, also was curious to know. So he thought, *under* the dress will be, of course, Mary. So what is Mary like? Yet that necessitated returning to *under* the floor, so down they all went again, the women this time less hesitant, as he drew them on, and down, and also more curious to explore, should he let them, this sudden, exciting inclination.

He let them explore, and as the yellow light reached all corners of the underfloor cavern, the two women went, hand in hand, to one after another of the sights which were there. As, for example, the stalactites and the stalagmites. Which had been formed by the dripping, and which hung, like icicles, from the roof of the cavern. The dripping itself was from a fissure, a cleft or split. But also, a narrow opening in an *organ*, as was now the case. A cleavage. *Findo.* To *cleave.* Peter had accomplished this by a daily *expenditure*, and these objects, precariously enough arrived at and/or created, were important to him.

The women moved incautiously, because these things were not what he had done, not, that is, what they had done for him. Mary did many things for him, as she now did, certainly, in the present place – by moving there at all – and by looking, touching, exploring. Louise, striking one of the pendular accumulations with the hard heel of her hand, said, listen! And from the hanging, or rather the hanging up spike-like accumulation, came notes, with each blow, like those of Big Ben chiming the hour, in London. Peter brusquely silenced her, and it was then that both women reminded him of their reason for coming to the cavern at all.

So again they sat in the room, with the dress material across Mary's knees, while she bent over it, as if to catch, now, in some pattern of the varied cloth, an instance of her own person. Finally, in short, this was to be her own *person*, or at least was, from, roughly, the knees to the neck, with arms and varied other areas left clear. Under it, of course, would be her own body.

Louise interposed the *idea* of, in New Mexico, Indian women, with their many layered dresses, built out into a raging, piled, and then formed piece of clothing. This, with the hair pulled back, long and left to hang down. Also, they had straight backs, fine clear features, a race altogether of clean, dark women. Under this onslaught, Mary buckled, adding for herself a host of other details, taken from pictures of Mexican women, Italian women, and the more known Spanish women. Peter himself saw his wife as *white*, and had known her as such. He added to the material which she held, on her knees, the memory of other materials, and, in particular, one thin worn black and purple-spotted dress, for which he had a great fondness. This dress, when she wore it, swelled into desirable proportions, the breasts forward, the waist drawn in, and for the neck, low and round, of the dress, a leaving open of the bones, which formed the height of the body, wide, then certain, down, into the complexity of the *flesh*.

It was the friend's *premise*, however, to make the wife not a wife? This was where Peter himself was confused. To take Louise, too, into the cavern – she was with Mary and that allowed it. Louise, looking at him, now, was *older* than he was. As, in some crowded neighbourhood, this building is older than that one, and, because it is, insists on itself as in that way more rightly there. Under any dress the body is this or that, older or younger, whiter or darker. Under the floor he had the cavern to think about, but Louise could not think *about* it. She was either there or not. Mary likewise.

Mary, the young wife, getting up, put the cloth on the table where it had first been, and went out to see about supper. In the room behind them Louise and Peter heard her speak, then the maid answer, then Mary speaking again. Whether or not the children had always been in the room, as they were now, looking at both Peter and Louise, covetously, was not certain. Could he take *Louise* into the cavern? Alone?

In the cavern Louise stood back from him, crouched under the warm yellow light, and hidden behind the multiplicity of forms which crowded from all sides. He spoke, yet the voice in finding her became too changed to be recognised. It was not his voice. Had he thought of her otherwise, he might well have approached her. But he did not. Soon other faces looked down from that point at which they had entered the cavern, little faces looked down, three in number. This time Louise did not strike the coagulated, hardened and depending forms with her hand. No tone at all broke the silence.

Yet the relief was in the *body*, both his and hers, and also Mary's. Who was not present, but was felt, among them, and each, Louise and himself, insisted on that knowledge. In the yellow light one group of stalactites and stalagmites appeared to be a castle. Another, not far from where Louise continued to *creep*, back, on hands and knees, was a snow scene, and reared, up and down, in sinuous, fixed motion.

When Mary re-entered the room Louise spoke to her, but Peter was unable to. He remained in the cavern. But concern soon brought him out, and closely listening, he accepted the invitation of their words and re-addressed himself to the problem of material.

Was the dress to be final – is in effect how he addressed it. The *body* was not final, yet women — or rather his wife – she was final. Louise was not. In the cavern, revealed, or veiled? In that light it was Louise, entire, who was revealed. In the mind, or idea, of Peter.

Picking up the material again, Mary let it spread over her knees and looked at Peter, and then at Louise. The concern was whether or not the dress was to be her own person, or Louise's. Or the Indian women. Or, in the cavern, all these forms were taken care of, redisposed, in, surely, a wide variety of *attitudes*. Peter wanted a dress, for Mary, that would not be Louise at all. He wanted desperately enough, to make the *body* present, all of it, by simply that clothing of Mary, which would not re-displace her, not again. Each time she left the room he thought she would never come back. He was left with Louise.

Left with Peter, Louise turned to Mary. It was Mary's suggestion that, in the cavern, they wear *no* clothes, because she was Peter's wife. But Louise wanted the *dress*. She arranged the dress on Mary, and then chose the intenser, more flaring design of green, yellow and blue, from the two materials, either one of which she might have added. To finish the dress, Peter laughed but felt dismayed too. This was to be Mary's *own* person. Mary readjusted the half-done dress upon herself, and held the material, which Louise had chosen, against it. The dress, with the material, became her.

But the *cavern* was and *is* an underfloor hollow, with a *horizontal* entrance, and is made by the *subsiding* or *giving inwards*, or *smashing in*, of *soil, walls*, etc. Cavern-dwellers are *prehistoric* men living in these huge or deep *hollows within solids*. Peter said.

The Book

HE WAS bringing the book in a gesture of final hope, something he had found in a bookstore just after leaving her. *Oh bright and sunny day*, and words to an old English time and tune, measure of clear voice and air. She liked to sing, in a high clear voice, a little thick at times, chirruped, like a secure bird. The book was a paperback collection of English Aires and Folksongs, edited by authentic people she would be careful to see.

Down the street, walking heavily along, it was time to be not drunk but the afternoon was heavy and slow, he was drunk with beer and dirtiness. All over his body, sluggish sweaty clothing under the dusty sun, walking more than he was used to, the streets were hard and barren.

She had a number of songs she would sing. At one time it is possible that she might have been trained to sing professionally. It was a leftover hope in that sense, a little of an ability put to fond memory's sake and trust to it to reappear, always. They do not forget what they meant to do, but just don't do it. She sang not happily altogether, not wildly, certainly, nor loudly, sadly, strongly, longly. Just enough to be the memory, turn on the radio, the Victrola, and listen. Concerts and early training were the strengths she had.

She had painted also. She had been trained in that in a large grey building along a dark avenue of the city. It was a timorous place, yet aggressive with age and authority of that kind. He once rented a room on that street. He had to go through the living-room of the owners to get to his own room, through theirs to the back. He moved his things in, sat on the bed for only a few minutes and then apologised and moved out. Had he apologised? The sins of walking are the sins of memory, and she was not in that at all.

He lit a cigarette and considered his direction. A drug-store lay on his left at some distance, a flat square with a few trees in a triangle beyond it, then across, a row of usual businesses along the same avenue.

She was there somewhere in that maze. At another crossing of a street, a hotel for women, Y.W.C.A., kindest of all refuges, heaps of people who must be secured, for a moment, against sex, age, and other identity.

Earlier, "I didn't expect you so quickly, I had just come down." He had called her, at the desk, a woman watching him in dull glasses, piled hair, but prim, and not friendly. Who came here? Ask for your wife, mother, sister, the girl friend, is she here? Like a morgue of women, that sex, all of them, beds and beds and beds of them. Think of the sound, snoring, wheezing, blowing, puffing, breathing, in beds in sleep.

"Not about that," he wanted to say. "Don't," she was saying, and she was crying. "I don't want to go through it all again. I can't tell you more. I don't know more. There isn't any more to tell."

Explain. I was raped on the boat, not raped but like that. I lost a thousand dollars in a purse, on the train. I bought a lot of Italian blouses. I do what I want to, now.

What is the English song? Something like, *I want to go where the birds go.* Not quite, but that flavor of old softness, a deep blanket of cold clear warmth. Hush, they are singing, *down in old Bethlehem the lights are low.* No but carefully, you can't get it right all the time. The note goes up there, then, one, two, down it goes. Lightly. *They came upon*, not so common, it is, *a statue, weeping at grief.*

It was a brutal dullness that he felt, walking. Having intended to do it, he wanted to do it, and with the book in his hand, wet with the sweat of his hand, from walking, it was not new. It was a dirty old plan, with the walking. The old book worn with the intention of taking it to her. As though next week he had remembered a plan which he had thought of and done, accomplished, paid bill of something or other. No history in that, nothing solved, no answer because he was being overcome by the action of walking towards her, the time climbing up on him as though it were a weight he accumulated step by step.

Can't you sing, too? No, I don't feel easy doing it, I try to hard enough, try too, hard enough. No but I can't. Can't you? No.

Would he ever see her again in this life, he thought. This day perhaps, again. Talking at lunch with food he did not like, want, to eat, a failure in that so reminiscent of his meals with her, and for years to come quite the same. Oh he wouldn't change. That was the song.

He had meant everything he had ever done. Not to do many things, to do a few also.

"Oh, where do the birds go when the summer's sun is through?"

No, but closer, a little closer, each time. The words go along a line in movement with the song, the song is in that way a song, of words. That tell what? Oh common things, of women and men, lads and lasses, hay, corn fields, horses, old roads, stones and crows, roses and one begins, "I remember, I remember, the house." Not so common but later, earlier, into some practice of ear and voice he knew nothing of. Say it slowly.

"Waley. Waley. Oh, love is bonny. A little whi(high)le while it is new." That was the true one, the right one. Sing it. It was in the book which he held in his hand. A documented pair who had done the selection assured her, would assure her, they were all there.

Sing:

> *The street is the book is*
> *in the garden*
> *sitting on your knee*
> *my dear old England . . .*

Sing of her, that is the garden's insolence, that bent the seat she sat in, broke the thorn to get a better hold, to stick it in the face of winter's thorn, bleak wind and cutting frost, aghast upon the frozen pane, the wind doth drive upon, fast night, fast moon, stuck fast in ice today. English songs are pretty little songs with a right, bright tune which followeth.

The book in his hand had a slight weight, but the heat of the hand as pressed against it, holding it, was the bother of it. He had no idea as to which street would most quickly get him there.

He wandered, a little drunk still, hence walking head forward steadily. People he supposed to be looking at him, or after, but he could not change his eyes. They went forward as his feet.

He listened slowly, closely, to all that she played him, on the phonograph. He had burnt out the fuses on two floors of the building in which they lived, fixing it better, more volume, more sound to it. The bump and grind of calypso, Charlie Parker. Listen to it. The song is, *oh where do the birds go, you don't see them any more now*. No but you can't hear it enough, so sweetly, so lightly. Hear it. Listen closely, then pick up the instrument and play it. Blow, this way, across, making the sound lift out of the long wood. Hold it firmly but do not over-press. A sound as in the woods' hollow, from furtive shadow and water, the reeds and willows of the wood. Not to be learned in an instant. Listen, and again, listen. He sang with a sharp croak, oh shut the door behind you. She was always not shutting the bathroom door.

In a maze of people, streets, then brought to doors, one after another of them, or parks like deserted, contaminated areas, as if cut off, out of the activity, as if to be rebuilt as parks one day, woods, hollows, water. A pipe dripped water into a stone basin. He wet his hands and then wiped them on his pants. He sat down to think of his direction.

"Not ever again," she said. No but one last time, say. This was outside the call of duty. One last look, book, like not forever, but one last time, Hey it's you! By god, it's you. I never expected to find you here like this. Oh say, what happy day, you came my way, and that was a song. Sing it.

He got up no longer knowing where he was. He asked the man passing where it was, and got a vague answer. The drunk with the book. Look, the drunk's got a book. A new book. They wouldn't answer him but went past quickly, smiling, frowning. Perhaps he would try to sell the book to them.

He wasn't that drunk. He was heartbroken. He was hot, tired with walking, wanted to drink beer, wanted friends, a home, wife and friends and beer. He sang a song for that sound. He kept on walking but it wasn't fair anymore.

You're not listening. Yes but he couldn't get the words. Like this, and one, and two, like this, and there, you hear it, now, and one, and two. *The boy stood in the burning bush. His hair was all on fire. He thought that he would burn to death. And very soon expire.* Yes but not, like this. Song it is, wrong it is. He kept walking because the plan had been made, no longer to be thought of as anything else. Get the book to her. Get the goddamn book to her. Show her what you can do. The book with the songs.

THE ISLAND

It is all one to me where I begin;
for I shall come back again there.
PARMENIDES

For Charles Olson

A SUSPICIOUSLY simple sense of life is that it is, in any one man, conclusive. Oh, for *him* – of course; but for this world I wonder, or rather think it is only in the relationships men manage, that they live at all. People try with an increasing despair to live, and to come to something, some place, or person. They want an island in which the world will be at last a place circumscribed by visible horizons. They want to love free of a community by visible horizons. They want to love free of a continuity of roads, and other places. This island is, finally, not real, however tangible it once seemed to me. I have found that time, even if it will not offer much more than a place to die in, nonetheless carries one on, away from this or any other island. The people, too, are gone.

Vancouver, British Columbia
1963

I

1

FROM THE north side of the island the carts began the journey into the city. The line of them wavered as it climbed in the blackness of the night, up the turning road of the hill in half circles, swinging in the darkness back and forth, slowly, up and up as their lights faded into the distance of the night. The town left below them faded also with only the slurring wash of the sea and a donkey, left high on the hill, to break the quiet.

It was a place marked by little, and once the carts had gone, and the people who had helped load them were again in their houses, the doors shut and lights put out, the town settled back into the darkness, blurring against the slope of the hill. Nothing changed. No one knew when the town had first come there, nor did any question it would not be, as ever, each time the sun returned to them over the edge of the mountains. There was no newness, no shifting strangeness, or oddness of people or of things. Whoever did come, as the one family from beyond their world that had, was taken in, and let live as all.

In the night the house in which the Americans were sleeping had settled into the same quiet as each shared. Only the taxi coming toward them through the darkness depended upon their difference, and it was their friend, Artie, sitting in the back, who wanted them to be specifically what Americans always were, generous, understanding, and naive. Half drunk, he wanted to reassure the driver, apparently an ordinary man though much excited by the lateness of the hour and the road, which grew worse.

As they dropped down toward the town, the carts, coming

up out of it, pulled over half asleep, and the driver of the taxi swept past them. The pitch of the road confused him and he expected each new curve to bring them at last to the flat far below. So into the town they came in the wheezing car at a mighty clip, sweeping past the sleeping houses, until Artie yelled it's the next road, and the driver braked hard and swung as the car leaped right and at last stopped in front of the house which Artie indicated.

The barber shop, occupying the first floor, was certainly closed, but the barber and his family were awake. They heard the car stop with old memories of half-light visits, and the silence which followed them, the disappearing friends. But this had to do with the Americans and so letting their door fall open a little, they saw Artie clumsily tip-toeing up the stairs to the second floor entrance. He waved a discreet acknowledgement of their presence. The man smiled back and Artie for a moment wanted to make him his destination. But he went on and coming to the door, knocked softly, then more desperately, then without question pounded and pounded. The barber called, they are still all asleep, mister, you had better come back again later, they are still asleep.

High above in the hall that made do as bedroom John was waking up, hearing through sleep the pounding of Artie below. His wife moved heavily beside him, also waking, and they got up. Artie, waiting, had stopped pounding. John opened the door and looked straight into Artie's vigorous smile, the short, bandy figure, all of Artie that there was to see. He was there all the way, and was saying something like, awfully sorry, John, such an hour, but had to see you, get canned you know, need to pay the chap, so obliging, such a long way, can you let me have the money, for the cab, pay you back this Friday. Godforsaken Artie with his thin hopes, impeccable courage, such bare affronteries, all of it compounded in a jerky, wistful, beautifully wise and at times quite horrible Cockney, which wasn't at that authentic. John was moving back to see him more clearly, but Artie followed him in, calling to the wife beyond, hello Joan, I'm sorry but I had to come, saying, it's me, Artie, wandering in past John to find a chair, then sat, making a gesture to John to please pay the man who might be coming up the stairs after them all. Dazedly John was getting the money from the table and then went down to pay the man, who left. Artie, left to his thoughts, praised the good John and also his own resourcefulness, because John was not a bad fellow, although slow, at least at five in the morning. He would listen and get him back to the city as well, to the job and the devils which beset him, very constant creatures bewildered only by much drinking for which his salary ill provided. And then his wife, Marge, whose heavy name was not her, whom he had thought to rescue, take away, and whom he *had* rescued, now vaguely, disinterestedly, disapproving, caught by love in a pattern she no longer much believed in, was enough, he thought, did Artie, to make a man drink, mightily.

Oh how I love her, John, he said. But you know what good that does, chuckling, a pointing finger toward the room that served as kitchen where the other wife was making them both a reluctant breakfast. I can't stop it. I know it will kill us all, but you know too, John, have to do it. Simply must. No peace otherwise.

John, seeing that his wife was out of sight, got the brandy bottle from the same table at which they sat, and glasses left from last night's supper, and poured them both a drink. They drank quickly, Artie gulping and smiling, John gagging, swallowing hard. What's up, said John. Why so far from home.

Artie relaxed, gave him the same old story but John liked it. The night he himself was usually so far away from, bedded down in a loneliness with wife and tired kids, the writer on perpetual vacation on his wife's money, all the weary terms of a reality he had tried to make serviceable for all of them, and she as well, working hard at it, both making huge mountains out of each and every molehill. Artie, slyly, saw John's excitement as he talked on, revived by the brandy, settled, at home now, and he made such a pleasure of it all, with an even kind acknowledgement of his friend's limits.

They were all there, John. I went into the Cave, you know, all the girls, and the two guitar players, no one there but an old Englishman, old rummy bloke, with a Spanish girl, bad show. So I got them all a drink and we ended all around that old man, with his poor girl, and other girls were teasing him, in Spanish of course, poor old stranger! Then Manny the painter came in, so we went over to the Burro's place, and got blotto, and that's where I got that taxi, because I couldn't go home in that condition. And now it's morning, is it, and the bloody old job to be done. I had to see you, John, because I miss you, you know, a night like that, and no John, it's not right.

John, coming awake, could see the light growing in the windows, and beyond, the roofs of the houses dropping off to the sea, not itself visible, but he could hear it as the wind lifted, a swelling mutter of water moving in against the rocky shore. It was day now. Joan brought in their breakfast of eggs and a little bacon, and some of yesterday's bread, coffee. They sat in a union of small necessities, not one removed from that, ever, as this time it was Artie's turn, but soon enough John's, and then, at last, Joan's. And what was it this time, Joan said and Artie shrugged, smiling. He knew her, the shyness of the hope in her, small woman also as he was a small man. So he could say, it's to see your smiling face and to eat your delicious cooking that I have come, fair lady, or words to the equivalent, a mocking pass of her criticism. She answered, it's too early for that, and Marge will be upset at your not getting home. Artie agreed but ate nonetheless. On the floor above them the children began to stir, and then the gawky and half-grown oldest appeared looking in at them from the doorway down from the stairs. Artie waved to him, and Joan got up to go back up the stairs with him, to help him find his clothes. The baby began to cry, and it was time to be moving.

They had a last quick drink for the road, and Artie followed John down and out onto the street, to where the car was parked, a ramshackle old vehicle, a sort of odd two-seater with the passenger's placed a little back of the driver's so forcing passenger to lean forward in order to be heard while in transit. It was parked in the shed of an old woman's house, for a low rent, but meant that the woman be greeted each time the car was used. Being so early, she was only peering out from a window at them as they got in. John nodded politely at her as they went past her view of them, onto the road.

2

As THEY came closer to the city, Artie's good humour began to slump. It is a lovely drive, and at times, most often unexpected, passing a field of olive trees and all the ancient twistedness of forms, a single voice will call out in a deep, plain song to be answered as it stops by another such voice, equally alone yet calling out of isolation and clear time, to be heard. It breaks the heart to hear it. These are men and women, both, picking olives, a laborious operation, painstaking in some ways, very slow at least for one watching. Artie thought of work as the one persistent qualification of his freedom.

The car battered along up the continuing hills, then down into the valleys, through small towns. John wanted to give Artie some of the sense he himself had of the job. Not working, he felt himself more capable of such a judgement, and more to the point, it was a job for which he envied Artie.

A problematic sense of self-respect. Something lost in trying to kick against the pricks unless the vision, call it, is complete, and secures itself in its own inviolability. Blake says, I am Socrates. John said that in the act of non-adaptation to the demands of an economic system may lie a commitment to the system's forms far more destructive an involvement than any simple-minded conformity. But such a long and dull sentence it had to seem. Is *this* philosophy? No, but it is a qualification of a dilemma, since men for the most part work in large clusters involving no definition of them but their own objective applicability, in a work guise, to a general program. What they do with their own time is their own business? Or else they fight through to, or are given, a direction of that program. Their elusive identity, by no means clear at birth (except as a statistic, an act of addition) seems even more muted as they move, as parts, toward the inner heart of the shifting complex. John shudders with a sense of his own uselessness.

Topping a rise, they heard through the noise of the motor someone singing. As they went past, they could see the man's figure far off among the olive trees, holding up the long, narrowing ladder, about to climb. The morning was fresh and green, but soon for Artie (Artie thought) it will be a small, close room with a dulled boy sitting across from him, impatient to be through.

Artie said, that other character who taught him wrote a whole bloody play with the kid just sitting there, watching. He used to tell him to keep quiet and study his Latin, whole bloody pages of translation, and now of course he's in London with the

B.B.C. and rich old ladies giving him all the money he can
bloody well carry.

John laughed. The job was a good one, a simple one, involving
only the boy, for relatively limited periods. But Artie tended to
argue its intrusions, into his own desperate enough privacy. The
employer, more properly a writer than either John or Artie,
being more than self-acknowledged and now famous, was a
variable figure.

You know he told Marge it was all right for her to have
intercourse up to the seventh month? As if we shouldn't know
that, he tells her, gets her alone and confides to her that little
piece of information.

(So you're going to have a baby, Artie? Yes, I am, rather she
is. It will no doubt kill us both. What do you want, Artie, a boy
or a girl? We'll get what we get, John, I think she'd rather it
was a girl. Are you pleased, Artie? I'm scared, John, I'm afraid
for it, and what can I give her to help? You'll think of something,
Artie.)

They began to come into the city. Here the road first changes
from dirt to hard top, with pot holes from the wear. To one side
a trolley track runs along and the trolley itself passes from time
to time, with a clanking bell, and many people inside. They
look out interestedly at everything that confronts them. At one
point the trolley swings off the road completely, runs through
the back yard and small orchard of a nearby house, then returns.
The first substantial building to be seen is a long, heavy barracks
for soldiers in sleazy uniforms which fit poorly, boys who are,
most of them, allowed much of the day off for working at jobs
in the city. They seem unsure of themselves and flock together,
laughing nervously but rarely drunk. Then come the small
apartments, new, cement block buildings with stucco surface
painted in light pastels, or white. The ground around these is
usually pounded-down dirt, an almost polished surface after a
rain from the many feet which make use of it. Children, inevitably, play with a complex variety of objects, as bottles, cans,
balls, balloons, sticks, stones, pieces of string. Their noise is
constant, a sudden shrieking, crying, or laughter.

The apartment in which the writer lived was only a few blocks
from this first approach, but they were to go to Artie's, which
was over a little, and closer. Artie had lived above the writer,
who rented two complete floors of the building, having a family

of some size himself. But here, Artie said, they had had no
privacy at all, because the writer at any moment might come
in upon them, to ask some question or to demand some service.
But then John remembered having seen him there once or twice
only, and one time when he had come with his own two boys,
the writer had suddenly appeared, as John sat there waiting for
Artie to return, and they had talked. Or rather he had found
himself confronted by the writer's long, childlike face, with
curling, greying hair, a face with eyes of intelligent kindness
John thought. As if all but the belief had been, at last, battered
out. He had with him a great collection of marbles, both glassies
and otherwise, and he had given each of the children, who liked
him, a large one. That much John remembered. In any case he
found himself thinking of the same man differently as they came
to the anonymous street on which Artie lived.

I'll tell her I was with you last night, at your place, I met
you in the city and you took me back, we started talking and it
got too late to come back. There was always a plan for Artie.
But inside the apartment his wife was not at first to be seen.
Then her voice came from the bedroom, calling, Arthur? Artie
went in to see her while John waited, a little uneasily for fear
of some argument though these rarely occurred publicly. It was
more usually a sudden flare of nervous temper that Marge used
on Artie, who tended to flinch from it like a whip's flicking.
Now John was motioned into the bedroom as well by Arthur.

The sight of Marge on the bed, in the bed, was in some way
disturbing to John. He said hello to her easily, but that was a
matter of training. He was again thinking of them both, as a
couple, a prurient curiosity putting them there together in the
bed, the more grotesque as Artie's subservience in her presence
made his size suddenly abject instead of ambitious. She was so
long and so pale and darkly blonde, with faint blue grey eyes,
yet clear eyes, eyes that saw through Artie with a painful
sharpness. How can they manage happiness, John was thinking.
There was an awkward pause.

Did you have a good talk, she was saying, propped up by the
pillows. Was she sick then? She was resting only.

Yes, we did. Your husband is a wise and provocative man.
But he didn't convince her. She was all but laughing at them,
the silly little boys with their silly little stories. It was Marge
who saw the writer only as a man amusing to her at times, and

at times not. She was a thoroughly bored woman, waiting, so she implied, for an impossible excitement to arrive and arouse her.

Well, he said, nobody got hurt, and that's a pleasure.

She smiled, but said, Arthur, you'll be late. Late for what? For the duties. There were great suspensions in a conversation with Marge that only conjecture could fill. Arthur wasn't even in the room, having gone to make himself a quick sandwich, or to drink something. John didn't know which. He called back out the door, do you want to go over now? I'll take you. Marge said to come back when he had finished and she would make him some coffee, and would be up. Arthur was in the small room, fluttering, saying good-by.

In the car Artie reminded John that Marge found him, John, an attractive man, which seemed a curious luxury of interest on Marge's part. Artie had told him some time earlier that Marge liked him, and that the reason why she liked him was because he was attractive, that vagary, confused the more by Marge's apparent somnolence, akin to a snake's whose attention can wake with an instant nervous presence.

John reminded Artie that he liked Marge also, and Artie as well. John and Joan were to Marge and Artie, as Marge and Artie, to John and Joan. The society which they enjoyed seemed to enforce a coupling for a reference beyond that of nature, the buddy system in short. No one got lost and there was a quick ally, most happily for purposes of mutual defence. And yet that fell apart. Lost in work or lost in marriage, American and English both were provided too often with buckets full of family, to put out whatever fires the lone eye might otherwise be drawn to.

Who the hell cares who likes who, John wanted to know. He envied intensely, whenever he thought of it, the proper European, French, Italian, Spanish, the male of the species, a connoisseur – all those French words in English dictionaries! – of his own emotional climate, and moved, it seemed, by no other logic than its well-being. In Europe they stalked his wife, while he huddled at home with the children, blurred by their self-assured insistences. On boats, trains, buses he saw himself loaded down with the luggage, the porter of the group, while there moved before him the cool image of Joan, followed by their attractive children. There was the living proof, he thought, of her effectiveness, whereas he could sell out his own part to anyone who wanted to carry baggage for a living. Not true either. Joan carried as much as he. In Marseilles, carrying two bags somehow, and the baby, she dropped the latter, catching it just before it landed, head down, on the concrete floor of the waiting room. It was then a nice gentleman had come up to rescue her, taking the bags, following after also, as John trailed forever in the rear.

Goddamnit, Artie, who cares if your wife likes me, he said again. Doesn't it ever get through to you that it's you I care about, do you always have to damn well beat yourself with that exposure, that deadly view? Wow! He stopped, quiet. They had arrived.

I'll be here when you get out, John said, over at your place or else I'll meet you here. Artie was out now, looking in at him through the car's window, a little wryly, admonishingly, too wisely perhaps, as if he pitied John his innocence. He nodded, and walked off into the building, John calling after, I'm off to make it with your wife! But Artie had disappeared.

Suddenly, then, there was time very heavy upon him, to be filled up somehow, against Artie's release. Better, he thought, that he should now go home, where he came from, but he was restless and impatient to talk again to Artie, feeling the conversation with him had been too brokenly stopped. Or what he wanted equally was to hear Artie's outrageous stories, of all the men he himself could only respect with a ghostlike reverence, of one great man's penis, for example, caught in the zipper of his pants in a public urinal in London. How odd that seemed to John, and still, very reasonable. It had also happened to him. Artie always flavored his concoctions with a sufficient dash of truth, to make their tentative acceptance at least a little more likely. John never questioned him, although he never believed him either.

Driving off, he decided to go to a bar close by which usually afforded him an unresolvable spectacle. It was a cyclists' bar, and on the wall, painted, was a large map of the route of the Tour de France. Elsewhere in the city were divers small bars frequented by the afficionados of the *fiesta brava*, the bloody bull fight, but John moved quietly and reverently in such places, studying the long lists of names and cities chalked on the small blackboards, the awards given, the *corridas* fought, to be fought, if that word were proper. But the cyclists were a little more malleable to his imagination, less strenuously present. He found them in the bar now as always, looking up, as he came in, with question, but too intent on their own concerns to bother with him. So he sat at a table somewhat away from them, having first got himself a cognac and coffee, and looked at them as they talked. They were not apparently strange people, at all. One, dressed in the official regalia, of undershirt and worn purple shorts, with high-laced sneakers, was wheeling his bicycle up and down in front of the others, pointing anxiously at the rear wheel. John could see nothing wrong with it. As he watched, another came in, sweating heavily, also pushing a bicycle. It was ten in the morning. John thought of the endless miles they might well have ridden, even so early, pushed, more accurately, against the resistance of the pedals and the road's slope. He often passed them in the car, bent double over the handle bars, bottoms up, crouched in a tension of effort. They never looked back, but always forward, at the road winding off in front of them.

Well, work, he thought, and seeing the girl behind the bar now bending over it, to see more closely the defect of the first bicycle's rear wheel, and so exposed as if in some timeless joke, always to occur somewhere and sometime, her breasts a large ripe pleasure of sight, work, John thought, and pleasure. Is it true? He himself did nothing, certainly not now, a pure voyeur if a restless one. When the girl at last straightened, she saw him looking, and shrugged, then looked back at him fiercely. He hoped she would not tell what she had seen. He got up, with a gesture of leaving, to the girl still watching and to whom he must by this time be familiar, and left. Adios to the friends of the bicycle.

Marge, true to her word, was dressed and had coffee for him. She asked about Joan, and the children, interrupting his fantastic transfer of the bar girl's breasts to her own long chest, and the image broke, leaving her sitting comfortably across from him at the table with her cup of coffee.

They're fine, said John, more settled now. You must come out to see us. Today if you want, I can bring you.

He wondered if she were listening. She did not answer. He saw that she was looking out of the window, at a clothesline, several, which intersected the space between their apartment building and that across the cluttered back yard, much the same as theirs, three blocky stories of cramped space. He said, would you like to do that?

She answered, no, not today, John. Sometime soon I think, but I have things to do today. Arthur has things too. She grimaced, but did not seem anxious to expose that problem further.

I'm sorry about last night, John said. You're lying she said, and laughed briefly. So he was. He hadn't even been there. Perhaps tonight he would be. He felt very uncomfortable. He remembered that Artie had said something about pills she was taking. Probably she was out of her mind? Out of her skull, rather, flipped, simply a remote carcass of tender nerve ends, jangling like a telephone. Oh well. There was no argument there.

Yet he liked her. Such a fierceness of regard, so peristently clear, he thought, so English. She was his dream too. Very tall she was, and very intelligent.

I'm a little tired, she said, John, I think I'll lie down again if you won't mind. If you want to stay, please do.

She was gone. He sat, reading. Elsewhere Artie worked on, chiding, cajoling, teaching the boy, in the other room, in the other block, in the other place.

3

THE ISLAND sits in the sea two hundred miles from the mainland, remote, filled with an oldness of time and place, complexly primitive and secure. The city (which Artie shared with the writer) is the port for the island's business, also the market for its produce and small manufactures. It has a proper season of bull fights, an old cathedral, and a few small suburbs running out at its edges to the hills in the north. So Artie's situation placed him at the heart of the island's significant activity and he knew many tourists and those more resident, whom he greeted continually in the street, with a whispered commentary to John who was often with him.

But John was uneasy in cities, a little frightened since they tended to make what small management of his house he was ever involved with, even more scattered and beyond him. The city demanded that he think when crossing a street, manage change quickly in restaurants and stores generally, or, literally, that he think of such complexities at all since they were for him complexities. Yet he spent much time in the city, as now, this afternoon, in the cafe with Artie.

The cafe itself had an air of business, of men sitting in good suits, discreet cups of coffee, dark wood, quiet, quick waiters, the owner himself a lean, unobtrusive figure back of the bar near the cash register. But he was also the impresario for the bull ring and had no need to assert himself. Even his smile was valuable, and he had smiled at Artie and John as they came in.

However, Artie was about to leave, having borrowed a little money from John for the down payment on a new radio, for Marge. He was to go quickly across the plaza to the shop where they were sold, returning quickly with the radio. John, too vague to move, returning the bulky collection of bills to his pocket, at first confused as to where they had come from, but then remembered he had been to Cook's with Artie to cash a small check, catching a waiter, went back to thinking and drinking, waiting for Artie, for whom he was there, he remembered, while Artie went to get the radio. He looked out the wide windows of the cafe, at the people passing, or sitting in the iron chairs outside, Parisian style. He felt a long way from home.

It was the other, the north side of the island (where the town was they had come from so early that morning) – quiet, steeply sloping to the sea, from small mountains, high up on which were towns of charcoal makers, black, smokey men like miners, big, white eyes, donkeys feeding among the pine trees, goats, few people until one had dropped down again back from the rock, and the sparse woods, to the shelf above the sea where the people had collected themselves and sufficient earth into shelf-like communities of terraces and small gardens, stone and mud houses, with orange tiled roofs, or a sudden castle-like structure (La Baronia, for example) owned at one time by the rightful Spaniard or Moor, not that population of terrified men and women who then, as now, wanted only to be left alone, hard-working, almost child-like in their lack of complexity – could not be taken lightly in the mind, was a paradise, was true in a most natural sense. As, too, the rhythm of the island's seasons, so mild and good, the winds which blew in from the sea, at evening, even the storms which crashed against the high cliffs shielding the town itself, the lights from the boats at night in such weather, the smugglers – and the store-keeper's wife in her excitement could not *not* speak of the typewriter, a grand new American model, which suddenly was present on the table like a god from the new world, but how? – who came in through the storm, hanging offshore roughly a mile distant, as the townsmen rowed out to them, then cached the divers articles in remote caves only they seemed to know of. But all the *guardias* had been paid off – leather-headed men, in green capes, and in this town of some five hundred people there were four (whose right it was to requisition any house which might suit them), and their families.

Days at the beach (below the town) one came, with his crippled son, a bird-like boy, favoring the twisted leg, impatient but as yet unaware of his difference, the father, now a man only, watching, seeing the other children stay away from him, the son, who shyly moved closer watching them.

There had been a baron at one time in this town, who swam alone in the morning, the whole stretch of rocky shore deserted by his order, though some crawled out on the over-hanging bluffs to see his stilted, thin figure move stiffly into the water. But he had gone, long ago dead, and La Baronia was divided into several living quarters, about the immense courtyard where the carriages had come in through the thirty-foot high door, and the priest lived there, the ambitious pension-keeper, trading on old memories, and others more quiet.

Some spring mornings the old men would move out of the confinement of their homes, now those of sons and daughters, to sit in the sun awhile, passive, looking out over terraces where their own lives had taken place, each receding back from that activity, until one morning the chair was empty and the bell in the church swung back and forth, ringing out the town's hope for their union with the good Lord. John moved closer in his mind, thought of his own children and their mother, the house now gathering itself for the evening meal, the sounds around it, men coming into other houses. A long time had passed it seemed.

I was thinking, John said. I'd like to move into that courtyard, you know, La Baronia. I wonder if there is room.

The radio in a sense moved before them, held by Artie. It was very new in appearance and cleared a way for them through the crowded streets as they looked for a taxi.

Perhaps we could get the States with it, Artie was saying. Make you feel more at home, John. Or the bloody B.B.C. Hear what that predecessor of mine is up to now, the bloody shyster.

A honking close to their ears in the darkening street made clear they had been successful. A man was pushing his head out through the window of the cab, motioning also in a constricted manner. John opened the door for Artie, waited for the radio to be secured on the seat, and then followed. Artie was giving directions and John sat down, carefully, as they started off.

In the hallway Maggie was eight feet tall, with eyes. Looking down at them, she said nothing. The two friends slipped past her and made with the radio for the bedroom, Marge behind them still silent. Once there, Artie set it carefully on the bedside table, plugged it in, gave it a swipe with his handkerchief to enhance its polish, then turned it on, a voice blaring, *if you, there must, we will!* John, very tired, could understand nothing of it, though it was, oddly enough, in English, even more oddly, American English, a flat, nasal tonality of, *send nothing, friends.* He thought? No, the voice was saying, *come to delightful Berchtesgaden for the finest leave of your life.* John started to say, that's where Hitler used to go, but stopped as Marge screamed, shut it off, her head was splitting, but Artie, still game, was switching the stations this way and that with a frantic insistence, voices and blurts of sudden music crashing in and out of the room at full volume.

Where were they? In the bathroom John sat down on the toilet seat and waited, the noise still audible from the bedroom, but now mostly Marge. Artie, at times, could be heard explaining, always a painful process. Then silence, then, a few moments later, a soft knock on the door, as from the bedroom, also, a softer music.

That was Stuttgart, said Artie, coming in. The American Forces Network. He closed the door behind him. I'm sorry to have involved you in all that, he went on. I'm afraid we've missed dinner. But she's quiet now, I think, with the radio.

He seemed to remember nothing, finally. He moved about

the limited space of the bathroom with an increasing confidence, while John sat, passive, still on the seat.

Where's my car, John asked at last. Artie, busy at the mirror, turned to answer, you left it by that first cafe, remember? Slowly, John did, and watched Artie take down a small bottle of pills from a high shelf on the wall. Her pills, you know, he said. But they're what we need now, old friend. Ok, Artie. Swallowing, he wondered what was about to happen, what else. The day, now night, was a chaos he had lost all sense of.

Do you think there might be any chance of getting into that place, John said. Artie looked at him impatiently. They were leaving.

La Baronia. I think I'll try that, he said. They went quietly out of the bathroom, through the kitchen, to the door of the apartment Artie, once in the hall outside, called back through the still open door, back soon, Marge, then shut the door. They went down the stairs to the street.

Well, John, all safe, said Artie. If he could only stop the goddamn self-justifications. John saw the man beside him with a clearing head, a head growing into luminous clarity much like that of a soft, white light. Artie, walking beside him, seemed to become a fumbling, disjointed poor fellow. But Artie's head, also, was growing, as John's. They regarded each other with good-natured suspicion. John felt thoroughly awake.

Boy, said John. What does she do with those things. Marge was a decent woman, and could no doubt prove generous if properly solicited. He imagined his own generous laughter as he said, oh no, Marge, not another! And then another.

It's a myth, John, Artie said. We are contributing to an unreality only we and countless millions like us may inhabit. He laughed, shouted *muerte mañana* at a huddled, passing figure who made no sign of hearing, pointed then to the car, squat by the curb. It was John's.

Returned to the car, it was impossible for either one to go home. The night was too young again. They were too hungry, or if not hungry, had not eaten. John drove to a small restaurant off the city's main plaza, the Great Square, where life was now concentrated in passing couples, clots of people engaged in rapid conversation, still single ladies of the evening, and a few odd black-plastered-haired young men, who looked at young women they felt to be staying at hotels. Surrounding the outer rim of the plaza were flanks of waiting taxis, there to perform any service. Lights, high on poles in the air, compacted the bright image. A few, small propped-up wooden counters were selling candy, beer, and the remains of the morning's flowers in hastily fixed corsages. Wiry boys hoarsely shouted headlines. John thought again of the curious fact that American cigarettes sold here more cheaply than they did in the States, much cheaper in fact. Was that, then, mute evidence of his own country's avarice? Everything sold more cheaply, it seemed to him. But was the value of a thing so relative to one's ability to pay for it? If so, why not give everything away. He wondered.

But the painting, *señor*, was not to be completed before his unfortunate death. What was all this about? John looked, concentrating on the act of focus until he could see in front of him a large, square painting, of a relatively young man, an awkward, lumpish, yet painfully (sincere?) hopeful young man, in the costume of the matador, the *traje de luces* (which always he wanted to call, the trapping of light, vestment more probably, certainly an investment of the poor wearer thereof, in this case, painfully acquired, bought, and why not give them to him? Certainly to do what he intended, with so little in the way of grace, unless the painter – who was this man? – were clumsily unable to capture, like they say, the nervous form, the mental presence, light on nervous feet, sure, graceful hands? Perhaps not. But he is dead?)

The painter turned to Artie, impatiently, nervous that the sale was not going well. Your friend, he said, seems a little confused, adding, too much to drink? The new air of this country disturbs him, and the water. Oh no, said Artie, old timer, John, he has much force in the head, and much heart also.

John, left to one side, remembered the restaurant, which Artie's games with the oranges had put them out of, the bar, where he had not felt like dancing, the next bar, where the neighborhood came in to watch, so they left. The next, too, quiet, the next, but not really. Where was the car?

Downstairs, said Artie, Manny drove us over for you. Frightful talent, don't you think? All that paint. This one, for example.

John saw again the young bull fighter. He is dead suddenly, Manny said. I paint it for him for *cartel*, many sittings, and I have the painting almost where I want it. He has *corrida* one afternoon and has *cogida*, the bad gore, eighty centimeters. He dies shortly, my best friend, *señor*. His second *corrida*, all is done.

John looked again at the painting, feeling humbled, dismayed, by the clumsy image of the awkward, heavy boy in the heavy, dully shining suit. Most like him worked in stores, part-time clerks, errand boys, waiting for the chance which seemed to come rarely to this island, so they practised with their friends, holding the mock horns, until one afternoon, unable to wait longer, they, one of them, jumped the fence, into the plaza, stumbled, running, half-falling, the worn white shirt flapping, small square of red cloth, stick to hold it open, calling, in breaking voice, high, *toro, toro*, till the bull turns, the peons too slow to prevent it, looks, sees, and charges, the small figure lifted and carried back against the heavy timbers of the fence in one shaking thud of hopeless sound. This boy had been luckier than such *espontaneos*, perhaps. Who could say.

I wait, said Manny, until the grief goes a little. Then I come back to it. But now he is dead, you understand. I paint him now as he is, dead, and to the whole painting now I come with blue, like my sorrow he is dead.

True enough. The blue was very visible, worked into all the planes on the face and hands, a ghostly, greyish blue, an awkward nightmare of Manny's ambition. The boy had been transformed into a garish nightmare of glowing blue.

It is hard to let it go, Manny said, but for you, I think you understand it, *señor*, cheaply. That would be well. He said an amount which John fumblingly put into dollars. It was not very much.

I'll buy it, said John, but I can only pay you a little now. The rest very soon, he added, sensing that Manny was offended by this use of his generosity. I would be very pleased to have it.

Bueno, said Manny. Now we have coffee for a celebration. He went off to get it.

Later, at the car, they helped John prop the painting against the passenger's seat, face up. It was time at last to go home, and Manny waved, then went off. Artie, still beside the car, asked a little anxiously if John were all right.

I'm sober, John said, if that's what you mean. Can I take you to your place? You can squeeze in.

In the light from a street lamp they both looked over at the dead friend, who looked forward only.

Well, said John. This is it. I'll see you. Soon, called Artie, waving, one way or another, watching the car go off.

4

I THINK of those changes by which an association is preserved, a process like that of decompression, for the diver, except that here the progress seems horizontal, insular, contained by oblique references to commitments already altered. John tried to commit himself, in all senses, though not to all things. To his wife, to begin with, the first free association, bred of loneliness, then of sex, then of mutual necessity, being now too known and too wise, they thought, to be innocent again.

The roads of this world, crossed by intersections of, "but I meant," "didn't you say that," laws, agreements, painful reinstatements, insistences of value stratified by centuries of enforcement, are often very painful. To walk them, to move from *a* to *b*, to *have* to move, no choice but that within that necessity, was for the moment John's own approach. He had somehow to prove the reality of his own footprint, there being no one else who could.

For him Joan seemed even a more complicated history, suddenly marked void by her presence at any instant. No roads quite led there. One arrived, just like that, or else never did, endlessly wandering about in the so-called approaches. Her sympathy was instant, or not at all.

To himself John made much of her being an orphan, thinking that by that she was freer. Not true, it seemed. How free was having to perform, for the chance of parents, at four, having had one failure, thus returned to try over? She spoke of the orphanage in which she grew too old (four), and stood taller than the other children, the toddlers, so cute and so available in that cuteness to the speculative eyes of would-be (but weren't) parents. Not at all to be hers, until one single woman accepted her, with love, and then died a year later. Losing that, she gained a problematic young woman for a guardian, a good *name*, and at last the income which the mother-woman had left her, and the house.

So John was to be all things to her, able to be none sufficiently. It isn't that one wants what one gets, or doesn't. One wants it, gets it, doesn't want it, does, gets it again. It is endless. John wanted Joan but contrived for himself a world in which continual separations occurred.

Joan spoke of her birthday party, when she was ten. The housekeeper, a tactful ally, worked hard to make it successful, and it was. The neighborhood's children crashed about the usually severe house with great pleasure. Joan ate a great deal of ice cream and cake. In the hall back where the coats were hung she let the boys feel her small breasts. It was a triumph.

But why, John asked, why did you let them? Did you like it? Did you let them all?

Later she had been sent by her guardian, to a farm in the country, where an almost English clergyman undertook to provide for his family by boarding girls as Joan, nice girls, who needed a healthy summer. One daughter of this man proved a shy and loyal friend. One son, however, older and impatient, drew her closer, coming to her room in the darkness, asking to lie beside her, to hold her, which she, being lonely, allowed.

John shook with impotence and despair. It was the *childhood magic* that he could not revoke, or even touch. Someone said, she uses it as a weapon. It is her bludgeon, her club. But that could not be true if in dreams he sweated to reach her, in that same place, that time so immaculate and clear. She says that her history is her own, John. You didn't make her. It made her.

A report of one of her teachers at college, "When I asked Joan what she wanted to do, she said she wanted to have babies." John left for the war, shaking as ever. At the last minute she called to tell him she no longer loved him, she had met someone else whom she was to marry, right away. He was gone before he could see her. A year later he came back, then found her. She had not married. She had been pregnant. She had aborted herself with a knitting needle. Where had he been? What could he do?

They married, he himself left college as she had earlier. They had three children, another dying shortly after being born. It all happened very quickly it seemed. They lived in various places, working toward a home, a place, but never staying long enough.

How could you let him? Let who? Touch you like that how could you do it? But that was when I was twelve.

She said, I promised myself that when I grew up I would never forget what it was like to be a child. I would never do the things to children that were done to me.

John often lived waiting for the other to come, the boy, young man, half-man, the whole man. It wasn't him. He hadn't been there. He saw the grossness of his own incapabilities, the treachery of his self-assurance.

He read a story in a French magazine, difficultly, unsure that what he supposed himself to be reading was really being said. The story spoke of the surrealist passage of two people into the sea, in diving suits, going down into the water together, touching through the suits and that subtle medium, speaking through tubes and wires. A picture accompanying the text seemed to imply a sexual encounter. Elsewhere in the same magazine was a thin, sure looking girl with full breasts, pushing out from the slight body.

In the sea the bodies rise and fall, but slowly, with careful regard for pressure. In the suits which cover them there is opportunity to adjust to the changes of pressure. Of this regard or of that, of this or that insistence. With care it can be controlled. The body will not be allowed to explode. It will rise or fall at the gradual pace of the will, the term of the communication.

He wanted to talk to Joan and he did. She told him that his conversation was very brilliant, and he was filled with an almost shameful gratitude. He told her everything he could think of, and she listened to him. In bed at night he talked on sometimes too long, beyond her ability physically to listen. Then he hated himself, having wanted to make love to her, feeling a confusion of strength and shame. She slept as he wondered.

She told him that her meals as a child had been rigorously limited, although there was no want. One cookie after dinner, two at the most. She spoke of the coldness of the house in winter. What could he do? They both ate great amounts of candy, usually in bed, after the children were asleep. They tried to move backward together.

But sudden ruptures occurred, creating digressive, floppy

losses of attention, leaving puddles of wasted time and self-regard. To maintain the area of childhood took much of their time, which was free enough, yet they were driven as well, compulsively, to be adult, grown-up, despite the loose world in which they lived. There cannot be childhood without the adult to define it, not at their age. The children knew that their parents needed the candy, in some inexplicable sense, not their own. They saw it gone in the morning. At times they never knew it had been there at all. Secrets grew in the house like mushrooms in a damp cellar.

What can be brought into such a house? A friend? Not simply. Flowers, picked at random on walks that tended to wander, were better. Something for the house, was better. Any *thing* that could be quickly, gracefully, dropped into place, in the whimsical plan of it all, was right.

But the picture was, to begin with, very large, and also, very ugly. Purposefully ugly, being dead. The image of the dead man could not easily be beautiful. The point of the picture was not that he had been beautiful in life, a memory. But that dead like this, and he was, he had been badly used, an irony, that he was an ugly instance of sudden death in the memory, his shining suit of beauty. It was also a very badly painted picture.

The drive back, then, was a slow process of sobering apprehension, an increasing realization that a mistake had been made. Moonlight came softly through the window of the car. Beyond, it made clear the hills, the olive trees, the quiet of the towns as John went through them. But on the face of the dead man, the picture, it brought to light a wearingly garish insistence of incompetent deadness, and it sat there, stayed there, with all the unconcern of any deadness, not caring, leaving the problem to another.

At last in the house, with the picture in his arms, John made his way carefully up the stairs. No one was as yet awake, although the first light of the morning had come, and in the town the people were beginning to move to their various occupations. All these he had happily avoided. Above him was the bedroom, toward which he climbed.

Coming in, he saw Joan's composed body, under the bed-clothes, tucked as always into sleep. He could see the flush of the morning white and growing at the windows. Could he wait? No, that was impossible. He leaned the picture against the wall, facing the bed, then went over to shake her gently, so that she grunted a little, shifted herself with reluctance, then opened her eyes to see him.

What, she said, what happened? Are you all right? She spoke heavily, clogged with sleep, as he touched her. She had not seen the picture.

No, he said, look, pointing. She did, suddenly jumped upright, and back, hard against the pillows. He heard her give a short, cut scream of shock. He put his hand on her shoulder but she pushed free, to look at him.

Where did you get it, she said, where. Where did you get it.

He tried to remember, quickly. Where did he get it. It was one of those things one gets. To explain Manny at such an hour was not to be thought of.

Did Artie make you get that, she said.

No, not Artie, this time. He had done it all by himself. For what reason? Any reason, no reason. He felt sorry for the dead man. What else would be left of him now. Only this grotesque incompetence. Couldn't they laugh about it, make of it a gentle joke, a soft, fumbling reminder of mortality?

Did you pay for it? Yes. How much? Twenty-five dollars. You fool!

He could hear, in his head, someone singing, *this time the dream's on me* . . . How did the rest of it go? No time to remember.

I met a painter, he said, young fellow, very interesting. He did it.

Why don't you stop drinking, she said, staying out all day and night, drinking. Why do you let Artie drag you around by the nose?

Tell her that I'm lonely this time, he thought. Can't stand this any more. But he could. Too much damn vagary. I hate myself. Do I? Not enough apparently. He looked back at the painting.

I sort of liked it, he said, sort of a weird quality he gets. That fellow was killed in a bull fight. Then this other fellow finished the painting.

He wanted to put it as, remember the time you hit me with the shovel? I didn't get mad. I know I do, did, often, but not that time. Other times like that, I didn't get mad. No time to, or it wasn't the time then. This time isn't either? Like that.

The time the baby died? Didn't I make it? You said that you

looked out the window and could see the spring coming, the first flowers, a feeling of warmth, wetness, and green. It was hard to see but it made it simpler to go on living like they say. Is this a crisis? A painting? No.

You do it all the time, John, she said. Why do you do it?

I get drinking, he said. You're right. There's an awkwardness to things. Someone has to do something. Buy a painting, say hello, anything. This time it was me.

You're always doing it, she said. It's always you. Always the sucker, the one left with the messy bag. To bring home, she said.

I only gave him five dollars, he said. I can take it back, somehow.

It's not the money, she said. It's that horrible looking thing. It's you gone all day and all night. Should I hang that thing up and not care? Look at it when you're not here? "Hello, John." "Hello, Joan." "You look very dead today." What do you want me to do about it?

It was time to go to work, to write the poem, story, novel, play, to earn the million dollars in the dream, once and for all to do it, day by day, forever and ever, to be able to say, finally, here's five thousand for you, and here's five thousand for you, and *this* five thousand is for me. Now everybody's got some.

He looked back at the painting, and found himself laughing. He said, we could put it up in the kids' room, give them something to think about? Hey, he said, let's not be mad.

He got up, walked over to the painting, turned it around to face to the wall. Joan slid down in the bed again, making herself comfortable, watching him. It was morning.

Then he took off his clothes, and got into bed with her. I'm sorry, he said, it's a horrible painting. He pushed his hand over, to touch her, and found her warm, heavy with sleepiness. I love you, he said. I really do, very much. He moved closer. Do you love me, he said.

Oh God, John, she said. Go to sleep. The children will be awake so soon. I'll have to be up. Please?

But Juana can, he thought, take care of them. He reached over, to stroke her, found the warmth of her leg, moved his hand over it. Please. The morning, the light, the sea somewhere below them. It was a lovely place. She was asleep.

5

SEVERAL WEEKS later they moved into a corner of La Baronia, but not by John's arrangement, rather by Joan's. She as well thought it would be happier, and by a contrivance of conversations went from maid to friend to owner, a farmer, who was pleased to have the Americans move in. This apartment, at the rear of the courtyard on the second floor with a large terrace above it, became their new home. It was as temporary as any other, but it had running water, more privacy, and was a section of a beautiful building, which made them proud to have a part in it. But the water was discontinuous, and gave frequent trouble, and there was no hot. The privacy was shared with the pension-keeper, who had use of the terrace also, and put his guests out on it to see the view. The building was beautiful, however, no matter they found it often uncomfortable.

Finally they were foreign, John at least was. Women move by a commonality of sex across all significant barriers, but men do not. Joan spoke the language more easily, feeling easier to begin with. She became intimate with the town's people. Questions took her over the town, into houses. When she baked her chocolate cake in the common oven, at the back of the store, many women came to watch, and, as it turned out, ruined the cake by taking it out repeatedly to see what was happening to it. Joan had gone back to the house to get something. She gave them all a piece when it was done, as much as she had to give. In consequence they took her in, held her on the common ground of their own existence, a woman with children.

The moving over, this afternoon they were going on a picnic, which Joan had made for them. They went under the large doorway to the street, across that to a path leading up the far hill, above the town, toward a farm that Joan had been to before, isolate and like a small village in itself, with friendly people who asked of the town and people there. What was the world at that end of it, were the days the same for all.

The path went on, above the terraces, changing to a steep slope, past small herds of goats, sheep, the tail-end of the small farms at the town's edge. Here the trees came in, stunted pines among the rock. The family came at last to a small clearing, beyond a cliff dropping off sharply. In the rock itself there was a small spring, a stream of water coming up out of the base, which had been cut back to hold it in a small pool. It was a fountain, and small shelves cut in also made a place for putting flowers or like things. It was said to be Greek, from the sailors who had skirted this coast, from Marseilles, or beyond, going back and forth. Looking out, one saw only the trees going down steeply, staggered and quickly diminishing points of fir, to the sea, endless on three sides, tipping out to the horizon.

A small fire was made to one side, and John contrived a grate, of stones, so the children might lean their hot dogs against it, at the ends of green sticks he had cut as well. Mustard and ketchup were put on split rolls. A bag was ready for the remnants. The children ate well, drank water from the spring, and began to wander out, to explore. They were soon lost among the trees.

Now, John thought, is the time. I love you, Joan, he said. It was after dinner, Friday night, the week's work done. She had just fed them with his own approval. They were not Greeks. Joan was content in the success. They looked together at the little spring, and thought of the men who might have made it. Probably only a farmer, a local instance. The Greeks and the Moors who had lived there, beyond doubt, were still book figures. But the sea could be their image. Out there it was all possible and likely.

Like this, she said, making for her hair a small crown of flowers quickly gathered. Just like that. An image of the goddess. She took them off and put them by the spring, on the small shelf.

Aren't you happy, she said. Isn't it a lovely place.

She had just performed a ritual. Out of grotestque approximation she had put her own body into the gesture of a sacrifice. Well, well.

Or seen otherwise, the success of American young womanhood. How else would she ever be in such a place, with hot dogs, and children, and a dull husband, a stunted image of manhood who squatted squinting up at her through the light of a sunset. The children were lost in the woods. The walk back was before them, rocky and difficult, unfamiliar.

At what time may love come, at what place, by what method or path, suddenly present. The altar of the goddess in the wood.

It is, he thought, it is a lovely place. Think of it. A lovely place. It is a lovely place.

No people exist, nothing is there. Sound of wind perhaps, something stirring in the trees. Cries of the children up the path. The town below, not seen, sound of far off people.

I love you, he said. I want to be true. I want to learn what to do and when to do it. Nothing seems that which I am but I would try to find an acceptable form for it.

Everybody laughs at it. Myself as well, the sense of an alternative to what has none. Everybody lives, loves, back and forth, shuttling that clutter of threads. All the singular hands and faces, mis-matched patterns, back and forth, against a shuttle of endless yarn, reaching and taking, and returning to reach, taking again, and giving. Love love, get used to it. Give love its due. It seems a song to me.

He touched her. One does it over and over, as he did. The tree is no different, the sun is no different. It comes again.

In love there is a hope that manages above all the others, the most efficient thing that ever was. The suddenness of its coming is only a gauge of how long it has been expected. Let everything be in love the way it ought to be and has to be, because it no other way can be.

The small woman had just performed a ritual. I love you, he said. A clutter.

Calling the children, they collected the food and utensils, and began the descent to the town. At the edge they saw the lights go on, as they did each night, at dark. In their own house the children were put to bed. They sat reading, talking. The house was around them, things they were aware of or had chosen, dishes and books, or baskets, clothes, walls they had come to use, doors that opened into expected areas. Finally in bed, they shut off the light, John did, felt his way back to the bed, lay looking up into the dark. They could see the window's outline in the black, a dark blue rectangle. The ceiling floated above them. The town was quiet again.

In the quiet they thought of each other. A hand moved, fingers extended. Something moved under the bedclothes ludicrous and humped. She had equipped herself. He felt her under him, his own legs slide over.

But the geography was darkness. From something unsure, fumbling, gaining distinctions. Certain areas of flesh and bone.

Calling into the funnel of the dark, are you there. It's me. I'm here now. Muttering words to himself, oh John, who had said it. The signature was lacking. He couldn't find anything in the dark. She moved closer.

It was I wanted you. It was me who was going to do it. (Who is speaking?) Your arms, your hair, your head is like a nut, firm as a nut. Say something, please.

Oh John. The pillows are far away, at the end of the bed there somewhere. The blankets go off, into the chasm of dark, down.

There are two people in bed together in a bubble of night, pure air, no space but occupied. Move over, there, now, I think you are ready. Skeleton laughter, harsh shatter, approximating a formal declaration. The lacking signature prevented it.

You can't do that now, you have to wait. Not now you can't not just now you can't do it, not now you can't.

The car sped into the darkness in the tunnel of its space, in, a toy projectile sped into the walls, which are supple and yield to the impact. A false door, a melting mirror. Something you went through years ago recoheres and is present, leaning. A slippery wetness, sudden chill.

Nobody wants to give that away. Nobody talks about it. The sale is over, go home. (Who is speaking?) Says the wise guy, image, flat face, head over heels, make no mistake about it. There now. How was that. The memory.

Couldn't you. What. Couldn't you wait. What are you saying. Who are you. Why didn't you wait for me.

The hallway in the collapsing house he ran back through, the walls falling behind him, crashing and echoing. The thumping sounds of the sea, crashing and crashing. Sound of nothing, a wire of silence, take your pick. It's nothing here at all. Officer, I never saw this woman before in my life. Don't say it. No, it's the truth. I don't even know her. Look.

The head is on the pillow again. Softly the blankets slide up and over, tuck into the edges of the bed. They lie breathing in the warm, sweet dark.

Early in the morning the church bell sounded out from the other side of the street. They woke to hear people passing by the large door of the courtyard on their way to the sea, a thin line of men and women, a curious sight in the half-dark. They went down the road in a sure file, singing, first man then woman, a song that seemed a hymn. But it was a dream-like occurrence, they seemed to be there but flitted past, ghosts under the window, wavering music. They carried something to the sea in a box, the men to the front. No one dead, but something, generation after generation. They had death in the box and they were going to throw him into the sea.

II

6

OUT OF ALL the clutter came some sense of things, and the town
(*¡que bonito!* with its up and down steps, cut in the rock face,
and the customs, so unexpected, and the people, so friendly to
them) and the sea beyond it echoed worlds and worlds of a
tenuous, consistent culture they felt but hardly knew. The children drew from it all a clutch of small intensities, feelings, and
things, a fish with glazed, sunken eyes, a square of bread wet
with oil, a stick with a small wheel attached to its end, and then
a terrified, fluttering, small bird, with a long string fixed to its
foot, held by their youngest child, and dragged from room to
room, a gift, until Joan insisted it be let go again, and offered
herself to pay for all such birds, caught with such insistent good
intention.

So they felt themselves well settled, when the taxi arrived one
morning, with many suitcases lashed to its top, and inside, a
curious aggregate of people, a father, a wife, two children, and
then a sister, with also a child, a goatish boy of eight. They
made their way to La Baronia with the help of the townspeople,
in this case several old women. They were here to find a house.
They had come from a great distance. The writer had sent them
to John with a note now given to him by the smiling, older man.
The various children held back a little, then wandered as John's
did, curious, tired but intent, in the bright sun of the fresh
morning.

All houses, however, were occupied. It was always true. Not
for twenty-five years had a new house been built in the town,
and all were owned, in fact were jammed with owners with such

families that the very walls seemed threatened. You want a house? Ha! But then there were such houses to want, perched, some of them, on the rock with all the sea falling out below them, or else tucked among the small, square fields, with half-doors opening into sparsely furnished white-washed kitchens. And fireplaces, and the walls that wandered as the hands had built them, and the small gardens, just beyond the door, and all of it, so delightful. Then perhaps someone has died in the twenty-five years, or the great tragedy has meant a certain hardship, and, however reluctantly, the family had withdrawn a little, back into the back of the house, to another, a relative's. It was possible that the owner of the other might know the owner of this one, which seemed to have no one in it. Yet any day they might come, the owners from Barcelona, in their new cars, pushing into the town for their particular *fiestas*, and who was to say the house was not theirs, the very one.

The husband was saying, however, that it need not be all that big. They sat on the terrace of the small hotel at the town's edge. It gave them a fine view of all the immediate houses. That one, perhaps, he said. They looked at his pointing finger, then at the house it pointed to, a close, somewhat quiet little one, some distance up the dusty road, with a few trees closely shading its front. But it was impossible, of course. Untold generations had lived there, did, although it was empty. One could never tell. Their helper shrugged with great bitterness. The outlanders had wings of gold.

So the family made their arrangements for renting the house, and after their bags had been brought there, John and the husband walked off down the road, leaving the women to put things where they would. John suggested a beer, but the husband was too restless, he had just arrived, as it were, and paced along the road with a good-natured abruptness. He wanted the peace and uncomplicated terms of it all, he said.

Why, look. There was the sea again. They had just come from New York, himself, and wife and children. But his wife was French, and showed it, good-looking, practical, and clearly she knew men and particularly her husband. He was an Australian, as was the sister, his, with the odd boy. This was her second time out of there, but he had made the break years ago, as a correspondent first for a chain of Australian papers, then later, during the war, for some Canadians, and finally Americans.

More specifically, he had been a war correspondent, and was lucky enough, if that was the word, to have been at the siege of Stalingrad. Now he was in some sense an expert concerning what the Russians had done or were now doing. He had written a novel, or was it two, about them. He had a grant from that, in any case, and now he wanted, as he said, a little peace and quiet.

Their feet tracked the dust of the road in little puffs, and at the edge of the rock wall, looking down over the plots of tomatoes, beans, odds and ends of vegetables, they saw the sea tilting back at them and at the land. The sky was clear, a slight breeze brought them sounds of voices from the gardens.

When did you get here, the husband asked. How did you happen to find it. In New York, you know, a place like this would hardly be believable, all that rush and fighting. I hated it, I didn't want it for my children. Living in the Village, with a Jaguar, some thought that strange to have such a car there, but I liked driving it. But I couldn't let the children play outside at all, there have been so many attacks and muggings. It's an ugly life.

John nodded, not knowing New York at all finally. Whenever he had himself gone there, all he felt was the excitement, the buildings, like any hick, he remembered. This man was very new to him and he was listening.

My sister, I'm afraid, feels I've deserted her in some way, but one can't always be what others want, I suppose. Well, this will be her vacation.

How long will you stay, John asked. The husband laughed, forever, perhaps forever. I love this peace. I've got a book to do.

That explained the writer's interest, but there had been no other writers exactly there, in this town, not in effect next door. What could John do with that? This man might well smother him with sheer paper, and all he could himself do, apparently, was resent it while smiling politely enough.

In New York, the husband said, if you broke a pencil you just threw it away, and got another, there were a dozen on the desk, all sharpened. There wasn't time to be bothered. And then there were those on the way up, fifteen fighting for five jobs, with houses mortgaged, big cars, for the right look, and god knows who would get them.

The day floated around them, warm, comfortable. John said, I'm writing. Letters at least, or how so quickly explain that he was not, after all, a very real writer, not the writer *the* writer was, and this man knew him, so knew that also. I am going to write, he thought, and when I do, I'll probably have a book too.

Do you know him very well, John said. The husband, confused, said, who? Oh, you mean Duddon? The guy who wrote the note for us, for you, that is, I mean to you. No, I don't really. He's a friend of a friend, he writes poems, doesn't he, novels, I think I've seen some. He's good, isn't he? He was very nice to us but didn't seem to think we'd get anything where he was.

He wouldn't, John thought. The son of a bitch. Make me your errand boy. Or was that village more real than this one. Perhaps it was. The writer seemed to have a very secure world there.

It's a nice town, John said, but a lot of people go there. The husband nodded, I suppose they would.

John thought, he was very nice to us also, finally. He walked the baby even, when it was crying, when they had first arrived. And something about, 'ole brother John in the pin-ey woo-oods . . .' And was that laughter, a little English? Something about an accent, apparently. The writer was delighted by the flatness of John's speech. He invited them to dinner, in his own town, while they stayed at the pension, the crying, sick children, the cold of the room. He handed John a small piece of sculpture John was to see, a figure of a man, compact and firm, Etruscan it was. John shook, afraid he might drop three thousand years of time in one gauche gesture.

But you have all this to yourself, said the husband. You're not so dumb. He laughed. Well, I certainly thank you for all the help. You'll have to come to dinner once we're a little more settled in.

Back in his own house, Joan asked him about the new people. She was pleased they had children. She feared a little the isolation of their own, although they were by no means isolated. But the other children did not speak English. These would. She also liked having other women whom she might see now.

John could not warn her of the disappointment, because he himself only sensed it, in his own defensive fashion. The French

wife was so very brisk and sure, and soon saw that Joan was
not at all so adept, either with men or with herself. It was a
brief but final turn, which they had together, and then all that
the French woman did became more than Joan ever would, and
both knew it.

The sister, however, was otherwise, thin, wirey, a grotesquely
cheerful woman, with so many real problems. She soon wandered in upon them, a little drunk with having visited the town's
store, she said, they insisted she drink a little wine with them.
Her son was with her, dragging back of her like an animal, a
goat. She loved the place, it was all that she hoped it would be.
Simpatico, she said, no doubt for the first time, trying out the
word.

This was to be her last time out of Australia, already final,
all those miles and miles of water, ticking like a meter. They
had had barely enough money for her to come, but her brother
had helped. It was clear he never would again.

John's curiosity found her very attractive. He loved the thin
pleasure of her excitement, the insistent exposure she seemed to
wear like skin. And how the French wife hated her and her
difficult child, fearing contamination of her own healthy children. The husband, the brother, fumbled between the two in
an increasing irritation.

And yet this painful woman had done things, so small, so
intense. She told them of her husband, a wool buyer for some
English firm, and himself, as she spoke of him, very clearly with
that connection, a visitor to Australia, not a native. She spoke
of the *group*, in Australia, the younger people, the hopeful, the
ones who had wanted to write, paint, or to do something. Her
brother had in fact been their success, and his first book was a
novel of just that world. Yet he had left it, and them. Ah, he
had gone.

She herself had been once only in England, as a bride, to
meet her husband's family. The father was dying. The mother
took care of him, washing the old body she had never, she told
the new daughter, seen without its clothes before that time. But
the bride got a bicycle and while the father died, she rode the
length and breadth of England, then crossed to Ireland, riding
along. The world seemed very open to her, although her
husband much feared her actions.

And she had read Lawrence, Lawrence that wonderful man

of hope, as pinched as her own. There was not a book by him she had not read, backwards and forwards, and John sat, intently listening, as she went on and on, with exclamations and sighs, about the *value* of the *work*.

Joan tired of her. She bored her, in fact, so much talk, so much useless intensity. The child was also a problem, and hung about his mother, tugging, as she talked. And then John, without intention but nonetheless persistently, kept giving her wine, which he himself drank too much of, so that the two of them would often end in a bleary comradeship of mutual attraction, which Joan found the more disgusting because the thin, hairy quality of the woman offered little apparent excuse.

In the town the first warmth became also a little ambiguous in its use of her. Now she was frequently an amusement for the men who were not used to drinking with women, and who found this one an odd sort to begin with, a foreigner who made difficulties for her family apparently. At least she was rarely with them, but instead she would be seen with her boy, at some far point of the beach scrabbling for shells or bits of stone she found beautiful. The fishermen, who were often there also, mending the large nets they used, holding out the torn parts with their toes while sewing over the tears with heavy fingers, watched her absorbedly. They would not speak to her finally. They simply looked. Her loneliness was not clear to them.

John's heart broke, watching her, and Joan's hardened. He was, more truly, waiting for what he felt must happen, some intensely beautiful impossibility she would perform. They had little contact with the family, beyond meeting them now and again when the mail came, but after the first exchange of dinners, there was no occasion to come closer to one another. Both John and the husband felt somewhat stupidly bewildered by what they knew was an antagonism between their wives, but they did not dare to seem sympathetic to stated enemies. Only the sister went between them now, and even she grew quieter, and sometimes sad, as she knew their stay was growing short.

It came one evening quietly enough. The family had gone out to the far beach to have a late lunch, it seemed. The sister suggested swimming, but the bathing suits had been forgotten. But she went anyhow, taking her son, despite the disapproval of the brother and wife.

Then, as the boats began to leave the closer beach, the harbor they used, one coming up the shore spotted her in the water, the fisherman standing stiff at the back of the boat looking down suddenly at her crying out so he should not hit her. To brother and wife who were watching it was clear that he must have seen her nakedness, her unattractive nudity. Such a thing in such a place was a great breach of custom, and though the fisherman passed on as stiffly as ever into the night water, there was no question of what he now knew.

Was it only a story to tell Artie then, John thought. It was the woman herself who told him, a little shyly, trying to see if what the family implied was true, that she had compromised them all. Or was the laughter only as general as it had always been. He could not answer her. When they left for good, he hardly said goodbye to her, not certainly as he had thought to. And was that friends, he wondered, because he knew that she was one. It was not to be answered.

The shame of it stayed awhile, despite Artie's suggestion that all Australians were a little nutty and not to be taken seriously. The French, of course, were worse. That explained the wife, and then the husband was hers, not the sister's. The man had been caught in the middle. But I didn't really like him, John said, nor her, only the sister.

Weeks later they got a card, from Australia. She thanked them again for their kindness to her. But again, it was not to be answered.

7

THE SHIFTING vagueness of friendship, all the people met in such random manner, filled his mind with much confusion. John could not sort them, even at times remember to whom in fact he had given his last loyalty. But the woman herself faded. Artie did not. The money trickled out to him, vaguely, but it was impossible ever to criticize this impeccable man, so immaculately fumbling all the terms of his life. Nights John would sometimes dream of Artie's voice, without, then, a real face at all, simply an insistent, quiet, slightly insidious voice. Could you let me have a little till pay day, it said, just to tide us over, to keep Marge happy, to keep the landlord happy, to keep any number of people happy.

Among the jumble of papers John called his work, there was a note from Artie. *For the record* (there was none): *can I straighten out that money I owe you* (no), *that you may not worry as I do as I owe it* (no). *Herewith calculations for you to confirm or deny, as you say.* No, there could be no answer to such a question, and John refused it. Or did he use it only to hurt Artie, whose wistful smile when discussing such subjects tempted John to rip it off with a pair of pliers. Yet love him he did. The *calculations* followed:

	John	Artie
Originally I lent you 370, you then lent me 2000.		*370*
	2000	
I gave you 2900 Francs —at the agreed 9 fr. to the peseta rate.		*322*
Marge bought £4. 3s. worth of stuff in England for you—at 100 pesetas to £1.		*455*
	2000	*1147*
	−1147	

853 I owe you.

This last underlined three times. What did he really want, John thought. He had everything he could give him. Why twist the heartstrings, or was it merely a habit. He read, *I won't be around for the next week or so: cold, miserable. Life is like this.* It became so international, pounds, francs, pesetas. None of it was anyone's money. It went on ... *I've no doubt I have it wrong, so tell me.* How answer that, he thought. You have it wrong, Artie, your whole system of *calculation* is wrong, Artie. You are not correct. *I can't help worrying about money because I haven't got any at all now.*

In the night he thought of Artie, tired, worn, smiling man. The shuffling gesture, the sidewise manner, the edged, confidential voice. The voice. He thought of their first meeting, like spies, on a wide street in Marseilles, high noon, with the people coming out of the buildings for lunch.

It was a poem had brought them together, romantically enough, one of Artie's in a small magazine in England. One about his wife, Marge, also present at that first meeting, harsh faced and glaring, sitting at a table in the cafe as they came up apologizing that they had taken so long to recognize each other. How had they not, in a way, the hopeful American, the hopeful Englishman, and all the world between them. He watched Artie placate his wife. He suggested beer, which they sat drinking glass after glass, for several hours, as Marge warmed again. Then concern with his own wife brought John to get them started on the drive back to the small town in which he and Joan and the children then lived, a fierce sort of village, considering the Americans a particularly dour blight upon them. There were no friends there finally.

Artie's face had been frozen on one side from the effects of an abscessed tooth, pulled, for the sake of cheapness, by one of the island's *practicantes*, the practical men, who confined their practice, Artie told them, mainly to children and the poor. In any case the frozen face caused Artie to speak in a tight-lipped fashion, making him seem all the more devious, and a little sinister.

His first impact upon Joan was considerable. He hovered, he followed her into the crowded kitchen back of the room in which they ate, he complimented her upon the cooking and upon the evident conditions of their living in such a way that she was both delighted, he seemed so story-book English to her, and dismayed, he was such an obvious liar.

And all this, John thought, from a letter, and even that written tentatively, out into the emptiness of other men's worlds, so hopefully, a little warmth to hold them together. I like your poem. Where are you.

They had certainly come quickly enough, almost by return mail. Artie, it seemed, had a holiday from his job, he explained, of tutoring the writer Duddon's oldest boy. A cushy job, but at times tedious, but John should by all means get out of France, and come to the island, so much cheaper and pleasant. They, on the other hand, needed a little break from it all, and now John could know why, but not then. He invited them, he was so eager for them to come, so happy that they really did seem to want to. And now Artie sat in the cramped, tight room under the eaves of the house, too low to stand in, but nonetheless where John tried to write, did write his letters at least, away from the movement of the house, looking out on the broad, flat leaves of a plane tree. Here they talked of literature, carefully, Artie telling of the writer whom John knew nothing of, of the poems he found useful. It was pleasure indeed.

So they had at last gone to the island, in stages, first John, to look and report. Then the whole family, arriving disjointed and out of sorts to sit in a pension for a month while Artie and John drove about the island in John's old car, looking for a house. Well, this had been the most fun perhaps, and he had not really been in a hurry at all. He loved the towns they drove through, stopping at the cafes to drink beer, sitting, talking, forgetting for that time that Joan was back in the dank pension washing diapers by hand.

Artie brought such pleasure. At times the air itself warmed, grew lighter, their beer sparkling and golden. They talked of all they could think of, and Artie's endless stories made a world for John such as he had never felt so possible, so close, to his own. These intimacies were the only value, surely. All the rest was dull, nagging responsibility, kept with a niggard care, dragging all down to dullness.

At least they had found the house. From a bar they had moved to a terrace overlooking the town. There is one there, the man told them and pointed. Hazily they collected themselves and went to look. It was the second floor, and the third, of a bare, tall building. Upstairs, in the loft, were hung tomatoes, down, the barber had his shop. Happily, in the middle, they would live. Artie had triumphed, and they returned to Joan with a great sense of victory.

When at last they were moved in, John found himself hating the darkness of the place, the bareness of the heavy walls, the criss-cross meaningless mosaic which covered the third floor, and the noise, constant, from the barber and his family. And the angry, ugly old woman who stamped through on her way to inspect the tomatoes above. What, really, had Artie got them but another makeshift mess in which to consider their dissatisfaction.

But, John thought, remembered, never look back. Consider the man who might sit now across from you, who has just taken another cigarette from your package, who drinks another beer you have bought for him. What is it that is expected, or wanted, what perpetual addition seems so necessary, or *calculation*, again. He returned to the note.

I only mean the list as a check from my financially worried point of view . . . It was time to see Artie again, clearly. The note was signed, *Yours, nada* . . . He hardly believed it. Perhaps he did, though, consider himself as such. There was a brother-in-law, for example, younger than Marge but equally decisive, a young doctor working with a team in Africa somewhere. He had arrived for his holiday, rented a motorcycle, and with Artie clinging to the back roared about the island, Artie being the guide. They had made a sudden visit, John remembered, the young man crisp, clear and polite. And healthy. Artie, in contrast, was for once pushed to the back, smothered by the determined energy of the other. And all faded.

In the afternoon he drove into the city, for the purpose of getting some things they needed, he told Joan. She did not want to go. He went straight to Artie's apartment, found only Marge there, so went off again, having told her he would be at a bar familiar to Artie, should he be able to come later. He did not like the way he sounded, saying it. He knew the money was equally her concern and that she must feel this a demand. But it wasn't. He wanted only to spend more, because it wasn't even his to spend.

He sat in the bar, in the late afternoon, waiting. Around him were the beginnings of the evening couples, secure people, among them a few English, French, Americans, and also the heavy, bright-faced Scandinavians. Some Germans also. He himself sat half-huddled at a table which gave him a clear view of the room. The jumping music someone was playing annoyed him but also kept him on edge, alert.

What had happened. Nothing perhaps, yet the money was a painful bore, a knot between them. Artie was someone he needed, so much he could not even say it. He was hungry for the pleasure of an uninvolved intimacy, but could any be that. And what was another man to him, at last. A fear he carried, a threat, a judgement, a confusion, feeling too often he could not himself make the measure implied, lacked the vocabulary even, had no words with which to make evident his own manhood, if words might accomplish that. He wanted a friend, of all things, another person simply to listen, to talk to, such a small fact. He wanted to be one of, the men.

Confused, he called for another beer, drinking quickly the one he had had, then saw Artie coming through the people toward him. He felt himself steady, even his voice grew firm in its order to the waiter, his world coming back. Artie, too, was talking as he sat down.

It's lucky you came in, he said. I was going to send this out on the bus. John saw he had money in his hand and was holding it out to him, John took it. He put it away in his pocket. What's happening, he asked. How are things?

Artie smiled, and said, the same, but a little better. I just got paid. That's some of what I owe you at least, a hundred pesetas. I'll have the rest soon, I hate to keep you waiting, but it's a hard time just now. You got my note?

John said, yes. But don't worry. God, money. Well, thanks. It all helps.

He felt dirty, vicious, tired. The squeezed wretch across from him was smiling into a hole of endless emptiness, his friend. That was a happy thought. Are you sure, he said, you won't need this you gave me? We have enough.

Artie answered, no, and drank his beer. John finished his also and ordered two more. They sat, quiet, watching the people, the men with their various women, some handsome, others not. The people came and went, the waiters moved back and forth between the close tables.

He could not place this man. The intelligence was curiously shadowed, held under, in a persistent self-mocking buffoonery. He made himself so available, and with such clear purpose, but the purpose might well change with the occasion. John could not allow that his only use to Artie was money, it couldn't be that. He had to have the friend, this friend. He tried, now, to regain the conversation between them, but the quiet persisted, the awkwardness stayed. They continued to drink, but their talk was broken, and the silence persisted.

Much later the bar closed, and John wanted to keep drinking, it quieted things, let him feel relaxed and sure, made even the friend closer despite the problems. He asked Artie where they might go and Artie got a taxi and took them to the broken edge of the city, where the houses ran out in sometimes half-finished buildings, open fronts, a melange of poverty and newness. The taxi driver himself opened the door, and went across the street in the dark with them, to knock on a door, which, opened, showed them a middle-aged woman, dirty clothes, asking what they wanted. Artie answered, a drink. She laughed then, and let the two in, the driver returning to his car.

Upstairs John found himself facing an unexpected line, of six women, across the room from him. The woman who had let them in was asking which he wanted. Of course he knew where he was now, he pointed to one, unsure, and she came over to him. They went together into one of the rooms at the back, but John wanted to drink, so the girl got him one. He asked where Artie was. She said, in the next room. What had happened, then, he wondered. She rubbed her hand along the crotch of his pants, he sat down, confused. As she undressed, he took off his own clothing, awkward, a little embarrassed. He hardly seemed to himself to see her, rather he could smell the harsh perfume, the sour bed, but felt the warmth, the rubbing, and heavily climbed on top of her, dazed, but feeling the skin warm, and made love to her as best he could. Then faded into a half-sleep, dizzy, confused.

In the night they all danced, around and around. People came together, separated, faces and hands, and there John sat, alone, and far across from him there was a man he recognized a little, not surely, but from the banging sounds, it must be that someone is trying to gain entrance to their enclosure. The bars, however, are fixed across the great door, but the heavy wood shakes and shudders under the impact of the blows. He calls. He hears a voice. They are swimming together across a great space of water. He feels secure, however, he has no fear because he knows the man is with him. There is the familiar voice, and now his hand is being taken, he is lifted from the danger of the water, so deep and far below him. He feels the movement of the hands as they grip him by the shoulders, now he is pulled clear, he feels the care. The other people have grown indistinct and the sounds they are making come only from an undefined place. It is far behind him. He has gone.

Are you all right now, Artie said. They were standing in the street, it was morning, Artie held him braced against the wall of a building. It was the same building, the same people. He felt sick, tired, but better. He nodded his head, trying to say something. When Artie had managed to get him to the apartment, he let himself be dropped in the bed. He knew only that Marge was not in it, he could not worry more where she might be. Artie was his friend.

8

THEN THINK back. As far as you can remember. What is the first thing. A crow has been hit by our car, we are going to the hospital where my mother, a nurse, has to see someone. Its wing is hurt. But by a trick they operate on me. I am at last taken home changed. We take the crow. We keep it in one of the many empty stalls in the barn. The whole place is empty now, my father is dead, I remember the tracks of the ambulance across the lawn that has come to take him, he is reading a story to me they used to print on the comics page, beside the pictures. There it is. He lies in the bed with me beside him, he is reading it to me.

She wanted to help him, Joan did, in her own way. She was in love with him, fumbling, she needed the love too. Poor little orphans in the snow, the marriage itself was such a shock to them though they had made love before it, but now they walked down the street in New York together, with a check but no way to cash it. Wasn't he the big husband, the capable man, then. She waited and waited.

He so loved the confidence of anyone, to be trusted, regarded. Like a dog, almost, the wagging smile. She told him his smile was lovely, it changed his whole face. But in the arguments he frightened her, she despaired of him, she shook, shook, shook, with sobs, caught, broken crying, over and over, shaking. The children stood stunned in the doorway, watching.

Can't you stop it, she said at last. You told me you would be back. You weren't. I thought you had been hurt somehow. I told the bus driver to look for you.

He shrugged, he couldn't answer her. Why should a crow, or a father, change so much. A broken grandfather, shouting, impatient, strange, trying to ram some manliness into the boy who heard his voice only as the one not soft, the only one, and

yet so much wanted. Talk to me. The women won't, there are
so many of them, five all told in the house counting his one,
older sister, the soft, sly voices, not men. The old man, and
perhaps himself if he could learn it, against them. He watched
his grandfather pare the apple, the strip coming off in one
continuous band, and then the spoon the old man used to eat
it, making straight, clean scoops. Teach me that.

But he got Joan out of her own broken house, the guardian,
the tight little woman all but screaming at them, her voice so
filled with hate and impacted impotence. They were taking
everything away from her, the house, the furniture, all she had
been given by the mother. Do you hear? The mother. She gave
it to me, not you. Are you going to strip me of everything after
all I've given you, my care, my love, my protection? She shook.
Joan could not answer. John held himself as firmly as he could,
he tried to answer her, seeing only the rage of the animal mind,
the tight, drab hate.

Let's go to the beach, he said finally, Juana can look after the
children. Won't they have a nap now? Let's go. I'm very sorry.

Once outside the house, it was a lovely walk. They went down
past the houses, of stone and mud, then to the small gardens,
past the washing place where a few women were still busy with
their clothes but waved to them. They were included now. It
was a happy, decent place.

Then the path came to a slight valley, where a brook ran
down to the edge of a bluff, dropping over the rock face to the
beach below. Bamboo grew thickly here, green high stalks of it,
with many sharp, spearlike leaves rustling in the slight wind.
Then up the other side the path went on, to the more arid edge
of the hillside, above the sea, where pines grew and few people
came. The goats were here, with a boy to watch them, who also
waved, delighted by even a passing company.

But weren't there woods, also, where it was, if no sea, but
then hay is like a sea, if the wind blows. You lie on your back
and look up. You see the clouds roll over you, so far up, you
think you could climb on them, jump up so high.

I played by myself a lot, though I had friends. But I liked
the silence of the woods, hiding there, listening. Finding a
sudden lady-slipper in the quiet of the woods, the feather of a
bird.

She walked behind him a little. There was not room on the

path for both and now it edged high over the sea, a drop of
many feet below. Looking back, the town had grown small and
indistinct in the bright sun. And then, ahead of them, they saw
the far beach, the neck of rock, the breakwater, reaching out,
the water white around it. Listening, they could hear the far,
faint crashing sounds.

Joan, he said, I meant to be back. I'm sorry. He wanted her
forgiveness, to regain her. To fight if necessary.

But fighting, often he was afraid. Deliberately he lost his
temper, knowing it would carry him, make him brave. He raged,
as his grandfather had taught him in some way to. Was it the
sound of the voice only? The old man had died shouting, swear-
ing, impatient. And yet he had been also quiet, so quiet, locked
in a weary stillness.

She reached forward to hold his hand briefly. They came to
the beach, and she went on, to follow the shore, while he went
back of a boat that had been pulled up, to change to his bathing
suit. He walked into the water, watching her go on, out of
sight, then reappear beyond the rocks again, waving to him. He
walked into the water, ducked, and began to swim out, relaxing.

You have to stand up for yourself. And that was clear enough.
He had to. If he was frightened, still he had to. In this family
there was nothing else to do but that, his mother, his sister, all
of them the same. There was no man now but him. His mother
was gentle with him, and she understood, he thought, but he
had to as she knew. You have no father, John, but I know he
would have been proud of you. If he could see you take it, stand
up for your rights, hit back when you have to. Don't start it but
don't let them run over you.

Clubbing the boy with the snowshovel, in the middle of the
snowball fight, his heavy, sullen cousin beaten with a rake
handle, his friends, pounding their heads with all his strength
into the dirt, fighting, trying with all his mind to win, win. He
had to. So don't get him mad, he loses his temper. Count ten,
his mother said. Then, if you have to, hit them, but use your
fists. But he still had to. And now he fought without the
movement of even one finger. He knew.

Somewhere back in the waste of it all, the empty place, he
knew the house and the woods too were someone else's. He
hated that invasion, that they could buy it. It seemed everything
was buried there, his pets, the dog, certain treasures of a small

kind. He had earned it, he felt, as one earns a thing by knowing it, all there is to know, every small thing. But without money they had to move out, to another side of the town, though otherwise there was little enough change. Yet it started the slippery sort of wandering he had come to, something had. There was an unending restlessness now, because nothing was in its place and all the continuity was just another fight. That done, he tended to move on.

He saw her against the grey rock and she was waving again to him. He pulled harder, against the yielding water, moving in to where she stood. She waited until he reached the edge of a rock which the water all but covered, and moved back then as he pulled himself up, spluttering and shaking himself like a dog.

Was it nice, she said. Is it cold. He wiped the water from his eyes, looking at her, bright and clean in the sun, smiling. It's wonderful, he said, not cold at all. Come in with me. She smiled at him, shaking her head. Let's have lunch, she said, and then I'll come.

He followed her back of the rock, to where several had fallen to make a shelf under which was a half cave, and there they sat down. The sea came close to their feet, and looking out they could see it reach to the edge of the sky, flat and blue. She took sandwiches from the basket she had brought, and gave one to him. She had tomatoes also, some olives, and white wine. She had put salt in a fold of wax paper, and offered it to him.

We fight too much, I wish we didn't. Do we have to, she said. She was talking to him. It was curiously apt, he had been thinking. Then, no. We don't have to. I am sorry. I had no intention of not coming back last night. She had stopped smiling, she ate more of the food.

He was not, he said, ever fighting her. It was to clear a place, to do what had to be done, somehow. It was that at any moment he never knew, it came, the occasion, and he threw her clear, as it were, he fought to stay responsible.

She looked at him, the sun became her, it brightened all her body into a lovely quickness. She said he was not being clear. Not as herself.

He drank some of the wine. Why fight, he said. I wouldn't fight you. Joan? She had begun to take off her clothes. What are you doing? She was going to lie in the sun for awhile, on

the rock in front of him. He looked at her white body in the
sun.

I want to go home, she said. Don't you get tired of living so
far from everything. How could he tell her. Where is home. Isn't
it here. I want the children to go to a proper school, she said.
I worry they can hardly speak English. She covered her eyes
with her hands, stretching.

There was no change to it, he thought. Bright, white, as the
sun, all was covered perhaps, an impersonal intensity of location.
And so now here, now there. What was the difference.

But what was the change. He thought of her as he had first
met her, an accident, an older party of another season, in the
winter of that year, and all the city was quiet with snow, the
white, light flakes of it falling and falling. He remembered the
first sight of her, what had he been involved with, some act or
other, for the party, the college house's celebration. And all the
people watched him and his drunken friends, and he was also
drunk, perform some charade or other, for amusement of them.
Drunken, as ever. There she sat, crossed legs, in the row in front
of him, with her nice green velvet dress, which was itself such
a courtesy of the season, so right for the occasion, and herself
so quietly careful, hopeful, watching with such childlike
intentness. Not at all wise, and not at all suspicious. After it all,
he had asked her to dance with him.

And now sun, but then the falling snow only. Then they
danced, his own shyness lost in her shy trust of him. That was
good, wasn't it. It was all, it seemed, good. When time came to
leave, he arranged for them to ride back to her dormitory with
other friends, the same stumbling ones which were always,
happily, his. The long car one had, had taken them all in, but
he was left, later, somehow still unclear, he was running down
the street after the fading image of it, trying to catch it, calling
to her. What had happened. He ran after it through the snow,
he ran after her through the snow.

He looked at her now. He knew her, each white inch, or
where the hair grew round each nipple, a very few black hairs.
Around the nipples of each breast butted from the tight barrel
of her chest. That was her. Like an old hag, a friend said, not
knowing nor meaning her at all, really, like some old ugly
woman with hair growing, like that. She had shivered, hearing
it, knowing herself or fearing it. The friends were always the

problem, talking, they would never stop, stumbling on, on to things they never intended. So that his protecting of her grew and grew, and she stood, it was he thought much too often the case, behind him, and he spoke for her, talking with her mouth for her. But then he would come upon her, suddenly, far from where he had come to believe her to live, and there she was with the friends, talking too, out there in that drifting, common world of all choices. Shocked, he tried to pull her back, and that was the fight again.

Now to go home, where was that. She lay white, hot, in front of him, her hands over her eyes. The sea sloshed in quiet, small waves against the rock's edge. What was the difference.

Where is this home, he said. Isn't it here. What's the use of fighting it all the time.

But there was no time for any of it. The sun, it seemed, had fallen half the side of the sky, so now it hung, jerking and bobbing as he opened his eyes and tried to look at it, in a confused impatience. Joan was shaking him, watching his face with amusement as he came back to wherever it was they were. It's time to go, she said, home. Home again it was. The old white house sliding down the long green hill, the half-heard shouts of the boys fading off, the car coming round the turn and up the worn drive, the dog, old man shouting through the late evening, the snow piled in thick drifts either side of the black street, the car fading as he ran. All sun and sea and rock again.

As they walked back to the town, she asked him again about his own sense of it, their living there and another sense of home they might have. Where was it. What did the children say but what they had to, or wanted to, as any. He thought they spoke well enough. So he heard them.

Aren't you concerned, she said. Yes, but perhaps differently. Shouldn't they have children as themselves to be with, and to speak English with. It was a curious problem, really a sense he could not quite get hold of. Where were they, because if here, then here it was, or there, then there it was. But how both, he thought. He could not answer her simply. It seemed an old nostalgia to him, that she took as concern. He had none to put with it, having taken himself to have lost home long ago, somewhere. Now friends were at best where they were, John and Joan, or simply themselves.

We're here, he said, and smiled. They had come to the edge

of the town and the people were again around them, passing, looking after them, some waving. It was here.

She left him, a little crossly, and he turned off the street to go for the mail, the pattern of the late afternoon insistent in his mind without his own awareness of it. At the small window alongside the store's front wall, because they were all homes, inside, and so people lived and worked in the same place, he asked if there were any letters for them, and saw the man at the other side of the window look through, then pull out the envelope. He took it, thanked the postman, and started back to his house, opening the letter as he walked.

9

ARTIE'S OWN reaction, when John told him the news, was a twitch of incredulity, and then a wild shake of laughter. John had, it seemed, done it again. Always that supine kindness, afraid of its own needs, did open the door, did in fact invite in whatever incongruity it could find. And this time it was apparently a lulu, a Liverpooler, a white, sour, sullen, first-time-from-homer, and Artie shrieked with enjoyment. It was going to be very good.

And again John felt that misfit desperation, that does, just as Artie suspected, play the rug to whatever occasion, this time England's. It begins so simply, as it had certainly with Artie himself, the letters, oh, the care of them. Such a tie across such distances, and when the young man said he had a short holiday and hoped that he might use it to come, for the first time, out of the dreary city of Liverpool, though he loved it, surely, to the sun-washed southern lands, what was there to be said but yes. God, what else.

Ah thoonk ooo be idiot, said Artie, or something like, *eee gone bee one big drag!* The giggles rode under the accent, the pinched face, hands, Artie now adopted, mincing about John in a greyish heaviness, bewildering him with the twitching face, the dour grey sounds that he was making, breaking into a quick fit of pointing finger and wild laughs.

It could not, however, be the young man who had written, not with that care of phrase John had so respected. And how are you today, and what is the weather there now like. Here, you see, it has been raining the past fortnight, or two, and I find my spirits depressed accordingly. By the care of a mother, in all senses, and the tedium of my employment at the hospital, comprising the sick, in all senses, so that I have become, as it were, their amanuensis, in all senses. But the holiday comes, and I have been planning, nay, hoping, that were it not a tedious inconvenience for you and your family, I might at last see you there. Which were a joy. Were it. Well, all were, like that. John had convinced Joan that such a visitor would restore them to the good spirits the young man so clearly lacked at present.

Artie saw it otherwise, and John confessed himself singularly unacquainted with England, supposing finally all were, of that country, just as possible, as violently to be enjoyed, as was the Artie of his heart. But then of course there were various places there, to be sure. Liverpool he had little sense of except for the notes given in one of his children's books, and there it was a little hazy. But the size seemed encouraging. "The city of Liverpool is a great English port, second only to London . . ." So that this in turn argued some equivalence of culture. But that word was also a hazy one. It said, "The industries in Liverpool itself use chiefly raw materials that come in by ship. There are tobacco factories, flour mills to handle grain, soap and margarine factories using animal and vegetable fats, and factories that make foodstuffs of all kinds . . ." There would be, clearly, much to talk about. And much to learn.

Yet Artie's amusement had had its effect, and a few days later John was relieved to have another letter, this time from a friend he did know, in France, who asked if he might pay them a visit also. John answered, telling him how much both he and Joan would enjoy it, if he might. This would help, he thought, offset the problem of the Englishman, Robert Willis, since the Frenchman, Rene Lely, was the one friend of their time in France, a painter who lived in narrow rooms in Paris while the remainder of his family maintained their aristocratic connections in Nice. But he was, more accurately, as colonial as was John in his restless singularity, having been brought up in Indochina, subject to very conscious politeness and great luxuriance of various jungle growths. There was no place, at last, for either of them and they tended to carry all that they might quite literally in their heads. Rene's intelligence was, for example, a clear, light character of the eyes, and a wit of insight that made him all but invulnerable to imbalances of all kinds.

But then there really was Robert Willis. Driving in to meet his plane John decided against seeing Artie again, even for a drink for reassurance. The last laughter still shook, and since the time of meeting was now so very close, Artie's humor would give it too much the character of a hopelessly garbled play into which John had floundered. Artie never laughed quietly.

So he went straight to the airport and parking the car, walked over the sun-hardened ground to the scant frame building that served as terminal. Here he found that Robert's plane had yet some fifteen minutes before its arrival, and sitting down to wait, he reconsidered all that he could think of for a sense of the man.

And thinking, why could it not be, that in that bleak city to the north some twisted occasion of parents, some painfully tight set of rooms, with the faded flowers, the dusty rubber plant, the sun-streaked umbrella, if sun there was, and then the child, from the stripped root, did grow albeit twisted, yet straight. And did sing, for example:

> *Sweet day, so cool, so calm, so bright,*
> *The bridall of the earth and skie:*
> *The dew shall weep thy fall to night;*
> *For thou must die . . .*

And wasn't that also England's, that north or south gave such tune to the mind, bred from the hardness of the land perhaps, though always he saw it as green, as Blake's, and pleasant in the sturdiness, the hardihood, of its people, the island of his own beginning, though split with the French, who seemed to hate with such quiet insistence those northern baby men. Lely seeing *les anglais* on the street, more often than not grew tight about the eyes, spit out something like, the infants. Their faces look like big babies.

And that was often true. He and Joan one time found themselves in a restaurant sitting within hearing of an Englishwoman, and her French friend, family friends they seemed, both in their forties, and she was telling him of some young man of their mutual acquaintance, most happily endowed with English stur-

diness it proved, who married a Lesbian, all unknowing, which
wife then set up her own menage, confining the dwindling
husband to parlor and couch, where he lived, she said, for a full
year in hope that Jessie would recover herself and prove him
right in his trust. The Frenchman had made a small mouth of
irritation, saying no young French would have been quite so
unaware of the nature of the problem. But the woman had
seemed almost to admire it, the good will, as it were. This
perhaps was England's strength. The Frenchman was not
convinced.

Now, suddenly, here was Robert Willis, unmistakeably,
walking toward him through the knot of embracing Spanish
with a stiff, sure intentness, each large foot proceeding with
braced will, through the foreign strangeness, the sounds, the
smells, the foreign sun. He looked very large and very white,
and as he slowly swiveled his large white face from side to side,
the pale blue eyes looking flatly for the man who might be John,
John heard the last echo of Artie's laughter, and got up to
identify himself.

The ride home found them sitting side by side in the car but
almost without speaking. Each time John said something, to
make it simpler, the answer he got so filled with Artie's laughing
mimicry that he dared not even look at the large-headed man
beside him. So he drove on, giggling silently, with tears in his
eyes.

Once Willis had been taken to the pension, and arranged
there, the fluttering servants were sent off to prepare his bath
and then he was to be led to John's part of the building. But
nothing was so simple. Willis suspected all, and what were they
doing with his luggage? John would guard it, but there was,
really no need. All were honest here, pathetically so, with their
large, warm eyes, so proud of their Englishman, so eager to be
commanded by such exotic foreignness as he possessed. But the
white, stiff figure, now half unclothed, sat on its bed, staring at
John who leaned against the door, trying tactfully to avoid the
question. Who were these people, it asked. What were these
odors, these colors of things? In England – and the greyness of
that place flooded into the room more awful than John had
thought possible, the dankness, the pain, the smallness, the tight
drab limits of that life before him, with its duties, its mother,
its pinched resentments. It was not England, it was the hatred

for that southern England, that high and mighty London. And that was the actual *foreign*, for this man, that wit, that quickness, that ease, that superiority over the pinched, grey north.

Oh, I know, Willis might now be saying, and hadn't he just, in each and every letter, come to think of it. Oh, yes, you can't know what it is there, that tram to the hospital, those lines of beds, all that tight, little suffering comes of it, every night, I walk through those halls and clean up after them, hearing their little voices bleating their little needs, and this one a tuck, that a bed pan, this one wants its little mess cleaned up, there, on the floor. Couldn't half yell if I weren't to, and didn't once when I might have caught it. Oh, the weary sick hearing only their own small voices. It's a real death, you know.

But he said, in fact, nothing, letting only his eyes, his bleak blue eyes, show the distrust he was feeling, even of John. After his bath he let John lead him to their own part of La Baronia, where Joan and Rene were waiting, a little nervously, for the expected guest. They had eaten, and Joan now brought out the food for John and Willis, the latter watching covertly the French Rene, and at times switching the heavy eyes to John as though to accuse him of some broken trust after all, there being this Frenchman indeed in his house. He spoke almost not at all, keeping to that required by the barest of politeness, and his comment to Joan's question, was the dinner enough, said simply, it will do. At that she joined Rene in watching Willis with much the same eyes as he looked at them, and John fumbled back and forth between the hostile silences until it was at last time to go to bed. Then he led Willis again back to his room in the pension. As he was leaving, Willis asked him about the Frenchman, was he a guest with them, or a visitor. John answered, guest. Willis looked bleak, shrugged, and said he supposed he was. An old friend, John added. But Willis had got the ground he was after, and that ended that.

In the few days following that the holiday allowed, nothing went very happily. They were even to become aware of a persistent odor Willis seemed to bring with him, as his person. It was the more embarrassing since it made even the air they shared with him difficult, and any suggestion of that only drew the bleak eyes to their usual sight of things. It had made a drear mistake in coming, it needed no reminding. Offered fruit common to the island, Willis tended to turn it over in his hands, examining it closely, but always gave it back with a gesture implying he was a little too quick to take the hemlock so simply. When he discovered tea was after all available he had asked about but had been told wasn't, then that also was the same trick, the lie, hovering over him, about to be the same as he might have expected from them, the easy Americans with their money. But we didn't know that brand was in the store, Joan would insist, with a reasonable impatience. How could we, we don't drink it. But it's the best, Willis said only. You would know that. You would drink it. Even now John couldn't remember its damned name. And later, having loaned him some money wherewith to buy the stuff, they asked him if they might borrow back the change left having run short themselves. No, said Willis, I have none of your money. But we gave you fifty pesetas, Joan said, we gave it to you. No, said Willis, I have none of your money. He was like a huge endless wall.

John did not dare to let Artie see him, although he knew sooner or later it would have to be Artie who got Willis off them. Willis himself had expressed some interest in meeting Artie, whom he had heard of, and was prepared to deal with more simply, since they were both English. He was also prepared to meet the writer, which he assumed Artie, or John if it had to be, might arrange.

It was all a hopeless mess. Rene had drawn back, smiling only in the background, talking to John as there was time to, but careful to keep well away from Willis. At last John asked him for help. Willis had not had a chance to swim since he had come, so they decided to take him.

Some revenge seeming reasonable, they chose a place well away from the common beach, at the side of a huge flat of rock going out into the sea, a wall quite equal to Willis, down the side of which one climbed to come to a narrow cavelike break in the side of the rock, where one could undress, put on a bathing suit, then dive into some thirty feet deep of open sea.

They could not persuade him to change to the rope-soled sandals commonly worn. He kept to his heavy leather shoes, and so he found the climb down difficult, even dangerous, sliding in places, but catching himself without a sound, looking hard before him. Below the sea washed against the grey rock, and the wind freshened, turning the tops of the ground swell's caps to frothy white. Far back they could see the beach and the people there from the village, but here it was silence except for the wind's sound and that of the water against the rock.

It was always a pleasure, and diving in, John swam clear of the sloshing kelp and headed out. Rene followed, and they both swam out together, stopping at last to rest and to watch Willis make his heavy way into the water. They saw him lunge down awkwardly, feet first, disappear under a wave's breaking against the rock, then paddle clear of it with dog-like motions, his head held stiffly up. It was painful, to be so heavy. The water had no care for him. He fought it doggedly, paddling heavily in the increasing swell, but made little headway against the wind and washing in of the waves. Slowly he pulled out from the rock a little but could not manage to come up to them, and so he lurched in the water by himself, fighting it with a persistent, sullen strength.

That was sad, not to have wings after all, nothing but weight. Would the words ever hold that up, John thought. If the water wasn't a way, what would be. He ducked under, pulled with his arms, went down into the quietness and depth, then up again, breaking to breathe in deeply. It was joy.

But now Willis was sinking, slowly but surely. His head no longer up, each wave caught him, slapped at his face, the motions becoming tired and uneven, jerking to support the stubborn weight. They saw him make a grab for the lip of the rock, but a wave hit, he was slapped against the rock's side, went under, came up again, managed to kick off with a foot, and broke clear to slap heavily at the water all around him, the head going under with each wave that rolled past the struggling body.

From within their own ease they watched him, and said without thinking, or speaking, let him go. Watch, but let him go. For minutes they saw the large head go under, reappear, go under, reappear. Rene's eyes were watching sharply, with a bright, open calm. He looked at nothing but the struggling man some twenty feet away from him, as he treaded water, rising, falling, easily with the waves. He is smiling, John thought, but himself then broke at some point within, terror of death only, and swam quickly to the exhausted Willis, dove and catching his legs, heaved him close to the rock, and then getting breath, dove again to grab his legs, broke the water with a yell, *grab the rock*, and Willis smashed up and over, but hung on. John dropped back deep in the water as Willis hauled himself onto the rock.

There was nothing more. Willis was even more silent than before, and at the house they separated, Rene and John returning to the apartment while Willis went to the pension, to rest. That night, while John was in another room, Willis said, out of a silence, to Joan, he saved my life this afternoon. He never said it to John. Instead he took out from a thick leather billfold a ragged brown clipping, from a newspaper, very old. It told of his father's having rescued a child in Liverpool, by jumping to throw her clear of an approaching tram. The father had gone under. It killed him. When Willis was how old, then. Probably no older than the child. But that was that. A day or so later, Willis went into the city, to visit with Artie he said, and to meet the writer. It was clear he would not be back.

10

THE TIME, then, with Rene grew more clear. There was time to talk, much needed, for the world had become too malleable, and John with it. The terms shifted, the look of things blurred, faded. Rene smiled at these complaints, because he assumed his friend to have much possibility. It was only a question of finding the use of it.

At least the house grew quiet again. Rene, in a loft above their rooms, began now to paint, and this in turn opened their eyes, forced them all back to seeing. They were given again the question of liking, or disliking, or rather of seeing or not seeing, whatever it was. The paintings offered no hold but that of shifting colors, weights, scratched, worn back to stains upon the paper, or an insistent line, a mass, suddenly present. Each late afternoon they climbed to the loft, to look, so that days themselves became again possibilities. An excitement returned.

In all of it John looked for what he might hold to, finally. He was not sure, shied from the easy good nature, the quick eyes. When their conversation grew relaxed and the sun settled in the corner of the room, through the far windows, the stone of the floor softened and the children, quick to sense their enjoyment, came closer, played in narrowing circles around their chairs. But, for his own part, John stiffened on the seat, heard the words, the laughter, the ease, as a fair displacement of his own concerns, and although he wanted most to let them go, could not, sat tight, listening, following with an intense uneasiness all that was said.

In the night, close to his wife, he heard her breathing heavily in sleep. He lay on his back looking off into the blackness, broken by the bands of yellow light from the outside street lamp, or moon, as it rose, reached its height, then dropped back, to break before the whitening day. Hours passed in his mind, lying there, thinking, at times reaching out to touch her next to him. She twitched in her sleep, shrugged off his hand, turned. He felt the tightness all about him, shifting, turning.

Through the distortions of furniture and vague intentions, he could see the children, in their normal day, at times coming to ask his help, or interest, and at times he walked off with them through the streets to see what they wanted him to, or to find what it was they had wanted. He saw his oldest son most clearly, standing stiff as himself, pushing out to the other boys of the village. Their pounding feet as they ran echoed past the walls of the houses, and now they broke clear of the town, over the hill, a straggled line of running children. There was his son among them, close to the front, pounding on.

In it all he wanted something, to the exclusion of all else, a wish as yet undefined but clear in his mind, a sense to allow him all of them. It was the purpose he felt most vaguely, and that was what had come to make his hands fumble, his head lock with frustration. Rene smiled, given much to smile at, blessed in turn with clear use, as John saw him. Joan also looked, and flattered by the sight, paid it increasing attention.

Days went, compounding the sea, finding in the mind a like flux, a wash of incident. He could not find it. He saw them all through the sliding water. And talking now, he was also thinking, trying to see them, to focus at last upon the center of their faces, the eyes, the smiling mouth. Echoes of it all came back, as Willis falling faintly apart in the city, so Artie told them. The shocked, drunken, bleak man holding at last to a lamp post, sick with impossible food and forced drinking. Artie screaming the *falangistas* are coming, run, the lurch up from the sinking table, Willis, stunned, falls out through the door, the black street, no one, Artie's cries, *police, police*, as Willis staggers over the sidewalk to grab the shaking pole, unwinds around it, falling, holding, and then vomits food and drink over his stiff clothes and hard leather shoes, breaks down into stunned, dulled helplessness. And Artie laughs, and walks away.

But you helped him, and what was that for. Simply that he could not see him go, like that. Could not. As if the sea would not want him at all, fought him, slapping his face again and again and again, broke against his chest, slammed him repeatedly into the coarse rock face, cutting his chest. Willis rose from the water streaming lines of blood, over the white chest, lurched free of it, silent, stunned, walked away. Was it all an echo.

And Rene smiled, he did not remember it that way. Joan watched in the hold of his clarity, and John slipped away. One afternoon, Rene gone again to the loft, and days now were short, he would soon leave they remembered, she seemed preoccupied, and John could not find her. There was no longer much at all to speak of, so far she was, so vague in her movements toward him. Asking what was the matter, he knew it was a misstep, but had taken it.

She said, I think I love him. And that was true enough. All the time had drawn that face, given washed colors to that impression, and her face twisted, answering, indignant that there should be one, that suspicion only should be the reason for her saying it. What answer, then, he thought, because she was echoing only the vagueness, the blur.

Rene moved back, smiling, there was no relation but an enjoyment of the friends, all of them, and the singularity that made his own life kept him clear, insisted. He knew them both and moved back.

But I love you, Joan, John said. It's me. She could not see him, she moved weakly in the confusions. At night they lay now in a careful distance, in the dark, as she felt, I love him. John felt it, and turned then, in suspicion, to Rene, who felt nothing, who was absorbed, interested, with other things, not their confusions, but themselves.

So it was all friends again. The last days of Rene's visit they went on picnics together, to the beach, to the hills above the town. All stayed in the neutrality of much diversion, as they moved from one end of their place to the other, back and forth, children and all. Then he had gone.

So there were, now, no diversions other than themselves. The friends had faded again. Joan went on, looking back, locked in a possibility she had seen, somewhere, even if nowhere. He watched the quiet pain of it and the carefully kept distance, wanting, hoping, to break through it, holding on. The days went by again.

Somewhere out on the sea there were boats. At evening John watched the fishermen of the village go out. They went always into the sunset, pushed on by the slow, sure oars. Then later they came back, through the dark, the moon at times marking their way by a road of light, as a dream's, fading, the slurred sound of the oars, pulling. He swam there too, reaching, lifting each arm to pull, over the surface of the black water, hearing the depth far under him in the blackness, dreamed of the distance in the black nights, and the sound of the sea reaching up into the room through the blackened windows. All slept in the sea's darkness, lulled by the faint, crashing repetitions of the shifting water.

Lacking other way, he began to make her up, to invest her with his own mind, no matter the twists, the shifts, the distortions of her, talking in his voice, from hers, impatient when she did in fact speak to him, now, came from whatever place she did live, out, to look for a moment at what he was, what they were together. He hated it, that naked look, the pain of it, and the anger. All came to the surface then, poured over them in a wash of stinging dislike.

He kept swimming, twisting, fighting the water, hearing the echoes. No letters came but for a note, thanking them. Rene wished all well. Willis wrote asking for something or other, some help with a magazine he now wished to begin. As though all he had come for, was just that. John wrote back immediately, grateful for the chance to rid himself of the last guilt, the failure they had all made of it. Willis shook, tried to grab the post, but fell foward into a pool of his own vomit. Rene smiled, and withdrew. And out on the sea the boats again moved out for the night's fishing.

Among the older men of the town there was memory of an older story, of a huge fish, a leviathan, which they had no measure for nor means to describe but as it had, once, appeared

to them, one night. Was it a whale. They didn't know. It was
very big, had come out of the depth of the water, suddenly,
upon them. Its great bulk reared under their boats as they tried
to beat it off with their oars. They fought it with what they
could, oars, anything, beating at it in the shaken sea. That was
the memory of it, then. A number of their boats had been
smashed, the great fish went under the sea, they came home.

And with each new sense he gave to her, put as a face on her
own, she fought it, quietly, but with stubborn, persistent will.
As she did, he also resisted, turning from device to device,
change of look, of gesture, smiling, frowning, moving here and
there, through their rooms, walking the floor, the ceiling, the
walls, until his face also became a mask to be expected from
any place at all, grinning, crying, out.

As relief they began to go into the city more frequently. They
found shops where tables and chairs might be made to their
own design, and John secured a long, spare table of dark wood,
on which he intended to write. Joan bought chests and chairs,
some with rockers, and also *braseros*, large copper braziers for
burning charcoal. They explored the city, stopping at odd places
for impromptu meals, or a single drink. They walked out along
the sea wall that skirted the docks and rocky beach beyond, and
watched the fishermen there, or else the ships coming in from
the mainland, the lines of anchored sailboats and small yachts.

It all passed time. They carried, despite intentions, much of
their emptiness with them, and talking, sitting in some small
cafe for rest, grew quiet and at the same time very restless. John
watched the movement beyond them, the restless people who
passed by them, and Joan slipped again past him, closed in her
own concerns.

Equally they turned to Artie and Marge, and neither had
seen Marge for some time, but for saying hello to her, briefly,
enroute to or from Artie. Now they came to her also, asking for
her help.

They talked to her of the recent visitors. Willis, she said, was
a fat bore, but Rene delighted her. The French it was, and within
her sharp, faint eyes was much liking for that phenomenon. So
she regretted not having seen more of him, sensing then what
Joan had seen. At that she drew the line, again bored. It was
simply none of her business.

So that was somehow that, and nothing more. Marge was

now heavy with the coming child, and that absorbed her also. Joan tried to reach her through this common term of women, but Marge again cut back to her own singleness, sharply, shrugging.

What was really the use of it. You may choose your own idiots to deal with, Marge told John, but don't expect my indulgence of them. Artie, of course, may do what he likes, as he most obviously does do. But aren't you being a little of a fool to be so trusting. Who are these friends of yours? Willis was certainly impossible. The other seems to have done you no service either. But it's all your very own business.

To Joan she said almost nothing, but would at times come back, from whatever world she happened to be in, to be warm, friendly, even playful. And Joan tried to hold on, but then the abrupt coldness would return, slamming nervous doors as Marge faded behind them.

One evening they had dinner together, meeting at a restaurant which Joan had found, arranged as a ship, outside a ship's wheel set in the side of the building above the entrance, and inside a clutter of life buoys, nets, glass floats, fixed to the walls. The room itself was long, and sparely furnished. A family owned it, the father acting as its manager, collecting the money paid for the meals, and taking orders. The two children, a half grown son and daughter, brought the food, and in the kitchen the mother cooked it. There were never many people in the place, and so it was comfortable, simple to feel safe in.

After they had ordered, Joan excused herself to go back to where the washroom was at the far end of the room. John watched her go, grow smaller with the room's length, dark in the shadows. They talked, and at last the food came. John ordered another beer, then looked for Joan who had not come back, then saw her sitting bent over, in the dark at the far end of the room, by herself. He walked back to her, almost slowly, trying to arrange the position in which she was sitting into an acceptable pattern.

She was crying without sound, tears slipping down her tightened face, and he asked her, what is it. She tried to say something, but doubled again in the effort. He felt her forehead quickly, there was no fever, and then her pulse, which was quick. Lifting her as he could, he gestured to the owner, now there also, to open the door at the back beyond them, then to

Marge and Artie now there as well, call the doctor, I'll take her over.

In the car he put her on the seat beside him, started it, drove through the muddling cars with bright headlights as quickly as he could to the doctor, the one who knew them, but arriving there, Joan now crying hard with the pain, he could find out only where the doctor might be, he was not there, and through the excited Spanish got the directions as best he could, to find the clinic where she should now be taken. In the car again he tried to reassure her, but the pain heard nothing. He saw, driving, what seemed a red cross bright above a door, assumed it was the clinic, stopped, took her, carrying her. But they were met by a small man, who muttered, fussing about Joan, that nothing was serious, said take twenty drops of something in a glass of water daily. It was not enough. John shook, grabbed the man by the throat trying to impress him, finally carried Joan out again, and on, till in the blackness another clinic's cross could be seen. In he took her again, faint with the fear she might be dying, now she was limp in his grasp, crying only. Terrified, he called for anyone and a nurse came down the hall. He gave the name of the doctor he was trying to find, stumbling with Joan's weight. They took her away from him, and pushed him back to a chair. He let their reasonableness hold him, it was the right place.

Later the doctor told him how very close it had been. A cyst had broken, as big as a fist, and flooded the intestinal cavity with pus. It was lucky it had not been worse. Marge and Artie had gone home, and Joan, in a room over his head, was asleep.

In the night, as he drove, sounds echoed, some crying, some the sea again, and the huge fish lifted and fell back. The water washed over. Out of it, too, came sudden sharp cries of another kind, at times a moaning only, blurred by the wind, the echo of the car's tires running on the packed dirt. The sea, when he came to it, was cut by a blur of shattered light, the moon clear above it, the hills in the blackness. He saw a shattered white face blurred with shifting water, a painful thing.

III

11

SUCH ARGUMENT as they had had between them was now, for the time, done with. It was not that all that much did change, but Joan was to be changed, quite literally, from whatever it was she had been to whatever it was she would now be. More than that the doctor was not prepared to say. His first concern was to deal with the infection, and to this end he gave her large injections of an antibiotic, so that the infection might be stopped and the cyst itself allowed to close again. Once it was clear that this had been effected, he said he would then remove the cyst, establish the extent of the involvement of other areas – specifically that of the reproductive organs – and act accordingly. The primary thing was now to rest, not to worry, to realize that whatever was to happen would be that which had to. You are not the first, he said, and smiled at them. You have already three fine children. And you, he said to Joan, have been living only with half your life. This thing (he made the fist) has been eating you up inside. You'll see. Once I get that out of you, you'll feel like dancing all the time.

He made this reference to the cyst itself become a kind of reassurance for them. It was at least specific. He insisted that they feel the extent of its size by taking their hands and pushing them down into the flesh of Joan's stomach until they felt the curiously resistant knob of growth take shape for them. It was, truly, very large, and why they had not found it before seemed strange. But then they had not looked for such a thing, and who would, except one hopeful of finding it.

Two days later the doctor let Joan go home, telling her to

return in a week. He gave John a prescription for a continuation of the injections of antibiotic. These were to be given her throughout the week to prevent any recurrence of the infection. When John asked who was to give them, the doctor smiled again and answered, you. Then he got a syringe and needle, and showed him the procedure, how care should be taken to avoid air, how to hold the needle for a quick, sure means of placing it, where to give it, and as he explained, John found that his interest had displaced his first discomfort. It would be another thing to do.

However, in the house it was not so simple. He fumbled with the needle. It seemed very dry to him, it would not fit easily onto the syringe. He had boiled it first but nearly all the water had dried up in the pan in the process. He tried to fill the syringe as he had seen the doctor do it. The liquid seemed to stick in the needle, clogging. Perhaps he had not allowed the powder to dissolve sufficiently in the solution. Joan lay on her stomach across the bed, waiting. Finally he had what seemed to him enough fluid in the syringe. He pressed slightly on the plunger so that it filled the needle, and a few drops spilled out. Then he raised her skirt, squeezed a pinch of flesh on the upper part of her buttock, and found himself looking at it.

What was so difficult. First, that it was her of course. It had to be right. The flesh looked blotched to him. There were small pimples, scratches, in certain places. He tried to balance the needle and syringe in his right hand, swinging it a little, pinching with the left hand, trying to get the rhythm of the intended gesture. Go ahead, she said. Please.

What could he do. He had to, clearly. There was to be no running, no explanations. There was nothing at all to talk about. It was a very simple thing to do. He lifted his hand, then swung it down, at the pinch of flesh, felt the needle seem to bend, stop, and saw the scratch, by his hand, across her skin. She jerked and pushed up with her hands.

What are you doing, she said, please, please get it over with. He took the pinch of flesh again between his fingers. He brought the needle close, and pushed it in, then pressed hard, too quickly, on the plunger of the syringe. She twitched but he continued. Seeing the syringe empty, he withdrew the needle, and then, having forgot the bit of cotton with some alcohol, to press on the puncture, did it with his thumb, nervously, while

reaching round for something else. He found the cotton he had
first used to swab the place with, where he wanted to put the
needle, now had, where it was now bleeding. He asked her to
hold it, putting her hand on the cotton and the place and went
off to the bathroom to get an adhesive pad. Finally he got this
on, relaxed, and she sat up, shaking.

Simply, the mirror had broken. One had. It was that what
had been a common sight was now not, and if he saw this or
that, in the continuity of arrangement familiar to their habits,
even to the enmities between them, and the love too, then that
was not now. Days ago such fumbling might well have irritated
her, and been cause of an argument. Now she looked at him
simply as one she could not trust, and yet had to.

Of course practice would make a little more perfect, and with
each successive attempt to give the injection quickly, competently, he did better. She suffered it quietly, his practicing. There
was a thin wire that had to be placed in the hollow of the needle
after the process, so as to prevent any possible clogging but
more to keep the point of the needle from dulling against the
metal of the pan in which it was boiled. This disappeared
altogether after the third injection. He had become careless, as
he felt more able. After he had finished, he looked for the wire,
to replace it in the needle. It was not there. He looked in the
pan, on the bed beside her, by the bottle of alcohol, in the box
in which he kept the needle and syringe. He could not find it.
She asked him what he was looking for, and he told her. He
looked again in the places where it might be, but could not find
it. Then, at last, he felt the flesh around the latest puncture.
Was there that which might feel like such a two inch piece of
thin wire. He could not be sure.

What had broken was only a mirror, and a very unreal one,
but it was all they saw themselves in. They had made it, both
of them, with what care they possessed. You here, me here,
together there. How many such mistakes could it contain, even
in its fragments. No one had wanted it broken. Even the arguments, and the distances between them, had kept the image
clear. It gave them back themselves as they saw themselves, and
if the faces should be angry, they understood. They recognized
themselves. The mirror broke because she was no longer to be
reflected there, as she had even agreed to be. Each thing he now

did, right or wrong, could not be placed in that reflection any longer. She had fallen out and broken too.

Toward the end of the week the doctor came, unexpectedly. He had not been before to their house and so they all felt an increase of intimacy between them. He became, in their dilemma, a primary conspirator. After his examination of Joan they sat together in the bedroom.

What you will now do, he said, is established. Both of you come to the city tomorrow, and you – with a finger to Joan – be prepared to stay for a few days. It will be a simple business. The cyst will now come out without difficulty. It is, in effect, all over, and you will be much relieved to be rid of it.

So they were, shortly, to be beyond any of their own intentions, but in the night, the last night before they would go, all the fears came. They thought, but what if she dies. He wanted to hold her from it, reach past the need and secure her with his own. I don't want to go, she said, don't make me. But then he found himself speaking as the doctor had, saying it would be better, that she would feel so much better, after it was over. But I don't want to, she said. Don't make me. They hardly slept.

In the morning as he prepared Juana for their going in, talked to the children, as she did, telling them she would be gone for a few days only, and that he would be back the next day, again she was crying, her face streaked, broken, like a small child's. She was terrified. The shattered fragments reflected only a thousand twisted small faces, grimacing, crying, a child in terrified horror, calling help me, help me.

He couldn't. He locked in knots, finally saying, if you don't want to go, don't. I don't care. What a specious thing it was to say, and who cares if he cared, or didn't, or said it, anything, or didn't. Was he the child after all. Were they taking something away from him, only. It was so hard. Wouldn't logic answer the question, and wasn't reason really what it wanted to be, so right. What presumption to be so frightened you really cannot worry about what someone else is worrying about, at all.

She looked at him, stopping her crying, almost without understanding. Was he quite serious. Again he told her she ought to go, and that they would be late for the time given them by the doctor. Everything had been arranged, and why should she disturb it. She would be all right. The doctor had said so.

Abruptly he turned and went out of the house, and she kissed the children, then followed him, without speaking.

Once in the clinic a nurse showed them to the room made ready for her, and left them, to return, when Joan was settled in the bed, with the preparatory medication. The operation would not be performed until the next morning, and now that they were in the clinic, with that decision behind them, the tightness relaxed. They sat there, Joan in the bed, John on the chair, looking at one another. Soon it would be all over. He reached out to take her hand.

Somewhat later the nurse returned, this time to give Joan a sedative, because rest was important, she said, and the doctor was anxious that she should have as much as possible. Joan took the pill, the nurse left, the afternoon grew drowsy and late. Sitting by the bed he saw her slide deeper into the blankets, and then fall asleep. He sat for a time, watching, but became restless and getting up, went out into the hall.

That much was clearly done. He might, if he wanted, have a bed moved into the room with her, and stay there. But he had promised the children he would be back the next day, and did not want, in any case, to lie there watching her sleep. Only when she was awake did he feel them at all close. Waiting was otherwise impossible, and she moved far away from him into the complexities of her situation. Which was new, bitterly so, and utterly singular to herself. She was being changed. No more hysteria then. What did it say? As any outbreak of wild, uncontrolled excitement or feeling, such as fits of laughing and crying. Suffering in the womb. No man would ever know that, and she would not, soon. It would be over.

Walking along the hall he looked in past the various doors, to see the packed families, odd to his own eyes, the patient very nearly crowded out by all the interested parties. It was actually a legal matter. Supposing the sick one to be mother, or daughter, then the custom was that someone should be there, as husband or father, to be the protector, the legal barrier against a possible misuse. Even in the operating room it was customary to have a male member of the family present, and as the doctor began to remove whatever part of the body, he either pointed to it, or otherwise exposed it, to this man, for permission to deal with it as he thought necessary.

Here is the hand, John thought. Take it off. The eye, take it out. What a barbarous process. And now the *hystera*, the womb. "Because women seemed to be hysterical more than men, hysteria was attributed by the ancients to disturbances of the uterus . . ." He walked down the hall, out the door, and into the street.

There was time to kill again, and he did not feel like driving, nor going to a bar, say, to drink. That would help little, and also seemed, under the circumstances, much too callous. But how feel what he could not feel, except as a dull, steady fear, an aching incompetence either to help or to understand. She was there, wherever there was, and the doctor, with his good-natured jokes and his steady, even sense of what, as he told them, was, and still was, necessary, he was closer, not John. John was still in the mirror, broken or not.

He found himself walking on toward Artie's, which was, as it happened, close. That would be a chance to talk, to let their concern take over, if only for a little while. They would sympathize, and he could use it no matter it might be selfish. They could all sit in their relatively terrified ignorances, knowing just as much as they knew, but no more. They could say, yes, surely there is no need to be worried. He is a good doctor. It is a relatively simple operation. Nothing will happen. Even so everything was happening. As he walked, he knew it was, as she was sleeping, as the time passed, quickly, quickly. He turned around and headed back to the clinic.

Later she woke again. He was sitting in the chair beside the bed, looking out at the night sky, the lights of the city, waiting. He had had a cot moved into the room and it sat along the wall under the windows, covered by a grey blanket. She looked at him, yawned, and asked how long she had slept. A few hours, he answered. And did you stay here all the time, she asked. Most of it, he said. Are you hungry. She nodded, and he went out to the hall to find a nurse.

A little later they brought her some soup, since she could have nothing more heavy, because of the operation the next morning. Then they gave her another sedative, and soon she was again asleep. He was tired also and arranged the blankets and sheets on the cot and undressing partly, lay down on it. Then, without thinking, he also fell asleep.

The light woke him, and he reached for his pants, fumbling, to put them on under the bedclothes. It was morning, a nurse was by her bed, it was time. Coming in, the doctor began to reassure them even before they could remember their questions. There would be no problems. She would go to sleep in this room, and she would wake up in this room. It would be all over.

Because in the old days, you know, sometimes the patient would be almost frightened to death, they would give him the anaesthetic in the operating room, with all the big lights, and the mask coming down over his face, very terrifying! One said to me once, don't start cutting yet, doctor! I'm still conscious! Poor fellow, we very nearly lost him then and there. Ha.

John went to the bed, gripped her hand, kissed her, but she was already deep in her own preoccupations. But she gripped back, hard. It would be all right. After she had been taken from the room, he sat in the chair, trying to read. The time passed but there was no relief. It had all changed and he could not find it.

Later still he looked up to see the doctor had come into the room, still with the long rubber gloves over his hands. He looked tired but told John it was all over and all right, it had been a hard, long job, there had been much to deal with. It was the fist, he said, like that, making one, and many others, smaller. Six months more and she would have been dead. You are both very lucky. Then he left again. Soon Joan was brought into the room, wheeled to the bed, then shifted off onto it. The nurse straightened the clothes around her, took her pulse, and went out also. John moved over to the bed and looked at her.

She was white, or more accurately, a greyish white. Her hair had streaked into lines on her forehead, apparently with sweat. Her mouth was open and she made snuffling, guttural sounds, breathing. He took her hand but it felt heavy, indifferent. Around her middle there was a large bunch, made by the bandages. All the flesh seemed to be listless, heavy. The sound of her heavy breathing made him feel uneasy, and he stepped back.

Who are you, then. Tell me what's happened, he thought. He took her hand, but he could not move closer.

12

REASSURING the children was not as difficult as he had assumed it might well be. What they wanted was not an explanation but just to let it go on, whatever it was. Philip, their oldest, but barely six, wanted to understand because it was from him that the two younger would find out, finally, what it all meant. He looked for a sign, however, rather than a reason, as all children do. It was the emotional wash of things, looks, ways of movement, how they all sat, that he moved to, and questioned.

How long since he had looked at them, John thought, and felt unsure. Where had they been. The days went by so quickly, so slyly. Then here they were, Philip and his sturdy legs, and William, solemn and large eyes, but with a humor back of it all, that laughed. And Jennie, the baby, round faced, stuffed, and round bodied, like a plump, content ball. What did he want from them.

None of it was intentional, if that mattered. They came, as all comes, because it does. No plans, no intentions. She had been so pregnant, terrifyingly, so often, before they were married even. They used some large oval brown pills to block it, to force it out. Footballs, she called them, gagging.

But that wasn't the whole truth. He had panicked, much more than that. Leaving her, but by a vicious twist not leaving, saying, I can't leave you like this, I must do something. What can we do. The fact was in her, not him.

She sent him away finally. She broke. It was just as he was to go to Burma, of all places. He was restless, and wanted to see the war. She had called him to tell him she was going to marry someone else, a soldier. It was far away. He spent a day, or was it two, three, getting there, trying to talk her out of it, but after he had left and gone back to wait for the boat, again she called. Then nothing for a year. But the sad, dreary, dragging love persisted. When he came back, a friend of hers arranged that they meet again, by accident. It all came back.

But the history, was what changed, the details, the things each faced, each by themselves. He didn't know even if that was what history was, what happened so, but it was that no matter. She told him of the months he hadn't been there. She said she

had wanted to marry the soldier simply to have a father for the
baby. There was to have been a baby. The soldier was in a
camp for those who had been badly shocked, a rehabilitation
center close to the college where she then was. By will, by
desperation, she caught this one, or did she. Did she fall again,
only. How did he know what had happened.

There was no marriage. Her stomach grew larger. She was
completely alone then. She sat in a shed with a knitting needle
and managed to abort herself. It streaked his face like a white
scar. There. You did that. Look. That was the history, and it
was not even for the first time.

Sometime later he had his own chance, in the apartment his
mother and sister lived in, in the bathroom, at the back, when
all the others but she and him were asleep. The pills again. The
cramps started, he followed her into the bathroom, held her,
felt the contractions through her arms, her body and then it was
born, the half developed foetus, into the toilet. They were safe
again.

He thought, how can there be a world so finally bleak that
all impulse ends as that child. Because it was even then a child,
a tiny blunted child, a boy. He had retrieved it from the water,
because it was too large to go down, and wrapping it in some
old newspaper, put it out in the ashcan in the alley. But they
were safe, and they had to be. It was nothing they wanted, and
it seemed at last that nothing they wanted could even be.

But is that your world, then. But how could he answer. Days
and nights and weeks and months at last years, one after
another. Here they were. That was the history. Take it, is quite
enough. In a fire it all turns to ash, all but what won't literally
burn, old cans perhaps, that go a twisted, rusty form there. But
it is not the same.

Marrying, they had hoped it would be their world. Who
doesn't, thinking of all the plans, the way the house will look,
the trees by the drive, and then back of the house perhaps an
old barn. The woods start out at the edge of the field and go
off to the very edge of the horizon. That's where he had grown
up, the old farm his father had bought when he was still a baby.
They put up a flagpole so high it could be seen driving out from
the city, twenty-five miles away. And then a friend of his father's
came out in a taxi-cab, all that distance, with a donkey in the
backseat he said he had brought from Texas. That's a world,

and you can make it. He remembered sitting on the donkey for hours, and it wouldn't move. It stood there, motionless, while he tried to kick its sides, his legs too short. His mother pulled at the halter. There was a photograph of this scene.

There was no need to feel sorry for anything. It goes on, it happens. All the bitterness with which it can be invested does not change it. Only it can change.

John felt himself free of such history when, at last, Philip was born. They had not planned it, and again she became pregnant just in that she did. The things, the devices, the precautions, were all at last, at some point, forgotten. Neither one could remember, when there was such need, or, very simply, pleasure. They could not confront it with a plan.

They had to drive some fifty miles to the hospital, through the night, the doctor behind them, a young, nervous man, but kind and quick to know the unsureness they themselves felt. Once there, the doctors who were regularly present became, somehow, the authority. The younger one became extraneous, and John almost as well, sitting in the waiting room under, as it was, the delivery room. He sat there waiting for the baby to be born, and could hear the sounds of the labor above, disjointed cries, grunts, did he only seem to, the sounds of his wife in labor. He saw a nurse coming through the room in which he sat, and asked her if she might find out for him how his wife was doing, if the baby had been born yet. Oh, she said, you're too young to be a father. But then he was.

He was free of history if only that he was now in it, and no longer something of someone else's. It happened to him, it was his son, and it was his, their life. They didn't have to worry more about being really alive, serious, committed, actually present. They had the proof.

Looking at him John saw the boy much as he might have liked himself to have been once seen. A son. And then he was the father. And what was it Joan had told him Philip had said, a week ago, was it, something. He had not listened, but remembered. Yes, she said she had said, he stumbled on a truth. And Philip: you mean he fell? Joan: yes, he stumbled. You mean, he fell on it to make everything true? And what else had he said, somewhere he had written it down, he thought. They had been coming up the hill, and the boy was tired, the other younger children already fast asleep, back in the house. And then later, he had said, was I asleep when I went up the hill last night? You were when you started certainly. And did you give me my hand? (You mean, give me *your* hand.) Joan said, he's probably got *give* and *take* mixed up. Yes, quite probably. Then he said, I'm in my skin.

The worst at least was over, changed, surely she was, but it was over. He made daily trips to the city, to see her, spending the afternoons sitting with her in the quiet room. She was still tired, vague, but he felt her beginning to open again as the incision itself healed. Soon they would remove the stitches, and her body would adapt, rid of the growth, and, as the doctor continued to tell her, she would feel a great increase of energy.

He brought flowers and put them by her bed, bunches of a light, white spray, mimosa. They talked of divers plans, things they would do when she was home again. It would not now be long. The time grew shorter. She asked about the children, if they missed her, and they did. But Juana's care was steady and complete. They were fine. And it was a few days more only that she would be there, and then home, for them all.

How are you, he said. He felt a weary loss of all his confidence, again and again. Where had she gone to. He saw another place in her eyes, in the tiredness, the shock still persisting.

She had no ready answer. Perhaps she did not know herself, and she did want to make him feel easier but she could not say more than she knew.

So she said, I feel changed. It's funny. I know that I can't have any more children. How many times I've wanted not to, but now it's different, because I can't.

Something like that, whatever it was she did say. As they sat into the evening, the sky black but for the few lights they could see still through the window, and below them the noise from the other rooms, and around them, the movements of the other people, it was a place they were in, just there. How could she say more than either had ever been able to, where it was, what it was, how she felt, what it meant. They could hear the faint music from a cafe, two blocks distant, guitars, and a high strident voice, of a woman, singing. It was a heart that was broken because it had been disregarded, and it was torn into black pieces, with a skirt, flaring, and hard, sharp staccato of heels, and the guitars insisted as always that it was true, it was true, it was true.

But it was not a heart, it was her, broken, if she had been, which she could not tell him, nor could he himself see, by looking, more than how, physically, she was to him. He felt great love, and then impatience, moving to anger, that she lay so confined. The wound itself looked like a long puckered mouth, with jagged tight teeth made by the black thread of the stitches. He wanted to tear it off, leaving the skin again white and free. He thought that if she pushed, or strained, it would talk, obscenely, that it would spill out on them all the hate and pain he had, obscenely, forced into it.

That, back of it all, was the fact, he felt. He was guilty, he had done it to her. How many times had he made her pregnant. Ten, she said. How many miscarriages, monstrous ill arrangements of her, tearing, until the knots drew tight and contracted all her hope into a tight, festered impossibility. That it should be his own mother, across that space, who should write to him, saying that such tumors could not be so caused, that they contained their own. How could he believe anything, and why should he want to. All he sensed was what had happened, and it was, absurdly, he who knew it, not Joan.

In the time she had, waiting, she wrote letters, which she did not write usually, to the few people she had kept touch with. One, an old friend of her dead mother, from all those years, answered.

She wrote, that is a pretty nice letter and I do appreciate it. I am typing the answer and asking your indulgence therefor, also hoping that you will forgive the mistakes. After three-score years and ten, one's body gives a bit at the seams here and there. While my oculist assures me that I never shall be blind, which is a comfort, I believe that my friends to whom I write are more kindly treated to typing, of sorts, than to the hen-tracks I make with a pen.

You must be a darling grown-up. I wish I could know you. Your late mother would love your letter with the way you accept an unchangeable status quo, with only the question of "Where do we go from here?" It really is a wonderful way to live, but I did not discover it until long after I was your age. I continually was trying to change the unchangeable and had no idea of realizing reality and building on that.

The children's pictures are mighty nice. My sisters and I would dearly love to get our hands on the children and play with them. Like all old maids, we think youngsters, if they are nice, are simply adorable. I am not particularly good for children, I suppose; I just give them everything I can and let them do anything they want which, as is easily understandable, does not always endear me to their long-suffering mothers.

Two of your mother's old classmates visited your island last winter. One of them, Mrs Pennel (Helen Vincent) tried to reach you, but did not make it, for some reason or other. The other one, Mrs. Hanlon (Sally Morris), did not get my letter in time to find out about you. At the college reunion last June, several people asked if I were in touch with you – you see, you are always May's daughter to us – but at that time I was not. I was delighted last Christmas time to receive a card, with a note, from your Aunt Jeanette, from whom I had not heard in over five years.

Do you see the *Reader's Digest?* In the current number, I believe, is a charming informal article on the virtue of just stopping in to call upon people, unannounced. It sounds delightful, but, in discussing it with a group of our college people at the Club the other day, we rather ruefully acknowledged that it simply does not seem to work in New York; there mostly is nobody home most of the time. So-o-o, if you come through, of course try to see me anyway, but notice beforehand is advised.

The letter continued for another brief paragraph. And again speaking of Joan's operation, it ended, "It sounds pretty horrible to be where you are and go through all that – even though you evidently did it creditably and very nicely . . ." My love to you. Affectionately. Aunt Bess.

When at last Joan was back in the house, the children were curious to know all about what had happened to her. John had not told them more than he had to, that she was sick, and would be better. Juana, however, just by the very mystery with which she referred to Joan's condition, had excited them and made them a little afraid. Now they wanted to see, and so Joan's stomach was uncovered and they looked. Philip especially did not like the sight, translating what he saw to the possibility of himself. He did not want to see such a thing. Jennie, staggering by the bed on which Joan was to stay until she felt stronger, put both small hands beside the long scar and, unexpectedly, leaned, shifting her weight, Joan made a quick face of pain, but patted her head, and John caught her arms and pulled her back.

It was William who looked, until they covered it again. He was very curious. He wanted to know how it felt, why it looked like that, what the thread was for, who sewed it. He drew a series of pictures, one having a small head at the far end of the paper, then the body trailing widely down in a sort of teardrop, with thin stick legs, lines only, at the bottom. On the body he put one straight long line, bisecting it. Across this he put short quick strokes, for the stitches. It became a body with a thing on it, the thing he had seen.

Slowly it went away or, more accurately, faded away. They grew used to it. The scar itself, when the stitches were taken out, followed the line from the navel to the crotch, stopping a few inches above the mound of hair. She wondered if it disfigured her, but it did not seem to, not like that. They had left an ovary and she would not face a premature stopping of usual functions. Had they not, she might have had an increase of nervousness, but that was of course now avoided.

It was all all right. After a time they began again to share the bed as before. They slept well, Joan's strength seemed to increase and even the energy which the doctor had spoken of. Perhaps it was a good thing, certainly it was a godsend the condition had been discovered before it had done more damage.

So, slowly, they began to live together again, and then one night John woke, felt her close, warm, the excitement came, and he reached for her. Then, shaken, she showed him the face, white, hating. She took all the emptiness, and gave it to him. That was the history, what it meant. All that was inside was now out.

13

IT ISN'T AT ALL what one believes in, or thinks to, plans, does, or fails in, or any of all the many proposals, of what now to do and what it may seem, then, to mean. All that endless rubbish of assumption will never change the least of things. Somewhere the pool, the puddle, begins to dry up, and as it does it leaves an edged ring, a series of rings, each day another. Finally there

is only a wet skin of mud at the center, and then, in the sun,
that also dries and cracks. What had been the flat slick of dusty
water is now simply that place where it was, some hollow in the
earth whose look recalls the water once there. The leaves, the
flies, or twigs caught at the edge of each day's ring are accumulations only. What do they mean.

Whatever irony, it was of no interest, and the habits of their
living together were of more use than any meaning. There was
nowhere to go, not quickly. Nothing to do, and nothing more
to be said. Joan wanted only to be let alone, and as he respected
that, she softened a little, let the habit rule in that way also,
and forgetting whatever it was she had intended, would be
smiling, unthinking, moving to his need.

He had now to do something, equally, because she was so
much in the act of herself, willing the pieces back together,
testing what it was had happened, bit by bit. He couldn't stand
there merely, the house whirling around him with such order,
and the village itself so steady in its own patterns, the tomatoes
ripening, the daily, rhythmic work of men and women, no matter
what it meant. Only the sea tilted back, at it all, poised on the
lip of the earth's edge, threatening, ironic, by a twist of sight
seeming to be balanced above the flat of the common ground.

What to say, then. Pinched by the sight, he began to write
as he was able, small, twisted sketches of things, stories of a
kind, distortions, fragments of acts that got displaced by the
words as he worked to test the meanings, the signs. There
was occasion enough to hold him, but what happened to the
possibility, say, or did it all have to mean what he meant by it.
There were endless positions, endless grinning heads, endless
places all were to be in, but then they slipped past to others,
sat where he had never wanted them to, slippery, undefined.
He thought that if he were able to begin with his own head, de-
tach that in some way, make it a possibility also, loose and free,
so that he could see the back of it, for example, and surprise
it by terms it would not yield to him if only some projection of
his neck, a growth, a thing that went with him, all of a piece . . .

No, pieces was what they all surely were, chips, fragments,
minor or major debris. Years ago he had asked his sister, older,
when she had her first child, a son, if she had had any inclination
to eat the afterbirth. She shuddered, and refused him any
answer. How could they find out if they wouldn't answer, would

not leap at the chance, at last, to be a part, a real live segment, of a larger thing. The sea shook the earth, but it stayed there. What was meaning to be if not at any time a meaning. He felt himself left out by some obscure slip of purpose. Behind the door when the brains . . . It didn't open.

But one can intrude here simply that all has become so small and detestable. They are so tiny and so far away now, with their little tears, and the little agonies and pinches. How stupidly she hates him, and how idiot-like is his pretension, that he is not hurt, but he secretes his resentment like pus.

What then does one want to say. Distrust any purpose, any proposal? The sea, the sea crashes, say, saying, say that, say if you have to, say that. Say it.

Not whatever anyone wanted, but then they were living, one day, and because they were, they wanted to live in some consequent manner, you know. Isn't it ridiculous. They did this, and then they did that, because they thought to. It was the plan. But all one does, or has to do, is simply to point and say, look at that man, the old one there, that fumbling grey-haired idiot. He's dying, you know. Oh yes, he's dying. What was it he said he wanted to do. Oh·yes, live.

And it isn't a big or a little, or an ironic, or any, meaning. It is. Let's all meet, somewhere, where only the dead won't come. Only the dead won't be there. Let's make it any time, but have just that one thing true, just be alive and there.

So I can see that street, after all, and even I know who will be there, or won't be, too late, will ask if another day will do, another place. Can't I see you next week, or then, or there, or wherever. Won't they say that. And you'll be given a plan to follow, and when you have got that done, you will be given a plan to follow, and when you have got that done, you will be given a plan to follow.

Try as they would, each separately, they couldn't break it, and they didn't want to. The habit was useful. Or how else would they know each other, even as their names were true to something they could recognize as a plan, as John and Joan. Then the children in consequent order. People laugh, but don't forget the fumble till the names are straight, the vagueness, the feeling, who is that, finally, that one, with the big head, the little head, the pin point, with the dirty yellow circle of light over it. Surely that can't be *Jesus Christ*, but didn't the name

fool you, after all. And wouldn't it be just that simple, if there
were, first, the last name, and then you put the first name with
it. It would be close enough.

So that was true, John thought, if you can distort it, whatever,
or try to, just enough to make whatever is hidden in it fight
back. Try to get it, get hold of it. If it hurts here, what is
hurting. In the order of his words he put the pieces he took
from each of them. Joan, in jagged variety, became all that he
suspected, his eye large and yellow, dirty. She did that to him,
so make her do it. Now she did it again, but this time in the
story. When he insisted she read it, she had to look in, a long
distance, to see the tiny figure of herself, twisted with all the
concern of his assumption. It wasn't true but somehow, viciously, the little thing did move as if alive.

Perversely, it worked for him, this twisting of things. He kept
busy through the days of her finding herself again, gaining
strength, going again to the beach, with him, and on picnics,
with the children. She was not at any time like a proper invalid,
only as someone trying to stand up, after a blow, slowly working
up to stand, by will, on shaking legs at first, then steadier, then
more surely, walking at last. He wondered where she would go
now.

Nights also grew simpler, and they had finally to love one
another, and it was true enough. There she was, and so was he.
Simply touching, they had to let go of the rancor and the
distrust. The dark helped. The faces weren't clear or if they
were, they were nonetheless softened, rid of the locked insistence
of the day.

How can it be otherwise, even if it is. Just that the warmth
is so close then, and whatever does grow, a common need
beyond the twists of understanding. How banal it sounds, but,
touching, it begins another sound, not that one, not ugly.

He was so awkward, trying, she almost laughed, and did
smile, at him. That's good. No more hiding under the bedclothes, twisting, turning, unable to do anything but ache with
irritation and bewilderment. Do you really hate me. Do you
really mean what you say. Am I like that to you. Is that what
you see. Piece by piece the sluggish block broke up and left
them softened, close in their feeling of one another, moving together, warm, wet, close, till the spasm of his ache broke also,

leaving them for a sudden moment, hot, arms locked, then relaxing.

In the night he looked then, seeing the wide apart eyes, the slight snub of her nose, the lift of the mouth. She was so clearly there. She shifted, eyes shut, relaxed, pushing closer to him again, soft legs, arms, against him.

He could not stay there. He tried for the closeness to stay as they were, but ended by an abrupt shift over, turning his back to her so that she was left with her arms around his chest, her belly, soft breasts, thighs, pushing against his back and legs. She hung on to him in the night, sleeping against him, riding the stiffness of him, the driven vagary of his relief.

It was like climbing out of the water, each time, dripping, with her holding on to him, exhausted, as he pulled clear of the heavy water. Again and again the same soft fall, the distance under them, and then the return so far, so sudden a need, as he climbed and climbed the heavy, repeated steps.

Were they returning only, coming back again. What is it they say, you never know till it's too late. It was late. In the room where they lay as he tried to sleep, it was dark and late. The day past, and the other days, back of it, all stringing out and along to some necessity he never got the hang of, or the feel of, the place of. One wants to ask a simple question, do I do it right, is it enough. This is the way it should be, they say.

One afternoon other friends came unexpectedly. They had lived close to them in France and had come at the same time to the island. But their house was in a town at the far end, and somehow they saw little of each other. Now they were here, getting off the bus, the husband carrying a speargun, for fishing, and other equipment, the wife with basket and bathing-suits, food. They had no children and could not have. They had a cat, a Siamese, and that had been brought also and followed them much as a willful child. They all went down to the beach together.

As ever they seemed, all of them, too distinct from all else that was there, the scrabbling children of the village, the fishermen preparing their boats for the night's fishing, or mending the brown nets, the younger men or girls there to swim as a kind of sophistication, as a show of their leisure. That world was dense and accurate somehow, was true to something just that it had been where it was now always. John watched his friend swim out with the frog goggles, the little rubber or was it plastic snout sticking up, the stick-like spear held upright from time to time in a meaningless gesture. It didn't look like swimming, there was no movement to it of that kind. It was a paddling, a puttering sort of aimlessness, back and forth across the mouth of the small bay. Up would bob the man's bottom, then he would disappear for an instant, then reappear, and if successful, would wave the stabbed fish, flopping, on the stick of the spear. It was an ugly, depressing sight, such an invasion of something as private as the sea. You can't walk under it like that. You can't pry, look, like that, a voyeur of a deepness that isn't to be dealt with like a convenience, a playpen for indifferent leisure. It made the whole beach shrink to a safeness, a stunned enclosure.

John felt cheapened, watching, and then all the more so, thinking, why should he so question his friend's enthusiastic pleasure. It pleased him, he liked it. That was enough, and why not let him alone. But he couldn't, he had to watch, saying nothing, eating the fish the friend had caught, when they cooked them over a fire they improvised there on the beach, another indignity, eating with a persistantly stressed indifference. When one of the younger fishermen came over to them, in curiosity, to look at the speargun, John stiffened uncomfortably hearing the pleasure in his friend's voice as he explained the complication of the gun's mechanism. It was so uselessly efficient, and for the fisherman himself, it must be a toy, it can't be a thing like a net, or a hook, not that I know anything about it, but isn't it just a toy. He watched the friend shoot the spear into a slab of driftwood, to the fisherman's delight. The rod shot through the pulpy wood with a vicious thunk. The friend reached down and pulled the steel shaft through. The fisherman then asked to hold it, impressed by the power he had seen.

But he would never fish with it. Can you imagine that solid, steady lump of man, the thick legs, the heaviness of that chest, all the rock of the heavy head, the blunted hands and fingers, the feet stubbed to leather, thick, hard, heavy, the whole blunt force of that holding such a toy, such a snickering trick. In what dream would that be possible. No, he held it only, turning the shaft, and then the gun, over in the dulled hands, only for the looking, the curiosity. The older men would not even touch it, stayed their own distance. This one was already himself a little tricked, a little cheapened, just that he let himself be caught by such deception.

Later, as it grew dark, the fishermen began to slide their boats down into the sea from the slant of the projecting shelf they had built out into the water. Now the old ritual began again as first one boat, then another, slid into the dark water in the order of the men who would use them, the oldest of the village first, then one after another, the younger, the less experienced, following the others clear of the small bay and on out into the deep, black sea. John watched them drift first with the push of the boat, hitting the water, then out, then lift the oars and place them, then begin to row, easily, the boat gaining way and then finding its place in the shifting faint line as it lengthened on the black water, streaked with the sun's last light. He could hear the creak of the oars, the slight wash of the sea, the sounds of all that repeated world.

It grew cold and they collected the remains of the meal, the children, and headed back to the house. He could hardly talk to them, even to Joan. He walked ahead with the children, impatiently. He felt a painful distance from all of them, and he could be neither the one nor the other, such world as the fishermen knew, nor this one he was given. In either he could only think, choose, take or not take. There was no law not to be broken, impossible to act against. He couldn't cry, simply take me. That isn't even a dream. He watched, merely, as so much he did was an evasive looking after, a faint sign, a fading odor, or sound.

But you did enjoy it. Of course. It had been, despite him, a good afternoon, good for them all. Friends were very much friends, and these were his. The husband especially he liked, despite speargun or whatever. He liked the large open eyes of the man, and the good nature, not hurting things somehow, again despite the gun. That was only a toy as they somehow did all agree.

Then what isn't. No games any more, really, he couldn't finally manage them. He dropped the ball, didn't take it seriously, or did, much too much so, all introspective and dull. How could people wait while he made up his mind as to how, this time, he would react. Your move, they said with some impatience.

Now they were out there, fishing, hardly the world's end for

what to do with one's life. If you moved them all a hundred
miles inland, perhaps they would simply die, like pained
Indians, without sound. Few even had motors for their boats,
none at the beach they had been at, only a few, more wealthy,
others, for whom the whole act had become a business. That is,
even these fishermen he wanted so to invest with such a place,
and given purpose, wouldn't yield it. It had to be put on them,
like a reason. They dumbly followed a pattern.

He wanted a boat then, simply, not to chase after. But what
did it look like, out there, or looking back, here, from there.
When he suggested to Joan that they might get one, she could
see no reason why not.

14

NEITHER HAD ever had a boat, that is, one, like a horse or pony,
specifically for their use, *theirs*. Each had been to some extent
around them, as John when still young had lived by the sea for
a short time, while his mother had the job of nurse for a small
seaside town. He could row, he was adept in the water more
generally. Joan was not quite so sure of herself but she stayed
afloat without any great effort. But what kind of boat was a
question. They both thought of a sailboat, instead of one that
had to be rowed, or used with a motor. They wanted one that
would be as natural as possible, to its element, and they had as
well the happy sense of boats as billowing sail and fair winds,
and. a bird-like grace of movement, riding the water as the air.

John made a trip to the city to see what might be found,
avoiding Artie despite the fact he could clearly help him, because
it was not now very possible to be close to anyone. Things had
changed. Sympathies, of that kind, were tired, on both sides.
Marge was daily growing larger with the baby, it seemed. She
had been there, and kind, while Joan was still at the clinic, but
as soon as Joan had returned home, it was as if Marge were
again bored with all that vague unsettledness, impatient of any
relation that would draw her from herself.

There was the money part of it as well, and a boat was a

sizeable thing to be buying. In that sense John was wary of Artie's reaction, since to be able to buy such a thing must mean to Artie one could. That in itself would separate them but if it might be got there, back to the town, without Artie's involvement, then the fact it was there, and theirs, would be simpler to deal with.

John went to the office of the travel agent, who kept listings of such things as boats, cars, random furniture, offered for sale, as well as literal houses open for rent or purchase. There he found little but was told to try the yacht club, where more might be possible. At the yacht club he was shown a looseleaf file of boats for sale, most of them huge things with powerful motors and many oak-panelled rooms, floating palatial houses, the thought of which emphasized the more his own inept sense of what he did precisely want. The attendant, showing him the file, looked at his clothes and grew bored with the whole question.

At last he did find one, suggested by the clerk aware finally of his customer, and although there was no price listed, the very size of the boat seemed to mean it could not be very expensive. Its actual length was twelve feet, as noted in the book, but this the clerk, now salesman, told him meant the boat had been modified. It was a suggestive word, that. It meant the boat had been sixteen feet long, as described by its class, a Monotype. There it was in the book, a modified Monotype, twelve feet. This was for speed, the clerk said, and so that the boat will draw less water, you see. The mast you will note is very high. That meant nothing to him, however, and he asked where he might see it. It is being repaired, the clerk said. It is somewhere out there along the dock, toward the end. You will see it there.

Walking out along the dock, he was nervous of all of it, anxious to see the boat and to get it over with. Here there were so many boats finally, all so decorous, a luxuria of relaxed means. He felt, in contrast, grubby and out of place, heavy-footed as he passed the brisk, tanned men who trotted in and out of the moored, bobbing boats, with their lovely tanned ladies. There were in fact only one or two who could in any sense be called such, either men or women, but there they were, by the implication of the boats, the network of bristling masts, the polished, painted wood. He felt them looking at him, and plodded on, impatient to find the boat and get out.

Then he saw it, almost at the end, pulled up on the dock

itself, lying tilted, the paint in places cracked and peeling, an old white, and on the butt-end, the name, *Pago Pago*, oddly enough, the two times said, *I pay I pay*. It was very small, almost squat, but with a happy wideness somehow, good natured, expansive, and, coming closer, he felt a wash of weak love, a choking taste of sentimental closeness, for just its exposure, its tubby proportions, its inappropriate place there among all the ease and rightness of the glib, sure fleet of the richly confident. He turned and went to get the name of its owner, then left.

Back in the village again, the boat grew remote in his mind, but the feeling of its rightness stayed. He wrote the owner, and a week later they made an appointment to see him. He was, it turned out, the harbor master, which reassured John that the boat must in some way be as special as he had felt it. Then, in the office of the man, seeing him come, with a dragging left foot and hanging arm, toward them, across the greyness of the old room in the old building, the maps on the walls, the windows beyond faced out to the sea, it was as much as he had felt, seeing the boat, in that strangeness of oddly inappropriate wealth. This was the sense of sea, ships and men he could feel as an echo of his own grandfather, no matter what distortions, hopes, shifts of actual things. It sang in his eyes and ears, and the sharp salt struck out from the air.

It was, altogether, a grand thing, and John went through the divers steps of possessing the boat much as he would accept a specific honor, a thing given him, to be trusted with, because its substance was alive and to be kept so at all cost.

Who could care that the old man might well be worn, or that he might not be exact as to what his own interest really was. Did he lie. But how say it. He had the conduct of all the harbor in his hands, each ship that came there came as he told it, placed it, in the washing sea past the neck of arching rock, the winds, the heavy, shifting sea. John felt safe with him, patient, honored. He took the paper of ownership as a man would his own name.

There was, however, the problem of getting the boat to the town. At the yacht club they were told it might be sailed there, it was not a difficult trip, though quite a long one, with uncertain winds, and possibly storms. One simply went due north, till the edge of the island was passed, then turned right, down the north front of the island, in an easterly direction, until the harbor of the village was reached. But those were directions for one on land, and he felt the contempt of the people who did say, to him, and then you turn right. There was a very large amount of water to go wrong in, and for one as himself, who had never sailed a boat, it was obviously a foolish thing to attempt. The next possibility was that the boat might be towed by another, but this meant hiring someone to do that specifically, and that would mean a large expense, to be added to what already the boat had cost them and would yet cost them, with necessary repairs and painting.

So they drove into the yacht club's grounds one afternoon, with ropes and blankets, having considered the road to the village as carefully as possible, the problem of hills, the narrow turns they would have to get past, the car's ability to sustain the added weight of the boat, the mast, the oars, the other rigging, and sails. They went to the attendant John had first talked to, who was surprised by their proposal, to put the boat on top of a car, but helped them to the extent of finding four of the men working in the boatyard to raise the boat onto the cab of the small car, then lash it in quick, tight knots, standing back finally to look at what they had done, amazed at the sight of the boat's hull extending far over both front and back of the car, and the mast, much, much further. As John tied a bit of red cloth to the end of it, he heard one say, what are they doing that for, which he took to mean, the boat on the roof of the car, and the other answered flatly, they're cheap.

But they made it, slowly, and at one point they did stall, close to the top of the most awkward hill, but now they were out of the city and all problems were common. A truck going past stopped to pull them to the top, then waited by the side of the road as they went slowly jerking past, the mast dipping and waving with the bumps.

Once safe in the town, John left all as it was until he should find out where he might bring the boat for the necessary painting and calking. Upside down, on the roof, it looked like a curious cap, or beak, and in the dark, as he walked around it with the children, both his own and those of the village who had come to see, he felt a little unsure of what they had done, what he had. The boat was now so far from where it should be, it made the clearer how much he had invested it with his own dream of things. Seen this way, he wondered if it would even float. How,

supposing it did, could he propose to sail it, who knew no more
of the procedure than what a drunken Dutchman had told him,
on learning he had just bought it, that he should always sail,
for the most speed, with the wind striking off either of his two
ears. These he now fingered, thinking. And when in doubt, the
man said, steer into the wind. That will stop the boat. To John,
then, it sounded certainly very simple, but here with the boat
in the half-dark, and the sea in the darker distance at the bottom
of the hill, and all the unsureness, wavering, the sense of the
fact, the upside down boat, and then all that yet to be dealt
with, the literal sea and the winds that would move them, it
was not so simple nor so sure.

The next morning, when Juana had come back to tell them
the town's boat builder, Mateo, could take it for repairs, John
drove it the last short distance, and with the help of some of
the younger men of the town got it off the car and brought it
into the yard through the gate of the wall surrounding. He had
never been here before, and he did not recognize the man
himself, small and quick moving, nor his wife, like a girl with
long hair, although both were sixty or older, the whole place
quite separate from the town, enclosed in the activity of the
man, the half-built boats, white, arched wood, the half-covered
ribs, and in one corner a curious, lovely tree that had flowers,
and stretched out over where the man worked, for shade. The
man looked at the boat with curiosity, thumped it here and
there, and smiled, approving it. He had sailed boats like it, he
said, when as a younger man he had worked in the shipyards
in the islands off Florida. He would help John sail this one, if
he liked. But now he would get it ready.

When time came to take it down to the sea, the young men
helped again, five of them, and John found himself lifting the
boat with them, the freshly painted, calked, white boat, up to
the shoulders, then out the gate, down the street, then another,
down to the sea, down the rock steps, almost falling John was,
to keep up to their quick strength, and they paid him quiet
respect, just that it was his boat, and they, though amused and
in great pleased excitement, would not displace him, let him in
fact stumble on with them, till they reached the edge of the
water, lowered the boat a little, and with a great heave threw
it into the sea. It shot out, bobbing, balanced on the water, light
and free as any wish for it he had had. He made a move toward

it but one of the younger men, unable to stop, waded in, caught the boat as the waves returned it toward the beach, swung up into it, and jumped with light, quick steps over its surface, displacing the center of its balance, so that it jerked and shifted with his movement, yet kept balanced, moving, as he did, under him. He laughed, then, standing in the stern, rocked heavily up and down so that the boat shook and then lunged forward, with each downthrust of the man's weight.

He wished they would go away, a little, and when the boat was brought to him, he took the oars someone had thought to bring, shifted himself into the boat, holding them awkwardly, then, as they gave him a great push out, settled them in the oarlocks, and began to row, out, past the edge of the harbor, thoughtlessly, until looking up, he saw all the village above him, hanging in the vague air, growing smaller, as he himself did on the widening sea. Then he brought the boat around to face in again and pulled for the far harbor, where he had been given place to beach it.

There he could go through the motions of bringing the boat up, clear of the water, with something like the plan he had had, at the beginning. There were only children here to watch him, his own three included, whom he had forgotten in his hurry to bring with him. But he excused himself, thinking it would not be safe till he knew more of how to manage the boat, with or without sails. The children pushed close to the new boat, and held it for him bumping against the gravelly sand in the slight wash of the waves while he went up the beach to get ropes and pulley, for pulling it out. He worked carefully, slowly, at each detail, fastening the rope to the front of the boat, placing the scarred logs of the fishermen crosswise in a line before it, as he had seen them do, leaving a space between each one. Then he began to pull the boat clear, picking up the logs it slid over to put them down again, in front, one after another, making his way with the boat and the children up the beach.

It could be that simple, if he would let it satisfy whatever it was he thought he wanted. He could bob at will on the water, up and down, even without the sails, in the boat, and he could learn.

When the time came for Mateo to help with the first real sailing, he had already rowed round and round the two small harbors, and beyond to a point where the land cut back and left the openness of the sea to the west clear before him. He had taken Joan and the children for rides, for picnics on the rocks beyond the beach, holding the boat steady while one after another carefully got out of it, and then, later, in again. He had let them try the oars, pull as he did with an increasing confidence, heading the boat about, or in, or out, or along the edge of the sea. By himself at times he would slip the oars under the decked-over bow, take off his shirt, then flop off into the water to swim beside the bobbing white boat, pushing it ahead of him, lazily, then grab hold and up and in again, and then back to the beach.

The people were a surprise, though he had expected some to come, to see the boat sail. There had never been such a boat in the town, but to have so many for the first attempt made him uneasy. They had collected on the neck of rock protecting the beach, and many were dressed in a conspicuously careful manner. It was a Sunday, but it seemed more nearly a kind of *fiesta*. He saw that someone had even carried the big tin container with the ice and ice cream in it all the way from the plaza to the beach, clearly expecting the crowd that was there. As he helped with the boat, bringing down the mast which was taken from him and put, by two men, into its place, and also the sails, the centerboard, the rudder, all of which were again taken from him, and placed in the boat as they should be, and the boat itself slid over the logs, with him at some distance behind it, in the knot of men around it, Mateo called to him and he pushed through in time to catch the back and to swing in, as those behind gave it a push. He moved forward and took the oars while Mateo prepared, then raised, the sails, and the wind caught them, Mateo calling that he should take the jib lines, and he ducked as the boom veered over, the sail stiffened, the boat leaned, and he realized they were indeed in the water but such as he had not known before, the speed increasing, wind snapping the sail, the old man behind him tight and vigorous, shifting the rudder from hand to hand as he managed the boom with the free one, yelling at times again to John, and he saw the ladies, the men, the white dresses, the yelling faces, the curiously dense crowd on the spikey rock they now shot past, until suddenly right before them was another black spine of it sticking up whitely, he gestured and yelled, Mateo pushed the rudder hard over, the boom snapped back, cracked him sharply on the head, the lines caught in a tangle round his neck, and John sat down, quite dazed.

Joan said they looked very impressive, and the children, as the town, were completely pleased by what they had seen. They had not seen John almost strangled, nor any or all of it drop round his knees in a hopeless, sudden self-exposure. His life! He walked from the beach, through the crowd, leaving the men who had first helped launch the boat to put it all back as before.

15

THERE WAS only back, a falling behind the others, as though, walking, one had not been able to keep up, saw them go on, ahead, the distance increase until it was only their tiny backs one could see. Let them go. It was more comfortable, useful, to walk at one's own pace, let the landscape come in again, see things where and as they might be. The perpetual rushing insistence of movement that only wants to keep alongside, inch by whipped inch, was done with, and with it the need to explain, to say this, to call back, ahead, after, behind. He no longer walked even after them. He fumbled in a distance of his own.

Days then he went by himself to the beach, and lay flat on the rocks by the deep water, thinking, the sun hard on him, flat, burning. He wanted a clarity, something stripped of the deadening pull of relations, all the facts and figures of people and their times and places. The sun dazed him, the water cooled and held him, and the time went on.

One morning, Joan having got up to care for the children, he lifted his head to be struck by the brightness of the outside day coming in through the window. He pushed his head back under the bedclothes and relaxed again, sensing the odors, where she had been, where he lay, breathing in the warmth of his own body. He felt quieted, secured, he wanted to keep there, in the warmth and quiet darkness. Pulling the covers more tightly down about his head, he shifted himself around, pushing deep under the blankets and sheet, into the end of the bed, so that his head now faced to the end and rested where usually his feet would. He held himself still, and listened. He could hear nothing. He opened his eyes as wide as possible. The dark looked to him as tiny flickered points of white, then an intense dark brown red of a deep space. He shifted again, feeling the close weight of the bedclothes, then lifted his head and shoulders, crouching, to make a pocket for himself, feeling the length of his own legs, then crossed them, letting his body hang over their length, down, so that his head, pressed by the weight of the blankets, came close to his spread knees. Then, looking intently at the black space, listening, breathing, he waited for something to happen.

It was not very different. He had grown, long ago, quite used to such separation. They went away, and it was reasonable. It was explained to him as having to happen and he was nervous simply that he should be stopped at all, caught there, for that instant, to be pinched by their needs, not his. Nothing had happened to him. He knew where to go, and under the long roof of the barn, high in the loft at the back, he burrowed a tunnel for himself through the useless hay someone had put there, years ago, down through the smelly darkness, and then out, falling, into the iron cage-like container for the horse's feed, squeezed clear through the bars, dropped to the battered plank floor. And was safe. There was no horse there. The door was locked from the outside. No one would reach him, call, come after, find him out.

Sickness made the same condition, and after the medicine was given to him, the bed tucked in, the book put close to where he might reach it, the light shaded, and whoever had left, then he came out, lay listening intently to all the sounds, the sudden bird beyond the window with the drawn curtains, the rustle of the other people down under him, moving, a truck passing out on the road. He felt and looked and saw things, a fly, a pattern, a blur of shadow.

Everyone smiled, from there, and didn't they say, at last, don't you know it, too, haven't you really lived there all this dull and passing time. Those places. Those things. Smelling, touching, feeling, all of it, in the thick safe dark that you can, if you have to, drop and still pick up again. You can go back anytime.

For Joan and himself it had been, very much, the first place, the one they went to, and even in their touching one another, it was the place they wanted, after the feeling. All the odd ones, really, they had got to, the cubbies for their time together, at the first, it could prove a cemetery, but there were flowers and no people, a friend's room and strange bed. But he wasn't there. Riding in cars, the others with them went away it seemed, not that either insisted but there was no place other for them to be together. They made it, the place, without thinking.

But it had come back to himself, only the one. He couldn't sit in the cave, peering out forever, and she wouldn't come in. He might call and call, himself, but then how silly it looked, a grown man crouched under the bedclothes, seeming to shout but how could one hear it, it was so muffled, and there were as well all those funny bumps the body made with all the bed-clothes heaped over it. She shrugged at it, assuming he would come out when hungry enough. Chase him out of there, if necessary. Ten o'clock in the morning and there he was, still in bed, if what he seemed to be, in that odd state, could really be called so.

The point was, you can't escape it by simply going away. It stays. You tried that once before. You were going to die by sitting in a chair instead of going to bed, where for once you should have been, since you were sick. Instead you sat in that ridiculous beach chair of yours, in that miserable house in France, day after day. Never moving it, even, never once leaving the house except when you had to, to relieve yourself. But that she never said, but he did, over and over, walking back and forth over the impossible distance in his own nature. He kept waiting, making that mute call, like a silent *oomph* it was, a whining silent groan that didn't have the decency to be audible. He couldn't look at her, speak to her, of whatever he did feel in such states. That broke the rules, which were, it must happen of itself, no one may invite it, it must be understood without explanations. This was the magic learned early, as they had left, first his father, then grandfather and grandmother, and pets, various animals of his concern, things, balloons lost hold of, soaring up, to tiny disappearing specks in the wide sky. You couldn't call after and you couldn't call to. You stayed, and waited.

When the children, looking round the edge of the door, saw the humped mound, without thinking they ran and jumped on it. They knew their father. But the mound reared up, shouting, and they jumped back. Later, as he dressed himself, John felt the dismay of his unexpected anger, and cheap that his own smallnesses should be so enlarged. He was, it seemed, pushing out the children with the insistence of his own childishness. There must be somewhere to grow up, he thought.

It had, clearly, to be broken, something had. All the coming and going, and things to be thought of, said, felt, decided, all were only the small trottings round about a small ring. She, in contrast, seemed to him always to live at least along something, a line or life equally, at least a change of time. Was he older. Older than what, he thought, which was a question, because they changed not at all in their relation that way. She was, in fact, older than he, if only by a few months. How to be in what life makes that time, where, when, what is supposed to happen that is waited for so patiently.

He fell back on Artie, going again into the city, waiting in the dusty cafes, for the hidden times with him. But that also was changing, without him. Marge would have the baby, momently, and Artie was quiet with that thought, shrugging, shifting, trying to find purchase on what had to happen. Marge had gone away from them all and spent days in her bed back of the small living room of the apartment making the fantasies of possibility altogether alone. There was no way more to reach her, she would not talk, would not, did not want to, even to Artie, or particularly to Artie, whose fluttering she seemed, to John, to detest now even more than she had. As he talked she would, abruptly, cut in with a harsh, insistent, oh Arthur, *do* shut up, and it was so quickly vicious, so completely stated, all shook a little with its impact.

Where then to go with it. Artie began to be busier than ever and at the moment contrived an arrangement to print magazines for a number of hopeful people too far away to be aware of how trustful they were. He went from printer to printer, in the city, contriving credit by a kind of domino stagger of leaning obligations. To John he showed incredible paper samples, some so sheer they seemed almost tissue, and on these he proposed the magazines might be printed. To save money, you know. For all. But it was Artie who pocketed the change. Most of the clients survived no more than the first shock of seeing their hope pushed into a wad of oily blur, which Artie insisted could be read, quite easily, and had been done at a very reasonable figure.

What was reasonable. John couldn't blame him, in fact he respected the crazy invention of such will. He watched his friend hold one of these fantastic products of his industry, in his hand, and without the least distortion compliment himself on the selection of such clean types, such neat arrangements of page, such sturdy papers and binding. And yet it was there, a shoddy mess. Artie saw nothing but that compromise between, first, his own need for what money he could manage from the people, and second, what the printer necessarily demanded also. Between these two poles Artie slipped through, leaving horror on the one hand, and bills on the other. John watched the whole process with a feeling akin to satisfaction, albeit stunned. He was amazed, and to his own confusion, pleased, that Artie could get away with it. He didn't so much talk to this man now as act as tester for the contrivance involved, and if Artie said to him, do you think, etc., he was not to argue, he was only to listen. In that sense he forgot completely his own involvement.

He wanted none, finally, with any of it. Let them all do what they would. He wished he could believe it, let the days come and go, look and listen, but stay back, let Artie make the necessary fool of himself, but he never quite did, he was canny. But let, anyhow, the women do what they would, Marge or Joan, make them make their own world they did so insist on, because they would no matter. It was strange enough that despite such distinctness of manner each did will the little mannies they lived with, the shrinking figures of men slipped through doors, shadows, little stone stubbornnesses to put on the table along with the knitting. Give them a real man, he thought, but what did he know of it. His own were vagaries of heroes as much King Arthur as the stumpy fishermen he saw at the beach. He didn't really want anyone at all to blow a bugle.

Coming into it so, Manus was, even with the odd name to begin with, odd, strange to the occasion because no one, least of all Artie, expected him. He was a client and it was his magazine that Artie presently was muddling. But to come that distance, from France, to check, as he put it, seemed unlikely. Artie he dealt with in short, sure manner, going round with him to the printer, checking the types, the paper, holding Artie very nearly by the scruff of the neck. It was a great indignity but one

was powerless to avoid it, so Artie reported in the outraged
notes John was sent via the bus.

When Manus himself arrived in the town, in the early afternoon, on a rented motorcycle he seemed to handle with easy
efficiency, John simply looked up to see him, answering the
knock, opening the shut door. The motorcycle had been rested
against a stone block behind him. Both looked in with a black,
clean purpose, or was that another distortion, wanting the one
to go with the other, the man with the thing he used. John had
heard the sharp sputter of the two coming, and he had always
wanted to ride a motorcycle. His uncle had, in the war, the first
war. The man stood, looking in, down, at John. He was tall,
taller, had a crooked face with a strong nose, it was that one
was first aware of, the beak-like strength of that nose, then the
eyes, blue, sharp in no simple sense, set into the projecting
forehead. Was he simply seeing it, wanting to, making it up
again. He liked the man on the instant, he wanted to be liked
by him also. He wanted someone to come for him. Was he, in
some odd way, melting, unable to stand to this, as he had so
long planned to, to speak, now called, to be able enough.

Behind him he sensed Joan was standing also, and he was
caught by their awkwardness, the two of them not even saying,
come in, but Manus relieved them by saying, I'm Manus, and
John said, come in, please, Artie had told me you were here.

Inside they sat at the table, Manus talking of his own plans,
and back and forth they went over the ground of who there was,
this man, that, what would work, what concern, who was
writing, where it was now. Manus was publishing the work of
two men in particular, one an Irishman displaced to France as it
happened, the other, more known at this time, French, brilliant,
distorted, perverse in his innocent clarity. It was the subject
John loved, the thing, to talk of it, all the days of locked mind
breaking up, melting, falling away. He wanted to see, as this
man did, the form of a ground they might both walk on, not
always the displaced skipping from stone to stone he had too
much the habit of. In this context Artie was already a small
faint crying, however much John's loyalty wanted to hold on to
him.

We want books, Manus said, we'd like to do one of yours, of
the stories, if you'll agree.

What was that. He didn't quite hear it. He said, but Artie,

you must take care with what he says he'll do. He means well enough, but things, for him, are an awful mess.

Manus said, I'm surprised you put up with him, but that's not on my mind. I'd like to know if you'd let us do a book, of your stories.

But he hadn't said that. You can't take the stories because you haven't read them, have you. You don't know them, you are paying me an impossibly kind compliment but I have no wish to make you take it seriously. I don't. I can't, I don't dare to. I can write but I can't do what you ask me to, that is, make you see them as my own necessity, and never as that literature we have, haven't we, been talking about. Not the books. I understand what you are saying to me but I can't let you have them, I don't even myself have them, in that way.

All of it, he thought, all of it, such a far away lonely distance. Manus, confused, but persistent, asked again. He explained what the plan was, the series they intended, the approval of the other men involved. He had come as much to ask this question as to hear whatever it might be that John did think of Artie.

Finally Manus stood up, he had to leave, or else it would be dark by the time he reached the city. He could not ask again, but left with a quiet, kind decency, John thought, getting up also, to see him out, watch him get onto the motorcycle, kick the pedal, the thing catching, the motor, then go off down the road, and John turned to see Joan standing directly behind him.

He said, did he really want them, and she answered, didn't you know. Then he turned again and began running down the town's street, out, round the corner at the far end, up. Far ahead he could see the dust of the motorcycle. He ran hoping that as it reached the steeper hill it would stop, the man would, would begin pushing the motorcycle, so that if he ran he could catch them, explain his own mistake. I didn't honestly know, he said. I thought you were being kind. I couldn't believe you really knew the stories and wanted them. He saw the dust of the motorcycle ahead but the sound continued. They were going up the hill. At last he stopped running, turned, and began to walk back.

In the house she said, you could write a note to him. He would understand that.

But he couldn't write the note. The error was too deep and he had to live as things were, he thought. He sat small in the room looking out at the darkening color of the sun going down, at the edge, the sea seeming to lift to it, so far from him, them, the room and street and town, and the afternoon fading out, sounds quietening, the air soft in the darkening room. He felt almost relieved, it had been so close.

IV

16

SUMMER WAS passing, they found, but it came neither as colder nor even, clearly, a sense of shorter days. Just the light shifted, a little, people worked more intently, and now and again there were strangers in the town as the charcoal men, their carts full of the blackened branches, sticks, or else the gritty dust of charred olive pits, making their rounds. Perhaps they were a sign of the season, brought down from the higher places of the island, now that the cold might be coming there.

But much more such sign were the gypsies, who one afternoon were found settled in a gully at the town's edge, overnight. There seemed to be several families, mostly of children, but they had no more than one or two carts, with donkeys which they turned loose to forage for themselves to the annoyance of the village.

They were, in fact, very different from the people of the town, who were, in contrast, stockily built, steady in manner, even stolid. These people were much more *fluttery*, birdlike in that respect, sudden in presence so that where no one had been a moment before it seemed in that instant they were, flutteringly ragged, and dark and laughing. It was impossible for John and Joan not to be delighted with them, although Juana grew more sullen than they had ever seen her, and pulled the children back from the strangers whenever they happened to meet them, shopping.

And yet no one, in the town, made any movement to put them out, and even more odd, they traded with them but in such a curiously shocked way it was quite clear that the gypsies had, in their minds, extraordinary virtue. John found, for example, a man standing in the street looking dully after a gypsy man, who had just given him an oddly small and twisted straw basket, ineptly made, clearly, in return for several large fish. Another stood by him, in much the same manner, and he had something that looked like a small, ragged banner, actually a stick with several short streamers of torn cloth tied to it. For this he had given a sizeable number of potatoes.

There were no simple senses to be given to it, and understanding had to stop short of the feeling it provoked. The people were, of course, paying for something, perhaps for the very town they had, and all the houses in it. If a gypsy man should call after one of the town's girls, or younger women, married or not, the town itself seemed almost to look away, and the girl, or woman, could only move stiffly, awkwardly, back from the heavy suggestion of pleasure, or equally frequent contempt, the man had put upon her like a hand. It was very strange, and when Joan questioned Juana about this part of it, she avoided the question by saying the gypsies *did good*, they gave little pieces of paper, with magic things, or signs of cloth and wood.

Then, as suddenly also, they were gone, leaving odds and ends of debris in the gully, marks of their fires, and among the people the signs, paper birds, flowers of cloth and wire, which they put on their tables or by windows until some child squeezed them too hard, tore them, or they were otherwise gone. John and Joan were left with a colored paper flower one young gypsy girl had brought them. They had given her some worn clothing in exchange. She laughed with pleasure and ran out, and they looked at the contrivance they were left with, a moment's work. Joan hung it in a window where it stayed till the sun had bleached out all its colors. Then she threw it away.

John, however, found himself returning to his impressions of their coming again and again. It was something he admired, so to speak, in that it was so oddly self-sufficient, it argued no great commitment of time or of thought. It simply was, and one was with it, whatever it was. But the actual circumstance continued to baffle him. Why did the town so simply accept these people so contrary to themselves. Was there a history of such acceptance, and did the people continue the form no matter they no longer knew the literal significance of what they were doing. As, for another instance, the children of the town played a game in all senses the same as the American's cops and robbers, except that theirs was Christians and Moors. *El Moro* also replaced the usual bogeyman, and he ate such children as were bad, etc. No one John managed to talk to remembered at all clearly who the Moors were, historically that is, and though in these frustrated conversations he found himself trying to tell them, their interest was markedly a courtesy. Yet the other sense of that figure was enough to scare their children half-silly into sleep.

It was all like that. There was a man who came repeatedly, he was told, to the celebration of the Three Kings. He had seen him for himself their first Christmas in the town, a man from beyond the island, probably a stranded entertainer of some kind, who now made a part living following the island's *fiestas*. His act was very simple, he proposed to play a guitar and to sing songs. He was dressed quite formally, as it was, and had a deliberately stern manner. Requesting, first, absolute quiet, he explained to the crowd what he would do, asked for donations, received them, and when he judged he had got enough, began to play and to sing. But he sang very badly, his voice wandered far from the actual melody, and soon the people began to giggle, unable not to, and then the man grew angry, stopped, asked them to be more courteous, and so on. The trick, in John's opinion, was ridiculously simple. The man sang badly to provoke the amusement of his audience, and then when all were unable not to laugh at his poor display of talent, with a great show of irritation he stopped. It all took less than five minutes, and off he went with their money.

But Juana's reaction to all this was that for five years now the poor man had been trying to sing and play his music but was unable to well enough, and so it was very funny and she had to laugh although she did not at all want to hurt his feelings.

But don't you see that it's all just a trick? That he doesn't have to sing at all because you've already given him the money?

No, she didn't. She hoped that by next year he would have had time to practice so that he could do it well enough to finish. She knew how hard he was trying.

Such an instance might be only evidence of the credulity of these people, and yet it was not just that. That is, why was this openness to such deception there to begin with, and what is deception, if everyone believes. The man with the guitar did not, nor did John, but they were only strangers. They didn't change the water by drinking it.

The gypsies, again, were otherwise, like the thing Joan told him she had seen some women of the town carrying in one of their endless processions. They were always having them. Each saint's day, and he had never realized there were so many, the appropriate image or a reasonable contrivance to stand for it was taken through the streets, to the beat of an old drum, to the church and then into it, where the priest blessed them all.

This day Joan noticed something odd about what they were carrying, and coming closer, found it was something not easily described about two and a half feet long, quite chunky, black in appearance but much like worn leather, and without any defined features although a roughly made head seemed there. What was it. No one clearly seemed to know, and all she got as answer was that they found it in the woods. Was it a saint? No, it was not a saint but it was something they had found in the woods. Why did they carry it in such a procession, so honoring it. Had they found it recently. They had found it quite awhile ago. It seemed best to have a procession for it, and they used as a date the day they had found it. But is it religious, Joan kept insisting, why do you take it to the church? They would not say, or could not. It was just what they did, and the priest blessed them all.

It was very frustrating, and John began to wonder if the whole town, as the writer had in fact suggested, was not some sort of coven of witches. The town next to it was supposed to be, or so the writer had told them, and all manner of odd rites were still practised there. But in broad daylight, and to the pounded insistence of a drum, it did seem unlikely, and that the priest should give it his blessing made it all the more doubtful. When Joan asked the priest about the black thing, he said that it was, as far as he knew, some relic of the town, perhaps the town's patron saint which the people had reduced to its present condition by repeated handling and had forgotten the actual date for. He saw no reason not to indulge the practice, and he allowed the thing to remain in the church for the week following its procession. It was the only one of its kind and in that sense it was not that difficult to overlook its strangeness.

There was no purchase, then, and nothing to take from any of it as a meaning more than to be witness to it. John asked

Joan, what do you think it was. She answered that it was some
pagan survival or other, just something that went back of the
Christian, and so they hung on to it, and put it in with the rest.
But does that explain it, he asked, can you believe it.

There was a little anger, he remembered, or was it his own
again. She had shrugged. I don't know, she said. Do you.

In that sense, the whole town was a conspiracy, even his
family. It wasn't that he didn't want his own children to have
even the grotesqueries of the place, if they really were that. How
can you be somewhere without being all there, and if they took
on the superstitions of the town, he was almost proud. They
were doing clearly what he couldn't.

Through the day the people went up and down their hills,
from house to terrace, to garden, to the tomato plants, the beans,
the other things they had there. Nothing seemed to stop growing,
and the tomatoes in particular kept on beyond any he had ever
seen before. The plants were now well over his head and had
reached their third flowering, and again the small tomatoes
began to grow from each bud.

At night it was simply darkness again, an ever increasing
density of waiting space, he thought. If the moon were large,
then it intensified the feeling of things out there, not frighten-
ingly, but thick, in the night. Sounds and echoes of people in
other houses, soon dark themselves once the night had come.
But a donkey, perhaps, restless, breaking the heavy waiting
silence.

He gave up trying to contrive explanations, or kept such
answers for closer questions, the life he lived. He knew that
there were witches all around them, things stewing in pots more
black than any shriveled lump they carried to a church for a
priest's blessing. Momently he would find himself snuffling bris-
tle-nosed to the sea along with them. Deaths in boxes seemed
to clutter the near water like strewn garbage.

I don't think that's funny, Joan said. He had forgotten just
what she might be correcting, and asked, what. She said, I mean
what these people do. Do you have to pry at it all the time. You
don't know anything about it.

It was a shock, her saying it like that. Rightly or wrongly,
women are almost smug in that sure way they have about
knowing so much of what they don't know, all that possessive
world of their intuitions. They are always saying things like, I

knew it was going to happen, I felt it coming, and no other explanation really interested them. And now that he was thinking of it, he felt Joan's sureness was particularly vicious, because it was always necessarily so *right*. He really hated that part of it.

In the woods back of the house he had grown up in there were little openings among the trees, where his sister, older, had made tiny houses of twigs and stones. She told him to put the cookies their mother sometimes gave them after supper into these houses. For the fairies, she said, and they will give you your wish. He always did. He could not remember one time not having done so. He must have rebelled, just against her, at least once, but what it felt like, after, the little fairies cold and lost and hungry in the little stone houses, he couldn't endure for long. He knew he never got his wishes, or at least with no regularity, and so he knew what did happen, that his sister and perhaps one of her nasty friends, another girl, took them, took them out of the little stone houses, probably laughing at him right there on the spot if they could stop eating his cookies long enough to. The fairies' cookies. Put your cookies in the little house for the fairies, Johnny. He knew they were giggling, they had a way of putting their hands over their mouths, or of looking sideways. Why couldn't he simply eat the cookies as soon as he was given them, and not wait till he was brought again to the woods, she said, to play, and then the little houses shown to him, always a new one, and always the, put your cookies in the house for the fairies, and he couldn't not. Very carefully he knelt down and slid the cookies, one by one, through the tiny door of the house, and then lying flat, squinted in to see the cookies filling almost the entire space of the house, wondering how long it would take the little people who lived there to eat such a large offering. But they were always gone the next morning when he looked again.

It was odd that such things as gypsies should so reduce him, make his life so suddenly a shriveled whining. Time was going by, and too often he sat watching it with a nearly querulous attention, wondering why it didn't make more difference to him. Get out and do something, he thought, and so, to Joan's relief, he took to walking off past the town, along the rim of the hill above the sea. He met, one afternoon, Juana's husband there, and he did not usually see him because the older man had a

way of staying home, while his sons went out fishing, or if he
did work, it seemed only a restlessness quickly exhausted. He
was neither too old nor otherwise unfit for fishing, which was
what he knew how to do, but he didn't. He was from the
mainland and looked upon his wife and family as akin to yokels.

He answered John's question about the gypsies with the same
feeling. It's that they're innocent, he said, the people here. They
don't know when they're being taken. In the city they know
better.

John asked him where he was from, and he named one of the
large cities on the coast of the mainland. John had been there,
and it was certainly a big one, dense with people and buildings.

Why did you come here, John said, and the man gave no
very clear answer. It was more of a laugh. Just that things had
happened, he said, and here I was. But one day, he added, I'll
go back and take them with me. Juana's never seen anything
bigger than the city here. He laughed again. Then they walked
together back along the hill to the town, seeing the lights come
on just as they came into it.

17

IN THE MEANTIME things went on no matter, whether or not they
understood. Nothing waited. Going to the city together one day,
they stopped at Artie's, for no real reason, and found to their
embarrassment that the baby had come. It was a girl and looked
very large and settled. In fact, it already seemed a definite part
of the household and they felt themselves regarding it as some
intimate friend of Marge's, as her brother had been when he had
come, who displaced their own weak acquaintance by claiming a
longer, deeper knowledge of the person involved. It had the
same blue eyes as its mother, and although all babies' eyes are
blue, this one's were more faint in their color, with an under-
edge of grey, quietly distant. It looked out at them steadily, as
its mother did, with no specified interest, and they fumbled with
their congratulations, saying how large it was, which they then
realized was not extraordinary. It was almost a month old.

So much for that, John thought, and shifted his attention to Marge. She looked tired, a little, and more vague than ever, more beyond them. He wondered where it was she did live, but now at least she had the occasion of the baby. No one could think her constant staying in the apartment, even in bed, all that strange. She had still the problem of whatever she was taking, and was even addicted, which was the word unhappily. It was easy enough to say it. He looked at her eyes again, supposing he could see the pupils condense to tiny bright pin-pricks of ecstatic concentration, but shied from the intense way she looked back at him. She shrugged and looked away from them all, holding on to the baby solid on her lap.

When he was able to talk to Artie more relaxedly, still there was distance, a distraction, a something else to be concerned with. What now, that is. It was already too complicated, and had been long before the baby had had to come. They had waited as long as possible, and this referred not to John at all but to them, Artie and Marge, and now Judith, which is what they named her. Little Judith, and one day big Judith, and very probably, big, big Judith, as its towering grey-blue-eyed Marge-mother. And together they would stand, in all the doorways, waiting for Artie to come home, and he would not come home.

John and Artie spent the usual night drinking, and at last John found himself sitting at a back table in the same non-descript nightclub Artie had first brought him to, he remem-bered, his first day in the city. So nothing had changed. He drank with a persistent, awkward care, afraid he might spill everything all over the table or on the people crowded at other tables all around him. The noise banged back and forth between the close walls, and in front of the low stage there were a half dozen men playing ragged music for the women dancing there. It was clearly the same old thing. But he could not locate Artie in the jumbled clutter of people and noise, and felt himself becoming lost and confused, and looked up to see Artie, though some distance away, because he had somehow got in front of the women, who were moving back to leave one by herself making a waving gesture at him, to bring him closer, and all the time she was shouting into the microphone a confusion of words John could not altogether understand, but could make out the sense that Artie was being invited to join her, and to dance.

If there has to be, dear Artie, anything of you I keep forever, one last sense not obliterated by all the mess of others, this will be it. It won't be the talking, good as that was, but this incredible picture of you there, which nothing could ever have led to, for either of us. You are dancing, Artie, your arms and legs are whirling up and about and down and around, and you are not at all, as they say, *out of place*. The men playing for you are laughing, surely, and they emphasize what has to be your grotesqueness, but you go beyond them, and by some device you only know, you make them play for you, as you dance, and the woman, who was laughing too, has been made to follow . . .

John saw, in drunken amazement, his friend hoisted up onto the stage, and the woman reach out for his hand, to pull him, then twist, and throw him, as the band began to play a rapid banging foxtrot with heavy emphasis. The people around John roared out with laughter, shouted *Olé!* delighted. Artie, much as a tired wrestler, got up again, sighted the woman, and reached out his hands toward her, which she took and again tried to lever, but he was now wary and forced her to jog with him, and for a time they lurched about the stage to the music, as the woman tried to break free and Artie tried to hold on to her. Then, unexpectedly, he began to whirl her around him, and the men playing picked up the rhythm of his gesture and brought it to crescendo, and then he abruptly let go, throwing the woman the full length of the stage. Again the crowd applauded.

When John tried to tell Joan about it, she couldn't see it the same way and questioned them being there to begin with, out half the night drinking with Marge home alone. With Judith. It was not kind of John to encourage Artie. Given that sense of it, he could say little more.

But he could not get it out of his mind, the extraordinary image of Artie there on the stage without the least embarrassment, in fact with such patent determination. It seemed very brave to him somehow. Because it was not so simply a drunken instance of exhibitionism. One had to be in some way a little sober even to get onto the stage, and then to outwit all that was against him, the devilish woman for one, and the mocking people, and the musicians who wanted to make fun of him as well.

John wondered if it were because Artie was English, that he could keep such dignity while so obviously unaware of it. In the war John had seen such instances, but they were really grotesque, and not at all funny, pathetic at last. He remembered the R.A.F. pilots who so envied the easy American fliers, and wanted to wear the same melodramatic leather jackets, with the big flag painted on the back, and the guns. Though they were the ones flying the combat missions, and the Americans only shuttling food back and forth between secure bases, one could never tell it by looking. Even in bars the English pilots never seemed to raise their voices.

It was his own embarrassment, however, that he was thinking about, and other memories of times when he had wanted to leap up, shout, outwit everyone in a grand flourish of laughter. There were times, more quiet, when had he been able to, he would never have done what he did do.

He remembered a hill he and Joan used to go to, for picnics, the year after they had met. At the top there was a large open meadow, skirted by trees, with no houses anywhere that they could see. He remembered lying in the grass with her there, unbuttoning her dress, then pulling down his own clothes, and making inept love to her. He remembered as they finished, and lay close together, he had heard a voice say to him, *boy, take that girl home*. He could hardly believe it real. He waited, feeling her shrink against his body, her face turned against his chest. A man, incongruously formal, stood wearing a neat blue suit, a not tall man, very stiff, about fifteen feet away from them, was standing looking down at his face, repeating his order.

John wanted to shout at him, *now*, fuck off you old fart, you vicious prying lascivious old monster. And even in the string of the imagined words (now) he felt the possibility of saying such a thing was still not his. Shaking with shame and embarrassment, he got up, pulled up his pants, feeling the man watching him but unable to look, knelt to cover Joan as she straightened her own clothes, and then, incredibly, collected the picnic things, picked up the basket, and with Joan walked in utter shaken fear away from the man, who stood still watching, and down the hill.

Somehow it was that that had been settled for, a fear that could only turn to anger, which couldn't laugh to keep its world. He could fight easily enough. He had all but strangled a clerk in a travel office in France, who had refused to have a friend's baggage taken to Marseilles after his promise to. Their whole afternoon was a tension of getting the bags to the office by the time the clerk had told them, but once there he tried to put them off, saying they had made a mistake. John's awkward French could not keep up to their talking, but he saw his friend begin to wilt under the man's sneering refusal. He stood waiting, helpless. Then he had his hands on the man's neck, squeezing, saying, *à Marseilles!* until a policeman pulled him off with the comment that he should contain himself. They had all laughed about it afterward, and the baggage had been sent as first promised.

Artie told him that things were becoming increasingly difficult. John saw that the baby was important to him, if that was how best to say it because it was for Artie something new to be dealt with, and he was both pleased and apprehensive. There was a lot to hold together, he said, and Marge had not been helped by the baby's coming. He was much more worried, finally. She used it to go farther away from him than ever, holding the new daughter between them as if Artie's irresponsibility must stop there.

The writer also was on him, now that the baby had been born. For a time he had been easy about what he considered Artie's laxness, in teaching the boy, but now Artie must demonstrate more responsibility. It was, not unreasonably, the obligation of a father.

I don't know what to do, Artie said to John, looking at him, wistful, a small smile in his eyes. He knew there was no answer and he didn't really care, he said, that there wasn't. But everything seemed to be coming apart. Never a bit of peace, really, since the baby came, what with those bills. The landlord after them, says he wants the place for some sister of his, and the rent's overdue. The printers after them, the people whose money he'd taken after them.

John said, can I help you, do you need money. He motioned for more beer, for the waiter in the dusty cafe in which they were sitting, and the afternoon came close with flat sounds of buzzing flies. Things faded.

Again Joan could not see it his way, and when he tried to explain his own sympathy for Artie's dilemma, she answered, he's trying to use you just as he always has. Why can't you see it?

He couldn't, he didn't want to. Let her criticize because it was her money. That he would never deny. But he couldn't feel the man wrong because he wanted to keep things together for his wife and child. Laugh as one would, that was true. They were in need, he said.

Well, what are we supposed to do about it, she answered. Take them in? Doesn't he have a job, and isn't the rent he complains about paid for them? She was right. He remembered that Artie had told them this was part of the contract.

Artie had told him so many things he couldn't sort them any longer, and he didn't want to face the complexity of trying to in any case. Let it go. He simply liked the man. He wanted to help him. But not any longer with our money, Joan insisted, and he couldn't argue with that.

But what so frightened him about it all, finally. He wasn't the one who was caught and he knew that. But he wanted the other man's friendship, his respect, very much, because it was, if he thought of it, a concern he could rarely secure. He was too often outside the terms of other men's worlds, like the people on the sidewalk watching the men put up, tear down, some building. It didn't matter which because the job in either case was clear. The people on the sidewalk were also secure because there were usually many of them there, looking. But, by himself, he was the only one looking, at all of them.

What said it better. One time hitch-hiking with two college friends back from New York to Boston, on the highway not far from New York they got a ride from a man in an old car. He told them it was his brother-in-law's and he had borrowed it to see about a job in the next town. They drove a little farther, and then he told them he had been out of work for several weeks and that this new factory opening in the next town might be his real chance. Finally he told them his wife had made him a lunch of the last food she had in the house, for herself and their children, and that he was hopeful of getting the factory people to give him a little advance, if he got the job, so he could wire it back to her that night. He was not fooling anyone. He was speaking quietly, steadily, but with that desperation that makes one talk to whomever will listen, in this case college kids he must have realized were just that, from their clothes, dusty but good, and from the way they spoke, almost formally, trying to be careful of what he must feel. Then he stopped to let them out, a good place to get another ride, he told them, as he was about to turn off for the town he was going to, and John and the others thanked him, and John picked up the paper bag with his soiled shirts he had had beside him on the seat, and got out. They waved goodbye as the man drove off down the road. Then John felt the weight of the bag was odd, and opened it, and saw that he had taken the man's lunch. There was a boiled egg and some sort of sandwich, peanut butter if he remembered correctly.

But he could not remember whether or not he had eaten it. He couldn't believe that he had, but to throw it away, all their food, was almost as difficult. He remembered waving at the car. But it was quickly gone.

And someone he'd known at college told John a story about people driving from Philadephia to New York for a party. They were late and had been drinking a little. They were driving something like a Jaguar, if he had it straight. They were going very fast, and suddenly they picked up in the lights an old Ford pulled over by the side but still on the highway, with an old man outside bent over the hood, with the door still open, on the left side as they came up. They swept past but hit the door, which caught the old man, and shot him clear of the car, catapulted him it must have been, but all they really saw was the amazed look on the little old lady's face who was inside the car, waiting. The person who told John the story said that was the first thing they said, when they came into the party, how surprised she looked. They kept on driving.

But back of them all, the stories, was one his grandmother had told him called Grandpa and the Indian. It was when his great grandfather and the family lived in Maine, an Indian – and there were still Indians, she said to himself and his sister – used to sneak into your great grandfather's shed at night and steal the molasses from a barrel he had there. Your great grandfather caught him one night, at his tricks, and threw him out right into the snow, with one hand. He was a strong man. Then later, when your great grandfather was coming back from town, it was in winter and he had the sleigh, he met the Indian by the road, and offered him a ride, to show that he had no hard feelings. The Indian got in and after they had gone a ways, he asked if he might feel your great grandfather's muscle because he now knew him, as he said, to be a very strong man because he had thrown him so far into the snow. Your great grandfather suspected a trick, but he let the Indian feel his muscle, making a great bunch of it by bending his arm. The Indian did, and said how large it was. Then your great grandfather asked to feel the Indian's muscle too, because he wanted to see how strong he was. But the Indian didn't want to let him, and kept saying that he knew your great grandfather was stronger than he was, and he would be ashamed to have him feel his small muscle. But your great grandfather kept insisting, because he knew there was a trick, and he grabbed the arm of the Indian, just above the elbow, and sure enough, the Indian had a big knife there, tucked under the shirt, and all he wanted to know was whether or not your great grandfather had one too, and that's why he had wanted to feel his muscle. So your great grandfather threw him out of the sleigh, into the snow, and the Indian never bothered him again.

Go to sleep, she had said then, he remembered, tucking them in, and he lay in the dark, thinking, seeing the things she had told them, and trying to understand what they meant.

18

REALITY becomes the shifting face of needs.

The water goes down the hill, and settles in whatever depressions occur there. And, equally, it does not, the holes the same. If people could be taken apart successfully, inside there would be a complexity of jutting hooks, and places for such hooks to fit into, and what people consider as relationships would be the fact of a complement of such hooks and places, fitting together, until some external shake or jarring pulled them apart. Or else the water coming down the hill filled everything, and rusted them. And it all wore out.

Nothing John tried to cover things with could manage. There was an increasing impatience in them all, and even the children were affected. But, wiser, they pulled back to Juana and the town, and were safe there.

But nothing happened, day after day, and even the weather would not fit to a recognized pattern, and if summer were now ending, what would fall be, and winter, and again the spring, with the almond trees in blossom ludicrously covered with snow. But the sun came out, and in an hour the snow was gone, and some hardy idiot, a random tourist, was actually in the water, swimming, with a thermometer to prove it was not all that cold.

John took to arranging his things with a cranky insistence. Should Joan take a book to read, which she had clear right to, he would suddenly break out at her in a rage, because she had not returned it to the place he had given it, had left it spread open face down on the bed or table, had got grease on its cover. Had she no care for things, he shouted, what was she trying to do. He spent hours sharpening a pocket knife, first with a carborundum block he had hung on to doggedly for years, enjoying the way it had worn down into a hollow where the blade was rubbed against it. And then with a hard smooth stone picked up on the beach, to give the knife as fine an edge as possible. Should he find her using this knife to cut anything he felt improper to its designed function, he became coldly furious and then, as she laughed at him, again raged back.

Everything between them was becoming niggardly and small, and at night, trying to grow warm again, he reached out to her to find her wary, and himself fumbling, wanting to be excused again, and again. He would say, I want to, and then her voice, in the dark, can't we wait. She would say, I am tired, I don't feel like it. But he would insist, I have to, I can't sleep if we don't.

Passively, then, she would let him, as she put it, pull open her heavy legs, reach down with his sullen hands, feel her. Then, as he climbed on, or else swung himself under the one raised leg, from the back, more usual, and felt against him the flatness of her back, in the silence, he heard her breathing grow heavier, more extended, to change at last into a snoring, as she fell asleep as he made love to her.

What had happened was beyond him, changing, in all the time that didn't change, going on and on into vagueness. He wanted, as he said, to be good, to manage, to be enough for her, and for the children, to be that one man who was for them father, and husband, and the man who made love to her with all the large gestures, the very heart shaken open. But she couldn't call him incapable, could she, not able to do anything enough, and fumbling with all that he tried to, and in his room he all but locked the door, and stared at the white wall, faced to see nothing but its flatness, the windows behind him looking out to the sea and the air, and wanted to give it up at last.

Take me in your hand, he said, please. She didn't want to, and he kept asking her. Please, do it that way. Because, if she did, it would be of that necessity a proof she would do it, for him, and would not only let him, as he had to, make love to her, quiet, not there at all.

In the blackness he thought of all that he had intended, his body stiff against her, and beginning to ache with the fact she was already asleep and he was tired of it. He kept on, pulling, pushing, in and out, against her, felt around with his hand under the edge of her nightgown, to find one of her breasts, held it, and kept on. At last the relief came in a small, expected manner, a deadened release. He pulled back, turned over to face to the window, with its squares of faint light, and lay waiting for the deadening to put him to sleep also.

What was it, he wondered, they didn't have or had forgotten, or made the wrong use of. The first year of their marriage they had, he had, taken pictures of themselves making love, as a kind of giggling defiance, a discovery of what it was, in the old jokes of the ant making his way across the vastness of Mae West, "and then there were these mountains," "and then this thick forest . . ." He was able with the projector to cover all the wall with her breasts, and they glowed there, blue-white, because the picture was under-exposed. On the same wall he stood eight feet tall, naked, with an embarrassed face, but the whole body hung there, visible. In the dark they lay together, changing the pictures, looking, until they came to themselves.

But there was nothing to see, and at this moment, he thought, less than nothing. Everything is waiting to be found, again. He shifted, restlessly, in the dark, he wanted to make love to her.

But it was now another night, and she was tired, impatient with all his insistence, the tenacity of all that he wanted from her, all the dreary time. What he never did do, if she had to say it, was more than such asking, wanting, waiting. He might, she said, if he wanted to make love to her, make love to her, and hold her, and excite her, and go slowly, and make it a pleasure, not a duty. She said, you never think of me, you do it just to get it over with.

What answer was possible, ever is, and what would be the question, then. Did they all just go to the well for whatever could be hauled up from it, the water, at best, or something someone threw in it. He could explain nothing. He could barely understand himself.

Outside the weather shifted, changed. It was curious. There were no familiar terms for it, although they had been there long enough to know what to expect, but it was not like that which one senses, before knows, and simply feels as natural because it has been known before any understanding. John missed the clarity of the days growing visibly shorter, and the leaves turning brown, the weather colder, and in the fields the stubble of corn stalks, the dead dry grass. Things go on and on, but if they are marked, placed, by some such sign, then one will know them. Now it is summer, and now it is fall, and now winter, and next it will be all the snow melting, the grass green again. And spring.

In a bar one night, where all the stranded entertainers came now the summer was gone, John looked up to see a man immediately familiar to him. He didn't know him, he only knew the kind he was, the way the hair was cut, short, the poplin jacket, all the tentative shy manner and the awkward age. When John got up and went over to him, the man was wary. He came from Springfield, Mass. He had worked all his life there as a clerk in a hardware store.

Why should he be here, of all places, but the man, more relaxed, explained his mother had died and had left him some money. He got leave from his job and was travelling around the world. As he always wanted to, he said. He was not married.

Back of them someone was playing a guitar, and it seemed inappropriately romantic, like a movie, the two men talking in the crowded bar, the night warm around them, and diamonds to be slipped from one to the other, and lovely ladies all faint and misty, in the background. There ought to be danger, a pervasive odor of risk and danger. But the man was frightened by what he saw around him, all the strange people and the noise. He doubted that he would enjoy any of it, when John asked him how it was going, and if it was all he hoped it might be. John told him he ought to give it up and go back, and the man thought he might do that.

Days later John was still thinking of him, and of how out of place he had looked, and of how in place he would look, if the store were back of him, the racks of tools, rope, the men in the grey or brown waiters' coats they wore. Like waiters, like the clerks in some drugstores he remembered. The mark of what they did. John thought the man must know where everything in the store was, and how many steps it took to get there. John wanted to say, let me at least get you laid, I know a place. But the man would have been frightened.

It had been interesting to meet him in any case. But John hated the despair in him, it was too familiar. More interesting was the middle-aged woman sent them by the travel agents, who wanted them to help her have a book of poems printed, her own. She lived in a hotel in New York which she managed, having a suite of her own on the first floor. The book was one long poem, with a religious subject, a tragic heroine dealt with at times sensually. The woman was not ambitious. She wanted the book printed for herself and her friends, although as they talked about it she was curious to know how it might be distributed, and if John thought it might sell.

In the pension where she was staying, she told them, a young man had just got married, the son of the pension owner, very handsome in the Spanish manner. His wife was such a lovely girl the woman had been shocked to learn that on their wedding night the young man had gone off with his mistress. Such a shame, she thought, with such a lovely girl at home. But it must be the custom. She went back to New York and the hotel, taking her book with her. She had sent them a card at Christmas.

The point was there were so many of them, and that if the door was opened, they all fell through, and they were endless. There was a retired American general and his wife, living in a suburb of the city, and every night, someone's maid had told them, these people came in to eat the meal their servant had prepared for them and they were dead drunk, and when the girl came back in the morning she found them passed out on the floor with broken dishes and thrown food all over the walls.

John thought, it was their life, let them. A friend, a painter, living also on the other side of the city had numbers of women coming to stay with him, a New York model, for one they had met, and then a Danish actress, who spent the war as mistress of an assassin. The actress said, you could imagine what that was like.

But no, he couldn't imagine what that was like. Who wanted to be pulled into each of their vicious little blocked hells, to sweat along with them, feel all their small agonies. He read somewhere the settlers coming across the plains in those covered wagons made something like two miles an hour, and at that had to throw out almost everything they had had the pathetic stupidity to bring with them, stuffed chairs, baby carriages, umbrellas probably. Every gully a mess of their ridiculous lives. Half of them didn't have the least sense of where it was they were going, and up in front some shell-shocked old bozo with long grey beard, croaking, this way, folks. Right into Death Valley.

He didn't want to go. Let the man from Springfield marry the lady from New York. He didn't want to listen any more to any of it. They broke his heart, every time, and he wanted to break his own heart. No more stories of the also drunken Swedish count who invites the Ceylonese male prostitute who is serving as bartender at a local nightclub home with him. They walk in, the Ceylonese and stoned count, and there are two chairs in the big living room, and the count says, take the good one, young man, and sits himself uneasily on the other, which has a broken leg. And then he says, perhaps we might have a little refreshment, and he goes into the sister's room, the young man right behind him, and on the bed they see the sister passed out, huge great-boned woman with her skirts around her neck, bloomers on view to all comers. But the count gets the bottle out of her hand, and remarks she is a little indisposed, but sees that as no occasion for their not drinking. Have one, dear boy.

We should go home, he thought, she was right. It was no place for them any more. It was all going strange and ridiculous. He couldn't face it any more, he didn't know what he wanted from any of it but that they should have something too, not be the ones always talked to, and leaned on, and left to put it all away.

But it wasn't she who had to make the mock protestations of changing it, telling the people to get out. Who wouldn't come, who weren't there. It was all himself as ever.

He looked at her, in the bed. He took off his pants, folded them and put them over the back of the chair. He took off his shirt, and hung it over the pants, took off his shoes, his stockings, and put them in the shoes, and took off his underpants and undershirt, and put them on the chair. He got his handkerchief, from the pants and put it under the pillow beside her. Then he shut off the light and got into bed with her.

It was dark again. One thinks, on such a night did love come, and make its boldness known. To all the waiting town. And all the waiting people there.

He felt her close to him, reached out to take her hand and put it on him, closing his fingers to make her own close over him. She started to pull her hand free, but stopped as he increased the pressure of his fingers on hers.

Please, he was thinking, do it. He was fading away, in the vagueness, he thought of other times, to pass the time. He thought of the first time they had made love, at night, in a shed wedged between the tools on the earth floor, her head against the blades of a lawnmower. To get out of the cold. She said to him, please, fuck me. The words were strange. He tried to, fumbling, because he didn't know clearly where even he might, or how to, till the excitement brought him hard against her but not in, and he spurted in a trembling incompetence all over her legs. Then, with his own hand, he rubbed her gently, slowly, insistently, until she gripped tight to him, shaking, and relaxed.

It was time again. She was looking at him. He could see her face faintly in the light from the window, and reached out to bring the face closer, turning her toward him, down on him, asking her, please, feeling her stiffen but with less force, then her mouth on him, wet, close, moving, as he relaxed his hold on her, and fell back.

For moments he lay tense there, as his back arched, his whole body tightened to the wet warmth of her mouth. Then as he felt all himself pulling to tightness, she stopped, suddenly, and lifted her head to look at his face.

19

JOHN WANTED to say, nothing changes that much, and if we try, it will come right again. He wanted the way it had been to come back. He was impatient, tired, unable to see what was wrong, yet kept talking. Each day, he thought, was another.

But the anger was unexpected, each time, and it spread not only between them, but over the children. In a sudden rage he would center on one of them, most often Philip or William, and would pick at them with tight-voiced questions, until they finally cried.

Where did you put it. I put it back. Where did you put it after you took it from my table. I put it back. It isn't there. Where did you put it after you took it.

The child wandered through the house, with John following him, stalking him, watching, persistently questioning, seeming at times to grow more sympathetic, saying, do you think it might be in this room. The child would sense the slight relaxation of the hard voice, and would look all around carefully. Perhaps it was a clue the father was giving him, and the scissors, eraser, pencil, whatever the object lost might be, would be there, at last, and he could go away.

The voice grew tight again, insistent. Where is it, Philip. I need it now. Then the procession began again, the sniffling child walking on and on, through room after room, looking. John followed with the questions.

Then followed, after the thing had been found in his own pocket, or else on the table covered by some papers he had put there, John's hate of himself but he couldn't open himself to get hold of it, and throw it clear of them all. He had to insist, and when Joan interfered, as he put it, his reaction was immediate and ugly.

I won't have them taking things and then losing them. I have to have those things where I can find them. But what were they, an eraser, or bit of pencil, for all the agony they provoked in such exact measure. He had chosen to make his children suffer each tension with him, so that they should, in a sense he recognized as indescribably bitter but all that he could offer, know his pain too.

But you can't expect them to remember, she would say to him, how can they at their age know what they did with each thing they play with. He wanted to answer, your own judgement is moral, as is mine. You are judging me. You hate me.

Reasonably, he thought, she turned away from him then, unable to credit such a distortion of what she had offered as a simple comment. She would not see the children threatened and terrified by him, and if they had to fight about it, then she was quite prepared to.

The world went on, the days dense with the confusions he felt, and the children grew wary as he used them, for his terms. Fight me, Joan said, if that's what you want. But even that she didn't say, but dealt with him briefly, surely, in ways she knew more effective.

He went back into his room, and spent days there, trying to write, looking at the white wall in front of him. At his back the window was open, for the air, and outside the sun shone hot, and the sea slipped down the far distance, as ever. There was nothing wrong. There was nothing right but there was nothing wrong that the least sentimentality wouldn't seize upon, and cry over, and put together again. If he could get up, and turn around, and look out the window for nothing but what he saw there, no figures, nothing to call to, just see air and sun and light and water. He heard the people on the terrace over to the right of the open window talking, in the language he could never understand clearly. Someone was laughing. Now they stopped, and began talking again.

For a time the house relaxed with a project which Joan began, for Philip but really for them all. The town had a small hall in which, at irregular intervals, movies were shown on a Saturday evening. John and Joan had gone once only, to see what it was like, but they had been uncomfortable sitting in the crowded small place, with the thick, smelly weight of all the people around them. It was an American movie they had seen. There was a pretty blonde heroine, young, brittle, and very familiar to them. The plot was dull, a usual account of bright success.

The people in the town were not interested in that sense of it, but saw it, from their world, as all that other of the American, and one girl whom Joan had made partly a friend asked her if she would teach her how to make the doughnuts like the girl in the movie.

Now the people who ran the cinema were having a competition, for the children, to see who could make the best costume. It was assumed that it was a really a competition of parents, and that the children would simply wear what they made. The whole town became absorbed in getting ready.

Joan decided that Philip would be their entry, because many of his friends would take part also. It was something to do, and

John as well began to be interested as the problems of making something for Philip to wear became more clear. Joan wanted to have some sort of head for him, out of papier mâché, and needed John's help with the frame for it. He made one, but in the making it became larger than he had intended, and gave the boy a height of at least two feet taller than he was. It was also a considerable weight when covered with the paper and flour Joan had mixed. They contrived a hole in the neck for Philip to look out of, while in the head, and covered that with gauze, which they painted as they painted the rest of the neck. But Philip could see out of it enough to find his way.

The night of the competition John went backstage with Philip, while Joan sat in front with the other children, and the rest of the people there. One by one the competitors walked out on the stage, from the back, in costumes which John found were really attempts to make the children look pretty. One young girl was dressed something like a ballerina, and a boy wore what appeared to be a conception of evening dress. Then it was Philip's turn.

John lifted the head over the boy's, and fitted it down on his shoulders. Then he put his own overcoat, which he had brought, on the boy, and buttoned it up about the neck of the head, then faced the boy toward the stage, and told him to walk out.

As Philip did, John realized there were two steps he must go down, in the center, to arrive at the main section of the stage on which he must stand to be seen by all the people sitting in front. At sight of the figure coming toward them clear of the wings of the stage, the people had begun to clap, but they hesitated, seeing the figure stop for a moment at the steps, feel with its foot for them, turn, then slowly manage to come down them, stiffly, apparently looking straight forward, John saw that their mistake had been in making the hole in the neck only large enough for Philip to look straight ahead, and not down also, but he had managed no matter, and the people were clapping again, and laughing with approval at his appearance. In the center of the stage the man announcing the children gave Philip's name, and there was more applause, and the announcer reached out his hand to shake that of the figure, and took the loose sleeve of the overcoat, lifted it to indicate its emptiness to those watching, made a mock gesture of surprise. Then Philip turned, got up the two steps again, and came off the stage to where John stood waiting.

But when the prizes were announced, Philip had not got one. The girl in the ballet costume, was given first, and then a boy, son of one of the *guardias*, got second.

It was so unmistakeably an instance of the town's rejection of them, to have been expected, he knew, but then he had supposed his son had more rapport with all the goings on he was himself too bored or careless to be involved by. Philip knew everyone, he spent all his time running in and out of their houses at least. Whenever he did want him, John knew it meant going out into the street and yelling, in full public view, *Phill-uppp!* Which in their echoed version became something like *Feeell-uppp!* They all called along with him, and as he had expected, Philip would appear in the middle of a gang of children, coming out of the door of some house he hadn't the least sense of who lived in, or else around another vague corner. If they didn't accept him, why should they make the boy the butt. He wasn't the one they were after.

John didn't want to talk about any of it. Joan carried the head, and the coat, and the three children came behind her. She felt, as John, that the prize ought to have been given them, but she didn't find it strange that it wasn't, and that two of the town's children should have won. She didn't see why they should have to spoil as well the fun of it all, and the fact of the real applause the people had given Philip. They had laughed harder at him than at anyone, and Juana said, too, he should have got the prize.

But why did the boy have to suffer their pettiness, John kept thinking, how explain that to him. That the world is a petty, abysmal sink of corrupted, dishonest pretensions, that every damn thing one tries to do is subject to that vicious limit?

But she said, it's not any of his business, John. You can't make him the excuse for your own sense of it. He doesn't know anything about that part. Let him have the pleasure he has.

So even she chose to twist it, and wanted to settle for the small portion, and would take the outrage he felt and make it another charge against him. Wrong again.

The next day they all went up on the terrace, put the head and coat on Philip, took pictures of him, and then put it all away. It was a relief to be done with it.

John went back to his room, to sit watching the wall, and in the emptiness could see the shape of himself, black and indecisive, a thing thrown large there, as if a fitful, flickering light were behind him. He could be, if they wanted, the night monster, who is let out only with the dark to wander, howling, through the empty halls. And if by hairy lips the kiss be given, then transforméd be he. And all the walls resound, etc.

He knew, John thought, so much better than she did, what it meant. He knew what each of them had twisted, appropriated, to push the boy out there, with that ridiculous over-sized head. He saw Philip, unable to see the steps, feel for them, with his foot, then get down them.

But if, as he thought of it, the only point was what they made him do, for them, and if Philip was never to get what was his, in spite of what they made him do, for them, then what was the point of it. John made the boy put on the head, too large, and walk out on the stage, and he didn't care whether or not he had to crawl there, or tripped on the steps, or could or couldn't see anything. He, John, said, go. And the prize was his.

That ended it. He couldn't justify what he felt, but he wouldn't try to, either. It was his son, and though his father died before he ever knew him, the same thing was true. He knew what his father had wanted and he was the last chance he'd ever had.

It became night, it became day. She tried to talk to him now, and what did she really want, but to excuse herself, and the children. That was all it meant. You can't get off the boat because you don't like it, you made a mistake, you want your money back. This is the only boat, and you are on it, and nothing stops and who cares what you think you think, and whether you are right or wrong or care or don't care any damn time at all. *You stay here*, John said, to the wall, you don't get away now.

She tried, even, to think of ways to relieve it all, since the tensions in the house were making them all rigid and constantly nervous, and anxious to be alone, so that they never were together, except to eat, and then the children ate with Juana in the kitchen, while she and John sat in the dining room, trying to talk. She could see the children through the doorway, in the kitchen, looking at her, and she smiled back at them as John ate, watching her, looking at moments, to catch her eyes, unexpectedly, as he went on eating. Then he went back to his room.

There he knew where he was. He could find all the pieces, and put them like pins on a map, against the wall, and make his painful information clear there. There was no longer need of any view, anything seen from a window, because all that was, was in. He knew what to do with it.

He contrived, one afternoon, when she had to go to the doctor to be checked, to be sitting with Artie, as he waited for her, in a cafe on the corner of the block where the doctor's office was. It was intentional, just as the fact of their drunkenness was, as it always was. No one was doing anything they didn't want to. When she came into the cafe, he waved to show her where they were sitting, and when she was settled in the booth with them, he said he had an errand to do and left them sitting there, and went outside the cafe to circle back around it, to look in through the window at them. He was careful to place himself so that she could not see him, and Artie's back was also toward him. Then he waited.

Some minutes later he saw Artie leaning forward, and apparently reaching out with his hand, for hers, and then he seemed to be trying to kiss her, which must mean he had before, since the cafe was so crowded and public and they would not do it if they were not used to it.

Weren't you, he said, didn't you want me out of there so that you could make a play for the one friend I have here. It was clear, and he didn't want the answer she tried to give him because it was the simple one, as she knew.

You can say, he said, as many times as you care to, that Artie was drunk, that he made the pass at you, that you pushed him away, that you didn't want to make a scene of what he'd done because you didn't want to do that in public, and you didn't want to blame him for what was a drunken thing to do.

He followed her through the house, from dining room to bedroom, to the kitchen, after Juana had gone to her own house and the children were in bed, and it was dark again, and he kept asking her, because he knew what the answer was but must make her say it, that she had done it and that it was what she wanted to do, and it was what she made happen, all by herself. I know, John said, you didn't think I did because all the time you were so careful always to be right, but now you have to be what you are.

He pushed at her. She went back, crying at him, asking him to stop it, and kept insisting, he was wrong, and crying, but he couldn't stop now, until she made a run for his room, which he tried to block, but he lost his grip on her arm, and then went after her, as she went through the door, into his room, and he came in, after her, to see her with his typewriter in her hands. As she lifted it, he kept talking at her, saying, it was no good, she couldn't change it, it happened, she had to say so, face it, stop trying to change it. She lifted the typewriter, yelled at him, and threw it at the floor, the whole frame breaking sideways, keys spilling, *there*, she yelled, *is that better*.

20

HE WAS SITTING in the room, at the table, with a book open in front of him. He read, returning from time to time to phrases his tiredness blurred, making his eyes wander from the white page. It was night, and when he turned, restless, to look toward the door, he could see, out the window beside it, an edge of the small room.

He sat as quietly as possible, forcing the relaxation in his body, feeling the hardness of the chair under him, the position of each foot against the floor. He put both hands carefully on either side of the open book, and when it came time to turn a page, he lifted each deliberately, pressing it down to the new one. Then he read.

Listening, he could hear nothing either in the house or outside that was not simply identified. The clock ticked faintly at the end of the hall. He heard a dog bark and then stop. There was a slight sound of wind or perhaps it was the sea, stirring against the shore. A donkey brayed suddenly. He got up, to stretch, then walked to the window to look out at the night. He could see no lights in any of the houses.

He was not worried. He knew each time he let that sense of things take him, all that he could feel was guilt. He felt that if he could hold to the reasons for the feelings he had, that he would come through without the problem of excusing them either to himself or to her. She was not a child but it was akin to that difficulty of spanking a child, when one says that it will not hurt him more than it will hurt the one who is spanking. He meant that it would not hurt the child more than it had to. If he became unsure of what he was doing, or saying, then it hurt only him.

Sitting, it was a pleasure that it should be so quiet. He thought he spent hours listening to fragments of undefined noise, which weren't merely interruptions, but as they lived together, all the time, so much that he heard was not what he was listening to. He was going to say something but before he could, as they lived, it was blotted out by something someone else was saying, or doing, making a noise. But it couldn't be, either, that everyone or everything all of a sudden stopped all talk, or movement, and all centered on him to hear, then, what it was he wanted to say.

The book was difficult to read. There was an order in it demanding he displace his own, for the moment, and he couldn't because he was waiting for her to come back to the house, listening to any sound that might be her approaching. When she had run out, he saw her take the flashlight they kept beside the outside door. He had followed her that far, wanting to go on talking, telling her what he felt about all of it. She had mistaken that as an argument, she was crying and then running down the hall and out the door into the darkness there. He wanted to follow her but at the door he was stopped by fear of people seeing them.

He sat, waiting, going over and over what he had been feeling and trying to say to her, to make clear not as an argument but as what he felt. He could only make it clear by telling her and she was not there to tell.

Getting up, he decided then to go out to find her. It was late and he was frightened that in the dark she might have fallen over something, from the wall of one of the terraces onto something hard that might hurt her. He was too impatient to go on sitting, passively. He went into the bedroom of the children to see if they were sleeping quietly, and without turning on a light, stood in the doorway of the room, waited until his eyes grew used to the dark, and then went to each, to make sure they were covered, and kissed them, moved by the tumbled manner in which they lay there. He went back out of the room and down the hall, and out of the house into the dark, quiet courtyard. He felt the air more moist, and the sky go a softer darkness, and looking up he could see the stars far over him like a misty web of small bright specks. He waited, and then he could see where he was more clearly in the faint moonlight. The great door of the courtyard was opened slightly where she had gone past it.

Walking, slowly, he tried to sense the probable place she might be, and where in the night she would go. He knew that without her actually there with him, there was no clear place she was. He could not imagine her as someone only escaping, running away from him. Then she would be as far as she could go and he had no way of knowing that distance. He knew that he himself would go to the sea, but that was no assurance to him that she might. In the dark it was impossible to go back of the town to the woods, and to attempt to look for her there, he felt, was useless. He went down the street, careful to make no noise that might be heard by the people sleeping back of the quiet walls.

Where was she. What was the point of hiding, and running away. It became hide and seek again, in the woods, with the children calling, calling. They counted so fast when it was their turn. Then he counted, he slipped as fast as he could past the ten-twenty-thirty-forty, blurring, and ran after them, he saw a sudden white mark of clothing, a leg disappearing round the corner. He ran but when he turned he could see no one there. He heard the laughter but he couldn't find them.

When he came to the path down through the gardens, he went more carefully, and by each of the small reservoirs, he stopped to go around it, looking for any sign that she might have fallen in. He could not believe it possible. There was so little light he saw only the vague reflection of himself looking down at the water, or the moon, above him, or nothing but the black water itself. There was no head there, nor arm hanging whitely, faintly, over the rough edge. He could see no clothing floating anywhere, and he could not see deeper than the vague surface.

From time to time he called, softly, Joan, and as he went by piles of brush the people had stacked by the side of the path, he poked at them, thinking she might be there.

But he couldn't find her. He could barely see the path, and managed to keep on it only because he had used it so often, going to the sea. What was supposed to be the point of it all, then. She knew he could not sit in the room all night waiting for her to come back, when she had decided he'd been properly punished, made to feel the arrogance of wanting to say anything to her at all. She wouldn't listen to him. She didn't care what he felt, what he tried with such insistence to say to her. Now she wanted him fumbling about in the dark on his hands and knees, poking at brush piles, and looking in pools of stagnant water for fear she might be hurt, in pain somewhere, unable to tell him she needed him.

He could not feel anything any more. He hated being out there, knowing that soon the people would be getting up and that they would find him out there when they came to their gardens. What would he say to them. They knew he was never there at such an hour.

Help me, he wanted to call out to her, and have her come and find him, not always himself the one who went looking. They ran farther and farther away, across the lawn and back of the trees, and then he couldn't find them anywhere. It wasn't fair any more.

Again he hated that he couldn't stop looking, wandering on after her, wherever she had gone to, or where she now was without doubt back in the house again, sleeping, and smiling in her sleep because she knew he was still out there in the vagueness, calling her name in bewildered impotence. Listen to me, he wanted to yell, listen to what I am trying to say to you, don't make me always the one so viciously guilty, so left in it, never you.

He was grinning but sickly, he was crying, he was trying to find her and he didn't want to find her. He wanted to go back to the house, have her be there, be safe, forget the argument or whatever she wanted to call it. He didn't mean it as one. He wanted to tell her simply what he felt, and why he felt what he felt. Listen, she had to, he was not wrong.

He went back to the house, and coming in thought she must be there, seeing the light still on in the room, but it was he who had left it. She was not there. He looked again at the children. They were still sleeping.

He went back into the darkness, to the rock above the sea in the chance that she might have thought that a place he would not look. He was tired but the fact she had not come back made him feel it more possible she had been in some way hurt, and might at that moment be crying for him. But because the wind now grew stronger as the night passed, and the light would come soon, and the sea kept crashing against the rock edge of the shore, how could he hear no matter how loudly she called him. He hurried as fast as he could in the windy blackness down the hill between the houses again, and then beyond them, out onto the rock, looking, calling for her. She was not there.

Making his way out toward the far edge of the rock, he stood high above the sea in the fading dark, now, as far back of him a faint light began to gather above the hill. It was almost morning and the people were moving in their houses, he could see the lights begin to come on in them.

The time was gone. Wherever she was, he would not find her. She had got away.

He began to walk out over the face of the rock, to its edge, then stopped as he felt a sudden terror he might himself make a misstep, and fall, in the vagueness of the dark and wind. He tried to see clearly where he was, but the light was still too faint to show more than what was directly under his feet. Beyond, there was only the indistinct sense of a flat space, and then the sky and sea meeting in a dark grey blur, far off. The wind blew against him, he tried to go on, and he could not. He knew she was there.

He had no reaction. He called, feeling immediately impotent, his voice go lost in the wind. He thought of pushing himself forward, of running, jumping off the rock to try to save her. But the fear even of falling made him again stop.

Behind him, on the hill, he knew the people were coming. He wanted to run back to meet them, to get their help, but instinctively he found himself afraid that they might think he had pushed her. He knew that he had made her do it, he thought of the black night and of how she must have come in it to where he stood now, trying to reach her, to hold her from the edge. But she had not waited for him, and he could not even go to where he might look down, and see her.

He was crying, and calling from time to time to her. Moments passed, and he found himself confused, and then embarrassed, by the fear that began to flood into him.

He moved back from the edge he could now see, feeling conspicuous as the light became stronger, and then made his way down the path at one side, but arriving at the bottom, level with the water, he found his view of it blocked by an unexpected ledge. He could see only the beach toward the town, and the place where the fishermen brought their boats. He found himself looking at the houses, now visible to him, and the gardens he had passed the night searching. It all went up in a pattern, gardens, houses, the woods, the rockier hills above it, then sky. He saw the sky growing lighter and lighter, with streaks of cloud, and then a red clear sun.

He sat down and thought of what he had to do, and of the children who would be awake soon, of Juana in the house already, getting the fire going, beginning to think of breakfast. He couldn't think of what he had still to face, the rocks, the thing caught, held by them, the grey waves sloshing over. The dead uncaring thing.

He would have done it, he thought, had she told him. But she wouldn't talk to him, she had left him no such choice. She had decided.

A great wash of painful hate went through him, and there was no more use in trying to block it, or excuse it, or say that she was dead and that he was sorry she was, and wished she wasn't dead. She was dead. He hated her. She left him with all of it, she had left him to explain his failure, her death, to their children, to the town, to her vicious guardian who would attack him, and would take the children away from him, and he couldn't now have them anyhow. She had taken everything. She stood on a vicious cliff, in a vicious blackness, and he had called her and called her and called her. He had come as she had made him, stumbling out into the vagueness, crawling after her, pleading, asking that she come back, into the house where they were.

He got up from the rock on which he had been sitting and climbed back up but could not go to the place where he would see, he knew, the rocks holding her in the grey water. He felt calmer, the air was cool and fresh. He began to walk back toward the house but slowly because he had still to think of how to recover her most simply. He did not want her to be found there casually, by a fisherman passing, who would look there by chance and thinking it odd, that something was there, then find her there, dead. He wanted to be the first to face her there, to see what had been done to her. As he walked, he was crying again, but he felt able to do now what he had to do, tell Juana there had been an accident, get her help to find someone to go with him out there, for what they had to recover.

He came to the courtyard and going in, he passed some people. He made a gesture of his hand, he could not speak to them. He wanted to get into the house before he was unable to hold himself together any longer. He opened the door of the house and walked in, and saw, first, Juana nod to him from the kitchen, and then Philip and William come running down the hall to see where he had been.

He was crying. Nothing could hold it back, and he felt it coming through him for all the years and years of his impotence and guilt, and the self-hate that wouldn't let go when it had to, but waited until it had killed itself and everything around it. His children, himself. He knelt down to them, they were looking at him, confused, one saying something he could not hear distinctly, but he took them, reached out for both, and pulled them, crying, into his arms.

He tried to say, your mother, but they were too close to him and he couldn't say it. He looked and in a sudden, blurred instant she was there, holding Jennie, looking down at them, asking incredibly with everything as it had been, what is it, John. What's the matter.

He pulled clear of the two boys, got up, and stood, looking at her face, and began to put out his hand, toward her, then stopped. I thought you were dead, he said, but I was wrong.

LISTEN

HE

I was thinking of you—I suppose in some ways being here again—even perhaps wondering whether memory's just this kind of insistent coming back and back. I don't even know really which one you are. It isn't a question of being afraid of something or being in various ways suspicious of whatever it is that does seem to come here. But, seeing people, out the window, looking at this kind of light, this fading pink, this fading blue, the trees towering up above this snow—I couldn't really be confident that something should so necessarily be wrong, always. Is it just a question of whether, let's say, it *was* right or wrong, always that kind of retrospective analysis or judgement? I suppose, very obviously, a question therefore, *does* the snow do what it's supposed to do?

SHE

I couldn't really see that you cared for me—that was always my dilemma.

HE

That makes you familiar, on the instant.

SHE

It's really the kind of sense you have, that you *can* assume who I am, that you always did feel that way—that I was supposed to feel this or that, had necessarily to know what you were *meaning*, this time.

HE

Yes, but—people *do* have ideas, like they say.

SHE

That doesn't mean that others have to agree with them.

HE

If I took your hand. . .

SHE

If you took my hand, you'd have a rather abstract situation of substance.

HE

Do you think this thinking has anything to do with anything?

SHE

Never that I was able to appreciate—like they say, *also*.

HE

One and another. Two girls run by, one in green coat, one in blue, one with red scarf with blue stripes, one with white scarf with blue stripes. They've gone.

SHE

You're not the same person forever.

HE

But sometimes I am.

SHE

My impatience was frankly the boredom that this kind of insistence inevitably created in me. I can't live without an actual place to live.

HE

I can remember you in different ways. I can remember, for example, the time I met you or at least that *you* you are, let's call you Christine, for the moment. That time, for example, I met you in that peculiarly dense small town in Wales, just after the war, your sister a telephone operator—you had such a lovely vulnerability.

SHE

I loved you.

HE

I couldn't—I couldn't *not* love you, in a funny way, I couldn't not love you, loving me. I didn't want to miss the appointment.

SHE

There's no room.

HE

I wanted very much to be there. I remember waking, that morning, seeing rain and thinking, "she won't be there."

SHE

I *was* there.

HE

Someone—I don't know who it could have been, since we almost momently were on a ship or a train, *then* on a ship, going back to Halifax and then back to a whole different context of being.

SHE

You remember.

HE

You at times overhears voices, hears over voices, has voices.

SHE

You is happy this morning.

HE

It's a good day.

SHE

What's so—different?

HE

It's outside, it's weather, it's sun, blue sky, here, *here*.

SHE

You listen to everything.

HE

There's no argument, just that there can't be.

SHE

What do *you* mean by that? Anything you thought you wanted I thought was what you finally didn't want—you always were changing *my* mind at least, if not yours.

HE
You didn't listen.

SHE
I was here.

HE
You didn't understand.

SHE
You think that's an excuse, each and every time.

HE
You didn't know.

SHE
Is that the only thing *you* think that *you* is?

HE
(singing)
   You stepped out of a dream,
   you are too wonderful,
   to be what you seem. . .
Let's *us*, you *and* me, me *and* you, let some others in here, right?
Open the window.

SHE
I don't like it. I think it's going to get cold in here. It's going
to get crowded.

HE
You—I keep thinking that it could have been different, it could
have been different each time it could have been.

SHE
You have such a roundabout way.

HE
I think that it's just that the world is round and one goes around
it.

SHE
Somebody, probably you, said it was a freight-boat enroute to
Uranus, drifting from god knows what previous time and space
through *now*—to there.

HE
A certan boredom.

SHE
You're certain?

HE
It just feels like that. It gets distracted, it gets tired.

SHE
The sun's shining still. You can hear the cars, can't you?

HE
Yes, but *I'm* here always in this funny, funny way. I'm always here. It's *you* that keep coming and going.

SHE
Are you getting fresh?

HE
No, I'm not, I'm——I couldn't and/or I wouldn't and/or I couldn't.

SHE
You were thinking of memory. . .

HE
I think memory is thinking. I think memory is thinking memory.

SHE
You were saying that you were sorry that you weren't where you were when you weren't there. That would be the way you would say it, wouldn't you.

HE
No, I simply meant that I regretted, like they say, places I hadn't been when I thought to be there, things I hadn't done when I thought to do them, ways in which I had obviously disappointed you—anyone, any one of you. I thought that I had been somewhere else when—as you know at least—it was always here that I was, even when I wasn't.

SHE
I didn't miss you, I didn't know *you* were somewhere else when you were here. I thought you were just gone away.

HE
I loved you.

SHE
I loved you too, if that's the point, but it really isn't. You missed
me insofar as you sent me a postcard?

HE
Mmmm, not like that, no. . .I want to be close. I want to feel
something, I want to be—with you. . .I think we should change
the subject. Let's be *you*, let's make *we* you and me. (half-singing,
slowly)
> *We*
>> *are going*
>>> *home.*

SHE
No we're not.

(pause)

HE
Can I?

SHE
Can you what?

HE
Can I hold you for a minute?

SHE
It's late. I don't want to be held. It's *too* late. All those excuses
you always bring into it—can't *you* just be there and *me* be just
here and maybe then you can be with me, but not because you
want to be—just because you *are*.

HE
I looked everywhere. I couldn't find a trace of it. I looked up
and I—I looked all over for it. I couldn't find it.

SHE
You were trying too hard as usual.

HE
Why is it that one's always—wrong, or even if one is right,
that somehow that's wrong because someone else is wrong and

therefore you're not wrong—or rather they are right and you're
wrong because you're wrong when they're right and they're
right when you're wrong. It seems an awfully sad kind of trait?

SHE
You were paid for that. That was an old car, you got enough
for it. You had I don't know how many thousands of miles on
that car when you sold it. You had no problems. You were fairly
paid.

HE
I'm not really talking to myself?

SHE
I'm not talking to you. We're obviously—I'm not sitting here
simply talking to you simply not talking—to *me*?

HE
I don't understand it.

SHE
It—isn't you. It—it is out there, that's what it is—it's *out there*.
Look at it. See it. Don't touch it.

HE
Let me hold you.

SHE
I don't want you to.

HE
Note for production: As this is taking place, try at various times
giving the voices, or at least the voice that's primarily answering,
the line of statement that the sense of *I*, let's call it, is producing.
Let the alternate voice at times get a physical differentiation by
seeming to move away, that is, by whomever's recording this
having the person speaking move away from the mike to get the
effect in hearing of someone moving in distance or in space away
from the other. The voice, in other words, can fade in that
respect, and get louder, as long as it continues to be basically
articulate and/or able to be heard. Then too, at this point, right
here, have a kind of a *pause*, not of any marked order, but simply
a kind of quiet, and then have sounds of breathing and/or some
human quality of sound in that way, with a sexual resonance,
that is, not dramatically involved with it but simply sounds of

some kind, not squealing exactly, but some kinds of sound to be involved with that, occur. And then have these not so much fade off but have these stop, let's say, momentarily, and then possibly a brief sequence of other kinds of sound, which the producer can make choice of in the actual context of having the thing come together, of kinds of rather sharp, intensive sounds, like a sudden entrance and fading away of something like a subway racket or a car's sudden brakes or a child crying—just have a kind of medley or melee, more accurately, of quick, decisive sounds, let's say, the hearer can locate but can't put together logically as a context. Then picking up at that point, this could take as long as the producer finds it interesting to hold it. Return, then, to the text. . .
Let's talk about something else.

SHE
You have been talking about something else. That's really what you've been talking about.

HE
Can't we really get around this endlessly elliptical dilemma? Really this reads like some, you know, late-night movie mock-up of existential hearsay. I don't want to be dumb all my life? I don't want to be hanging around here as though there were no other place to hang around.

SHE
You're hung up.

HE
I don't want to be sitting in a hotel room with a pink lamp shade and a half-drunk bottle of whiskey and some picture on the wall that shows a silo and a barn and some hay with clouds floating by, and a window that shows a salmon-pink house and an elm tree and lots of snow. I don't want to go skiing this afternoon. I'm too old to go skiing.

SHE
You're five years old.

HE
I don't want to go out.

SHE
The other kids are out.

HE
I don't want to *do* what the other kids are doing all the time, I want to do what *I* want to do.

SHE
You don't know what you want to do. How do you know you don't want to go out unless you go out? The other kids are calling. They're banging on the door. Go on out.

HE
I don't want to go out.

SHE
You miss so much just by not trying it.

HE
I know what I want to do.

SHE
What do you want to do.

HE
I want to stay here.

SHE
Look. I've got work to do. You've got to go out. Put on your boots, put on your mittens, make sure you have your scarf, and you go outside. Now it's not going to hurt you. Go on out.

HE
I don't want to go out. I want to stay here.

SHE
(with voice much quieter, more questioning)
You think it makes any difference?

HE
I think it's what one's doing, I suppose, which makes any difference. I think it's simply what we do, and what we choose to do, and what we've got to do—things like that. Isn't that what we agreed to?

SHE
Do you think I'm going to be here forever?

HE

I don't think that really is the point.

SHE

You certainly make it seem as though it was the point. Earlier you were saying that you were sorry you didn't make that picnic scene—you remember that? You didn't talk like that then.

HE

Ok. I didn't talk like that then. I talk like that now. You know it's twenty years later, for god's sake. I obviously changed.

SHE

I didn't.

HE

What do you mean, *you* didn't change? I can't even see *you*. I saw you twenty years ago. You were standing. . .the last time I saw you I remember it must have been about eleven o'clock at night, we were in that street, I think you kissed me, I can't really remember twenty years quite so simply and I've certainly done something else since.

SHE

I—I—I—remember.

HE

Well, you certainly have a convenient memory if you can remember only what you want to remember, and I'm supposed to remember only what you want to remember, and there's nothing else that you think that *can* be remembered. *I* can tell you what happened. I don't want to go out. I don't know how one person, to put it confusedly, can think he, she, or it has so much authority, so much privilege, so much dominance, that *quote* no one else *unquote* is supposed to have any at all. I'm going to tell you what—I'm making a change. Here, for example. Would you turn that down?

SHE

I don't want to turn "that" down. Turn *what* down? There's nothing to be turned down or up or sideways or backwards. There's no *sound*.

HE

Listen.

SHE
What are you doing—trying—*get*—*stop* that!

HE
Stop what?

SHE
That. That thing you've got there, that. You know you look pretty funny?

HE
You liked me five minutes ago.

SHE
So did you like *you* five minutes ago. If you like *you* now, you certainly are very—generous, in your affections.

HE
It's going to be Valentine's Day soon.

SHE
They—are beating—on the pipes.

HE
This isn't a tenement, we're not—you know, we don't have it hard?

SHE
I don't know what *that* sound is. Is that the cat you keep in the closet?

HE
Note for production. This possibly—I'd have to check it later—this could possibly be a place for some kind of, you know, some kind of rising, rather quiet noise, like the growl of a tiger, let's say, simply get a sound track or some kind of tape of, like, simply a lion and/or tiger, some kind of cat of that order, growling, ominously, and let it rise a little in volume so that when there is a hiatus in the speaking, you know, it can rise up back of the speaking and then suddenly dominate it for a moment and then become very silent. There can be throughout the pacing of the text, there can be moments again which in working the script over and/or in the production of the script, there can be moments where decisive silence occurs, simply to isolate that the patterning I'm trying to get here is of one voice as center,

speaking, and another voice or—*and* voices, actually, voices which can change, so that at moments in the text *you* will be saying something. . .we have basically the situation of an *I* and a *you*. At times the *you* will be conversely the *I* who is speaking and/or in the reference of the text, and at times the *you* will change, even it could happen as the *you* is speaking, the *you* can change into a diversity, e.g., when the *mother* voice is saying, "get your boots on and go out, etc.", that could possibly change to the voice of the primary, the first woman who is speaking. Let's see. Thus far I think we've got basically three or four *yous*. That is, assuming the *I* is the center of the speaking, there's the *you* of the girl remembered in Wales, there's the *you* of the first wife, there's the *you* of some contemporary woman (it's not necessarily—it isn't Bobbie, for example), and there's a *you* that could be of the mother, for example—so that's actually four—and as this continues, I'd like to get a *you* to speak in a diversity of tones, and I'd like to have it play against the situation of *I* but I wouldn't necessarily feel it has to in each case locate the situation of *I* or even recognize the situation of *I*. That is, the identity of *I* can be spoken to in a diversity of ways so that clearly at times that identity won't even be the point—like we say, "Hey, Harry, how are *you?*" It can be that kind of circumstance also. So anyhow, that's the end of that note, and back to the text. . .
I want to get serious.

SHE
Not about me?

HE
Not about *you*—*I* want to get serious. I'm not getting serious about *you*.

SHE
What. . .

HE
I want to get *serious*. "Now, if you are sitting opposite me, I can see you as another person like myself, without *you* changing or doing anything differently. I can now see you as a complex physical-chemical system, perhaps with its own idiosyncracies but chemical nonetheless for that; seen in this way, you are no longer a person but an organism. Expressed in the language of

existential phenomenology, the other, as seen as a person or as seen as an organism, is the object of different intentional acts. There is no dualism in the sense of the coexistence of two different essences or substances there in the object, psyche and soma; there are two different experiential Gestalts: person and organism.

One's *relationship* to an organism is different from one's relation to a person."

SHE
You can't even read it straight. Why don't you speak for yourself?

HE
Why. . .why. . . .are you angry?

SHE
You're angry—that I'm bored.

HE
I'm not bored.

HE
You are angry. I mean *me*, not you—*me*.

HE
I'm *me* too.

SHE
No, but not *that* me—*this* me.

HE
That me is *this* me.
   "The I, the I is what is deeply mysterious!
   "The I is not an object.
   "I objectively confront every object. But
      not the I. . ."

SHE
Do you have to read it over and over?

HE
I—I have to think of it.

SHE
Well, think of something else.

HE
(singing)
> *You*
> *stepped out of a dream. . .*
> *You are too wonderful*
> *to be what you seem. . .*
> *Have there blah blah bla-blah. . .*

(pause)
Note: put as much of that text of that song in as seems useful
for some kind of fading or various extension there. It could be
used, tacitly, satirically, it could be used so that the music
disintegrates, the voices distorted in some particular way probably into some. . .I wouldn't change the *spread* of the singing
but I might change. . .I think the range or the *character* of the
singing more accurately could be changed, not by distortion
mechanically produced, not by distortion necessarily in the voice
itself. And again one might in producing this have it end in
some physical distortion or have it suddenly—*not* suddenly—but
have it just get into distortion that's impossible quite to be
understood, and then have a pause of silence and/or silence that
has essentially some kind of humming or some kind of vibratory
or under-sound of: *bonng-onng-onng.* . .Some sound of that order,
again mechanically produced. Then, I think that the *disjunctive*,
some kind of scattered music here, might be useful so as to give
a *phasing.* An undertone, voices in that way could be here used
as well. And then there's the other song I want to get into the
text, which is:
> *Where*
> *are you?*
> *Dum da da dum da dum dum. . .*

I want that song in, again for whatever length seems possible,
and you could—or *one* could, rather, the producer or whatever
way this is finally to be put together—there could be a kind of,
this could be a place where kinds of so-called sound-effect could
be used in a diversity of ways, where increasing noise of some
order might come in, simply the banging of a box, or some kind
of banging of some physical object, could begin to occur. In
other words, as this is got together, I'm going to have to at some
point figure out what the activity is as some *duration*. That's

what I can't really at the moment get clear. Anyhow, that's the
possibility as it now occurs.
Anybody home?

SHE
Here I am.

HE
Where?

SHE
In here. I'm here.

HE
Who's out there?

SHE
Me.

HE
There you are!—I wonder, let's say, if one, or if I had it, or if
you had it, if one had it, to do over again, do you think, do you
think it *would* be that different, so to speak, do you think if one
could, or if you could, I could, go back and start it all over
again, do you think, for example, that the picnic would have
been that interesting? I don't mean "interesting", but I sure
didn't mean to hurt anybody like that. I don't even know if I
did hurt anybody like that. All I remember, for example, was
that—all I *now* remember is that I had this awfully painful sense
of having left someone in an expectation of something far more
actual than I'd anticipated, and simply never showed up.

SHE
It doesn't show up. There's nothing that shows up. In other
words, we've looked at these. We've looked at all the records
and, frankly, no disposition of any disorder is apparent. There's
nothing that shows up.

HE
That's not what I was feeling. I meant, simply—do you think
that if one did it over and over again, that it would be in any
way different?

SHE
Of course it would be *different*. This moment, this place. . .

HE
Do you remember, for example, when we were sitting there and
we saw the couple sitting across from us, and the man looked
rather older than the woman?

SHE
Who *are* you?

HE
I mean the time we were sitting there and we saw in the
restaurant—we were having lunch—and we looked over—

SHE
But I mean *you*.

HE
I'm talking to you. This is who I am. I mean the time that we
saw the man and the woman sitting in the restaurant, and we
were struck by the fact that they looked pleasant, and that I
remarked, I remember, that the man was, could be, possibly,
the father of the woman? Possibly, simply, an uncle, or possibly,
even a markedly older brother—something like that—and there
was a very kind of clear, sturdy—a kind of pleasant, accurate
tone to the woman. She wasn't a girl nor was she in any
sense—old, perhaps, or older? Sort of like, you might say—

SHE
I didn't say anything and I find this very distracting, this kind
of trying to remember something I'm supposed to have knowledge of that *you* say that *I* was involved with. *I* wasn't there.

HE
No, the time—

SHE
What you're saying is, the time *you* saw something, the time *you*
saw someone, in some restaurant, with someone else. That
sounds like a—a soap opera.

HE
No, simply they—

SHE
No, I'm not saying this—you are.

HE
Simply—
(a slight knocking at door)

SHE
There's somebody at the door.

HE
It's not you?

SHE
It's not you.

HE
Why don't you and I go somewhere else?

SHE
We tried that.

HE
Finally we're together. It's you *and* I.

SHE
It isn't that we were ever apart.

HE
Is there any—anything really more?

SHE
There's an incredible amount of undone business.

HE
I hope so.

SHE
I always loved you. I always wanted you.

HE
Me?

SHE
No, *me*. I wanted *you*.

HE
Listen. . .

MABEL: A STORY

SOME TIME AGO a collection of poems which I had studded with various dots and divisions was occasion of some confusion, because readers were uncertain of my intent. No doubt a more accomplished writer would have devised a scaffolding that could be taken away, once its work was done. But I wanted this one to stay there, if it could, continuing that fact of process.

The texts here collected – more accurately, coming together here – have long been in mind as a possibility: not especially for what they have to say, but in the ways in which they have chosen to say it. So again a scaffolding becomes significant, and the number *three* seems finally to be its insistent term.

Why *three?* possibly because I had tried to read Flaubert's *Trois Contes* as a young man – "three countings (accounts)" or "three tallys (tales)" – and myself then wrote *Three Tales*, adding the word *Fate*. Or it might have been the three wishes of the fisherman, or the fact that two is company, three's a crowd.

Briefly, as to the literal writing – R. B. Kitaj had invited me to provide a text which might serve as a basis for a sequence of prints. I wanted it to be 'long enough' – whatever that can mean – and hit upon *thirty* as feeling right. So "A Day Book" is precisely what it says it is, thirty single-spaced pages of writing in thirty similarly spaced days of living. Later I came upon two coincidences. I discovered that Thoreau had defined

a "day book" as a literal record of the day's activities and
thoughts, without attempt to understand or digest or to reflect
upon them. That was perfectly my own intent. Then I
discovered that St. Jerome, commenting on Matthew 13:8,
identifies *thirty* as "a symbol of marriage" – and *marriage* is
insistently the preoccupation of this text, in spite of the fact
that a *one* is its center.

"Presences" began with the publication of "Numbers" insofar
as the sculptor Marisol had seen that collaboration of Robert
Indiana and myself, and considered I might be the appropriate
writer of a text to accompany photographs of her work, which
a New York publisher had then in mind to bring out as a book.
I wanted a focus, or frame, with which to work, and *one, two,
three* seemed an interesting periodicity or phrasing. That is,
using a base of one-page, two-page, and three-page units
(again single-spaced in their initial compositions on the
typewriter), each section of the text was then six pages, and
that times five was thirty – returning me to a *three*. I then hit
upon a simple way of avoiding intensive repetition of units in
the sequence, simply by taking the last number of 123 and
putting it first, making it 312, etc. The subsequent history of
this text suggests a "spell" very much unintended, insofar as
its publication met with particular physical difficulties and
confusions, e.g., the New York firm, which had contracted to
bring it out, at one point discovered that the manuscript had
been lost.

Happily, that spell is reversed in the order of the last text,
"Mabel: A Story", where *one* is no longer predominant. If you
look at the grid of numbers appearing on the title page of
"Presences", you will discover that 1 begins the progress, and
also ends it. There is another interesting pattern found in
looking from the upper left hand corner of the grid diagonally
down to the lower right: 1, 22, 333, 111, 222, 33, 1. But now
the order is gained by taking the first number of 123 and
putting it last, thus 231, etc. And the diagonal pattern now
moves from the right hand upper corner's 3 to its recurrence
in the lower left hand corner. The text itself, begun as an
imagination of women for a collaboration with Jim Dine, is,

of course, of "the world", and the poem which concludes it
was, remarkably enough, on view at the Library of Congress
about a week after its writing.

So much for that. Better to thank one's friends for their very
dear help: Bobbie (forever), Bill Katz (again and again), Kitaj
(who really started it), Marisol (sister witch!), and Jim Dine
(heart's friend). They are the explanation, finally.

Otherwise, there was "An old Sakai in Malacca [who], on
being asked his age, replied, 'Sir, I am three years old.'"
That seems a good place to begin.

Buffalo, New York
1975

A Day Book

'To build itself a hideaway high up in the city,
a room in a tower, timbered with art,
was all it aimed at, if only it might . . .'

from THE RIDDLES, 29
translated by Michael Alexander

HE IS waking to two particulars. One, that he is to make, before sending it, a copy of the letter, and then realizes the letter has been mailed. And two, that all the assumptions involved in what has happened to himself and his wife, in their so-called fantasy, are literally assumptions. They are not right or wrong. How is the intersection possible? The light is faint in the room. Overhead he makes out the long beams of the ceiling. There seems to them a faint silvery tone, which he reasons is so because they are as the expression goes rough hewn. Light grows slightly in the windows, behind him, just by his head, two slits, then across the room from the bed, a French door with cloth now hanging in front of it. This has a curious yellow tone, as the light increases, and shows the lines of the windows running up and down on either side of the door, which also shows as a series of dark lines, marking its windows.

The descriptions are such that he cannot trust them or rather, would say, fucking is fucking. Having said that, what to say. She lifts her leg. It sounds like a cow. All the tone is wrong. Rather, he can see, behind him, his head magnified, as he turns to look at it, on the white wall close back of him, possibly five times magnified. He raises his hand so that it too appears, darkly but still with the tone of the door, a faint almost powder blue, a lovely hand, four fingers, one thumb. He thinks of the possibilities of fucking. That that part of him, the penis, grows hard, erect, in the dark, he pushes himself onto her, into her. Such dull progress, in the head. Elsewhere in the house as the light increases he hears the sounds of them, wife and children, moving about, faint voices, they are getting ready for school.

The letter leads only to further complications. He will pay the money if required to. The man for whom it is committed is in jail in Mexico. He has never met nor seen him. There is only a somewhat vast emptiness of sentimental assumption to make reason. He had been told of the circumstance weeks ago, slightly, perhaps altogether, drunk, sitting at a table with two younger men who had come to see him, one to interview him for a small local radio station. His so-called, his actual, ego swelled. He saw his head again magnified as the penis now huge he thinks is taken in the hand, then mouth, is sucked in a wetly rhythmic insistence until he feels it, or something in him gathered to a locus, explode, implode, into her face.

Fuck her. Like something lightly in the hand he flips her to the other, in the mind, sees the slight twisting of her body trying to avoid that consequence, then drops to the waiting hands. Always hands, which interrupt, roughly, her gestures, or equally now his own. The man, men, maul her body. He does not want to look nor think of it, but finds himself, in the increasing light, looking. He cannot see, think, clearly what happens. Whatever he thinks of seems to twist away, like a fish turning.

On the wall in front of him a paper he had attached to it, of notices of movies, has loosened at one corner, and now hangs vertically, Science Fiction, Three Cities of Spain. It is all some-what too linear as if thinking were, he thinks, a line to be followed. Another day will be that one. This one, the new morning of a day.

November 19, 1968

I KNOW the condition of those around me, or rather think that I do. One wants to say, *these days*. There is a tacit paranoia I have begun to enter into all such accounting. Again, I do not know if it is an age, my own, biological, or something so patently the case that no one moves apart from it. When Leslie comes he speaks, in his lecture, of the fact, to him, that prose has rejected the self image or 'The Sorrows of Werther' kind of fiction. I can feel that sentence just written pacing itself to some argument with him. What will I do without that possibility? But then who cares, in any sense at all. How the head winds itself in the pretension of its own reality.

Actively the words provoke this patter of images. Wind over hollows, so that there is a mutter of sighing voices, something said in some other now past time. Everything this morning, perhaps or almost certainly from the tiredness, has a drifting float to it. Hence write hardly. He picked up the axe and chopped down the tree, which are two of the directions. But if you are in the system, you go out, or out, in. He thinks briefly, is that yin and yang?

But he cannot arouse himself. Nothing stirs, really. In front of him is the Shiva image, the arms so multiple and yet each, in the photograph, of such tactile solidity. The clock is ticking. Ten minutes past seven, and as Alan had noted the night before, the light is viable, changes in the shaded window, to a curious insistent whiteness, and I cannot take hold of things with intention – too vague, too tired to worry.

What I did think of was that I could not really expect it to happen, never quite enough. First love like that. Really the time we were finally lying on the floor of the house, in Maine, way up in Maine on a large island, the girl whose name I forget but will at some point soon remember? Passing in time. Or the imagination of time, or world of whatever creates its experience. He says grandly, we are wound within ourselves, and unwind – that being that. But I do remember the pressure of us then, a straining through our clothing, she flat on the floor and myself on top of her. The he, myself, like a photograph that seems to move floating in air before the other apparent containment, the I. It's all tentative enough. She wants to be fucked. That's what they all want, says someone years away, in my ear, kid. Tease them a bit, chew their ear, they'll give it to you. There was a joke of girl at water fountain in factory who bending over to· drink finds herself then caught by nipples of each breast by fingers which pinch, twisting them. The sharp, quick flood of wanting. She gasps. But couldn't it be equally, someone else's voice interrupts, it just hurts like hell? That's the joke probably, either way. And for years is sense of, if one does it, that way, the consequence is as stated. These space suits we float in. Gravity keeps us on the same so-called plane, so that the measure of possible presences is the fact we call distance between them. What I always wanted, really, was one of those rigs you put on your back, a sort of jet power pack, like Buck Rogers had, that let him move then at various levels from the ground. Fuck in the air, I say, and that's what Alex uses as climax in all senses, for that novel has the heroine and pilot demon lover fuck as the plane is going into final loop and dive from failure of gas. Fuck anywhere, "now that man has no oar to screw into the earth." Alan is talking of those gods from above, the air, and of the destruction they have made.

November 20, 1968

EVEN TO GET HERE, I find myself moving letters and other accumulations out of the way, and to have this one sheet of paper, again move paper clips, and again letters out of the way. But why not. One lives as much in that detritus as in some other possibility. Thinking of places I've known wherein there was a most simple order either of poverty or of intent, there was still inevitably that residue – or so I think now, something like the wake of a boat, or echo of sound, smoke vapor.

I was moved, extraordinarily, listening to the journal last night, three pages, that the fellow was reading. He had put it, as he said, in a time capsule when eight years old. Now he was something like twenty. We were sitting in the small room, the so-called 'class' – there was such a feeling, in myself at least, of turgidity, stale feelings, either intensely programmatic as my own had become in the attempt to make something clear, or else just baffled. I watched the eyes of the girl across from me on the couch, trying to see what she was feeling beyond the mask of her makeup. The body was at least attentive, one thought. The journal was literally a small spiral-ring notebook. He said his family had given him one each Christmas. The writing began with a boy who immediately became a girl who in turn then qualified the boy, and the sex moved back and forth in that identity. I had been trying to make clear that words might be lived in, in this way, and now he had, unexpectedly, "off the subject", as he said, given me my demonstration. Pre-pubescent, we thought. Yet the sexual was very insistent – and in this play of *he* and *she*, I was also exploring the change, now woman, now man.

Outside Spot barking, the morning shifting again through the oblique window I can see to my right. To the left, the square of light in the door, covered by the red cloth. The watch, hung on a nail, makes a lovely deliberate ticking. Looking then at the small post card of Shelley "By Amelia Curan, 1819" which was painted, then, three years before his death, I can make nothing of it – no sense clear of who he is in the image. He holds, hieratically, a feather quill pen in his right hand. The face seems utterly opaque except for something about the eyes and the curiously firm set of the mouth in an intent he is feeling, a way of being there. Allen's sense of writing as a time capsule. The myriad deaths and births, the systems exploding, going out, sending the fading messages, the space sea of times and places.

Mrs. Gutierrez, come to get the wash yesterday, sitting at the kitchen table, describes what the doctor has told her of stroke, to wit, fat people – her own problem being overweight – don't die, they have strokes, and then their own people don't want to have to do with them. Once or twice, perhaps, but then the smell, the condition, repels them. She doesn't say it like that, but I do. She speaks in a quick heavy manner of accent. But the picture, so to speak, of such an almost delightful obesity, sunk in sloth, like they say, stricken, the wandering eyes, speech-less, "going out", as the related turn away in repulsion. Also a note in the paper of a few days ago apropos a doctor's report of what he considers the fact of a biological information of death in the system previous to its consciousness – roughly a year previous. We seem to live in one, scattered by the particular occasion, and spend so-called life attempting to recover coher-ence. The parts of a body, the chapters of a book.

November 21, 1968

THIS TIME, NIGHT. Some sense obviously of when does the story start, or more, what point the going on and on. I can do that, i.e., know it can be an exercise I simply continue till I'm either altogether bored with it, or have to assume it can't come to more than such boredom. But what's the other side – not what had earlier been attractive in Olson's use of Rimbaud's, "the other side of despair" – which *is* the drama, somehow, immediately, but not what this is involved with, somehow.

Night, now or day, now, or ten o'clock in the morning, or at night, or some time whitely between, or there. Or here. Where else would it be. Alan's: now here/nowhere.

But you are here. Say it that way. Drawing the face in. So that the mouth, like the Cheshire cat's, appears. So that a sudden slap obviously makes you wince, and wonder why there should be such sudden anger at your appearance. Where have you been. No need, really, to explain. If you thought to, you would have, and myself would also appear, provided with that summons. We can surely see the two of us sitting, now that the initial discomfort is past, all that left behind, and what fears or confusions either one of us might have been feeling would be done with too.

Twenty past twelve midnight. The girls just returned home from the school carnival, delayed by Mr. Muench's having tried to try out a bongo board, apparently has slipped in the process, and hurt himself.

"There's a bongo board you know? Mr. Muench fell off it, and bruised his ribs." Kate gets ready for bed. Hear sounds of her taking off sweater, rest of clothing. The cat's in there somewhere. It's late. It's been a long day. I took Alan with me up to Taos to bring Sascha the plastic for the windows of his house. We don't see Sascha, but it's a pleasure to see where he is living, small house south down a valley, facing from the west side, the length of the Sangre de Cristos. Brook runs along the road. Lovely brilliant glitter of sun on the water. Lovely sounds, wetness. Opening fence, walking up field to his house, there is a flock of sheep, then a few cows, and horse. Try to think of when young, seventeen as he is. Alan says, not that again. Me too, I guess. But what a lovely place to think of, be at, at that age, or possibly only idealism of not being there, nor that age. But the sun is so yellow, so slanting across the fields. Kids coming home from school, I watch one hoist himself over the fence, to cross short field to his yard. Another, about seven, looks up as I wave and waves back. There is a lovely brilliant clarity to the air, all the detail of the mountains very distinct, and also, the closer edges of the trees. We follow the dirt road back, cross over the bridge, past the store and on the porch a girl Alan has spoken of noticing on the way is still there, with her boy now, leaning toward him. I see them kiss.

What one wants, after tiredness, after all the day of driving, some nostalgia of such kind. When I was young, like they say. I thought, seeing the water of that brook, of New Hampshire brooks. But it was really in Massachusetts. Alan says, like Vermont, how he loved it, the place and tone of people, the aunt who was really not related but would come for divers family festivities like Christmas.

November 22, 1968

EIGHT DAYS LATER. Which seems incredible, like, just a moment ago it was I was sitting here, but it's morning, like they say, about seven, and Bobbie's gone back to bed. Then the old friend's arrival and my own sense we do get older, just by virtue of the juxtaposition, chum. Two old gaffers chatting. Or rather – a curiously abstract tone given to anything we say by the drifting vagueness of his junkie-ism. I want to warm him, or reach him. It's a sentimental insistence I have as habit, but don't longer feel as meaning much. Nor does he really need it. That's what I think then.

But the eight days absent, gone through, now more to the point. It's night. Then it *was* morning, when I was writing here, at the same table, same Shelley-face, Shiva. What is that space comes between. It becomes for the time impossible to put in that place an actual time passage. Only bits and pieces, e.g., the apparently broken nose I now have, Alan's leaving, Ed's arrival with his girl, the flu, the car's not starting day after day. Like the old business of notches on a stick, or rows of x's. Accounting for it.

You won't pay half through, not what you've spent. You couldn't begin to. You might now want to settle accounts but after all you've done, you'd be another lifetime paying. And paying – and paying. That's a sense of proper delight makes the wind warm to its work. It would do better to simply rage when able, and be quiet for the rest, than pay it back to where it never damn well came from. So I say, or think to.

Fucking visitors anyhow. Ed says, are we bothering you – at point I feel so literally sick I could vomit on him, and know the question, in my Machiavellian yet fever, is only to reassure him. Is it hurting you, love. Do you mind I ate the last of the meat. Are you sure you've no use for it. Fuck 'em. I am a proper beast when ill and what the hell else should I be. For once the body dictates, and the only problem is not to stay ill, for the sheer delight of that fact. As, for example, that lovely part, was it, in Mann, *The Magic Mountain*, wanting to spit on the unsick so as to convert them. There is such malice in a little edge of sickness, that is, when one's not sick enough just to whimper, but feels the particular shift from 'normal' to 'ill' just enough to place the difference, and therefore have use of it.

There was one lovely night of sheer drunkenness, beyond anger happily, so the body floated in its own roundness, and stand or fall, it was all one. The next morning I was bruised from head to foot, including the nose, but such a relief, so much had got backed up on Alan's own restlessness and confusions, and the talking so unremittingly of goddamn zen and goddamn revolution, and nothing *here*, or just literally *what* one could put one's hand on. I had to wait till I was drunk, to let it out – and then it came out sans some sneer against him. Which was not the point, at all. He is as painfully about his life as anyone I might think of – which is or is not the point.

Fading a little. Can't reach it, in time. Over that way, or this way. Was it there, etc. You can't remember anymore nor is there much reason to. It'll be by again, if intended to. It's all a plan somehow, or they'll tell us. Lovely to think there's an occasion more than what you think. To eat and sleep.

November 30, 1968

DRIVEN TO IT, not by need of some external kind, but rather because he wanted to, or thought he did – to *see* something, be witness to it, yet not possible to see in that, he could propose at least, it did not exist. That sense of, how do I know what I'm going to say before I've said it, a convenience at best surely for what might be as little known after said, as before. But there at least. He wasn't really interested in that fact at all. What was there, or would be. More problems, if it were then up to him either to defend or to justify. He simply liked the fact of writing, both in doing it and as it then became, in the intimacy still possible at that moment, something just done and not as yet involved with other possible questions.

Formalist, he found himself straightening the rug, dumping ashtrays, insistently checking his experience of the room, rooms, to see if the familiar order were continuingly the case. But otherwise had also impulse or something made him jump when no chance of landing anywhere seemed likely.

But the girl said, *practical* of him – almost a threat, he felt. She was instantly attractive, crazy long body, great energy in it, black, but literally brown, or in fact such words, or color, were not at all the fact of skin. *We all wear leather*, said Ed Dorn, *i.e., skin*. She was lovely, briefly to be there. One of those people one finds oneself looking at so openly there is almost a wince, one's own, at what an intimacy has been recognized. She was, I suppose, womanly just that she took such fact very happily, and wasn't in the least put off, or if so, looked simply about her with a womanly, and slight, confusion. But the "practical" stuck somehow, she said it so wisely, next morning before they were off again, enroute to San Francisco, for the first time west, both herself and the other girl, with his own friend John like a weirdly wise tourguide. It was his car but the ladies were providing money for the gas, etc. Some of the first conversation had been about the way the money went. Her eyes were particularly lovely, very direct, very warm, so that the head seemed somehow to pull back from them, like hair pulled back, as at times hers was, to make even more emphasized the center her eyes were, in her face. Yet "practical" – making the edge between so-called Taurus and so-called Gemini, his own situation, on the "cusp", someone had told him – perhaps his mother since he could now hear her voice in his head saying that final "sp" (ss-peh, but not separated, just said *clearly*) – making that sense of Taurus, its fine dependable dogged dreariness, "practical", seem even more what he was than he'd dared to fear. By day a mild schizophrenic, by night a tireless pragmatist.

He wanted to fuck his wife all the time now. Yet having done so, would have his head fill with 'things to do', almost lists of them, as if the relief of coming, like they say – and though understandable, it's an odd phrase finally to mean the emission of semen, but must mean something like, *it's me, I'm here!*, whereas 'emission' would have the slightly military sense of, that which has been sent forth. . . . As if the relief of coming cleared the way back into one's self, and the world, of the particular, not the imagined, thereby vanished till it recurred again in the need either to find place to piss or place one's member elsewhere, in the act of love. Or eat, or sleep, or whatever all that was constitutes bodily needs and functions. Did one fuck more in the fear of fucking less. Possibly. But there had never been the experience of great bounding leaps of frustration. At best, deep comfort. At worst, the inappropriate, and hence the lack of a place to be. Betimes – so-called wet dreams or else masturbation. In such wise had days and nights been passed.

January 14, 1969

WHAT DOESN'T SATISFY is what had, at the outset, seemed the specific permission possible. Say anything, i.e., shit, fuck, cunt, etc. In my own head these words are now so much a faded condition, in themselves, no energy seems to come from them. You have to have them somewhere, not placed, but met – in the literal *cunt*, the legs now open to expose it. Or coming home, the *catshit* on the rug with its almost acrid smell. Or *fuck you*, he says, daring what he hopes will be the reaction, so that he is freed to club me.

Not one without the other, nothing else in the fading sea, with whatever winds move its surface. So that what had seemed the utterly placid surface, glassy, as they say, becomes otherwise. I remember one time in teaching, at that point Latin to a group of eighth graders, there was always an almost attractive whispering as I'd come into the room, like leaves rustling, but with sudden quick bursts of sharper sounds, giggling, or the high-pitched blurt of just those words I had thought, at my age, to have use of. At first I paid no attention, depending on that sense of it, that it would go away by itself once the interest had been exhausted. But, witness myself, the interest doesn't exhaust itself. There grows a habit, so to speak, of the possibility and power which the words possess. But now I remember her, the first woman I ever did, saying, almost in hysteria, *fuck* me – *Do* it. It's the one time the word does stay in my head, forever. But now, with the giggling, impatient just to get them settled enough to begin with the day's work, and so be that much the sooner rid of it, what can I do. I get up, look at them, then go to the board while they continue, paying me only covert attention, and then write on it as quickly and with as large letters as I can manage, *SHIT!* They all grow immediately silent, some blush, and so I say to them in that convenience I think mistakenly given to adults, *shit*. That is the word. Are there any others you would like to consider? And continue then with some vague lecture on 'power' words, and how of course we all make use of them, and are also, equally, attracted to them.

But that other time, in the fumbling, despairing fact of its demand – the word was as fierce as an axe, and as practical. And as deeply the mystery she was as I could ever find other sense of. It seems to me at times as if, at the center of all that these women are, and that literal mystery to which they invite me, or Homer was a fucking idiot with his Circe, and she more full of shit than even Odysseus – the dumb cunt . . . . No, but a quiet almost murmured babble, so that you have to come closer, and listen hard, to catch in the mumbling, and in even the incredibly ugly and aged face pushed at you, with all that repulsion of broken teeth and hairs growing out of moles and foul, hissing breath and bleared obscene eyes, *those words*. And love it, incredibly *her*, as she transforms into that imagined delight you had held of her so long before the sight of her actual fact. She delights, you are held in the succulent wonder, fondled, teased, and just those words come whispering into your ear.

I had read somewhere that men are much more apt to engage in sexual activity with an image, a fantasy, in their heads, than are women. Perhaps that relates to their fact as form-makers, whatever finally that comes to – but also true seems the other fact I have been held by at least, that women are source, are the material condition. I avoid my pompous intent by giving over all arbitration, by anyone, or argument. Laughing, the proof is in the pudding. One reason I have not been attracted sexually to animals is possibly because they cannot speak. I hear that incredible lore, in those words, echoing, remembering all there ever was or ever could be of any of it.

January 15, 1969

EVEN TO BEGIN to say this takes extraordinary care, i.e., the paper gets jammed, the wrong key gets punched, and what literally *is* to be said gets as adamant as the timetable for an eastern railroad, or the seating arrangements at some unimaginable ball. And what *is*, to be said: Today – to mark it – I came into the waiting room of the dentist's office where my two daughters (the two still at home) had been brought, with Bobbie, my wife, to have their teeth cleaned. (But like some horrible pun I find myself typing, probably drunk, 'teetch' for 'teeth' – even *now* having to erase the horrid *c*. . . .) I had been to the airport, after leaving them there, I felt shocked, had neither eaten nor done more than dress, after an elaborate shower and so on, getting myself dressed to teach, though it seemed as though the sun could scarcely have risen, and all had a sluggish sullen air to it. God knows the children no more interested (were) in the getting cleaned (teeth) than me in getting them (there).

All like that. Inertia, difficulty, resentment. Sullen, silent, opaque and consistently resistant, the whole damn day a sort of tribunal of impossibilities. Like some idiot, though graced with an acceptance, his own and the idiot Department's (English), of his own qualifications as a so-called Ph.D.

I had been to the airport, to get a ticket for a flight (not to anywhere by any instinct), and all having gone well, drove, happily without incident, to where I had left them all. I went into the waiting room – in brick building coincident with jail, courthouse, school, factory, store, as Mailer intelligently insists – and saw two people sitting, and could not recognize any, in that curious dimness such places have, for my own view of things. Was, of course, instantly paranoid, expecting, hoping, to be identified momently by them so as to have *place* there, too. So *saw* a young woman, pleasant in appearance, sitting to the left with legs crossed, attractive, and a lovely fall of brown hair, absorbed, as they say, in a magazine. And across from her, one of those inevitable bitches of the late forties (her own age) who 'checks out,' as the expression is, any *late* arrival to her own environs, whether same be a garbage pail or the Ritz. So felt therefore instant displacement and paranoia, and looked desperately for any sign of the three people I had brought there some half hour before. The so-called problem with doctors' or dentists' offices, as jails, is, *where* are people in them. Not to mention, *in* what circumstance.

So now, *where* – were they. Not to panic, I walked over to a shelf, rack, of magazines, and began to look through them, and then looking, covertly, at the girl sitting to the left, with that lovely hair, saw she was literally my daughter Sarah. Who had, she said, been so absorbed simply to avoid the engagement of the bitch, the soured and vicious person (I stake my life on such assumptions), was sitting across the room from her.

What *is* to say, is, this day, I give testament to my daughter's having entered the opaque state, for me, god knows male, of whatever it is, is womanhood. I did not recognize her, but saw, instead, a young woman of viable and attractive form – and liked her, and wanted therefore to know more of her. In short, a momentous day – to be swept clean of idiot distraction, persons, the dead student, the vicious elder woman, the time-table, the clutter – to be clearly, Sarah, age eleven, *is* a woman.

January 16, 1969

HAD DRIVEN DOWN to Bernalillo, in the valley below us here – we are up in a small town, Placitas, at the north end of the Sandia Mountains, in the foothills about 7000 feet – to mail letters, restless, about two in the afternoon, with Bobbie and the girls having gone into Albuquerque, etc. Flat sort of chilled afternoon. High, faint sun, which as I turn off the highway into the mainstreet of Bernalillo, sits directly in front of me. The street here is wide, very western in look now since a few years ago what had been the store fronts and look of various houses along it were cut back to permit the widening of the road. It's predominantly Mexican, and is used also by the Pueblo Indians – Sandia, Santa Ana, Zia, San Felipe, et al. Just about as I get to the highschool, on the right, I suddenly confront a parade coming up the other side of the street towards me, led by one of the town's police cars, with that heavy anonymous-looking dark glasses policeman, smiling, happily, with, behind him, about four abreast and some six to eight deep in rows, horsemen, with yellow flashes on their right sleeves I can not read – Sheriff's Posse? – and god knows authentic in appearance, of various ages, all predominantly Mexican, young and old, with those about in their thirties, say, very conscious of their style and riding with a very upright, almost fierce sort of pride. I pull over to the right and stop completely, Spot back of me on the seat, panting, so I roll down the window, and watch, and listen, as the parade goes on past me to the left. So now simply the notes thereof: Parade – first police car; horses & men; firetruck (this is local and from time to time sounds its siren, as does the police car); drum majorettes (Mexican again – with the same style as the riders, very conscious somehow, or else in that reputed sense, *sleepy*, drowsing almost in the movement); band number one: red tunics, grey pants – (this is) Bernalillo High School Band; (then) four cars, then float – yellow and light blue – CUBA HIGH SCHOOL RAMS (which then explains the occasion, i.e., it must be two teams are playing against each other, basketball? hardly anything else on January 17, 1969) – with their band – dark blue and gold. High faint sun – from head of street. Spot pants back of me. Floats then numbered (1, 2, 3, 4, etc.) – Frank's Conoco – etc. "Put a bear in your pot" (referring to Bernalillo).

I turn off finally onto a dirt road runs back of the town, off to the west mesa, the houses moving back toward it, all one story, mostly adobe, or else cement block, and to the left, the east, about five or six miles distant, the bulk of the Sandias like a section of the earth has lifted, broken clear, and raised up on edge. Then turn back toward the main street, having driven parallel to it for a while, coming out just below the post office, in the one block of businesses, so turn back toward it, go in, am greeted by the post office official, like they say, who asks me, am I still living in Placitas, after I've mentioned the parade, and says he is going to run for the school board, and will be up to see us. I demur, in a way, saying my wife has much interest, which she had had but I question if she continues to. Going out, drive then back up the street, back of the parade, and at one point come abreast of it, in the left lane, realizing it is making an about-turn opposite the highschool, so stop there back of a car to wait for the street to clear – as floats, people, go by now on both sides. Slogans on floats like, Flush the Bears! (on float with teddy bear, purple and white, on toilet) or Stone the Bears! (with kids sitting in car with big display bottles of whiskey) – and against the wire mesh of the highschool fence, kids on the inside watching, in a lovely delight.

January 17, 1969

ALL THE DAY has seemed echo after echo of previous condition – in whatever person or sense of person was ever real in it. I don't know any longer what actually is the proposal but for some hopefully initial sense of who was there, literally, and what I felt myself to have to do with them. I am speaking of children – the first child and son ever born to me, for one, and his brother, and sister. What a curious rhetoric seems to come even in saying it. But now, knowing even if briefly the latter two, humanly there is for me at least such persistent resonance in that relation. I don't want to make them subject to my own feelings, nor do I really think that will be the occasion in any case.

But such damned echoes. . . . Speaking to their mother this morning on the phone, cross-country like they say, from a place I feel myself almost literally to have earned, a life with people I love and who love me – all that cagey, double edge of statement is so insistently distasteful, all that dull 'I know better' that comes in her voice, and the almost shocked manner of the childlike 'saying of the piece' – what is it makes it be so.

I've been trying to know what it is to be specifically myself in this point of age, almost asking people how they are feeling in it, as one would fellow travelers in some situation, shipwreck or great happiness, possibly. Such confoundings of myself, in the past, are seemingly now absent. Fears, ways of stating oneself, and so on, do seem truly to have taken themselves off. I don't think it's a question really of having done anything, though I've reassured myself of that fact, perhaps more in teaching than in writing – or in the last there is no point of rest permits one to feel at rest with, 'there, I've done it, and that's that.' Curious that Benjamin DeMott this morning on the phone should say, I hear you're the hero now – or so-called words to that effect, but sans some convenient self-demurring, or whatever, I could answer, I'm not – very much to him, who would know, I think, the incredible deadness inherent in any term of that assumption. Straight forward is forever the only way.

And whereas now these dilemmas of how to be of use to these people, hardly though still inevitably children, hopefully in some sense of mine, – all the rest of such facts as one calls 'human relations,' all these so densely apparent, almost daily, and so changingly and variously open, adamantly so it would seem. Think, though no sophistication, two days ago one was entering, by a process of self-reality like either a huge sky or else an incredibly absolute tunnel, the possibility of that woman one called 'wife's' fucking a randomly met though pleasant man. 'Why not' would prove the social history of our so-called age, but the literal possibility, in fact, like they say, would prove the alternate truth of human condition. No one owns. I think the most useful truth I've been given to acknowledge of others, as a man, is that in one's own experience another's is not necessarily denied nor increased. Years ago now, remembering that situation of separating from that first wife, Olson's parallel, in his own confusions, put as he said, that one could love *two* – or myriad, as I now find, either in myself or in another, and the relation to *one* is not of that fact lost. Will it be that someday we come to some relation with those who make up our condition, *humans*, that will not argue their histories as all that they depend upon for relation – or else, more accurately, that what they do is more relevant to all their lives, one by one or all in all, than what they didn't. I feel such trust in life, once I stop all that previous qualification – just that I know I'm alive, and witness it with such pleasure in others, *we are here* – I'm happy, in the most simplistic of senses. I've thought a lot, like they say, but more than that I've not found.

January 20, 1969

I MUST NOW FATHOM an old judgment which, I believe, is but one of Condillac's ideas: it was that it's useless to read books of logic; it's essential to try to reason correctly, and that's all.

The rules that Tracy prescribes at the end of his *Science de Nos Moyens de Connaître* are so simple that I can quite well try to put them into practice. They consist in retracing the memory of the thing on which one wishes to reason, and then in being careful to see that the subject always contains the attribute given it.

But this happy temporary release from cares and troubles I enjoyed but a few moments, when I was awakened and greatly surprised by the terrifying screams of owls in the deep swamps around me; and what increased my extreme misery was the difficulty of getting quite awake; and yet hearing at the same time such screaming and shouting which increased and spread every way for miles around, in dreadful peals vibrating through the dark extensive forests, meadows, and lakes. I could not after this surprise recover my former peaceable state and tranquility of mind and repose, during the long night; and I believe it was happy for me that I was awakened, for at that moment the crocodile was dashing my canoe against the roots of the tree, endeavouring to get into her for the fish, which I however prevented.

Even here though I myself am pursuing the same instinctive course as the veriest human animal you can think of – I am however young [old] writing at random – straining at particles of light in the midst of a great darkness – without knowing the bearing of any one assertion of any one opinion. Yet may I not be in this free from sin? May there not be superior beings amused with any graceful, though instinctive attitude my mind may fall into, as I am entertained with the alertness of a stoat or the anxiety of a deer? Though a quarrel in the streets is a thing to be hated, the energies displayed in it are fine; the commonest man shows a grace in his quarrel. By a superior being our reasonings may take the same tone – though erroneous they may be fine. This is the very thing in which consists poetry; and if so it is not so fine a thing as philosophy – for the same reason that an eagle is not so fine a thing as a truth. Give me this credit. Do you not think I strive – to know myself?

Finding then everything is due tone and order, I remembered
my fears, only to make a jest of them to myself. And now,
palpably mistress of any size of man, and triumphing in my
double achievement of pleasure and revenge, I abandoned
myself entirely to the ideas of all the delight I had swam in. I
lay stretching out, glowingly alive all over, and tossing with a
burning impatience for the renewal of joys that had sinned but
in a sweet excess; nor did I lose my longing, for about ten in
the morning, according to expectation, Will, my new humble
sweetheart, came with a message from his Master, Mr H., to
know how I did. I had taken care to send my maid on an errand
into the city, that I was sure would take up time enough; and,
from the people of the house, I had nothing to fear, as they were
plain good sort of folks, and wise enough to mind no other
people's business than they could well help.

One path only is left for us to speak of, namely, that *It is*. In
this path are very many tokens that what is is uncreated and
indestructible; for it is complete, immoveable, and without end.
Nor was it ever, nor will it be; for now *it is*, all at once, a
continuous one.

January 21, 1969

SHE WAS LOVELY, then, in the darkness. Tired, but with that
sweet tone of an almost playful if protesting abandon, *not to now*,
as one says. What had he been thinking? Simply that, sitting at
the table in the kitchen with the friend, literally, the other man,
it was inextricably time to know a fact. In his own response to
her, or hers to him, they were so entangled in their own feelings,
and if she became object to him, then by that he had withdrawn
from her, so as to know her more clearly. She could not be in
that the specific woman she was.

So now he came in, with the other still in the hall back of him,
or perhaps he had not left the kitchen as yet. That was it. The
other man was still back there, in the outer room, possibly as
displaced, but eager, as he was, turning on the light, so that she
turned sleepily around and looked up, smiling, I think, with
that moist soft tone of muzziness. His cock was already hard,
excited by even what he was saying, that he wanted to fuck her

with the other, or really the other way round, and when he had gone to get the other man, reassuring her, who was aroused also, that it would be all right, both took off their clothes, as she had, lying with sharply white body, red and white and black, her hair, with the bedclothes pulled off, and as they both in an awkwardness moved toward her, she eased them by smiling, and reached to take the other against her, so that he now took position beside them, back of her, reaching over the arch of her back to stroke her tits, as the other was now down on her, sucking, the cunt, as she moved against him, making soft sweet moans, as one says, and became, before him, the two, her incredible whiteness, smaller in body literally than he had known, and now the man on her, sucking, as she pushed against him and shuddered. They clung together. He, back of them, had fallen into a curious object of his own, as if he were looking in a window, a long space, but her hand came back of her to feel his cock, then as the man seized her harder, locked again with him, arched and fucking in completed intensity.

There was another moment, somewhere in the time, he lay by her buttocks, stroking, as she had knelt over the other to take his cock in her mouth, with both hands cupped over it, below her mouth, with the lips extended around it, and hair falling over his stomach, up and down, with quick sudden intensity, the man up then pushing, to go *ahhh*, and come.

Later, it was already faint morning, at the windows, the long french door, the man and the woman with him were kneeling nude on the floor before them as they now themselves fucked slowly, lazily, on the bed. He was fucking her from the back, his cock up the crotch of her legs to her cunt and his fingers rubbing her clitoris. The two in front of them, hierarchically, slowly, made love. The woman sucked the man's cock, up and down, slowly, the mouth moving back and forth, and the long hair falling, the body almost stern in its concentration. He had placed both hands on her shoulders and drew her back and forth as she at times stroked his cock, or else placed her hands on his hips. Slowly, almost gravely, it went on, while on the bed, he watched, felt his own cock tense with it, could not see the eyes facing also toward the sight, hers, erotic, lovely, tight with interest, his own, fucking, fucking in knowledge of animals, in delight and permission of animals, gravely, sweetly, humans

without fear or jealousy, but intensive increasing provocation.
So that now, in dreams as it were, he unclothed her, beckoned
them forward, saw their own clothes fall, the cocks stiff, engaged
them with her, one after one after one.

January 21, 1969

PIVOTS UPON EVERYTHING, that business if you don't see it now,
you'll never have another chance. Like bagels, bacon, bedpost
rhymes with b, or else the rhythm does, uncle, irish, or offen-
s(ive). You play with it. His broke soon after he got it. That
Christmas. That night.

Sweating profusely. He profuses to be a teacher of the young.
He is tired. He is sitting in a room facing wall some twenty
miles from Chicago. White tired. It's getting close to six o'clock
and the shops will be closing, the people coming home. A
memory of white streets, freshly fallen snow, the light catches
in a lovely glow around it, somehow the sense of aureole, apart
from aura, a halo of roses, green dreams but none so dominant
it makes a sense to get home to.

Small animals in well contrived cage, of glass, with open top
the very pleasant orange brown dog, a mut, looks down into
but does not touch. Kangaroo mouses, seem bright, fresh, at
least pleasing to human attention and valuation insofar as same
in the system admitting them, and/or has brought them, from
Tibet, or Mongolia, or any name you want to, to make them
hear. One jumps into revolving wire cage, making it spin round,
and by clasping its belly to the ladderlike interstices, goes round
and round, rightside up, upside down, and then in a particularly attractive way, flips out, at the top of the spin, and somehow lands rightside up.

Students, viz., those who study in this case, but more, a present
social condition of person, those who are, at these institutions
of various size and density, and talking, talking, we all talk, the
first time I was seen hereabouts, but had slipped in, when he
was looking, I wasn't, came in the only way you get in, by just
opening the so-called door.

He can't make heads nor tails of this, he can't. Nor can I. What

was he saying, i.e., no sooner had he said it I was thinking,
that's a pretty glib assumption, for such a serious man who says
he is. No but I think what's actually on his mind is some filling
of paper, like he wants to, like dinner he can't eat, but asked
for. You said you were hungry. Or in love. Or tired. Or many
things indeed, and now you're stuck with it. Try climbing out
of that skin by your neat little agencies. Or get a computer
remembers that, for one thing – you said you were tired. You
don't resolve the argument that way. So hits him, full in the
face, such a delicious relaxation after all these years of disappointment, really, in what were the endless expectations, better
job, at least more pertinent to his background and actual experience, not to mention what, underneath, he was really feeling.
Say, for example, that he is employed to eat shit in the subway.
One, you don't find much. Two, it tastes bad. Or good. It's the
same, and/or what they call, or used to call, or perhaps even did
call, when I is or was a boy, since you don't know what I is
except as you says so. That wasn't any job any man ever had
in any case. But it was shit sure enough. You could smell it on
him, not a smell easily removed. You speaks metaphorically?
Quick perception of the relation between things, hallmark of
genius – and didn't have to think it, just wrote it, baby, just
damn well wrote it.

So the old girl must be out she don't answer phone, and probably tired of hearing it all in any case. Lord love a duck, go
fuck a tiger. But he really wants to go home he says. Must have
been awful, on those moors, hearing those people about to be
used in horrible sex acts, just children, saying, I wants to go
home. Not funny, old sport. No laugh when you find yourself
gone, down the drain, just flushed with the end of it. Dirty
trickle, that's all. Now the drain's stopped, and there will not
be another this evening. Crazy trail end of smoke, like there
used to be, down the tracks, through Acton, when he was a kid,
and over that intervale and river, going to sleep or trying to,
would come sound of, chuff, chuff, chuff. Whoo, whoo.

January 29, 1969

IN THE BOAT OF IT, so to speak, going, but rather in the fact that from *here* is *there*, and the past a wake of curious resonance, and forward no more than the body's movement, in walking, the one foot lifting, to find place ahead of itself, else behind.

So that, at times, there are experiences, suppose them, of oneself, or whatever it is does manage the containment, at least so experienced, and nothing falls in or out of it but fluids, effluvia, spit, shit, little flakes of dried skin, and occasional 'parts' lost for a variety of reasons, and also the whole bulk of words constituting, also, actions, as if one hit the future, saw the stone skip a myriad number of times, light dazzle, on the water's surface, and then, as the boat continues, looks back, as they say, to see the stone disappear. Words. Such a lovely particular abstraction, torn out of whatever else can be felt as coincident. 'I can't find the right words. . . .' Or, in no possession thereof, but now insistently possessed of them, choked, stuffed, spills out all the possibilities of there being, one, no reason, two, all reason, three, rage, four, confusion, five, pain, six, pleasure, seven, *use* certainly, eight, a possibility, nine, delight in any *material* condition, and zero, or ten, put the one in front of it, and return thereto – one can suppose them then to enter the room, probably the bedroom (bathroom?), him screaming hers, her's, substance, in him. A curious twist on all occasions.

So that – there is a curious mirror, when one reflects the other, and in that, other sees not one, but other as one. 'Be neat, speak courteously, make a good impression' – and hence the false face carried so persistently front of what might be seen, and must be. What else to look at. But surely there is a relief in that intention, if any has any possibility. Oh, so sorry. Here, take this chair. Yes, it probably will rain.

But – "It was funny. You went in and out, like, you weren't what I supposed you would be. You were simply talking. At the luncheon, for example. But when you read, it was both you, that way, then I saw you with almost an aura, all around you like a very large halo, Olson, Duncan, Ginsberg. . . ." Or words to that effect. Something like that said. It was so late, dark, nothing really very clear in hearing it. Such a lovely solid body somehow. Attractive. Really, in that basic sense, drawing to itself the alternate energy. Not me really, one thought. Real – it's a different thing, of course. Gets tired, older, certainly, but is *here* – has only itself to be in. Can't be image only of some other experience of it.

When you were young. . . . When one was young, it becomes a memory to say so. It is another image, nostalgia perhaps. But she says, don't talk about *age*. Such an interesting subject, though. Williams – "You reach for it, you feel the impulse, your mind is sharp enough, but when you reach, your fingers can't articulate, you can't keep up with the impulse, you *want* to, but it all fails you, won't work. . . ." He certainly didn't like it. But others – possibly. He said, it's supposed to be a fruition, the accumulation and success, most hopefully, of all you've intended – the time you can decently rest from it, see what's become of what you've meant to do, and, having as one's wont to say, succeeded, enjoy it. Decently earned rest from it. But it's not like that. You reach for it, you feel the impulse, your mind is sharp enough, but when you reach, your fingers can't articulate, you can't keep up with the impulse, you *want* to, but it all fails you, won't work. . . .

Someone was speaking of the elderly lady who, looking in the mirror, saw the face she couldn't accept as hers, all the wrinkles, the change in it, in that *inside* she was a girl still. *Me.* . . .

Unacceptable, that the mountain can break up, the sea diminish? How is that possible. Ah. All one's life one was alive! Do you think they're happy up there? Where. Oh, wherever they are now. Who knows. What? Oh, whether or not they are. Well, not for us to think of. We're here.

January 30, 1969

ENTHUSIASMS, THE ENERGIES that come therefrom – like, 'My heart leaps up when I behold. . . .' With such insistent fact. Wondering if one's response, to the younger man, is possibly just a way to experience this state, so lovely, fresh, renewing, in its possibility. And not, or then again perhaps, some unrecognized edge of homosexual content in oneself. But that too, acknowledged. So beautiful they really are, at just that moment of so-called age all is poised on the possibility, and their own energies are so moving.

Coming out of the post office, the town so curious or not at all so in its rather insistent, comfortable and apparent wealth – like the lovely time Duncan, in the house of the pleasantly wealthy woman, is saying in that high-pitched excitement of his, "Money, money, money! I can almost smell it!" – anyhow that tone, and the lady following behind suddenly says, "Are you *English*?" – meaning apparently the tones of the conversation she is overhearing, and says, "Suddenly I thought we were back in London! You know, we just came from there," herself unequivocally American and the answer is, no, *New* England, and now living in *New* Mexico, and very *much* American. And so forth.

A bright sunlit day – after a long time, it seems, of rain, snow, fog, a chill in all the air. The vagueness, in that sense, of the hotel room now shifts to a particularity, and one is *at home*, knows where the things familiar to oneself are, moves in the space with pleasure and interest, familiarly. Like John Cage's saying, why not a motel, and what else does one need – and surely for those who live primarily in their own condition, almost a skin not to absent from nor could one be, the place of the body is the place one lives in, and the mind follows and makes do. But – as Olson – that fact of *habits* and *haunts*, so hardly earned in a way, and found. As New England – odors, sounds, senses of wetness, ways streets move, trees, the movement of the ground, sense of distance, smells, tones of voices, light. One wants to, at last, *be there* beyond the intention in all senses, simply there.

Faded, dull? Not really. *Elsewhere* in one's self, another part, as one might say, another function possibly – if life, whatever it is, can be so divided into contents. Chapter one, head, chapter two, heart, etc. Who knows – but it can't be a discretion, whatever it is. But what had happened to love, so to speak – when its person is absent. Desire continues, but cannot find its response. Or rather turns to other terms of it, talking, talking, talking, talking – god knows a deluge of it, and when the young man comes up to the room, almost a shyness one feels, it is so curiously intimate, so flooded with a privileged meaning.

So anyhow. Who is out there, oneself, looking at oneself, from within. The mirror. Real because it is there? The man who looks in the mirror and sees no image of himself reflected? Lost in time and space? Etc. Or Narcissus, kneeling, sees the wavering beauty, the body of his own life, there reflected.

Aunt Bernice – in trailer with Mother, crunky, derelict somehow trailer park, Nokomis, Florida. Route something or other, at the scrub edge of town, within which an almost terrifying institutional-like boys' school, military. And the sea there is a bay, a salt lake – though hurricanes give it the semblance of more, a more organic, let us say, activity. They walk along the breakwater by the beach. Is it Mother slipped on the rocks, and broke her arm? Or Aunt Bernice? One did. The visit of the friend, the woman – they report it as most pleasant. They are impressed, perhaps even displaced by intimidation, that she is so obviously socially *well-fixed* – they smell it with old habits. My aunt. My mother. Aunt Bernice tells story of her first employment, in a one room factory, in a sort of warehouse, where they are put to work, she and the other girls, affixing hat bands to hats, and since they are apprentices, receive nothing for this work, but are told that in a few weeks they will be sufficiently competent to be paid, like the other girls they are told are behind the door, in another room adjacent, who are being paid. Then one day, the employer absent, they get sufficient nerve to open the door, and see the girls on the other side, who, like themselves, have been told the same story. So they all protest. And quit. How one thinks – how true, there is only *one* condition.

January 31, 1969

BAR TALK. Bartok, just the same thing, in this case, like the piano scenes he'd write for children, kids, you might say, play like the bear walks through that forest, and woof, woof, not like that, but of course the drunken bear dances in crazy cadenzas, and in the bar the light falls, goes, the length of that long wooden surface. You could scream at them, hey, let's play Bartok – one of those middle Europeans had joy in his heart.

All serious people end up being serious. All whites white, all blacks black – so they say. Intellectuals are people got sex in the head, would Lawrence say, because they can't get it up, or once up, down. There was a story, told years ago, and last night repeated, about Orwell, was in bar with working people, ordered drink for working man next him, a pint, which is supposed to be read as question, no says he, have to get out of here soon, a half pint will do, says Orwell, but that's not what people of your class want, it's a pint, or nothing. It really is nothing. The syntax all dislocated. No working man would be that patient, to hear the end.

It must be the person does, even unintentionally, precede the definition. Now pay attention to your class, which must be Aristotle again. Play with your own kind. But they won't talk to me, much less indulge in games with me. Never you mind, those are your people. But they got a funny look to them. Never mind, them's it for you, young man. Oh, is that what I am – or is? Or what is that, on you. I's your ma – well, not like that, I'm your mother, whence, from which, and to for, your eyes are decently averted. Not look at your own mother, but instead at them dirty things? Keep to your kind lad, – not do, to mix.

Buddy's comment upon Max, who had told Julie, *yellowbird*, he called her that too once, when the revolution comes, or he must have had use of another vocabulary, not such a dull one, like wind the clock, it's the end of the week, pay day sort of stuff, no revolution there – oh dear, the wheel's going round – no, he said, when the revolution comes, you've got to go, all your sort, blonde aryans, or whatever term he used to describe of course the very delightful blue-eyed blonde-haired softness of her person, no less her heart, dear, very sweet girl she was always, in all the confusions she did experience with men, source of all evil, they only want one thing, but circumstances, which needed her, first time met in fog, that haze of L.A., stopped for a moment at the intersection, turning on, the roach passing round, look out to see the car adjacent, shades, glasses, also shades, also turning on, with the white headed white gloved possibly policeman in the middle of said intersection, get the hell out of there, that's revolution, later, had she come home then, or been there all the time, like out in field, somehow a town, of oil derricks, a house, someone, the wife was it, is passing a plate of pot, and some opium, smoke, and the master of the house, an incredible and serious young man, person, plays baritone, onk, onk, and crazy guttural under-ride of sounds, he should live in the cellar, but at least no neighbors, drive home, their home, Julie's, through L.A., to drive two Porsches back to Albuquerque, Race, and Buddy, and him. This was yellowbird – instant love therefor, and also her sweet shrewd husband Manny, a local boy, played trumpet, later in crazy dinge of N.Y. was waiter sat in, you dig, on relaxed occasions, with the band.

All that. No, comes the revolution, baby, you got to go – despite subsequent hook, of junk, another husband, bull fighter, at least on the way, all the way she went, each time, with must have been physical condition just as much as the toothache she has first meeting, all her lovely mouth swollen, so sweet, like a bee stung. Like bartoc, bar none – Max, you play it. Tell how make her the one meets the edge, no color, but her the so-called victim. Would rather kick a dead horse, i.e., he'd understand. She comes back, tells Buddy, in perplexity, but Max says, comes the revel, which is the misspelling, the revolution, I have to go. Like, your mother's calling. All into damnwell fade, now. Max freaked on speed, or not to propose like libel, like, he was never the one.

February 1, 1969

EXPERIENCE (in a manner usual enough) created by a system – The spatial relations made by a house, for example, the distribution of movement in an arrangement of streets, etc. Ralph Ellison's use of the term, *conscious consciousness* apropos his proposal of Malraux's *Man's Fate* as an instance of a 'classic' text – mind experience, or however to isolate it if that's possible, taken as the possibility of system.

Watching the markedly tall man leaving the dining room – he makes the actually over-large hallway and stairs going up to the lobby seem of a size his own body is the measure of, i.e., it's his size, not the overly big space others make of it. Now there is an awkwardness in the size of this typewriter, the way the keys are placed almost 'beside it' – in front – so that its literal operation seems to be somehow in another place, as one types. The resistant difficulty it seems to make of the action of thinking, in words, that this form of writing seems to be –

The days' form, the wondering rather insistently just what one is 'doing' here, and yet much liking, also, the kind of intensities the literally random talking of the afternoons, with the so-called students – actually a pleasantly dense and various collection of young and happily fresh-feeling younger human beings. Letting it be there, much like 'letting the song lie in itself.' Paying attention – letting the fact of the circumstance come out. So boring does seem the alternative, among many others, god knows, of trying to give it 'point', to direct it to some 'purpose'. What is that purpose, unless clearly one of a very immediate and direct context of, the building's on fire, that door will get you out – or else, to share in the doing of this, and/or to do it yourself, like they say, these skills and materials are needed. At some point, perhaps invariably, the relation between this thing being done, or being used in the doing of something possibly else, and the information system used to convey the fact or nature of its occasion to another – The occasion of so-called abstraction *there*, in fact, the experience then of that 'there,' as opposed – really – to *here* – I. A. Richards speaking of his method of teaching people who've had great difficulty in learning to read and write, his use of the *tensions* in language systems, – not that, this, here, there, now, and so on.

Whether errors, as meaning to write *Echoes* becomes *Whether*, as the finger meant to strike the E key, hits the W – and the thought moves to include it, to use it in the thought, and so on.

Echoes. And, ands. Possible possibilities. . . . Syntax making articulate, i.e., coming literally to sound in the context, fact of fatigue and distraction. The machine talking too, as one fumbles in use of it. Barking doors. Crying tables. Spilt lights. All that clutter – book at that moment falling down back of typewriter, so that head becomes attentive and yields momently to record of it, and now is again back in the difficulty of the typewriter, how wide the paper is, where is one, or where are the words now in their occupation of the paper – how much left, to go, to be said, before the end of it has been come to. How much time is there left. The ease of it, also – being tired, wants to relax in that continuum, to yawn, stretch, let go of attention as a preoccupation. What's that all about.

Bill wants a situation, call it, wherein he can take a daily photo of himself – he was talking with Marisol – that can accumulate that content of a face, nothing fancy, just getting up, a sort of business like the slot-machine photo booths, like you wash your face, take a picture, go about the day's content as ever. So that you get a year's accumulation of face, so recorded. Like Bob, yesterday, involved with a photograph that tracks movement, in the essentially static context of the photo-image itself – so that you 'anchor' the image by having some of its detail, anything, or one, or more, stay in very particularized containment of focus, very sharp; and then let the hand, head, whatever, move – and with strobes, you get a one, two, three phasing manifest in the image. Like Bobbie's 'trace' in the move of objects on Xerox. Like this – writing – "fitful tracing. . . ." No copies, nor intent, nor much at all – but *phases*, be they phases of the moon. Or mine(d). Or the *d* added, and paper gone.

February 3, 1969

WHATEVER IT WAS they must have been thinking about, they were there too, certainly, as much as the rest, like they say. Funny what they hear, or seem to. 'Objective,' for example, becomes a sense of something apart from oneself, something in the world – though what 'world' or how 'in,' it must be they can't then think of. Age again, possibly – being young. Always that insistent organism 'doing its own thing' – being one. Fascinated by modes of age, really, especially in girls somehow – is it the fact of sexual complement, being male, one is drawn to, or just that it is a denser, more various condition. Possibly.

At the curiously dense house of people visited on Sunday, a very pleasant, large and comfortable house, very socially comfortable – at first surrounded by the young, so that the hostess, a straight-seeming vigorous woman in her forties, attractive, suggests the study would be a quieter, more relaxed place for all thus interested to be. There, literally, one sits with them all surrounding, all young, with one exception of the older woman has some specific question in mind to ask, something literary – whereas they either look at one intensely, measuring, or else try it on, their own condition, especially the young women. Of which there is one unequivocal beauty, tall, very relaxed sense of flesh, black hair, looking always a little flushed, pleasantly so, a little arrogant in manner, sharp, quick eyes, pouting, like a 19th century heroine. Wears very large, round, charming glasses. A young woman of no little means, one would think.

Lovely, as it were, to be the village blacksmith, at least doing something can be attended, taken as literal and having an active information. Remembering Tom, when still very young, in Mallorca, caught in the chaos and, to him, it must have been, terror of the occasion, a pig-killing, goes directly to the man he feels most securely – who is, in fact, the man killing the pig, hence the center of all that energy.

Where do they come from, where do they go – etc. Lovely the round and around of it, over and over and over. Delicious people – as the man, yesterday, in the coffee shop one's come to, for a coke, so dry in the goddamn mouth at that point, as it's time to go, notes the tape recorder, he's apparently the owner of the place, and asks what it is. Then, as he is told, shows in turn a watch he has on his wrist, which needs no winding, runs by means of an electronically stimulated 'vibration' – and says, listen to it. So that one puts it to the ear and hears a sharp, insistent, rather high-pitched humming. Like some incredible seashell.

Lovely all – days, the tiredness accumulating and time become phase of immediate temper and energy. Crazy wash and fall of water remembered as a kid, living then in Northeast Harbor, Maine – that endlessly insistent movement. Could never make any meaning of it. Whitman most to be respected in his sense of it, "Out of the cradle endlessly rocking. . . ." Not, god knows, the metaphor only, but the "cradle, endlessly, rocking. . . ." The words themselves that don't stop.

Would track along, down, otherwise, brooks – most in spring, would follow, thinking to come to some place they led to. Had somehow the conviction, though more felt then as simple feeling, 'they led some place'. Very intrigued by sense you could go from town to town, following brooks, which in turn became rivers, which in turn at last gained the sea. One winter, things so froze you could skate from West Acton to South Acton, on Teel's Brook, and did so, having to jump over branches and roots, and hummocks, had frozen at points in the ice, oneself and a friend, or possibly more, all the way, till at last it widens and you come to the pond that sits, or then did, under the railroad bridge, must have been a small factory there somewhere, and made a great space of ice. Back a year ago, very strange seeing that brook, could have been stepped over, with a slight hop, filled for the most part with a wavy marsh grass and cat tails, and occasional skunk cabbages too. All shrunk as somehow one hadn't really thought would be the case, though many indeed attest to it. Imagining life as growing, growing – into a giant, a huge illimitable form.

February 4, 1969

Voice from lovely nowhere – Art Murphy, young guy had set some poems, also worked with Williams' material, was at that time at Juilliard, friend of Paul Zukofsky's – was struck by what he'd taken to use, also the translation, into sound, really a spatial situation, of what the words were as material. Someone later saying it's like Webern? Perhaps – but how else does one come into it. It always sounds like something else, at first, then makes itself or else stops.

The dumdedumdum, dumdum, accents – can hear the prose sound same, up above there, "Voice from lovely nowhere. . . ." Always from lovely nowhere.

That girl saying, lovely exact face, quite long, that well-washed long blonde hair young ladies of good families do seem to favor, saying, she'd been at the Country Day School for ten years, over half her actual life, at this point. That was the family sense of the place, as the other woman said, we have the younger children come to these events, because we feel they are taught effectually by the experience of the older ones, and so on, and so. Or again, of the young lady – her teeth in bands, made her at times close her mouth, as one shared the seat, back, with her on the ride returning to the hotel, awkward a bit because of them – horrid things to put on teeth, in one's mouth, most awkward sans any question. Such a pleasant long straight nose, high forehead, good clear grey blue sort of eyes. All of them look usefully healthy, good breeders one thinks – not at all uglily.

But like Karen's crazy mut female dog, wispy, terrier, bristly hair, incredible energy of excitement, endless restlessness, provoked by any movement in a wild range of feelings – *that* has survived, leaped through, come without the breeding, just *made* it. Always moved god knows by that occasion, just the *luck* of it.

So back to Art, who's there in that same school now, for the same arts festival business, with Steve Reich, who is thus by the young people's bulletin identified: "STEVE REICH has been composer/performer at the San Francisco Tape Music Center, at Yale University and at the New School. . . ." Und so weiter.

Time really now insistent, e.g., in one hour, for example. Will that then be there forever? Where, etc. In one hour. In one hour there are sixty minutes, or then the division into seconds, but has to be place to be in one, or any, for that matter. I.e., when it's not in one hour, it will be in another.

Thought you'd like to hear so having a minute, would just drop a line. To say, thought you'd like to hear, so having a minute. So have a minute, thought, to hear. You'd like to. All that sort of stuff you never put anywhere anyhow, it just comes in, goes out, up and down, in and out the system, as Buckminster Fuller says – one thinks one heard that – Or music: Go in and out the system, go in and out the system, go in and out the system – Words then misplaced, forgotten, i.e., how it ends there. Something about roses, it seemed it was. Not a mulberry bush in any case.

He looked through them all and found no cases of mulberry etc. Case dismissed. Next case. That's television. But pleasant to think, would you please return that. Like, who's rerunning this business. Who's recharged here.

Such a card. Not comic however – nor intent to be. At all. Not at all funny. Ferlinghetti: if I told them my mother just died, they'd break up. The rest of the story is really another story. Well, his, among others, also hers, obviously, if she's implied as dying. Them too, since they're the ones got it started in the first place. If they hadn't laughed all evening, at anything he'd said, he wouldn't have said that. That wouldn't have been anything then to say, but something else. He said enough, surely, to make his point. At least it was understood, what he was saying, even if what he otherwise said was not. That's what it was all about.

February 5, 1969

SOMETHING THAT STICKS in mind, actually a familiar question – why are the arts insistent on technological possibility. But more, does writing involve that same interest – etc., etc. Etc. Of course. Etc. Phasing. System again, really – or wanting some information as to the context, call it, in which language is being experienced. Not simply to be told, like they say, to go to bed or whatever, but to have use of how one is hearing that, literally. Not 'psychologically' – but as physical situation. Always fascinated by Olson's movement – a literal situation of phrasing, manifest in the words. Or Duncan, almost like tape loops – in fact, very much like them, not at all 'metaphorically'. One of the people in the so-called class remarking Beethoven's means of working, not 'linearly' as, now this is to be done, now done, now that it is to be done, now that – but in a situation almost spatial (he was speaking of the drafts of the 5th symphony, of B's taking this from that, and putting it in there, then taking that out, putting in something else, so that the material was both an accumulation and a collection variably possible, i.e., could be 'shifted around' in a various formal situation, etc.) Too, John Linsley's interest to explore neural and physiological relations in language, to possibly make explicit Olson's proposals about breath and speech relations, and also the 'proprioceptive' – again much insistent on the contextual, as agency.

– Spill of names now, losing ability to identify who it is has been met, and now reappears. E.g., have apparently made arrangements to talk to a man, at noon, and find that it was actually two men, but go off with the first, leaving the second to arrive and find no one there – but happily no hurt feelings, like they say, but again, what can be the sense this man has, having made what seems to him an agreeably simple arrangement to meet for conversation, and he finds he's been mistaken for another man – who in turn is unaware of any of it. Must be some sense of his faintness, inability to make himself known to others – while the case is simply too many faces, voices, people, too much to thus locate and remember, as Allen once confronted by young man in someplace like San Francisco, who says, remember me?, can only answer, if your life did not actually involve mine in some intensive manner, some event of relation would make a focus for memory, I am afraid I really can't. And yet one obviously does want to be remembered, especially, by someone, as Allen, one very much admires and wants a place with. So he'd take them all, if he could, but it's just not possible. Bound to get lost in it, something inevitably left behind.

– One's own so-called identity becomes equally vague, so much is separated from how it is one would feel, or possibly act, with another company. Fact of sudden direct intimacies, call them, pushed on people in the most social of gatherings, just that that habit (at home) is so much the so-called case of one's way of being with others it 'will out' etc.

The lady speaking at dinner of, was it your father's book (this, to another younger woman there) that described his wife's intention not to have the children be fearful of their bodies by themselves going about naked in the house. The other answers, I was the only child, perhaps my uncle? No, it was your father's book – and then another woman speaks of their intent, hers, and her husband's, to do the same thing – and found their oldest daughter was extremely fearful, in school, of being nude in front of the other children, for showers, examinations, etc. All of that curiously awkward and false psychology, i.e., that proposes *a* must be followed by *b* – but so often misplaces what might be called the 'terms'. I didn't know it was loaded. No, he didn't even know it was a 'gun' –

But now. But "tired," still – what does that propose to describe? A so-called level of energy, possibly, a way of feeling the body respond, as going up and down stairs, shade of some sense possibly a cold is being contracted? For? Cigarettes very harsh – no 'desire' in the sense, really no sexual response to anything. The real comfort, moments before sleep, then also, just at waking. A grey-like warmth.

February 6, 1969

HOME NOW – a deep relaxation, of feeling, also a restlessness permeates much response, to others here, Sarah, Kate, or Bobbie. But the *physical* relief, the letting go – fucking, or eating, talking, moving about the house now in one's own body, a great need happily resolved.

Ron called last night to tell me of John's sudden, absolutely unexpected death. They had been together, with Billy Al Bengston, etc., at a party – later, as Billy Al and John left, apparently not long after John had a heart attack, dead shortly after if not then and there. Described as a "massive coronary". A very few years older than myself, perhaps one or two, but no more. Bobbie's saying, this will happen more frequently now, as a gauge obviously of what will be increasingly our own experience. As Frank O'Hara's death then. But neither does she mean, nor would I, some curious 'economy' of that possibility. Somehow I knew one would die when about eighteen, i.e., physically experienced that limit, and then came upon it again aged about thirty-five.

I couldn't feel a regret for John's death – he *was* dead, when I heard, instantly had become that somehow. What I felt myself relieved by was so close to that sense, of Allen's, "Death's let you out . . ." but not in sense of 'escape' but that it had occurred as an instant, merciful, in human sense, no long painful lingering of the knowledge of limit and impending death. I couldn't make that, couldn't at all, for a friend. Fear at times my mother, aunt, will be momently in that bitter economy. I *know* people die. Then let it be *quick*.

Elsewhere – a swirl somehow to things, to relationships. I sense the friends we do have here, really the one couple we might be utterly open with – not that others god knows don't prove friends also, but it is really that intuitive economy, that knowledge, of others I am speaking of – that things are hard for them, she's off to a job she much wants, needs, and will be respected by, as a visiting potter, he restless in himself, wanting reassurance therefore from another 'age', younger, or whatever, wants the casual perhaps. She is impatient with that, I sense. A funny, fucking world at times. So many – is it again some fact of 'biological' age? Or doddering fools. Or what the hell. I seem intent on making everything the condition, dependent, on everything else. Lovely note in Tom's letter: "I have just finished writing a paper for theo. on what truth was. I said it was relative naturally. . . ." He's had a history teacher he spoke of when visiting last month, who apparently had told him *all* condition of person could be described, and/or was determined, by terms of social, physical environment. That's ass-end-to, one wanted to say – just that it isn't known, or *what* isn't known, 'until later' (like what you may get for Xmas etc.), is *not* experienced in hindsight (or is only thus regarded) only. Even that banal story of the 'little locomotive', *I think I can, I think I can*, is preferable to that teacher's dreary and perhaps called for stoicism.

At last. Jim Dine writes: "i just returned from a football match, and i am frozen and bruised. my oldest son and i were thrown and crunched to the ground by a partisan crowd. these english are a queer bunch. . . ." Allen, also recent card: " "Leaky lifeboat" Gregory C. said about the body – it certainly doesn't stand up to the cosmic metal crunch – so maybe I'm all wrong about wanting to "feel" "good." Help! down the drain again! Gotta get new Metaphysics!. . ."

February 9, 1969

NAGGING SENSE of not having got to it yet, i.e., best done with in whatever manner it can be, before I fall off completely, at something like four in the afternoon. But had woke up so early, or equally from the other end, late, hardly able to keep eyes open etc. Not that bad really – just dazed, as driving down to the post office again, had hazy senses, at moments, the car was drifting, which it probably was. One thing interesting: stepping out to get to the car, i.e., out the door, had sudden sharp dusty smell, like the smell of a day, had not smelled quite like that for some time, years, in fact. It may be that smoking cigars only is proving its point, whatever it is, at least beyond impossibly burned mouth it seems from eight in the morning till whatever hour one goes to sleep.

Gabbling, really. Note all of this, i.e., e.g., etc., all seem to start with, I guess they are, noun clusters, what did they call them – substantive clauses. The one thing Santa isn't. Faint humor indeed makes the day even greyer, although the sun shines almost fiercely, despite so-called winter, and the blue of sky is almost metallically clear etc.

Bobbie and the girls coming in now, can hear them at other end of us (had meant to say "house") – Kate saying, "mommy," etc. Funny how they enter on a lean of some purpose, want, etc. Elsewise they are silent, and say nothing. She's also in now. Can hear her too, talking back. Sort of a scutter of sounds back there, makes a kind of pitch of babble against the tv, other end though closer, hence heard more distinctly, but also rejected, hence not.

Why woke so early, was sense, in dream, person I'd depended on to take and play tapes for classes, hadn't, so I then had to face either enraged (I doubt they would ever be so, for such reason – too sluggish about such expectations) or contemptuous students. That's a dream – faint sneering faces, "But I tried to help you!" Oneself pleading, "It was all I knew how to say!" Aie . . . Must be sense from previous years of teaching when at times the relation, with the Students, was almost of necessity a politic solicitude. Their parents the custodians, no, the owners, of possibility. They hired one etc. Or the so-called headmaster did, but was their servant also. The fact of what does happen persistently to teachers, all forms of it, no matter 'high' or 'low'. Remember at U.B.C. that summer, Allen meeting the visiting professors from Toronto, talking, then asking one, what he was doing – and the answer, "I'm only a teacher. . . ." Rank with self-contempt, so much so it sounds only faintly. His own imagination of its being the lowest of the low. So – what *does* that have to do with "Oh fathers and teachers. . . ." Another order of reality altogether. I can't imagine teaching from a feeling of self-contempt or even a sense one was worthless etc. Have obviously come close, in several very specific situations – as, for one, teaching in Guatemala where Joe would tell me, "The reason I pay that man more to run the *finca* store, is because he is worth more, it's more important etc." So that was that, or whatever it was – god knows. Joe must have driven himself finally too fast, into a box of some kind, he had a crazily persistent wish to kill himself – but almost gaily, it seemed, no real sadness in it, just an absolutely clear sense of 'ending it' that way. What was sad was his love for his wife, who couldn't, it so appeared at last, really 'credit' him with that feeling, or wouldn't, more accurately, accept it. She really didn't like him much. But I did, and so did Bobbie I think – there was a very human toughness, and perception, and gentleness to him. But I don't know finally, in that he was 'my boss' – an odd use of that possessive pronoun, as Bob B . . . once said. All said one way or another – I can't really believe it's more than a 'thing to be doing', and that's what it's all about. I.e., talking.

February 11, 1969

FADING OFF – mind rising, at best, much like fish used to, in bottom of pool, coming up slowly in a series of spiraling circles. When was that. West Acton, again. Somewhere back there – as though time were a distance, and it is most often, it seems, imagined as such, the fading wake, etc.

A brief catalog of plans, like they say: summer to be spent in the house in Annisquam, where we'd been two summers ago. Get out of this one – possibly sell it? Come June. Not much else in mind – no more thought of now to do, than what I sit here literally writing. So-called books about to be: *Pieces, A Quick Graph, The Charm.* Even to name such possibilities used to be like telling beads. Now, not so much.

What is that useful sense of the 'future' – viz, its occurrence resolves all conjecture. Words to that effect, i.e., on hands and knees trying to find book (P. W. Bridgeman's writing apropos, specifically the discussion of *time*), am confused by sense of where it should be, in the muddle of the bookshelves back of me, and then remember, or do I, Moe has it – something he wanted to read for himself there, respectably enough. But why not then get the damn thing back. Ah well again. *If* he has it to begin with. So it goes on, actually another 'track' from what the 'real' might be supposed to consist of – but which is so-called which, and where is it one is, in either. Or elsewhere. I get now altered sense of, "But that was in another country. And besides, the wench is dead. . . ." Like Olson's report from Whorf of Hopi sense: what's happening over *there* cannot be accepted as happening at the same time as what's happening *here.* Space is a time modifier. Try catching a train that ain't there.

Through the wall, hear in a curious intimacy – in the pleasant almost cubicle of the workroom I have, Donovan's singing, Sarah playing it. She's probably in the kitchen, or in Asia – having seen to that. But no, sudden lift of her own voice, singing just over his, through the wall. Now she must be putting another record on, hear her moving it, and what's she's done is to replay the one just heard. I love that sense, though obviously its real occasion might be hopeless indeed, of making scratching noises, or banging, to be heard through walls, rock, that "I hear them!" Awful when the fact of men caught in a collapsed mine shaft. Awful, as kid, that one must have been somewhere in Pennsylvania, days it lasted, crazy scratching kind of possibility. "*I hear them!*" Somehow hope contained still in the utterly hopeless fact of something. Time passes.

The man met briefly in Lake Forest, at the Deerpath Inn, we were all having lunch, speaking of Poe's house in Baltimore I think. How it was in poor repair, should be some sort of state concern or whatever to keep it in repair – but what he then described as Poe's bedroom, and how one got to it, a very actual garret not permitting one to stand, not him at least, reached by a stair so low and so constricted he was on his hands and knees in order to squeeze through, into it. And Poe's young wife then on the floor below, to which the stairs led apparently, and the woman attached (aunt?) in bedroom adjacent not even separated from the wife's room, but more in the order of a sitting room adjoining. All there: the claustrophobic sense of enclosure, the paranoia about being surprised in some act.

Imagination of one's own life. Boat still? A thing taken in hand, found there – what one could do with oneself, all the sexual echo, or implication, of that. No wonder the head and heart got separated – one had to be left outside. Anyhow – not for long, at all, at all. Or goes on thinking, in the night, hours after, *working* – which has root somewhere back there in to 'make sacrifice'. It's the same.

February 12, 1969

"To tell what subsequently I saw, and what heard. . . ." Williams – also like Allen's "What did I notice? Particulars!"

Brought again and again to fact of, what is it – here, there. The time of it. Agency's modality, i.e., my own.

Conversation: what will you have for lunch, Alan. We don't eat lunch, Alan. . . . Unexpected visit now, he'd come flying in apparently last night around five, from NYC – there with John, I guess. Anyhow a simple man to get on with, and with an interesting condition, like they say – the habits, orders, of a wealthy Englishman – Irishman, more literally, as he would remind one, etc. Having just put his rented car, a Mustang, on edge of bank backend of house (here), so it's all about to slide down same, happily now moves it sans problem – and is off to park it elsewhere. Contrast I keep thinking of, that is, his intent of a couple of years ago, to make movie in Yucatan centered on Maya – and ends up with John making *The Secret Life of Hernando Cortez* starring Taylor Mead and Ultra Violet. Like, some resolution of that hope. Have not seen film – though think I'm old enough – which is, apparently, interminably fucking in variety of situations, places, etc. Talking to John at Xmas, he says: objectifying, reifying, all that range of sexual fact – so as to 'place' it, so as to see it as there, etc. Something like that. Céline, early in novel (*Castle to Castle*), makes point: words make pricks soft. Cock softer. Mullen-sucker. Bong-banger. Ideas are not always appropriate, no more than the sun shines forever where the sun is always shining. Thinking: that bit of Zukofsky's, "a dog that runs never lies down. . . ." "A dog, *that* runs, never lies down. . . ." He says. I was thinking: *that* runs, and the dog keeps on lying down? And did you get the license plate number sir etc. How about a sir etcetera and a glass of mud. Two over lightly, and fork.

Anyhow *that* Alan is here, the other Alan – there are many Alans in the world at one time, but only one by one do they seem evident – or ask the queston: will all those named Alan please signify by raising their right hand. No one does, i.e., no one here other than Bob, Robert, Bobby, boy man – Boyman. Willie Boyman. You put your little foot right here, and your left foot right here, and your right foot right here, and there. Burble through walls again. The one so-called constant. The other Alan saying, in NYC a winter ago – the psychic energy of so many people in the buildings surrounding, can literally feel the weight of its force, pushing on him etc. Squeezing his head possibly into shape of insufficient turnip. A lone blade of grass on a broken sandhill. Echoes. The pun they couldn't kill. Eccos. Necco wafers. Thinking of 'future' – somewhere in time and space there awaits some number like fifteen people, various sorts and sizes, expect to be dealt with in some manner for period of two hours – in roughly two hours.

Gap then of some fifteen, twenty minutes – no evidence of same immediately clear, to me at least. So could write one word, say, wait ten minutes, twenty, hour, hours, day, days, weeks, months, years, – but there the limit does begin to be manifest, like they say – and so on. No one the wiser. And what would be 'hidden' – in some intent – to begin with? Ho, ho. You thought I just wrote it straight out, like. But I didn't. I wrote one word. Waited five days. But think of the arithmetic and/or is it *possible*, mind you, is it possible to write (how much?) in what length of time, given that means of proceeding. Can we *wait* for it. Would you rather sit in the car. Are you tired, of waiting. What, are you waiting for? Why wait. A simple downpayment secures your order.

February 13, 1969

THE MESCALIN CLEARED out a lot of gunk, just that tensions and an almost active depression apropos the time now to be got through before we can leave had become increasingly difficult to deal with. We went – Bobbie and I – first to meet Bill Merwin and company for dinner. No one showed for about a half hour, which was pleasant enough, i.e., Bobbie had spent most of the afternoon getting through a birthday party for Kate (which also went happily), and I went over to their school, to talk to kids interested in writing, etc. So the time in the restaurant, waiting for the others, was a useful chance to unwind. Then, after the reading – the kids now at their grandmother's for the weekend – we went to a party back in Placitas, then came back to our house about twelve or so, and decided to take the mescalin.

I wasn't sure just how much would be needed, but wanted to avoid the awful dragging waiting of the previous business of the acid given us about a month before – which must have been mostly 'speed' and left me particularly with a frustrated sense of nothing ever really taking off. Like waiting in the bus station, for the damn bus that never get there. Anyhow this time, wisely or not, I took what we had, some six pills of one batch, and two of another, and split them, and we took them all. Wisely enough – since any less would have been another drag, and as it was, we had mainly four to six hours of useful float, mainly verbal – in fact, without visual shifts of any marked order at all – and a great sense of a cleaning out of tensions, and then a very happy sense of inner peace and relaxation. Too, I loved the intensity of verbal play – even to lovely physical experience of words' sound in my head and mouth. Very happy clarity. Later, – it must have been nine or ten in the morning – Bobbie went then to sleep, and I spent about four hours sitting in the livingroom listening to records and reading – Sappho, for one, which book I must have had for almost a year without really reading it. Then Beckett's poems, as:

> what would I do without this world faceless incurious
> where to be lasts but an instant where every instant
> spills in the void the ignorance of having been
> without this wave where in the end
> body and shadow together are engulfed. . .

What becomes – to my own mind deeply useful – so explicit with either mescalin, or acid, is the *finite* system of the *form* of human-body life, i.e., that that phase, call it, of energy qua form is of no permanent order whatsoever, in the single instance, however much the species' form is continued genetically, etc. That night, with the mescalin, I had insistently in my head this earlier poem of my own, called "The Skeleton":

> The element in which they live,
> the shell going outward until
> it never can end, formless,
> seen on a clear night as stars,
> the term of life given them
> to come back to, down to,
> and then to be in
> themselves only, only skin.

Which had then the edge of obvious irony, previous to that information I've been talking about – but now is altogether the obvious and yet sans edge of fear any longer, or even so-called regret. That the 'I' can accept its impermanent form and yet realize the energy-field, call it, in which it is one of many, also *one*. Nothing, in that sense, as Louis says, can ever leave.

February 16, 1969

ALL THE PLEASURE of the last two days somehow lost as tedium recurs, the week starts again – though the weather is good, in fact, dazzling, sharp blue sky, springlike. The house somehow on us, on me – and I land it on Bobbie – as *thing* now makes an impossibly heavy limit as to what can be next. Sits as dead center for endless self-depression. I feel disloyal to it, having had such pleasure in it, earlier. Must be literal *fact* of so-called objects is unacceptable. That nothing can be held on to, and that which holds on in reverse – as this house is now somehow our 'responsibility' – is deadlier than attachments the other way round. Like children who never leave home.

But more to the point – I hate leaving. I hate what was the hope of something proving thus limit and dilemma. I hate damn baggage one gets willynilly attached to, and then has to push off, each time a little more restlessly, yet with less energy in that act. I feel a deadly tiredness, and what prove 'solutions' and/or small victories of so-called intention are inevitably the same dreary accumulation and drabness. There's nothing comes of it. Children don't grow to succeed their parents' ambitions. Nothing has that pattern in any sense one can respect. This morning, driving back here from the city, I picked up two kids, like tattered gypsies, seeming about 16 or so – 'on the road' and headed for the hippy community just above us, The Lower Farm. Despite the fadedness, already, of both of them, the kind of vague, passive excitement – the 'lore' of their situation, and the half-furtive manner they at times use as address – at least they are in the world unequivocally, I mean they are literally on the road, in a fact of their own bodies, literally somewhere. No imagination of them ever quite gets them there elsewise – certainly not that of their parents with mom's tears and dad's irritation. Fuck 'em all. . . .

Were one to change, so to speak – the impulse would be so

located, just to drop the whole fucking mess of such context. Let damn well go of it. Is life, so to speak, like the village idiot who's given a job polishing the town's cannon, in the square, and then saves all the money given him – finally gives up the job, and when asked why, says, he's now bought his own cannon. Would that be the best of its apparent occasion – "self-action," as Olson would say. Seeing this morning, in a letter, title of an earlier book of Tom Raworth's – *The Relation Ship* – but what about Lawrence's death ship, "The Ship of Death": "The apples falling like drops of dew/to bruise themselves an exit from themselves. . . ." Something of that onus in the house, itself now some curious scab of previous condition, to be shed like that, picked off and got rid of – no longer a place made clear in living, at all.

Cage's sense again, that motels suffice as 'homes' – that all the locatable shell of usual existence has to break down, and be let go of – all that impinges so insistently as purpose, gain, success in intention. Fearful, one realizes the house as shared vocabulary – that each time one's let go of, all its accumulated resonance falls too. What then to move to, but the place of whatever renewal of energies seems to be possible? Isn't that why, in this point of age, there is fear of losing relationship, being 'dropped', just that the place one can make for another diminishes as energies also do – or seem to, except as frustration provokes them – sad, sad echo of Dennie's poem: "We have not spoken of these tired/risings of the sun. . . ." Or the fantasies, my own so often, of Bobbie's shift off from me sexually, to someone else – not as it used to be, in my head, almost a warcry of belligerent suspicion, i.e., a rush of anger and dismay – but now, half-curious, in my mind, a sense of provision, a sly shift, an acknowl-edgment of my own change of condition. An accommodation without alternatives.

February 17, 1969

INSISTENT BREAKUP of forms, things. Sister calling this noon, or a little after, mother had called her from Florida, unlikely it now seems that Aunt Bernice will survive. Eighty-five she is, having still insistently told the doctor (even now) she's seventy-

six. The women draw together I sense – though Helen says
mother had mislaid, understandably, my telephone number
(which I'd sent her again only a few days previous). So Helen
will go, must now be enroute there – and I'm to call on Friday,
when it will be noon there, to see how things are. My mother
apparently much upset now, crying on the phone, Helen said –
she'd been, previously, such an adamant containment of her
emotions, must have been trained to that both by having been
a nurse, and also, when my father died, the necessity of carrying
on, not showing what must have been her actual situation. Not
necessarily a poverty thereby enforced – but bleak, surely, at
times, not to let go, let it wash out, in an openness of other
people, her literal family.

She's old now too. Can't be much less than Aunt Bernice, and
Helen says, on the phone, she must now think of herself as next
– that damn history again, the chronological – though it so
rarely proves the actual sequence, as my own father's death
would demonstrate, or John Altoon's – or so many, from the
war, or otherwise. The chance, that changes all of it. There's
no listing proves the way it has to be as 1, 2, 3, etc.

I don't know. I don't feel grief as yet. Helen says she is not
conscious, recognizes no one apparently. I like her, love her,
almost shyly. No real occasion, like they say, we should have
such feeling for one another – but what I sensed in her, I
think, even as a boy, was that she really liked men – was that
incorrigible though proper coquette. Delighted doctors, among
others – "your sister is quite a lady. . . ." That kind of report
our mother would then tell us of, later. The care she took with
herself, in that sense – despite the awkwardness of the colostomy,
for her of all people – her, not daintiness, but very literal femi-
nity. Her impatience, with either self-indulgent sentiment or any
attempt to get round some actual state of feeling. Sneer, she
would – very truly. Tough – yet respectful, somehow, of actual
innocence in men, that tender state – as my Uncle Ward, despite
the impatience she often seemed to feel with him, his unwitting
sillinesses, and his dogged loyalty to his previous and very much
dead first wife – he had named their daughter Thoreau – which
drove her up the wall with irritable impatience. But never, I
felt, simply she wanted someone to lean on – wanted really,
always, more than that, a context, one might say – a man. Was

discreet, but had to have one, unlike my mother somehow –
who made other adjustments, having children, ourselves. And
density of persons, at first at least, the job – with all the various
patients – then the household, with Theresa (the girl effectually
rescued from home for the feeble-minded by my father, who
comes to work for us, then, after his death, stays on, and is
really the closest and most stable person I have to relate to, as
a daily event in the house, all the years I'm growing up). Then
grandmother, grandfather – both lovely, tough people – my aunt
much their complex, grandfather's will and emotion, grandmother's will and wit (which, though seemingly cold, I can
remember as a very actual smile, to herself often, of what charms
both awkwardness and its concomitant humanness do combine).
A deeply decent, straight woman – makes both my mother and
aunt, and the humanity of my Uncle Will – who was the happy
nature somehow, of that family, as my uncle, younger, Uncle
Hap(py), was very decisively not. His the will elsewise: five
years our next-door neighbor, with his sullen family, decides on
impulse and 'reason' not to speak to me, myself aged about 14
forward. Aunt Bernice never accepted that shit, bless her. She
knew.

February 19, 1969

BACK HERE YESTERDAY, about three or so – come from Salt Lake,
first east across the mountains to Denver, then down, so that
we come in over Taos, then down following the mountains to
Albuquerque. A deep wash of nostalgia. Upland meadows,
bowls, filled now with snow. A scale that much attracts me, a dry
asperity to things, distances – a great range of space, horizontally
balanced.

Then, having drunk some on plane, at home continue, in somewhat desultory manner, and turn on when Bobbie's gone to the
store – a float then, which lasts much of the evening, going on,
with brief time at Bill P's house, having gone down, Bobbie and
me, with Steve Katonah and friends. Sitting all in front of big
tv set, like a fire – two lovely kids, girls, about six and three –
hierarchal look to each, the older, sharp, very tense quick look,
likes being placed in mind games, e.g., that everything in my

house is named 'Creeley.' The younger, blonde with classic short braids, great apple cheeks, very alert kid – and finally both come up close to where I'm sitting on the floor, make themselves beds of blankets and sleeping bags, curl up by my legs, and I can reach over to tuck them in. Sharp insistent nostalgia, then, for that age of children – so open, simple to address.

Then back here – again sexual insistence I feel, wanting to fuck on and on, the fantasies, again, of Bobbie being fucked by others, an orgy in my own head – till she falls off to sleep, myself too.

In the night, wake several times with terrific dryness, mouth, body – probably the drinking, though have smoked endless amounts of so-called grass. Which continues into the night, i.e., into dreams, so at one point there is very vivid sense of being in what seems a small town, with John Altoon, Bobbie, one or two others I can't now identify or remember. Sense of lane going down to houses, a little like Mallorca – whites and blues, green of trees, grass at edges of cobblestone-like paths. We are talking about impending bust, there's been word of it – waiting, in half-sense, for arrival of police. We expect them to come in one or two cars, probably black, to get out and 'look around'. We anticipate being object of their curiosity, like they say. But have, somehow, a very desultory sense of any impending hang-up, rather, it's something we should pay attention to, but since it isn't now the case, hasn't 'got here' yet, it's hard to do anything. Too, sense of waste somehow in getting rid of the pot before there is literal occasion – however hopeful that obviously is, which, in dream, is also part of our thinking. Then John, first in conversation with Bobbie, apropos her work, talking of senses of painting. Looking then at drawings he's been doing, sense of looking at them right then and there, in the open – a great portfolio, call it, of them, in large dimensions he worked with – great boards, etc. And insistence, his, from time to time, *that's pencil* – which at first I'm confused by, and then see he means it's done of a piece, so to speak, all at once – which he must relate to working in pencil. And one with various trees, one, in particular, dead center, he points to and says, *that's sincerity* – which I take as meaning, that's as much tree as was possible to realize there, that's all of it, all at once, all I see. And it is – i.e., is crazily intensive seeing, and all *at once*. He speaks of fact he does not work comfortably in 'accumulating' the image, has to be 'all at once'. He is so present, in the dream, it becomes for me like other times I remember talking with him, and what measure of things then came of it continuingly. I see why paint was always (or in some ways) hang-up for him, too slow for what he was doing. As times in Mallorca he was mixing pigments as he worked, finally just dumping turpentine on piles of dry pigment, not even looking so intent he was on the canvas.

My aunt – goodbye. Also John. She had written poem for George Washington's birthday, for paper – would have been printed two days after. She had that 'thing to do.'

February 23, 1969

SOMETHING PROPOSED in time and space – then, as you'd say – but not as consequence, rather a point of time. But *time* and *space* may well be subjective impressions, like they say. And why not. Speaking of the several 'I's' so to speak, the habit of saying, what did you think you were, and I answers. Phil Whalen's poem, "Self Portrait In Another Direction" – was an instruction of that time. The layers, but more, the place of where one is, in what constituted, etc.

All of that – tired, a little, against some drag, insistent, of having to get somewhere. Not here. Only included in the action, nothing elsewise 'to be'. It was to be some accumulated so-called 'record' – 'some of my time. . . .'

How to know it. Most real measure now in mind is the saw which the Ainsworths had hanging on the wall in their kitchen in North Lisbon, New Hampshire, of the father, dead by that time – the one he'd made and used. The way such saws were made – first, finding the specific wood for the frame, letting it season, soaking it to get the arch, shaping with knife, etc. Then the saw blade, filed from steel band. The saw become specific to the man using it. Is that sentimental. Going by motels – would there be any use in knowing the specific lives have been lived in them. Or suburbs. Or any such generalization. As against the abandoned cellar holes in woods in New Hampshire, up roads themselves no longer in use. One had sense of the lives that had been there. Or sites of Indian pueblos – a specific locus, a situation that must have been more than coincident.

Two senses, really – the so-called 'individual' and the species group. This is for your own good. Bigger than both of us. But I like it. Back and forth, in some endless interchange, apparently (but of no actual?) necessity. The consciousness *thinks* it has experience of this or that. Conceptualizes. Like Alpert's note of the ratio between conceptual units and the content admissible in perception, something like 1 to 20,000 per second. Itself a somewhat unwieldy 'idea'.

Going to sleep. Waking up. Moving. Waking with stomach ache, sudden premonition of death – probably echo of the past weeks and fear of one's own 'time'. What would it be like. Nothing much – certainly nothing you can live in. Aunt's apparent tiredness. Doctor's sense, she didn't want to try to continue living. Better – she knew what she didn't want to do anymore. Arrangements within self, rapport with the surrounding. Keep it moving. Can *thinking* be prior to action, *is* an action, etc. Never felt one would or could think of something previous to its 'circumstances' and/or recognition. Couldn't somehow 'get ahead' of it. Always in situation of 'seeing it' now that 'it's' there.

Go to sleep. Different situation. Time to, go to, sleep. Time to wake up. No time, moving along – no sense of it, no concern. Time enough. But she got caught in it. Whoever she was. Get it over with. Can't wait for this to happen forever. Nor need you. "Relax and die. Be born! Be born!" How to get somewhere without trying, and *where* is somewhere, etc.

In airport in Denver, lined up with people, about eight in the evening, to take plane to Salt Lake – our category is clear enough, we are going somewhere, for various reasons, in various condition of age, income, etc., in various experience. But all, or genetically all, with eyes, ears, nose and throat. Etc. Tired of dying. Wanted only a trace. A sense of deer tracks, or rabbit – out there, in the snow. Sentimental – thought full of feeling. Welcome, stranger! Come in the door with bag in hand, smiling. Anyone. Anywhere.

February 26, 1969

Sun's intensity at the window much like the day it all began.

Crazy washed-out red, not a pink – but a white red. Must be seven-thirty or so, the day beginning, the kids now off to school and Bobbie returned to bed. Quite quiet – but for stoves cracking, as they light or cool. Hum, it must be, from the refrigerator in the kitchen. Now light of lamp looks very white as other light to the left floods the table. . . .

Had thought of sending, messages, of a sort, information from whatever system it is that one is, *keep sending* – Burroughs' 'back to base. . . .' No 'over and out' as yet, no completion finally of anything. No rest in it, no shape certainly, nothing to do but be doing it. Image of lone telegraph operator, da da dee, da da. Through the long night, so-called. The train roaring toward the trestle, god knows in what hopeless condition, the sagging etceteras. Will help arrive in time.

No help either. Image of person with carefully balanced bunch of packages, another says, oh, let me help you, moves to do so, and because his enthusiasm, or some benighted sense of what he's about to be able to do, makes him unable to recognize what the kingpin of the whole mess is, he so shifts it, in grabbing, the whole bit falls to the ground. Instantly.

Someone saying, someone in Southern Methodist University no less, *The Finger* is too loose. How's that for surrealism by the dozen. Myself was another man, in another country. Or better, that kind of address, years later, of, sir, your son is stepping on our daughter. Get him off. Not possible in that all the skin changes, every seven years – no relative of mine. Law of eternal transcendence.

Back to base. In closing moments already clear in night's dream, a bicycle of some order, now faded, something about some people, a sense of turning occasion. Down the hill.

What the fuck do they think it is. For ages hence? "No thought, of it, but such, pleasure, all women, must be in her, as you." It's clear enough. I do keep looking, in that sense. Out. In. God knows why except that nagging sense of responsibility is somehow still adamant.

So explain myself, to myself. For that you couldn't be blamed, but in other respects, or literally this one, you did not perform in agreement with either your intentions or your stated obligations. But *how* – i.e., dead, does that still 'obligate'? *Outside*, the quotation mark? Was my father, like they say, a deadbeat? He was dead without question. Was that wrong. Now son makes deathly silence, in return, as though he were the tradition somehow of that deadening silence. Retribution of some order one hadn't given a thought to. They won't speak to me either way. In time. But 'myself' am system of an endlessly proliferating consequence. At least I won't live to see the end of it, any more than did Philip, the elder of my two half-brothers, dead of some cause, and Tom, the younger, now with a store in Miami Beach somewhere. How did they know about it – when they started off in Watertown, Massachusetts. What was the 'hidden factor' then. No, they, at least the older, would 'rather be right' than 'wrong' and no doubt was, all his life. At least it was his without question – it never came this far.

So of course there was an end to it, even as it began. That's what's always known – you feel it even as you feel anything, beginning, you have that uncanny, under sense, it will end, I can feel it, the wind, already, drops a little, a waver, something clear enough. But that hardly makes one not want to go, so I always have and will, etc. It's nothing new, wanting to be included.

February 27, 1969

Presences

A Text for Marisol

1 · 2 · 3
2 · 3 · 1
3 · 1 · 2
1 · 2 · 3
2 · 3 · 1

Classicism is based on presence.
It does not consider that it has come
or that it will go away; it merely
proposes to be there where it is.
DONALD SUTHERLAND

1 · 2 · 3
One

BIG THINGS. And little things. The weight, the lightness of it. The place it takes. Walking around, it comes forward, or to the side, or sides, or backward, on a foot, on feet, on several feet.

There is a top, and a bottom. From the one to the other may be a distance. Equally it may be so dense, or vaporous, so tangential to touch, that an inextricable time passes in the simplest way. If it were to fall, either over, or up, or down, what spaces were there to accomplish would be of necessity measured later. Time runs to keep up, in other words. Already days have apparently gone by in the presence of one.

This is the first time he has spoken in some time, in weeks, in fact. The mouth was, or had been in the sense of what was seen, sealed over with some sort of substance, waxy in look, and, touching it, the feeling was of something sticky, as sticky rubber or sticky gum. This substance, translucent, made the lips seem preternaturally large. Very, very large. To which a footnote: *"He bore a preternatural resemblance to his caricatures in the evening newspapers"* (Evelyn Waugh). But his lips had been sealed. Sealing wax then. Had not someone, possessed of a stamp describing an intricate sphinx, therein and on imprinted that image, on his lips? A cruel, thoughtless joke possibly. The person who did this one thinks of as caring little for others. It must have been an evening, when this occurred. There was nothing else to do insofar as the day had come to nothing. It was rainy, a little chill to the air. One wanted the sun, the sun. There was a beach. Small figures at one far end of it, never quite clear in their detail. Somewhat clifflike rocks surrounded. High above, there seemed to be an open space, which might have been the sky, and yet, in the inexorably close weather, it had to be assumed. Top and bottom, the world?

What was he doing on the beach? No, it was a chair he sat in. He continued to sit in the chair. As if he had been thrown there. He had been thrown there. His small, unobtrusive body lay crumpled against one of the arm rests and his eyes, photographic blurs of grey, were pleading, mutely. In a book of the same order, so to speak, of the ungenerous kinds of people who do not love but nonetheless expect to be loved. Why was he forsaken? He was not. He was placed, in a place.

She picked him up and threw him into another place. His little seersucker coat tightly hugged the space under his arms, his armpits, and his diminutive body became rumpled with the impact of being elsewhere. His tie, however, fell straight, undisturbed. Always the gentleman. Being alive, she felt contempt but moved away from it to get some ice from the refrigerator. This, as one says, she put into glasses which she then filled with gin.

The glass was very large. The ice cubes were huge blocks of solidified water.

•

X SPOKE of having been wakened by sirens towards the middle of the night. Then assumed the police were abroad. In a town of eight hundred people, at midnight, so that they might be coerced into subservience and made to comply with the police imagination of a decent order. Awful. Y wrings hands and wonders why, why. There is, was, a full moon. Perhaps that is why the police have chosen that night? Later Z tells story of being roused at five to answer fire alarm and when they got there, find empty house now gutted with flames, and they are helpless to do more than water down the outbuildings, the barns, and watch the house burn into the rosy dawn. Z lifts the bottle to drink, and becomes, languorously, the sucking, lips smoothed over the nozzle. The nuzzle. The puzzle. The police.

In a free country, in a country where police enter the imagination as free, free agents, their uniforms are very blue and their badges very large and silver. They make a glittering array, formally. From any point not occupied by them, we see, as few, or others, or many. They may be the same. It is their way of dress that disarms that which stands as us. They can't stand us? Nobody comes, having none. Z recalls Wrentham, Massachusetts at the time of the 1938 hurricane in which many elms fell, a sadly stalwart army. He is puzzled that they all do not fall in the same direction, to point the same way. But interlace, across the streets, holding hands or limbs. All day the wind roars. They wait outside, to see what the next move will be. We include them. We take them outside. They have died many times before or else have moved away, into other towns, and take off their sad uniforms, one by one, and lay down at last in holes which they have dug in the earth. It is sad, to think of autumn, and the wind blowing, and the elm trees having leaves blown off, and the police and us moving to other towns and taking off our uniforms. We prefer fire. We would that it were firemen we were. We were.

Big firemen. Little firemen. In the flames they are dancing. *Fire delights in its form.* Firemen delight in their form? Inform us, policemen. We call upon them to inform us. Hence all the beatings and the shootings and the putting into closed places behind doors. Firemen and snowmen share other fates, the one burning, the one melting. Snow delights in its form, being mutable. It is the immutable that despairs. At least for a time, for any other time, for all time, for bygone times, for times past, for time enough, for in time. Time will tell.

The clock, on the wall, walks to the door. The door, in the wall, walks to the stair. The stair, up the wall, walks to the window, both ways.

X speaks of which way the road should be one way, whether to go up the hill, which results in the grinding roar of motors and less speed. Or down the hill, which results in the smoothing lag of motors and more speed. Principles of activity are first. Because they are first, they are not second, and so what is second has uniquely the condition of being first, in that respect. Or if what is first is not second, then the first of being second is to be the first second. There are sixty seconds in a minute but no firsts. The first second is that moment when the gun is

caused to fire, and whatever activity it signals to begin, does
begin. That is the first second. The second second is the one
that comes after. In the ritual of *count down*, there is a curious
reversal experienced as five, four, three, two, one. Five. Four.
Three. Two. One. Note that one is not only not first, or second,
but last, which is immutable, therefore despairs. Being neither
first, nor second, nor even fifth, which in other worlds it might
be in that hope might there exist, it is the last one. Despair is
the absence of hope. X speaks of the despair of the road being
presently both ways. There is no way to go on a road that goes
always. One way will not be another way.

X speaks of the necessity of deciding, before the police come.
We call the firemen and they come. They have uniforms too but
they do not all have them or they do not have all of them. The
uniforms have whatever firemen they have and so do the
firemen. There is instantly, first and second, a relaxation of
tensions. They fight fire, for example, but though they burn,
they do not fight themselves. We all burn and enjoy the paradox
of firemen. Snowmen melt, with the first soft breeze, with the
trickle of freshening water, with the budding crocus, with the
warmth returning. *Où sont les neiges d'antan?* Oh, watery bodies!
X speaks of the road on which snow has never fallen. Oh,
trackless wastes, oh, driving snow. You have driven away from
us, melting friend, wet hand. Your gentle, fluttering flakes must
live in other climes. A hill elsewhere.

This is the despair of being none, or last, or first. Upon that
trackless waste, faceless, upon a hill in Darien, Connecticut
where the traffic is endless, the cars immutable albeit they rust,
both ways. The traffic goes all ways. Call the police, please.

Call the president. He is first, and second to none. His road
goes one way and the cars go slowly, thoughtfully, upon it. The
snow falls upon it and the snowmen come. The firemen come
and the house burns. The wind blows. The elms fall down,
pointing one way. Melting away.

Y speaks of other needs, bodily needs, needs of the mind. She
wears two hats, of which one is put upon another, but each is
first. Her head is small and comfortable. Her hair is long and
brown. Her hats are black and brown. Her eyes are brown, her

dress is brown, her feet are brown, her house is burning. Call the firemen.

Please. Call the police please.

•

How do you know someone? These typical meetings, and all the people that come of them and to them. The rain on the roof makes a persistent, nostalgic pattering and the music seems a faintly saccharine sadness and he sits with that expected catch in the throat, thinking back and back. He wants to locate a specific place he thinks to remember, and also the company of that afternoon, a then pleasant woman he had known at first almost casually and then with increasingly confused desperation.

It is a somewhat flat place, this area, with unobtrusively present trees in designed patterns. It seems to him that a discretion of paths leads to a common center at which point occurs a statue of some sort, of a person, modestly contained. It is not, as he recalls, a soldier or figure of that sort. Rather, it seems to him a man who is standing, but possibly sitting, with hands rather close to the body, although extended. But there is no assertion, either of offering or of taking, in the gesture.

They have chosen a bench adjacent to the statue and now look out upon the diversity of the regular paths coming to this one center. There seem to be hedges, in his memory, but again they make no abrupt intrusion upon the view. They are of such height and substance that they permit sight of those approaching, or retreating, from approximately the waist, or in some cases the chest, of persons thus passing to and fro. Children are seen as specific heads and at times raised arms or active gestures of one sort and another. It is all very quiet in tone. The sky is typically English, as one says, a severely grey overcast although rain falls only as a drizzle, and this occurs but rarely.

It is comfortable, to be sitting here. The rain seems forgotten, the music fades. Their comfort is secure as they sit, and they have eaten but shortly before and done the divers things they had thought to, a phone call or two as also the mailing of his several letters.

There are also birds, distinctly. He cannot remember of what kind, precisely, since they also take place in this grey condition and have neither size nor plumage that would make them appear distinctive. Possibly they are pigeons of the common variety, grey checks or bars with occasional splashes of dull white. If there is an occasional red, it is so flattened by both birds' condition and the greyness that it becomes as if one with the others. Or they are sparrows, unobtrusively fluttering and pecking, almost noiseless.

There is much to talk about, it seems, but for the moment they are content to sit. Quite probably he has taken her hand, or she his, and they lean back together against the bench's support. The hour argues no necessities, and for this moment the complexities of what either considers their lives are in abeyance. Think, then, of a muted calm much like the edges of lakes at twilight.

Looking, he sees, marked by the hedges, the line of the people coming and going. For a moment, one in particular appears as a head only, but it is not a child's. It has a decided mustache, carefully clipped, and wears on its head a homburg. He looks as intently as he dares but realises that the man is becoming aware of his staring, so turns quickly to look elsewhere. In the new direction he sees nothing untoward for some time. Children, with their nurse, whom they are exhorting in clear, high voices to accompany them to the statue, are the only immediate presences. Reassured, he follows them with his eyes, so that he finds himself with them, as a group, centered upon the statue. But this also, he recognises, has changed. As the children come up to it, the youngest, a boy, climbs up on its slight pedestal, then stands upright, holding on to the statue's back. Remarkably he seems to tower above it, and waves to the nurse, and the two small girls who must be his sisters, to see him in his new vantage. The nurse calls the boy down, impatiently, seemingly irritated that the public monument might be injured in some way.

Here the rain has now stopped and moments ago the kitten was playing on the bed, then moved about the small room until it mewed to be let out again. The music has changed to "Back in the Saddle Again. . ." by Gabby Hayes. He is discomforted by both sides of the reality, the mirror. He had not remembered the place so vividly as he now seemed to. There are patches of

wet steam on the lower panes of the windows. The flame of the
small pipelike stove burns blue. The light beside his right hand
makes an intensive center of illumination upon the paper. Something like that. He lights a cigarette again.

It was in memory that this scale of things shifting was particularly interesting to him. He knew of those constructed rooms
used for purposes of psychoanalytic research in which perspec-
tives may be altered to accommodate the patient's experience
of the spatial relationships of substances on an apparently fixed
plane of reference. But he could not remember, now, whether it
was the father whose chair grew large, in perspective, or was it
the father himself? The room tilted. That door, so looming, was
actually the measure of a small box. He could see everything.
There were no darknesses despite the greyness of the weather.
But the scale was insistently changing. She continued to have
his hand in her own and both sat without speaking, in a pleasant
quiet. He was curious to know whether or not she had been also
witness to what now so displaced him despite its lack of threat.
The boy, certainly, was none, was, in fact, charming, with his
red cheeks and alert movement. Although he could not see him
as clearly, hidden, in a sense, as both now were back of the
statue, with only the nurse's torso fully apparent, the girls too
he found cheering.

He reviewed his initial sense of the place. Its absence in time
gave it curiously vague location finally but by a process of
pacing, in his mind, he felt himself to have placed it with some
accuracy. If one moved that way, then the street was along the
path a short walk's distance. If left, then again a street appeared
in a relatively brief time. The park itself he saw as basically a
square whose diagonals were the paths, or the major ones
because he thought there were possibly two others whose direction ran parallel to the outline of the park itself, composing two
smaller squares, in that way, within it. He was sure that hedges
outlined all the paths and that there were also trees at various
intervals, in fixed pattern, and that flowers grew, in discreet
beds, at various points but these he could not give decisive place
to. In like confusion he could not distinctly remember the color
of his friend's dress, or coat, or whether she sat to his left or to
his right. He was reluctant to disturb their own quiet and so
said nothing to her.

People continued passing up and down the various walks. He found that he could continue to watch them without their awareness of it by fixing his eyes on some object slightly beyond their actual location. A woman with an extraordinarily elongated chest but with head markedly smaller came past, her lower half cut off by the hedge. Two large heads followed her. A dog, barking, jumped suddenly above the hedge, like a whale sounding. The statue itself seemed to dwindle increasingly. Perhaps it was the lengthening of the afternoon that created the impression. He looked at his watch and saw that they would soon have to move in order to keep an appointment for tea. Yet he could not shift his attention from what he was seeing it was so calmly fascinating.

He recalls now many things, many people. He thinks of a beach in Truro, in Deya, in Gloucester, in San Diego. He puts people on it, many men and many women, and many children. Dogs run past. Divers things are dropped, lost in the sand. The water comes up on the beach, goes back on the beach, with the tides. Why should *size* be so insistent a center? Is it simply that a toy car won't hurt you and a real one will? He couldn't accept the isolation of condition implicit in that logic. The big man wants to help you, the little one hasn't the strength?

But their heads and *that* insistent variation was a matter of different kind. He felt the pressure of her hand tighten and, looking at her, felt it then simple to call her attention to the phenomenon with which he had been, for so long, preoccupied. But how could he reach her, then? Way off she was somewhere, truly somewhere else. He could take an actual map and with a pin make precise her location, but here she was not. He crawled into the core of the telephone wires and pushed with all his strength to make a way. Foolish. He wrapped himself with paper, scrunched down into the ink, licked, then patted, and sealed it all over him, then stamped it. All the same, impossible. He was always too big, too small, it didn't really matter.

The people go on walking. It is really a matter of indifference who comes and goes there, assuming they treat one another with courtesy.

$$\frac{2 \cdot 3 \cdot 1}{\text{Two}}$$

Look, look. The road home. Someone. The road knows. The rose nose. He sees what he says. And says what he sees. There. Here. It isn't very big. But then. It isn't very small. It. Is in the middle.

Come in. At last the door opens and into the warmth of the small but humanly cosy room step two onions. Neither knows what road they have taken, or been taken, or even will take. They will not talk about it. Their faces betray a green and ruddy reverence. Their reference is belief. True believers two, too. They come in also. Chairs are offered all four, but sans legs or even arms wherewith to balance upon the center of such possibility they choose to roll down on the floor, all four thus on all fours. A heap.

The fire burns low. No other light or lights lighten the living room, which it is. Discover that wood speaks. Never to be forgotten the first saw it saw. It hurts, ripping the tender interlocking tissues, rasping, ripping, scraping, unfeeling such saws. Agh. Onions were better although knives come too, often in pairs. The road follows its nose. The house will not burn. The fire burns low. Wood speaks. Chairs are awful. On all fours, onions.

It becomes time to cook. They have always liked cooking, the empty pots and pans, the torn paper, little bits of this and that. Too many cooks, or two mommy cooks. They will. And it is ready. Eat. But wait for mommy, or many, as they come. It is too low for the window, but gets a chair, careful to step on no onion, or fire. Sees out. There, there, there. She is coming. Down the road. How good the hills of home, or wherever they are met with. Up and down, a delightful pastime. They are sure. Dancing is for girls. And boys. Boys and girls and onions make a delightful repast. Just in time.

Mommy is here. First her feet, first her hair, first her before, first her behind. The door knows the doorknob. Opens and in the openness of the opening, mommy comes in, all over. Mommy comes all over everything. With everything. Just in time insofar as it is a place to be. So happy to have her come. Eat.

Without the road no one knows. Without the door. Without the window. Without the wind blowing. Without the sky is blue. Without the moon shines on. Without the rain and April flowers. Where have we been, then. So long. So far. So big. So little. So much. So what. Always comes true, two of them. Bringing home the onions. Bringing home the bacon. Unfriendly persons. Diga me, las personas vayan. Right on, old buddy. You speak good. In two tongues. In two heads, too. Two is the number for you.

Stretching out, having eaten. Everything. All done. No more. It's all gone now. Poor wood. Poor house. Think. Doors on everything, all locked. Her arms full of packages, she fumbles for the key. The door opens and looks out. She, full of packages, looks in. In and out. Up and down. Same thing. She knows she is home. Home free, they say, the whole house shouting. Come in. Pleasure is such a delight. Yes, yes. How good. How bad to be good. How good to be bad. Up and down. In and out. Here. There. The window. Moves the chair over, awful to see there. Two. Mommy. Full of onions, who have things they can too do. By mommy. Sit down. You have been long gone, you have come. Home. The hills. The valleys. The sun. The moon. The ups. The downs. The moors. The arabs. Singing light flies forth through valley floor to topmost tip of tree stands up to see the singing light. Lights and livers, clouds and onions. Eat. You are home. You may rest assured. This is what home has come to know and be known as home. Forever.

But outside you can look in, or inside you can look out, or up, down, or down, up. Think. Who is mommy, who is she, that all those saints have fainted? The sky, guy, the lid, kid. Can you ride a rocking horse, billy boy, billy boy. Singing light. The sun has come and made the moon to shine again on all, on all fours on the floor. Takes a load off its feet. A load in his pants. Her hand in his. Just under the skin. They dance with ants in their pants. New arrivals. Telegrams. Boats pulled up on the shore for the night. Low voices. Muttering fires. Silent stars. The universe is one. Universe.

A place in the sun, a place in the dark, how good to be home, when it comes time to sit down, just in time, her arms full of packages, a load in his pants. The couple are truly two and too true. The sun is shining. Singing light. At night he walks out under the stars, and looks up. At night he wakes up under the stairs and lets down. A huge load. A big one. But bigger two. Two heads are better than one, requiring no hat. Where did you leave it? Out there. Incredible, ecstatic distances discovered narrowly missing. Take your onions with you. When you go out to play. Stay. Out of the road. A voice singing light. And low. And know to go home before asked to. Good manners. Good night. Good day to you, dos personas. You have come far, to come here. Come in. Home. Come in, billy. Over and out. By which action leans heavily on her head, causing her pain.

The first night. Home. The second night, home, the third, home, the fourth, night. Home game. Plays in the park. A ball.

Always does what told to. Always. Mommy. Remembers mommy as onions, full of packages. Buys boys. Just in time. This time. That time. A time too.

Quicker, slower. The hills seem to lengthen in the last light. Stretching. So far to get to know. Home. No one home. Always two. One wants two. Dig it. Me too, las personas. So charming they have come. Home. Home to mommy more than one to keep the home fires burning. Saw a saw. The wood works. Without the rain but safe inside, again. They have always liked cooking, little bits of this and that. Mommy comes too. But only once. A heap. Right on. In two tongues. In two heads. Is the number for you too.

Mommy. Come home.

•

ONE MORNING you wake up in bed five feet tall, or six, or eight feet tall. Something has happened. You lie and look at your feet, way down there. Your hands extend on the ends of two elongated arms and if you move them in arcs, they seem the measure of the spheres. Neither securing nor disquieting, this change. More probably it has happened to you because you have come upon it, fallen upon it, as it were, and stretching, it's all very true.

You were out all night, possibly, and perhaps the night, even nights, before. You were walking but in the dark and given the faint path you were trying to follow, you had fallen several times. At one time you went down several feet, into a somewhat steep though small ravine, and lay at the bottom, looking up to see the dense dark forms of trees against a faintly lighter blue-black sky. Fog lay deeper than yourself, in soft pockets down the lower traces of the ravine. No sounds, really. Now and then some snatch of talking, some creak of wood, a falling star possibly, sounding a streak of peripheral tears.

You wanted to cry, you were so happy. Sad? Could not altogether remember. The one thing changes the other. No two at the same time, somehow, despite it insistently happens. What you were was young. Old? More probably older, as it's said of those who have come to be here. There. "He finally got here." But he was going there.

You watch him as backward, into, a mirror you, in looking, are. He does not see you, he is you. Or her, or them. They are several ones all in one. You love him because you love yourself, loving him, yourself.

You move, looking for places where you may meet. She must be somewhere else now. No wish to take her life into yours in just this way. Falling down is hard to do. Certainly as an accompaniment to someone else's. Though they fall into each other's arms every time.

This warm specificness of bodies, you think. Eight feet tall, eight inches, six or five. The trees look across at you, equal height. A level regard as on a plain or bus station, eyes meet. You meet her walking and look into her eyes, so lovely, lovely wit to them, seeing you. You climb over her body. You remember mountains in New Hampshire. You think of things to do. Rainy days in

Massachusetts, a barn with hay mows. You wriggle into the hay, burrowing down, and come, head first, to the metal basket for the horse's hay, placed at the edge of the ceiling and wall. You look out, upside down, taking deep breaths since you have just arrived at the surface, into the horse's deeply soft dark eyes. It loves you. It is not your horse. The barn creaks with sounds of timber shifting, loose boards, and on the main floor with its heavy planking, your feet resonate with heavy sure footsteps.

Today you are a man. Yesterday you were a man. A week ago you were a man but no one had told you. A letter, indescribable, had been mailed years before. There was need to establish your own identity before it could be given you insofar as it was specific, although you didn't know it. It was waiting.

You were waiting, all your life. It was not a long time. You woke up, in bed, elongated. Your mother was far away. Your father, dead. These specific relationships, all wrong. Unmeaning more than being there, too, you thought. The sun burned through the window and seized your face warmly.

You wanted to be in France, Spain, but you were not. You insisted on home as a place you knew, and forgot it. People you loved, had loved, cried out in pain, unwitting, inconstant, helpless. You saw children in large crowds coming toward you, arms up in the air, calling out to you to acknowledge them, to come to them, with them. You wanted to, you thought, but your size as you stood out and up from the bed brushed the ceiling. You were irrevocably in the room.

You would never leave it. You had come to it, into it, and gone to sleep, her long warm hair over your face. Breathing deeply. Unthinking, slept there, with her. You woke up and explored her, climbed all over her, took with your hand, her hand, and touched her. Deeply. Soft, wet, warmly, and talks to you of yourself, all alone.

A voice in your ear shouts, *mangia!* An agreement to eat as the huge boat flounders on through waves of water. You have consented, through need, to be put in its very bottom, and sleep on one of a rack of beds, which reach up to the ceiling. You wake up and see a face, eagerly intent, very close to your own, shouting. He cares for you as an old world person cares for his brothers. He is sweet and thoughtful, but very loud. It is time to eat. It is not time to eat. An hour goes by. You walk through the maze of stairs and gangways to the dining room and join your friends, a man and woman, sitting at a small table, waiting, smiling, as you sit down too. She has lovely deep breasts, long waist, full body. He is intelligently wry, open to amusement, and blond. They like to dance.

You step out, you jump, back, forward. You find yourself confused in the literal place. You reach around yourself, feel bodies, women. You know them but are restless, and twist away. Someone on the stairs, going up, takes your hand and looks at it, smiling. She admires its strength and width of palm. He tells you you have painters' hands. You smile with pleasure, you never forget either of them, but they do not really know each other, nor ever did, or will. It is several places you live in, the horse's nuzzling as you pull clear of the hay and drop into its stall, the woman, the women's nuzzling, the man's smile.

You step over them, you drop back into the bed, alone now. The sun rises steadily, into the sky. You go with it, fall back, get up, lie down, walk slowly forward, then run. You can make out the forms of the trees, in the fog, darkness. No moon this night to help you. You remember your way, feeling forward with your feet the nature of the path you are trying to follow. You have come back to leave again. You want no one to see you come or go.

You are very big, you think. You were small, a speck merely, a twinkle in the universe. You have come here to continue and will never stop again. You think it all goes on forever and will go insistently with it. Here, there, you run back and forth. You are in love again.

You love it that you are in love again. You are eight feet tall, waking up. You are alone. You are crying, you are smiling with simple pleasures, you know everything, you know nothing.

You want to get home now. The boat plunges on. You walk to the bow with your two friends. She places herself at the very point of ship's forward timbers. The wind blows strongly. The man watches, smiling, and from time to time asks questions about life in Spain. She does a little dance, long hair swinging, and you mime it with gestures of your strong hands.

The woman is back of you, behind you at a great distance, driving a small sports car whose owner had been her sister's husband. She is going somewhere but thoughts do not show it clearly. You look around intently and recognise nothing. It is fall, or spring, with the leaves coming out, or dropping off, the trees. You feel the changes insistently. You want to go back, or forward, to where it all was, is, will be.

You have suddenly changed your name again. It is unpronounceable. Something like Harry, or Bill, or Jim perhaps. You cannot remember. It seems to go with the great size of your body. The boat is nearing land, you think. You try to get the small number of your possessions together and put within simple reach. You go again to the bow of the boat and look out, thinking to see something. The effect is of much water, sky, and a few circling birds you note are gulls. There will be a last party tonight, on ship board, a farewell. You know that your friends will not leave you since they are going to the same place. You sit at table with them and drink all of the red wine that the ship provides. Later you go with them to the bar, then dance with them.

You are thinking of explanations. It is as if it never happened so you cannot believe there is reason to be more concerned than that. Then you are crying, uncontrollably, and you are, insistently, asking all who will stop for your questions, what it has all been about. You rehearse your own explanations over and over but they are incomplete. You wait for it to end. You see the end coming, you think.

You have been away. The boat approaches the dock assigned to it and modestly the trip is over. You see your friends already taking place in the line of people who will shortly be leaving. You want to wave to them but realize you are leaving too.

Perhaps it is too late. At last you get into the line and are slowly taken off the boat as it moves forward. You look shyly out of your eyes to see who is waiting. You see her at some distance, at the edge of the crowd. She is very small, perhaps shrunken. You ease your bulk forward, waving to her, and her eyes meet the middle of your chest. You lift her in your arms with your hands to kiss her. You both go home.

•

THE DAY GROWS misty with incoming fog. Just out the window a large, leaning tree-stump and an oil barrel, upended, gone green in lovely manner. A slow day, waiting for rain. Flowers lift to go stiff at the edges of their leaves, curling. Things grow, crashing up, and tops then die, and the lower parts of the plant go brown and die too. Everything expanding, as far as it can.

There are monsters in the desert, who prey on the unwary. Tales record as much as such ever leaves behind. Windy bones bleaching, like they say. This time they got wise, they thought, and made extensive preparations so as not to let these monsters have their way with them, however many there were in fact in the company. Forty, say. More like two hundred. At least a very distinct number of these people. What they do is get lots of water in big casks and water bags and all that sort of container and they load the mules and the camels, all that they have to hoist this stuff forward into the desert of their desire. They have the monsters completely buffaloed, so they figure, because they are not going to run out of water out there and drop down on their knees in the sand with their tongues going black and their eyes popping out, etc.

So off they go, a great day, bands playing, mothers waving, wives, daughters, the otherwise left at home. This is really going to be it. The monsters know they are coming just that that is what monsters are there to know, but they just let it keep happening as these others think it really is. First night comes and the enthusiasts really think they've got it made as they guzzle their plenteous water. They are even splashing it around a little until the one who has got the whole idea in his head, the leader, says to quiet down and get some sleep and don't waste the water needlessly. He says that not harshly because he knows there is so much water on those mules and camels they could almost float to that other place they are going to. Next day dawns bright and early, and they plunge on. Things are creaking a bit, water is heavy, but they keep moving in the same good spirits, rolling along. Comes the third day, the fourth day, things are basically the same, but the fifth day it is really getting a little heavy. Like, who needs all that water.

So the commander gets them all around the campfire that night and gives it to them straight. Men, desert is dry and this one has monsters, and that water is all we've got. Right. So up again the next morning, and onward. But this is not a morning like any other because now they see coming toward them another huge caravan in a factually weird condition. All the people are wet, really soaking, and they are slogging along as if it was raining cats and dogs. All the wagons are slugging through mud and the people's hair is plastered down and it really is totally wet. They see one guy with his mouth full of watercress, then another. Wow.

Naturally they ask what's up. Oh, say these wet people, you see that green line way over there. Past that line, it's raining all the time and that's where we've come from and you're going. So that's what, say the first guys, and instantly smash all their casks of water and their barrels. Forget it. Then they go on, find no water, drop down in desert, and the monsters eat them.

3 · 1 · 2
Three

In THOSE DAYS we were trying to play football in the lot back of the school close to the pine trees. Mr. Scribner was our coach, volunteer, and also Harry's father. His clothing is hard to remember except that every Memorial Day he put on his old army uniform and marched with the VFW section of the parade down the main street of the town and finally to the cemetery not far from where we were then living. On the days we played football he often wore an old-style football helmet, with distinct pieces it seemed, so that the ear flaps especially hung down like sewed on patches. He, Harry, and the others, Marilyn, Stevie, younger children and Mrs. Scribner, all lived in an apartment in a house owned by Miss Boston, a curious English woman who often went riding on an old horse in complete riding habit. The Scribner family were her especial responsibility and so she provided both dwelling and odd jobs for Mr. Scribner, who did no other work we knew of.

So he was free to teach us, as now football, and that we learned in the classic form of the early 1900's. To block the opposing team, our line, on the snap of the ball back, turned to face sideways the persons next to us, not our opponents but our teammates, whereupon we fell down and rolled over. This proposed an instant jumble and thus a confusion of bodies through which the other team's players would not be able to pass. We practised this manoeuver persistently and it is the one thing clearly remembered from all those afternoons, late sun and tumbling and lots of shouting and the trees that kept still and watched.

Marching along those streets, uniform always feeling incomplete, perhaps the kerchief wrong, or the shoes not the kind stipulated by assumed regulations, or the body just not fitting it, even the feet trying to catch up, Mr. Scribner was so quietly and generously reassuring to ourselves. We wanted it. We would do anything to be with it. One Halloween night we were trying to think of some immense displacement of the town's usual conduct but only the big boys could really make it. They took the billboards with the political campaign images and hoisted them on to roofs, and even got an old car up on top of Mr. Grey's house. But they were too fast for us. We'd get there but whatever we had had in mind would be gone. So this night we were soaping, slowly, the window of the town's one dry goods store and were so absorbed by that activity, that we didn't see or hear Pat Foley, the town policeman, coming up behind us in the dark. So there he was and because he couldn't grab all us, he grabbed one, saying, I've got you, Fred Bird. Boys, come back. Somehow, with an instant agreement, we jumped him, amazed, and held on, whereupon he let go of Fred and we all ran off, scared and heroic, into the dark.

Then one day Ralph and me, Luxie we used to call him, had wandered off from school down to Mac MacGregor's, who owned the town's garage and kept homers, racing pigeons, in a big attic over the garage itself. That was where Rat used to work, a bullet-headed, muscled young man with slicked back blond hair and scarey insistent eyes. His information attracted us, as did Mac's, but Mac, being older, got bored with our interest. Rat, on the other hand, would hint endlessly of thefts and deals, and of women seduced, fucked, buggered, raped, torn, eaten. We always stood a little way back from him but we listened to every word he said. His obscenities particularly now come back, the hissing almost spit tone of his words. Later we heard he was taken off to prison.

This afternoon we were just walking toward the garage and were involved with a sort of chant concerning the school's principal. It was a lazy late spring day and we kicked stones or occasional bottles as we went, keeping the unison of *Huff, Huff, the great big puff.* We came into the garage still chanting and to our so-called consternation, suddenly woke to Mr. Huff's actuality, literally before us. His car, a Model A, sat with hood up just beyond him. He looked at us very harshly, asked us what we thought we were doing, and gave instructions that we should see him in his office the next morning. That subsequent encounter now fades though the memory of the way the boards of the school room floor were oiled, and how they smelled, and of wet coats and boots hung in the hall, and light through windows into large rooms, and the varnish – even of faces, of the girl who had epilepsy, who sat in the desk in front of me so that her head, during a seizure, would fall back on my desk top – all that stays put.

She was a shy girl and the seizures really embarrassed her. I felt for her very much since I had a glass eye that would with my rubbing at it as the school day got tedious occasionally fall out and roll across the floor under the desks. Always some pleasantly intrigued and brave kid would pick it up, ask permission to leave his seat, and bring it back to me. I would rub it with my handkerchief, an instance of which I still compulsively keep with me, though the eye itself is long gone, and put it back in. At recess kids I wasn't friends with would tease me by asking, did I take it out with a spoon, and then plead to see it. Was it round and so forth. One so maddened me I remember jumping him and finally pounding his head against the metal supports for the swings until friends of us both pulled me off.

I couldn't keep my temper easily. My mother used to say, count ten. My friends had an endless variation of ritual for not letting them get you. I would be fine for a while but then it would just blow up in my head, and I'd jump. Often it was sadly actual friends I attacked, like Buddy Butler, with whom I fought when we were both in the seventh grade, out in the school grounds, surrounded by those specious, provoking onlookers, until we were both so exhausted we could neither of us hold on to anything nor lift our arms anymore. One other kid, a bully, really wore down on me until one day, as I was going through the hall to get the bus, he flashed past slapping my books out of my arms to the floor. Happily I nailed him, with a quick punch on the nose, which bled, transforming him to a weeping, sad kid.

Myself is what one comes to think of, then, letting the well fill up, things happen. Others out there, like June Welsh, who was a welfare kid living on the DeSouza farm up from where we did. Beauteous June, round faced, short bob, so tough and so tender. She caught at one's heart with her human vulnerability and to walk home with her was to enter such deep pride and confusion. Or Helen, seemingly tall, Scandinavian, her brother for a time my sister's boyfriend so that she and I were likewise linked. Tilda, whose brother was my own friend and whose father thought I should devote myself to Latin, and the outwitting of the Catholic conspiracy. Days and nights no doubt forever.

Persons and things moving in and out of that place make a part of it. The Batemans came late, moving into a house down the street from us, two boys, mother and father, which last opened a small store in the main part of the town. Both parents were faint sort of people, that is, ok but we sure didn't figure they were like Mr. Scribner or Mac or Mrs. Locke, who made the traditionally world's greatest chocolate cake. These people tended to keep to themselves, nice but really not there. The kids thus had no real center either to come from or to bring us to. The older was our age and came into what we were doing as we needed someone to play right field or to keep a look out or to ask some awkward question of people we'd prefer not to talk to. So he got along.

But the younger was really alone, there being no kids of his own age close enough to get to nor our own real permission, and particularly not his brother's who was told by his parents to take care of him, hence wanted him gone. This kid was spunky. You could knock him down time after time, tease him endlessly, but when the dust cleared, there he was, coming back. He even got a kind of mad clarity out of it and that tinge of really heroic singleness which can be entirely present, no matter the circumstance. He believed everything we said so that was our advantage. For example, we played our version of cowboys and indians in the woods back of my house. It was really settlers and indians and so we had the clearing, which was where the settlers were established, and then all the woods around it, thick with impending indians. Word would come that the indians were massing for an attack on our humble defences. So we'd hold a conference, to which this kid was also invited, and come to common decision that our best defence was offence, and so all of us set out to attack the indians with the one exception of the kid whom we told had to be there, to keep the camp together. Once out of his sight we were instant indians and howled horrible execrations on the white man and his encroachments on the red man's lands. These consisted mainly of threats to cut off the heads of, the testicles of, the hands and feet of any white dog met with. From time to time one of us would dash through the clearing where the kid sat by this time bawling with terror, to scream, they're right behind me, then disappear.

Only literal fatigue ever ended that one, and it always worked. The sobbing kid would be reassured it was all a game, then he would slowly stop crying, pleased we were all back, and then, very possibly, it would all begin again. We just couldn't believe it was so simple.

But one time I remember it went, in that classic way, beyond expectation. It was an afternoon and both of his parents were gone, his brother too, and him, and me, and possibly one other kid were out in a small pasture, partly an apple orchard, close to his house. It was fall and the apples apparently were of no interest to the farmer who owned the pasture. We found a few we could eat but most were on the ground, rotten. So we were fooling around with the rotten apples, throwing them at rocks, the trees, occasionally at each other, until we hit on the plan of daring the kid to throw them at his own house, which was white clapboards. We helped him by hauling large quantities to a place where he'd have an easy chance of hitting it, and so he began. Big brown splotches began to appear as the kid lobbed one after another, delighted with his own ability. Finally we wanted him to stop, fearing he'd spill our whole involvement to his parents, but he was far beyond us and the last memory is him still throwing, it's almost dark now, and the car drives into the yard.

•

"AND THERE'S some milk." "It's very interesting." "That's out of sight."

It's a funny experience, you see? To go see something like that. A lot of the time I'm in, I think. Like a hole, to keep in one place. You're thinking. Tom leaving, and going over to visit Magda. Not heavily, he's got a beautiful, wise, intuitive sense of where it is. If I started doing the thing with my head, it would be very hard to keep doing this.

"A rhythmic experience." "The steady thing."

Making that be your secret guide but not your outspoken guide. Oh, I think so. Beautiful, wise, intuitive sense of where it is. Turned on. Waist deep, amidst the encircling gloom. The intimacy of the sounds in the house were first, like they say, a kind of displacement. Yah. Music interferes, spheres.

"You get here are mostly all your own sounds."

To get it on, but it sounds like. The kind of music that was happening around here when everybody just sits in and tries to make music together. Peter turned me on to African music. To create it if you were particularly serious. I didn't find that experience anything like what I'd think it would be at all.

"Particularly serious and disciplined." "Just because I realized the kind of music that was happening around here."

Harmony is just like what your ear says like. Your own sounds except for cars. I love the sounds though. Open, marshmallow? That's the same thing with clapping. Ah, ecstatic. Open note to the possibility of something happening. Open. Swamp mellow. What are you saying, you like this house? It's entirely intimate.

"Like they say, a kind of displacement." "Tum, tum." "What do you mean by being turned on?"

Know any keep doing this. Making that be your secret guide but not your outspoken guide. There's some milk. Then I've already thought of it. Like I got into a hole. A whole imaginary trip. It stays steady. Making that be your secret guide but not your outspoken guide. Intuitive sense of where it is. It's absolutely everything.

"Then it's impeccable." "Ah, ecstatic."

Cut it out! I really like this though. Way down upon. There's such a metronomic. Tum, tum. Like resonates all through. Weird discomfort. You do? Just basic beats. Like I'd been listening to African music, you know. Made music seem like what you could only manage to listen to. I was playing second violin. It's the same experience when it starts happening.

"They really mean it. Coming back, I realized I played in music. Only what you could manage to create if you were particularly serious and disciplined. The beats, and then the variation on the beats. Yah. Tum, tum. Open up anything. How do you get yourself turned on then. Beautiful, wise, intuitive sense of where it is. But not your outspoken guide. A whole imaginary trip."

•

VOICES FADING fast. He turns in a circle to find them again. Sense from movies of fun house mirrors and, *this way, Harry, I'm over here*. Bang. Another mirror bites the dust. He throws his now useless gun at the multiple images and turns, to think.

Perchance to dream, like they say. Think it over and come back on Monday. No one ever quite wrong enough. So far. No one ever quiet enough. To hear them.

Meeting Mabel again after forty years, he was struck by the fact she was still alive. In fact, pretty. Pretty good enough is enough for me, he was thinking. He turned to smile. She was thinking of the time they had first met, on a dock in downtown Boston. Waiting for a bust.

Not funny, McGee. Simple laughter from the outside looking in. Pains of growing up. Growing pains of larger sizes. Places inside wanting outside. Things to do while waiting to do something.

Why *do* things, she was saying. He stopped as if at a real intersection. I do what comes to hand, he said. Painful, inept moralist, she was thinking, let him eat cake.

Mabel grew incontinently while waiting for time to pass, in the several places she found herself in, waiting. The voices fade fast, in fact, the first to go, leaving the rest to follow if they can. She was a girl, then woman, then a fading voice of herself in inept moral circumstance, waiting. She loves everything, he thought. He remembered the first time in Boston as if the dream were really true. Is this him, he said to Mabel, as they sat in a room, looking at one another. The man on the can is the owner perhaps. See baby food image of man now big, with life changed by hitting wall in race car at excessive speed. Nothing changes he hadn't thought of. Instant real. Truth's inexorable circumstance. Later.

They were driving under a long succession of viaducts, or overpasses, in a slight rain. The other man's wife was extraordinarily attractive, and she was driving them home. The other man drove the other car. At some point not simply to be determined the lines of movement were no longer congruent and they became divergent, flooded with memories. She could not smile simply as if nothing had happened. She was dreaming a dream of alternatives. She nuzzled the bottle like a horse and laughed at her previous fears. You have nothing to fear but fear itself, looking in the store windows, wanting shoes. Congruence of clothing had made them appear the same. An army of marching men. And women. Raincoats and rain hats and galoshes protect them from the heavy downpour. The car passes, spraying sheets of water. They were in love and took no notice of the shouting people. He reached over to take her hand and it came off in his. Her head rolled on the floor. Her eyes dribbled forth. Her ears shattered, face breaking like a tired child's. He took out a gun and shot what was left, disgusted. Then he walked away.

Mabel dusted the furniture again and checked the provisions for the drinks. Ice, water, glasses. All was in readiness. She went to the mirror and fell in. Guests arriving a half hour later found the house apparently as ever but water had flooded the basement and was rising rapidly. Also numerous icebergs bumped up under the livingroom floor, nine tenths of them under water, as they knew from childhood. Silly boy, she said, and ripped his clothes from him with one hand tied behind her back.

They regretted they had not known one another better when the first opportunity had offered. In retrospect they were perfect for one another but now he lived in Africa and she had lost his address. He was also dead, she thought, surely, after all that had happened. He, however, still loved her too, and was sitting beside her on the couch. Mabel, he said, and ripped her clothes from her without even thinking. He lit a cigarette and walked away without a backward glance.

Backward people more retentive of what's present, he thought, waiting for the first signs of life. When the truck hit him, he was really not there. Mabel, unknowing, still waited for the sound of his footsteps, coming up the walk. She had put on her best dress and after seeing to the drinks, she sat on the couch with both hands in her lap. After all these years she knew it was about to happen.

She was in love with another man's life, and wanted to, *go crazy*. When the car hit the wall, he broke everything in his body including the bottle of gin he was bringing to her. It was to have been a happy reunion but it would be some time now, if ever, before it could be thought of. Thoughtful of his condition, the ambulance dropped him off at her corner, waving goodbye.

Mabel knows enough to know better. She listens with both ears. Her head is a radio. Rialto rose, love is the bed she lies in, heat what she turns on. Or up. Smiles through broken teeth. Old rumpled mattress. She felt his hands on her body although he lived in Africa, she remembered. It was a dream in which many things have happened all at once.

Sodden, dreary expectations. He had no impulse even to ring the bell, much less to go into a room he could only feel revolting. How dare she interrupt his life with inept solicitations. He threw the roses to the ground and stamped on them, then left, to his own devices.

Voices fade fast. In the desert the sound extends in asymetric manner, over hill and hollow, until exhausted, fades out. The last rose of summer, the same. He listens with a marked intentness, turning the volume higher and higher. At last there is a faint, scratching sound. It is from the attic, over his head, where she sleeps alone, head buried in pillow, her eyes a smear of tears.

As soon as you're born, they make you feel small. They are bigger, she says, sneering. He lurches against the fireplace and falls in. She turns off the radio and leaves the room. She says, that's the last time. He is soundless, in the fire. He is thinking of old times, when they tucked him softly into bed, with a good night kiss.

Mabel is the big time but he's blown it, years ago, on the dock in Boston. A grape for your thoughts. Pettiness floods his mind. He rips her clothes from his body with one mind. I do what comes to hand, he said.

$$\frac{1 \cdot 2 \cdot 3}{\text{Four}}$$

IT IS A SCENE with some distance so that a lake, or sky, floats in the far perspective. Immediately to the left, at the front, is a woman with upper torso clothed in a light hazy autumn brown colored tunic with lower half swathed in an apparent sheet. A naked child, holding a wreath stands just by her left knee. She holds a staff, that is, a long stick but not really a pole or something one could really belabor anyone with, and she does not appear to rest on it with any weight. She dallies with it, so to speak. Just to the child's left, is the major presence of the group, discounting, for the moment, the poet, and this is a man, or more accurately, a god, whose right arm reaches across his chest at shoulder height, to point with index finger at the poet's notebook or papers or text, which he has resting on his knee, his left hand securing them. The man or god's right arm is resting, close to the armpit, on a golden lyre, which catches the light (all figures and things are illumined by a strong frontal light coming from their right or, as one looks in, the viewer's left – a setting sun?). This figure has no clothing on the upper part of his body, but has a short skirt of crimson which breaks just above his knee as he sits. He wears a wreath, possibly of laurel, and his look is directed to the poet's pages. The poet, since this is *Inspiration of the Poet, L'Inspiration du Poête, Die Einge-bung*, has a remarkably unformed face and long hair, as have all figures in sight with degree depending on age and condition. He looks up, poised in some tentative thought, and is holding an instrument of writing, silver, which also catches the light. Just above him, to the viewer's left, poised between the god and the man, is a small baby, naked with outstretched arms holding a great wreath as if he were about to encircle the neck of the poet therewith. The woman, the more she is observed, seems to be waiting for the god, as if he were shortly to be finished and they might go somewhere else together. Or else she waits for the poet? It seems to be her child, that is, the one standing close to her. He is also holding an object in his other hand, the one not occupied with the wreath, but it is not clearly discernible. There is a postmark which includes a section of the god's head, and then a sequence of six horizontal wavy lines to the right of it, moving across the image, but neither the printing nor date is legible. The god wears silver or possibly gold sandals, which also catch the light from the viewer's left. It is now clearly a sky, blue, which appears beyond them, far reaching clouds catching the fading sunset in tones primarily of orange and brownish-grey. The poet's left foot is posed so that it seems to drag back of him, a curious crouch, in fact. Listening carefully, the viewer hears now a voice speaking.

Check it out. I'd like to tell you about something truly exciting. It may be the god who speaks thus. *It's a soft little cup which adapts to you individually.* There is sadness, remembering. The words come from other times and the poet knows that the *twenty-first is tomorrow.* Also other people will speak. It is as if Poussin had anticipated these possibilities, and it is a lovely thought. "I send greetings with this card and the wish for a sustained and sustaining inspiration." The sun sets and all disperse, leaving the three trees they had chosen to sit by, for the accomplishment of their severally appointed ends.

•

STOPPED AT THE intersection and asked to give directions, they cannot remember clearly if the house is below the one they are thinking of, or just above it, or on right side or left. They themselves have come through the grove of cedars and are heading for the lights of the small city below them. They are a little surprised by the articulation of the questions because these people cannot be expected to speak English. The Dane, with them, laughs and says that he avoids the problem by living in a castle. He says that it is easy to find.

Romantic histories? Or fragile symbols of an uncertain light. It is not clear to them why the car has stopped so far from the town to ask such directions, or why it should be of them, so faintly apparent from the roadside where the car has been pulled over. There seems an invincible arrogance, a secular power, to the reason, whatever it may prove to be.

But there are two wings, two wings that go nowhere. To the house, or to the castle perhaps. No, it is a bird, that is silent and sad, the Dane says. There is no sound from the car as the people in it, not quite possible to see clearly, wait for further explanations. In case the terrible sun of the tropics shines for an instant, she wears sun glasses, a profound night of the eyes. This is the woman to the left of the driver, hooded figure, they now discern, with long talonlike fingers holding the wheel. The night prepares to fly from these depths of quiet objects. They think to move on but the immanent presence of those in the car will not let them. The lights below them appear to waver and flicker, and the city itself becomes inactual as they try to replace it. Without a look in their direction, the driver suggests it would be most helpful if they might come into the car, and go with it, until the house is found. Then they would be taken to whatever place they wished. He dictates, they realise, the mode, the custom, the domestic use of memory, and they are powerless to retrieve another purpose.

What a day it has been. Nights follow, one thinks. What a day after day after day, now, presently they are walking and talking about it, their strange lives. They have not as yet come to the car, already waiting for them, one thinks. The dog has found a resplendent bone in the garden but the castle is empty until evening, when the lamps are lit and men and women come into the great dining room for their food and water and ample meat, the bread, the other things to be eaten. Sly, he uses the occasion also to fondle attractively the various women or men who attract his amorousness, since the night will wear on.

The car has by this time left the city. Hours earlier, it swung in the air, at the end of a magnificent crane used for unloading cargo, hooded in canvas, and was dropped, four wheels square, onto the dock. Four persons, undeterminable, but for the fact one seemed to be a woman, and a lovely one, go directly to the car, once it has been freed of its encumbrances, open its doors, get into it, and start, abruptly, its motor. Without further sign to any of those who observe them, they have driven off into the city's winding streets. They leave behind them the feeling of the day's fragments, years in conflict, and an indescribably solemn clamor. Those still watching suddenly put their hands, in apparent anguish, to their ears.

Backwards, they are turning the pages in their heads, looking for the place they had left off being there. The sight of the woman has stilled them. They see the petrified flower, the antique bird, the lips so sensually and forever sealed. In the car the driver spins the wheel right, left, independent of direction. Although the woman sits directly next to him, her hands moving from time to time to his face, his hair, his leg, he makes no response. It is the limit of a hundred distinct possibilities, a retrogression to nothing, possibly, and they are fearful of breaking the profound silence or of provoking these angels of the tedious.

How wise to have the simple answer. The Dane is laughing insofar as the castle has fallen into his hands, kings and queens and all. He is insolent but right, indefatigable position. All obey his ownership and subserve his underlying purpose, which is to use them one and all. The great halls resound to his pleasure, laughing, and night is turned into day with the merry-making. Only the great oaken beams supporting it all know the mystery of its diverse information. It is that wood is shaped by its maker, earth, water, or hands. Inside the walls, pinioned by the mortar's weight, the workmen look out through the cracks, sadly, at the lovely sight.

The Dane, in the car, longs for his castle. He makes shift to invite these new informants to come to it, not the house they have had in mind. He assures them of great and insistent provision, gives them all his heart in a flood of pain.

They think of love as they had known it, hands shaped as hearts, and held with inexpressibly tender containment. They think of mouths, opened, closed. Eyes and hands, with hair, fingers pointing them on. They think of sudden ambitions, regrets, plans, recognitions. Impossible Pegasus for impossible heroes, the car does not answer them but continues.

There is one way into the king, having at one time had a king, remembered. There are crowns, inextricably headed. Bearded figures in long gowns with boots of strict leather. There are places the people themselves will recall, summon back in fits of irritation, to have one word more. They want the car to stop since the house will not come to them, however fast or slow they approach it. The Dane is only their friend and the most helpless of them all. In the castle his bags sit unpacked by the bed he has never laid down on. The defiant gesture, the inert adamacy, are history of the moment only, and fall back of them in the car's movement forward. There follow years and centuries, generation after generation. They push and pull, discreetly, hopefully, but to no avail.

Unity is the essence of all, the force which holds it all together. The woman extends her hands, her body, toward them, mockingly loving. Whether as mother or lover, she lures them to her own amusement.

Why do they fear. It will not hurt them. Why do they ask so tentatively. They will not be answered. Where do they think to go or to return to. They will not.

•

BACK TO BACK, these situations of *tortured sensibility*. Does that mean the sound of finger nails scraping a blackboard, the old proposal of sliding down razor blades on your heels, or simply the sharpened stick pushed into your eye, tongue cut out, penis slit, fingers crushed, both legs broken at the ankle. Coincident with consciousness is an ability not only to know things, but to recognise and anticipate *feelings*, even to propose them, the terror or pleasure in that act notwithstanding, so that the reality so engendered becomes the experience of the world entirely.

Angered, outraged, they got on the plane in Chicago. There was shaky agreement in London, but insistent flarings of temper and irritation. Friends put up with them, with him in particular, and at one point late at night in an alley retrieved the garbage he drunkenly poured out of the cans standing along the edge of the street while also picking up the clothing his wife in rage pulled off to throw at him in rejection. Then Paris, exhausted, quieter, walking again with friends after a brief and confused lecture he had given at the Sorbonne, the lovely spaces and tones of the city, their hosts' argument relieving their own. And finally Italy, where they were to stay for a month at a villa in the north, on Lake Como, facing across to the Alps in late spring. They were met at the airport in Milan by a car and driver bearing the villa's insignia and then driven through flat city streets, then fields and increasingly winding roads to the villa itself, sitting above the town on a high promontory so that the intersection of two lakes met at its point. They were greeted by the director of the villa and his wife, introduced to those also in residence, some ten or eleven men and women, and taken to their rooms.

His own outrage was involved entirely with proposal, and with, he considered, what he had accomplished, their present situation being its latest condition. He loved her as he had assumed her to love him also, and he had been away, returning with the usual nervous hysteria and demand, to be, hopefully, comforted by her, his laundry seen to, and then he was off again, to make more money in a manner he found both egocentrically pleasing and hateful, by public lecture. They were to meet in Chicago at the airport. He remembered precisely the table they sat at, after he had asked her, obviously expecting no answer to confuse him, if she had fallen in love with anyone during his absence. When she answered, in her usual truth, that she had, but that it could not work, and that she continued to love him also, he was dumbstruck. A myriad of possible details, pruriently demanding, flooded his head. He insisted on facts, as he said, going over and over the dilemma of the information in his own increasingly drunken mind until they realised they had missed the flight to London. He called a friend and they went to his house, but the difficulty would not be eased, and they fought there too, himself falling and cutting one wrist on a glass that had been broken in their struggling together. The friend got them to a hospital where his wrist was sewn up by a contemptuous young doctor, without anaesthetic, possibly to make him feel the ugliness he was exuding. The friend left and after some walking, they found a hotel still open and spent the night in a restless attempt to sleep.

He was at the villa ostensibly to write. Both realized that it was markedly difficult to be long alone with each other in that his obsessively recurrent questions brought them again and again to bitterly useless argument. Too, the privacy necessary to her own life was being battered by his attacks. The alternatives were the other people, of course, but most were occupied during the day, either with their own work or with trips out into the surrounding country which he could not afford for his wife and himself. So he asked if it might be possible to have a small room apart from the suite given him in which to work.

At one point in the villa's history one of the militant Sforzas, who then owned it, designed a retreat for his monastic brother in the form of lovely gardens and walks through charming copses of trees. Small cells, or *casetas*, were erected at various points along the edges of the cliff for meditation, and it was one of these he was now given, in which to work. Its space was roughly six feet square, with a large window extending almost to the floor overlooking the lake. It seemed a small tower, of stone, and delighted him entirely.

So each morning he would retire to the caseta, while she went on up the path to the ruins of a small castle on the very head of the hill which the villa occupied. This was encircled with a low wall of stone and again the view was impressive. At noon he would break off whatever he was doing and go up to join her, and both would wait for the appearance of two of the villa's servants, in white jackets, carrying a lunch for them in a wicker basket complete with fruit, wine and napkins. Sitting there, it was possible for him to let go of his resentment and to be with her in a way actual to the place itself.

He had come to Europe first as a young man, after the war, but only briefly and then only to England. His group was being repatriated and while they waited for other priorities to be respected, they sat in a small army camp close to Cardiff. That had acquainted him with the *oldness* of Europe, but it was a very faint sense. He had been with these people in a war, the most contemporary of realities, and continuing with them elsewhere did not lessen that impact of the present. After marriage, he returned to Europe with his family, and lived for two years near Aix in the south of France, then for about the same period in a small town in the Balearic Islands of Spain. His self-conscious use of either French or Spanish kept him from ever really being there as an actual person of the place, but the daily involvement of his family certainly made him common. Especially in France, when he went out into nearby woods to attempt to find wood for a fire, he had the feeling he was walking on ground that innumerable persons had also walked on, over and over, making a weight of time he had not thought of as possible. Human life he had begun to recognize as an accumulation of persistent, small gestures and acts, intensively recurrent in their need if not, finally, very much more than that. The *ideas* they delighted in, or suffered, however much they did affect the actuality of all, were nonetheless of a very small measure of possibility. Hunger or happiness, exhaustion or the security of home, both the measure and the vocabulary were extraordinarily simple.

At meals he considered, somewhat defensively, the facts of their company. He felt *nouveau*, an upstart, among them. He recognized their names as those of an eminent company. One, affable and in no wise condescending, had directed the Marshall Plan in Europe after the war. Another was a markedly famous journalist and spoke very easily of presidents and the worlds they are found in. A third, English, an accomplished historian, had been previous Vice Chancellor of Cambridge. To him he referred the poems of Basil Bunting, which the older man took off to his room with some interest. But himself, complacently angry and despairingly unable to regain a place familiar to him, was unwittingly awkward and almost hostile. In private he was both contemptuous and defensive. His wife, as love, had gone to hide her head among the stars.

A small brochure, given them on their arrival along with details of the times of meals and other daily activities, noted the history of the villa. Its first recorded possession was by Pliny the Elder, who had used it apparently as a farm and retreat from the hotter southland. Both Plinys make mention of it. Subsequently it was owned by the Sforzas previously mentioned and must have remained for some time in their family. Leonardo de Vinci speaks of the view from that ruin where his wife and he ate lunch daily and, in his *Journals*, remarks that one may see the waterfall across the lake in the small town of Fiumetta. Stendhal had been a visitor, as had also Flaubert, and in modern times, as one says, Mussolini, fleeing for his life, had been apprehended as he was trying to reach it. It was finally purchased by the daughter and heir of a wealthy American whiskey manufacturer and then given by her to the foundation whose grantee he now was. The Kennedys had used it, for conferences, despite the irritation of its administrators. It went on and on.

One night, after a particularly nattering attack on her, his wife left their room, still in nightgown and robe, and went off through the interminable corridors and passageways to escape him. He thought to go after her, but at the door, looking out at the silence of the dark halls, he could not. Later she reappeared, smiling, to tell him that one of the eldest servants, an old man who worked as night watchman, had seen her and deferentially offered to follow with his lamp so that she might find her way. How simple the intrusion of factual needs upon affairs of conjecture and assumption.

As he sat in the caseta, sunlight flooding the window, the lake far below, what was so adamantly there to be written. "Sun bright,/trees dark green, . . ./a little movement/in the leaves." He could hear the sound of a small outboard motor on a boat below him, voices talking, laughing. Best that one's needs be simple because there seemed no true alternative to that condition. No one of those previously to have been here, not the farmer nor soldier nor monk nor artist nor writer nor dictator nor anyone at all, were more actual, after all. It came and then went. "Birds singing/measure distance,/intervals between/echo silence."

$$2 \cdot 3 \cdot 1$$

Five

WAITING FOR THE door to open, they think that Betty's teeth are equally present in Marjorie's mouth. They look the same, large, white, hard. The horse seizes upon the carrot in the small child's hand not because he is hungry, but because he has extraordinary teeth. Teeth work in the mastication of food in a manner mutually agreed upon by uppers and lowers insofar as these do meet, upon the jaw's being closed. Open or closed, the doorway itself stood empty although they waited still. His mother would often both delight and frighten him by popping forward the two plates of her false teeth to make an extraordinary face. Most people know that George Washington's teeth were made of wood. Teeth is the plural of tooth in much the same manner as wives is the plural of wife, or *rooves* possibly means more than one roof, though it is entirely a situation of personal choice, depending on the person or persons involved with saying such things. People waiting in fixed circumstances of anticipation often find themselves committed to speaking in a manner frequently without interest.

Raise the roof, he said, biting his teeth in anger. He ground his teeth in his sleep. He had frequently a toothache. Dentists take care of teeth for payment and spend much of their waking hours looking into mouths. They wait for the door to open without apparent interest, knowing it will only be more teeth. Sometimes they are committed to pulling out teeth, no doubt feeling relief in getting rid of them. Young boys are often told that the vagina contains teeth. The tooth mother (*mater dentata*) is one of the significant guises of the great mother herself. Teeth are frequently hung around the neck in the form of a necklace. Dark spots on the teeth may signify caries or cavities in the tooth itself. People frequently make an inordinate sound chewing celery, a noise attributable to the action of the teeth. One knows a number of people who are proud of their teeth. Others may have buck teeth, a term possibly having to do with rabbits. Others have broken teeth, or possibly missing teeth, where some blow has caused the specific tooth to loosen and fall out. 'I'll knock your teeth down your throat,' is a phrase used to intimidate anticipated opponents in some muscular struggle.

"The rat has teeth" is the first line of a poem translated from the Chinese by Ezra Pound. "Habet dentes" is part of the phrase with which he was involved. I have a car and will drive you to Des Moines, says Betty. Marjorie notes the population of Des Moines is 209,000. Although neither has as yet come, they are close friends of the assembled people who wait for them with unabated interest.

What is anger that, when she at last arrives, Betty's teeth are knocked down her throat? Marjorie's mother has teeth and will not let her come. They have all gathered in a bus station while waiting to be driven to Des Moines. One of the more thoughtful of the group takes out a small volume of Ezra Pound's Chinese translations and begins reading the one about the rat's having teeth. It is well received by all who listen. Betty, tickled by the parallel reference, laughs through broken teeth. The door at last opens and those who come in realise they know none of those who are there. Where are we, is one of the first statements made by persons in both groups. The question, questions, hangs, hang, in the air.

One thinks the most distasteful of possible human practices is the knocking out of teeth on battle fields so as possess the gold to be found in them. He can recall no instance of dentists' offices being burgled for the gold to be found in them in anticipation of using that metal for inlays. Nor is there clear sense of what happens to removed teeth, unless one is still a child. He dreams of the tooth fairy, come to reward him for letting his grandmother pull out the dangling front tooth. The tooth itself is under his pillow but the subsequent hand, reaching under there to possess it and leave the money in its place, moves with such assured stealth the sleeper has no consciousness of what is really going on.

One will never forget the large gold tooth hanging outside the office of the hero in a novel by Frank Norris, although one has never literally seen it. In like sense one tends to remember God, although he has not frequently been seen either. The mind has a power, like teeth, and immediately bites into what it has anticipated as prospective reality. One friend was a dentist for the mentally disturbed and recounted innumerable stories involved with teeth in sexual associations. The skulls of skeletons contain teeth more frequently than any other remnant of the clearly human condition, excepting the bone itself.

Teeth are permanent fingernails, that require no cutting. The blades of the harrow are often called teeth. Gears have teeth as do a great variety of fish. He wants to throw away his teeth in the anticipation of freedom. The sowing of the dragon's teeth resulted in the instant growth of formidable warriors, who attacked forthwith those who confronted them. The false teeth still kept in the drawer, although the actual owner had died, were subject of great interest to the young. Teeth are gall stones, in the mouth, with sharp edges. The teeth of the saw had been dulled by attempting to cut into metal. Some persons file their teeth, primarily for the appearance thus gained. Horses have their teeth filed to permit them to eat more comfortably. Who has not had his tooth removed by being sawed into four sections, and does not remember it? Steel teeth, despite rusting, might prove more convenient than wooden teeth, which would become soggy by constant immersion in the mouth itself.

The love bite, or nip, is practiced by animals and humans. The ear, especially, is seized upon. Betty's teeth were attractive, as were Marjorie's, but upon being hit in the mouth she realized that they were now gone. One forgets that walking into the teeth of the blizzard is an unfortunate circumstance. The police want teeth put into laws because they are hungry. Toot, toot. To sound a horn or whistle in short blasts. He showed his teeth, expecting trouble.

The door was a mouth without teeth. The broken windows of the vacant factory looked like teeth in a broken mouth. The teeth lying on the beach apparently belonged to no one. They could not remove the dog's teeth from the shoulder of the small victim. Remembering Betty and Marjorie, and going to Des Moines, is true. Getting one's teeth into it clears the head and the air.

●

THE STORIES KEEP coming back even if the people themselves are long gone. Memory seems to stay active no matter anyone really wants it that way, and the old *do you remember the time* number is a really heavy one. I went back last summer to see what the place looked like now, and I found they had moved the road from out in front of the stone wall, where it used to be, to even further out front, so that you can't even see that the house is there at all. The house itself and the barn and shed look much the same, but they have added some other buildings toward the back of the field, and it looks pretty settled in a way it never did when we were there.

Those days it seemed we would go the whole winter without much company at all, except for the few families that lived within a mile or so of us, up the road. When summer came, we were always pretty eager to have friends from the city come up and spend some time with us. One friend even took a job working in the woods, to help us keep the scene together. That was the summer we lived for the most part on chickens and blackberries since that was all we could get hold of. The garden hadn't come in yet and what we had canned ran out in the early spring. It was all an idea, in a way, but we were certainly serious and we were also young enough to bumble along without falling completely on our faces.

There was a lovely pool, up in the woods, formed by the river that came through part of our land, then angled off to make the lower boundary down by the railroad tracks where the large garden was. There was a smaller garden, for the kitchen, close to the house, but the big one was where we had the potatoes, corn, beans, all the vegetables we used primarily for canning. The pool used to get a lot of attention and it was well known to all our neighbors and even to the people in the outlying towns. One motel owner used to tell the people staying there, that they were free to use the pool, and that bothered us. In the summer the woods often got so dry that people smoking, or trying to make fires for cooking, could burn the whole woods down quicker than anyone could ever stop it. We tried to keep people out, just making it open to our neighbors, who knew what the risks were and were equally concerned, and still the other people kept coming. We even put up a big gate, anchored to posts that were sunk in cement, and somehow they got the whole thing out, posts, cement, and all. One time a travelling carnival, that had been in town over the weekend, chose our pool, or actually the road up to it, to dump all their garbage in. It took weeks to clean all that up.

So it was an idea, in mind, as to whether or not really to want people, any people, to come at all, much as we often did love them. Quail, and sometimes pheasant, would come to eat with the chickens, and that was a pleasure. During hunting season, when people were really careless and often drunk as well, we kept our dog close to home and sometimes other dogs, who had got on a scent, then lost themselves following it, would straggle into our yard. We'd check their tags, call the owners, usually local, and then they would come and get them. Our dog was a bitch and there was one particular old basset hound who would come, each year we lived there, and get himself stuck in the cat door, trying to get into the house. There we'd find him in the morning, wheezing away.

The people simplest to visit with were, in some ways, the various travelling salesmen that came through. By the time they had got to our place, they probably knew they weren't going to make any sales of any great amount, just that it was a poor part of the state and our place was obviously no exception. But it was lovely, especially in the summer, and they would come in anyhow, just to talk and look around a little. We would give them some coffee, or beer if we had it, and then we would all sit around telling whatever stories came to mind. There were two men selling siding for Johns Manville I especially remember, both of them sort of brash but good-natured and finally not really meaning to bother anyone. They tried to sell us some siding at first but when they realized we were broke, they just sat down and talked. They would joke about the siding itself, although it seemed as good as any other. One would take a piece of it, say, this is the strongest we got, never will break, then slap it down on his knee and it would shatter into a dozen pieces. That somehow seemed awful to us, just that we were the people who would usually be buying such stuff, and when the salesmen said, this is really strong, we found ourselves believing them more often than not. It was the idea again, that had really got hold of us. The same men had a sort of game they would play, to pass the time that must have got pretty boring, driving all those miles to all those old farms they hoped would buy some of their asbestos shingles. They came in all colors, some of them pretty loud for that part of the country, and so the salesmen would try to see what sort of wild color combinations they could get some unsuspecting farmer to let them put all over his house and barn. They would talk about a blue and orange one they had done over near St. Johnsbury, or else a pink and green one they had done down near Plymouth. Then they would laugh and we did too. It made us feel cheap but thankfully they weren't talking about our house and barn. It was a small blessing.

It was the idea of it all, that we could never get entirely clear. The salesmen were one small part of it. They were real in it, certainly. The farmers around us were, the people in town. One man we knew had never gone more than twenty-five miles from the place he was born. When we asked him one time if he'd like to drive down to Boston with us, his answer was he didn't know anybody there so he didn't see any point in going. A lot of people were like that, even those who had gone into the army and been shipped to Germany or the Phillipines. They just stayed there and when someone had gone away and then come back again, their usual greeting was something like, I haven't seen you around lately, and then whoever was talking would just pick up there as though the other person hadn't been gone more than a few days at most. That idea of people being in a place so completely we never could get to ourselves. We saw the people as moving in places and they apparently saw it the other way round.

There was one man I remember, who seemed a little different but no less of the place. We had geese that year and I let them range pretty much at will. One day a car stopped and this man got out to enquire if I had a gander for sale since he had several geese but no gander, and he wanted to breed them. I didn't, as it happened, but we got talking about geese, and then one thing and another, and I invited him in to meet my wife and have some coffee, and he accepted. I remember particularly his look, rather quiet and shy and a little withdrawn in that sense. He said he was the northern New Hampshire and Vermont representative for the International Correspondence School. He was also a deacon in his local church, over near St. Johnsbury. He was dressed neatly, in an old black suit, carefully so. He told us he was married to, as he put it, a very sweet and very godly woman. He said she really had one aim in her life, and that was to make him happy and to do what he wanted her to. She never raised her voice nor let any of her own needs become more important than his. He said, in fact, that his only confusion in living with her was that he never really knew what she wanted or even if she wanted anything at all. He would try to please her at times, by bringing something back from one of his visits to get people to sign up for the correspondence courses, and she always liked it. It didn't seem to matter much what it was. It could be a flower he picked coming up the walk into the house or a new iron or even a new shawl or hat. She always liked it and said it was so good of him to think of her. He didn't make much money with his work and she knew that, and she never complained. One time, he was ashamed to say, he had lost his temper, he was so worried about what they might do next, they had no money, and she just said she knew it would be all right and that he would do just fine. He said he had hit her, and she never said a word or complained after that about it. He felt lonely at times just that he didn't feel he really knew what she wanted at all. It was almost too good, he said, her never wanting anything or saying anything, really, to him at all. He found he was driving a lot, and the car was not in very good shape, it was an old Pontiac, and he should keep it just for the business he had to, but at times he had to get out of the house. He loved her, she was his wife, but he wished she would talk to him and tell him what she really felt underneath.

His son worried him too, he said. He was a good boy, and a strong one, for thirteen, but he would forget things. He would start out walking to school and somehow never get there. School would be over and someone would come tell them that the boy hadn't been there and ask if he was sick. Sometimes it would even be dark before they could find him. He would just be sitting there, most often out in the woods by himself, and when they asked him what he was doing and why he hadn't gone to school, he couldn't answer them. All the boy would or could say was that he'd forgot.

•

VOICES FROM the silence. Silencio inmenso. Darkness falls from the air. When I show myself as I am, I return to reality. Vestida con mantos negros. Somewhere else, sometime. Walking in the rain.

When I show myself as I am, I return to reality. Piensa que el mundo es chiquito. Goes green, goes white. Weather falls out, raining. Applause at the edges. Seeing wind. When I show myself as I am, I return to reality. People should think of themselves when they live alone. Goes white.

Vestida con mantos negros, piensa que el mundo es chiquito. Thinks white. Falls from the air. Sees green, sees white. People should think of themselves when they live alone. Now I am not so sure. In the big city, you are your own best friend. I see you. Walks streets at night. Goes green, goes white.

I began to make self-portraits because working at night I had no other model. Thinks that the world is little. Weather walking, in rain. I used myself over and over again. Sees green. Passing people, goes forward, goes green, goes white. I would learn about myself. Y el corazón es inmenso, laughing. Seeing tears, feeling edges. Pause of applause, in the big city. You are your own best friend.

I put things where they belong. I return to reality. People should think of themselves. Walks streets at night, working at night. I had no other model. I used myself over and over. I see you. In the big city. People should think of themselves. Goes green, goes white.

Turning. I like to make combinations that seem incongruous. I love you. I think they are coming. I wrote you last week. I want to sit here awhile by myself. I think it's better this way. I put things where they belong. A hand at the end of an arm. Goes green. Walks streets at night. Little world. She thinks the heart is big. Bigger. Biggest. I used myself over and over again. A mouth a little below the nose. Goes white.

Piensa que el mundo es chiquito. Small. Little. Not very much. I would learn about myself. I used myself. I show myself as I am. Goes green, goes white. The heart. Y el corazon es immenso. Large. Immense. Sees rain. A hand at the end of an arm.

I was very sad. I was very happy. I was thinking of rain, walking. People should think of themselves. I started doing something funny. I need a lot of affection. I return to reality. I had no other model. I used myself over and over. I put things where they belong. I show myself as I am. I started doing something funny so I would become happier. People I met were so depressing. And it worked. You are your own best friend. Vestida con mantos negros.

Postscript

"My death," said a certain ogre, "is far from here and hard
to find, on the wide ocean. In that sea is an island, and
on the island there grows a green oak, and beneath
the oak is an iron chest, and in the chest is a
small basket, and in the basket is a hare,
and in the hare is a duck, and in the
duck is an egg; and he who finds
the egg and breaks it, kills
me at the same
time."

Mabel: A Story

1 · 2 · 3
3 · 1 · 2
2 · 3 · 1
1 · 2 · 3
3 · 1 · 2

Points define a periphery.
EZRA POUND

*Oh Mabel, we
will never walk
again the streets*

*we walked in
1884, my love,
my love.*

1 · 2 · 3

One Again

SENSING, moving out, or not to move out but rather, *be there*, quiet, after months of impatient and restless crisis, or voices endlessly breaking, rising, so much continual anger.

A sound. Says, *don't try to move it, we'll help*. Hair. Hear. Here. Don't try to move it. But not in English. Reaches down to the legs, or feet. Cannot absorb distance. Feels no space surrounding, or going out. Feels late, but present. A moment late. Wants nothing or for nothing. Completely provided for, either way.

I sense your eyes, my dear. Are upon me. All a babble, baby's. Babies. Eats them for lunch. Hurry. Ridiculous instruction. To sit in the car, waiting.

Sensing sheets. Of blood. Paper. Cloth. Don't try to move it. Feels head, side, empty, wet, wants patterns. Thinks to slam the fist down. No hand. To help with everything. Anything.

Bloody sheets. The first time in Nova Scotia. The first time in the hotel. The first time in that room, returned, coming to it through history. Now.

The room has been taken. So says the room clerk, the manager. Who knew anything. Before. Years to come to. Still.

Feels him all over. Screaming. Don't try to move it. The sheets. Are wet. Sticky.

To know, in the beginning, the end. Cannot hear hair. Here. Stand still, and let it. Bloody. Wants to move out and say hello.

Having been there, or rather, is coming. Wants to join the others. Through history. Feels films over eyes, feels hands, over head. Not touching. Feels fine, feels awful. Sensing the rest of it. Wants to come back to, go to. Babies.

Girl boys, boy girls. People. In streets, in places. Staggering buildings of brick and sand, up, up, up. All fall down, grumpa. Number one. Number one and number two. Together. Hair to the knees. Through the blood. Eat it. Shit. Fuck. Cunt. Eat it.

Up and at them. *Don't try to move.* It. Her. Him. Argument of no avail. No hole. No place. No pattern. No head. No top. No bottom.

No feelings in it anywhere. No nice people with long hair. Nowhere in the faces before they come here.

Talking says to fix it up simply. Sea. Sew, rather. Saw. Can't see. Sheets of blood looks red through, at people possibly. Is sitting. Waiting. *Every normal person. Inside the mother. The fetal to the adult. This possible future.* Quote.

Quack. Quaint. *Queynt.* Cunt. And a jolly good time to lie fallow. Fellow. "Literally a laying together of property." Quote. As if stuck. In the throat. Her a hymn heard of her. Him. Gets out.

First mention of person to whom all coming was going to get there and sat down at last freed of encumbrance and stared at the world thus constituted as daily menu and peace and quiet and love and hands across the sea, mon cher. *Ma belle.* I want to sit at *Mabel's* table. No tell hotel.

•

HEARSAY. M's determination at times to be singular, so proposes a sadly endless consequence of herself shall be trailed through minds of her time like roses. She wants to count, and does, as she puts it, count. She is a large, rather sturdy, young woman. She does not particularly enjoy this aspect of herself except that it carries her through, so to speak. She can be, variously, the expected demure young lady, or else the bar-stool swinging drunken broad. It doesn't really seem to matter that much to her. She is an age hard to determine. Very young quite probably, five or six, in her own mind, but also markedly old, looking down on it, whatever, some other persons or circumstance, from that abstract wiseness.

She is attractive, was, either way. Be her daddy, if you want to, or brother, also possible. She tells you she is a bastard, and smiles. She likes uniqueness. She takes off her clothes somewhat slowly, or begins to, then shucks them like husks from ears of corn.

The story is that her father was some sort of musician, or singer, possibly an opera singer, in the provinces, who, as so many, does fade off in a pattern of incompetences. She meets him once when in her late teens, possibly for tea, and sees the seedy sad person she has so long anticipated. Daddy. There seems no longer much point in securing the acquaintance.

Her brother dies in his early twenties, she says. She speaks of it quite frequently, his promise, the handsomeness of his body, the almost delicate gentleness she associates with him. He has or had a wife, but she is forgotten.

Possibly it is the bleeding, victimized 'Christ' of her girls' school, all the 'victims' the nuns so eulogize. One experiences the sensation of nails pressing into palms, scarifying, making driplets of pale blood. She wants to enclose this creature in her head, secure him with pale tendrils of barbed wire, lash him with whips. She knows very surely that he will succumb, give in, she says, to her budding desires. At this time she is approximately twelve or thirteen years old.

Her mum has humor equal to her own. They roar together, at times, making the company a little nervous. They also drink heavily together one suspects, knocking back glass after glass of pale whiskey. They are Irish together, with a little Scots thrown in for endurance. Tough, independent ladies, so they say.

Mum takes orders for reputable functionary medicines. Migraine, things that ladies need, an ampule or two. No joke to it. She has been long in the business, has the tone, in fact, of a clearly practical woman. One wonders what they think of one another, other than being 'mum' or the daughter. Other than the jokes.

She wants the man, so to speak, to fantasize their relation, be the bleeding moors boy, be the brother. And into her, against her fainting protests, put it. She apostrophizes often. Ooooooh. It is yummy in proximity to her moony belly, bottoms up then, sits in the lap. From the back, she says, happy. One can still hear her laughter, apart from it, looking down with her insistently wry amusement.

She works herself as an artist, competently and in some ways successfully. But her income is either a meager allowance from things that have been sold by her dealers, or else her employment as a secretary. She types like a drummer, ratatatatat, fast. She says she dislikes it but finds work. But it interrupts, as she says, her own.

Her place is one room, with the loo and bath down a flight, shilling for the geyser. The bed jams up against the wall, a table is fixed alongside the sink, on which she has her typewriter, her other utensils for work. As paints, etc. Sometimes she uses a friend's studio, for the larger space. Her clothes hang against the wall, on hangers, neat enough. She brushes her hair with short, decisive strokes, teasing it into an attractive bush. Her eyes are quite large, blue, and her nose somewhat snub, her mouth capable of much expression as is said. She is unequivocally a large young woman.

Her dreams are factually modest and what extensions they have she undertakes to provide for herself. As being the victim, as going to Egypt. Under the moon. She does not particularly want to hurt anybody, just to have it happen coincidentally. When she is apprehended destroying papers in one office she frequents, she glares at the woman whose 'business' she is attacking, but also winks.

She lives a life quite specific, dresses well, is known as an interesting woman generally, leaves decisive friends in her wake. But still falls in love disastrously, so say her friends, with fops, phonies, people waiting for her touch. She brings such enthusiasm to her encounters, possibly for this time to be forever.

She finds herself in her thirties somewhat confusedly. She did not want it to happen. There is a younger, considerate, even pleasant man in her life, but she cannot find direction in their occasion together. Introducing him, she is uncertain as to how to locate him in the company. Possibly she forgets him, walks off.

She has herself gained even more competences. She sits in bars looking them over, easily, at home. She goes *out of it* from time to time, crashing in publicly afforded sanitariums, being dragged back from Stockholm. Recovered, she wonders if she can handle acid again. Or is it too soon. One doctor, commenting, says that verbal therapy is useless. She is absolute. She wants something, someone, to change it.

The days shrink, the place grows smaller and smaller. She says the room is unlivable, now another, she says the people who lived in it shat all over her books, destroying them. The man has dissolved somehow.

The sun must be flooding into her mum's room now, where she's sitting, writing a letter to a friend, telling him she's in love, the wonder of it, the insistent, giddy-making pleasure, the man, the woman, wanting just to say hello.

•

SEEING VIDEO-TAPE interview last night of four women, mostly young, who had been raped – one four times in a two-week period, newly arrived in New York from an upstate small town. And when she goes home, to be safe, walking down street she knows by heart, someone there tries it. And at this point she's so frustrated, freaked, and just plain angry, she beats him up.

And. Who is it. Who's inside all this, who outside – where. Carolee laughs, saying, "they think there's some kind of broken glass in there." Or, "don't call me *strong*, lay off that 'male' 'measure' of 'reality'."

Is it water, ma. My hair's wet, my hands are all blood. *A sandwich of pure meat*, he used to say, floats by like a disattached pier. I got kids, man, I got kids – who are 'girls' their mother (put quotes around that) 'bore' – through the water, let us say, to that far distant shore.

In the head, mind pounding at the image, that hysterical face, very possibly one's own. He didn't know he was homosexual until they had tied both hands behind his back, spread his legs, and fucked him – having beaten him for some hours previous.

Or – androgyne. Melt me. C. says, no go – we ain't got it, nothing out front, no *tool*, so to speak, nothing to *prick* with, no club to wave in the air, threatening.

There is a sense, you have to give it to me, you're holding out, you cock teaser, you bitch. The Chief of Police in Berkeley says quite quietly he believes it must be the provocation these young women offer, for example, hitch-hiking, or simply walking the streets after six in the evening, say, with their present modes of dress. "No young woman . . ." or, more accurately, I cannot quote him because his language has rotted in my mind like garbage, "No girl of mine would . . ." But you would, and have – and endlessly fantasize its substance. The Chief of Police of any city in the country seems now a *falsie, a dildo*, an instrument of obscene intent factually.

You know they all want it. He dances, wiggling and croaking in falsetto. Oh, my dear . . . "That is just absolutely terrific! The only thing we can now do is play another piece by Bach . . ." Again. And if they were home, and if they were safe, and if they were good, and if they would listen – as the monstrously gross thing, with breasts, with spread legs, lifts up, in Sweden, with sweetly sick candy colors, permits the entry, into her, of daily crowds, hordes, of persons, rushing to be born no doubt – or just to see what it's like inside – there. They never knew it was so roomy, for example, nor that they'd have friends eating popcorn alongside.

This is not the 'play house' in the park's playground, for the kids, where they watch as the guy keeps the knife at her throat while groping her, and someone, a volunteer, steps up from the audience to light his cigarette since his hands are busy. Back home they wonder how Mabel is making out and hope she has remembered to write them as she said she would.

But my own hair, brown, grows long and tickles my back, and my breasts point provocatively, and my clit grows slick, and I finger it, faster, and faster, and – ahhh. And I am only a man, and a husband, and a father. I am not to blame.

I used to pray in the night for the unexpected though devoutly hoped for advent of some heavy number with unidentifiable 'arms' and 'legs' though the wings I could spot on the instant as 'it' flew through the window, and into my arms. I thought it was God in drag, possibly. I thought that no one would blame me for this communion. With this dear thing. Libel laws alone would prevent the violation of personal privacy. Elsewise they dragged her through the field by her hair, claiming that she had asked for it – that insistent phrase – and for two thousand years had done nothing else but bother them at their labors. Whereas the *thing* had no possible occasion finally but that created in our meeting – despite it was only in my mind or its – and was not offensive in the least.

Is it a 'hank of hair' – a table, a chair? Did you sit down, or stand up – in that body. Can't we dance, can't we melt, into one another – so good? Dear thing.

I feel so righteous, really cool! I have the world, no less, altogether within the strictness of my entirely just and responsive mind. And, dear ladies, no possible harm shall now come to you – because? Because I am *here*, and my wise and fond regard protects you from all harm, from all misunderstanding or misuse – and hand in hand, you and us, me-s, will stagger on until I really get tired, or bored, or just forget the whole business until some meat package thumps me to consciousness – and I smile, and love, and be, most truly, a man.

Here homage to Leonard Cohen, who remarked that more has gone down apropos the two inch pinch of skin just fore of a woman's vent than possibly from any other cause whatsoever. Which is to say, real estate, man's estate, to sit in state – Les États-Unis! God bless George Washington, the first president to put wooden teeth in the place he most expected to find them – his own mouth. How simple, once one knows the answer. And you walk around in the echoing tunnels, nothing at all to be feared, these sewers which are *shores*, my dear: a channel for draining a pond.

Was it *Voyage to the Bottom of the Night*, or *The Mill Pond's Gone* that most influenced you as a youth? Did you walk hand in hand with yourself? Did you hide around the corner when your sister, you gay devil, stomped from the bathroom with fresh flesh gleaming rose? Was your mother your first love? Jim goes out for a long one and the setting sun catches his extended quivering body in its last glowing so-called ray. There are sighs deep down in Rosedale for this youth's acquiescent ability. We'll have him for supper! We'll eat him on the spot.

Therefore why was it, when discovered on the parking lot's pavement with the young woman who was at that time my best friend's girl, that the policeman said, *go home?* We sat, sad years later, she and I, and we were waiting to hear Charlie Parker for the first time for either of us. She told me attempts to become an actress had foundered and that she was living with a practically famous novelist who was in Palm Springs for awhile, and the world had got vague and out of hand. Across from us was an old friend who eventually put me down as well, but that night he just looked at her, distant, didn't he said remember her, although she tried to locate herself for him, *Helen*, but he didn't respond and no doubt had his reasons.

There was another friend who'd come to the island we then lived in, or on, for an abortion, and I happened to run into her at the restaurant of the small pension where she was staying. She looked down and markedly ill, she had just had the operation and was still bleeding heavily. I was a young man thoughtful, I thought, of women, but beyond that – because it is a true abstraction – I really liked her and invited her to come back to the house with me, and stay with us until she felt better. Later that same evening another friend, a warmly decent one, came on to her, she was very handsome, and she tried to explain her disinterest, but he couldn't let go of it till some one of us made clear what was cause of her preoccupation. Then, of course, he backed off, confused, suspicious even that she might now not like men at all.

In my head, in men's heads generally, put it, is something like a memory or perhaps more accurately the *sound*, the *feel*, of water. One cannot live finally, too far from the sea, it is endlessly a place of initial being. I want, one day, to sail away on it, go out, forever.

Today, in the meantime, we were talking after the class was over, of ways in which men might be called, or referred to, by women. One woman suggested, *brother*. This, another friend, a man, said at least implies, *family*. With men, with my grandson, for instance, I would welcome, even yearn for, the hierarchic title that gives our relation its place in our male imagination of the world: *grandpa*. My own father died when I was so young I never felt that experience articulately, which is to say, I can never remember calling anyone consciously 'father' in that precise way.

And yet. I don't know. So much has rotted in the distortions of this consciousness, this presumption of reality, that I would yield its rationales and logics not very painfully at all. Or not – perhaps. Even would fight without mind at all, to protect them.

More literally, I had been thinking of Mabel, dumb, poor thing, in this case, hoping for help possibly if she thought of anything at all. She is drab beyond description, and invites really nothing of any consequence. She is poor, in body, in pocket, in life. Myself, who so projects *beauty*, a clarity of women, am impatient and irritated by her simple fact. I do not want my own life to know her. She frightens me. She invites a penitence I do not yet understand.

3 · 1 · 2
Two
Also

HE WAS TRYING to recall what, in any sense, he either did clearly know, or else might assume someone else to. There was no age specific to himself that he could think of. That is, twenty-eight? Or thirty-eight? Or forty-eight. Or what, biologically speaking, did the atrophying cells, so-called, of his body have to tell him more than that they were not as much *there* (did he know that?) as seemingly elsewhere. They had gone away, he thought – not dead, just gone.

He was now home. He was sitting in a chair adjacent to a television set, not as yet turned on, that he thought perhaps to turn on. Just like that. He could feel the markedly large *pieces of meat* (he laughed?) not too far from him, although he was certain enough of their very possible location, in the house. The sounds of pans, or pots, dishes, moving in the kitchen. That was Mabel undoubtedly. Noises from the floor above him – seem-ingly more Mabels, these younger, more critical in the sense, a critical mass. Nothing, however, struck him as being potentially disaster.

How long, he thought, had he lived there? Years and years. No real sense of any of its having begun at any one time, and not at all of its having ended. It was a more or less stable environ-ment. Meat eats meat, even the vegetables.

He patted the dog, male, who was pushing his hand with its head. *Good old boy*, he thought, *nice dog*. Truly the one other male to be considered – as when persons approached unexpectedly, and it barked, or else chased cars, aggressively, faced down other dogs, sniffed, licked, ran with them, after them. Its kind, of an order unlike the human, in some respects, but also like too – as sexes, etc.

The meat called, *eat* – and he gave up the inclination to watch the news as his hunger, stimulated, located itself and rose to walk out to the kitchen with his legs under it and his head on top as ever. The other persons joined him in a various pattern, as did that which had called, and he sat in the accustomed seat for him, male, at a sidewise authority, alongside that situation he had long ago felt incompetent to deal with, that is, the actual dispensing of the food itself, with its attendant circumstance of cutting, apportioning, handing over, and the like. Possibly he, as the dog, was most involved with just eating, and had the further reassurance, such as it was, that the food was possible insofar as he was possible. They came together, at least in the terms of the present arrangement. Therefore the others had themselves to justify, as their appetites, their various realities might propose. He could not finally help them with that dilemma because it was not his own, thankfully, and he had no *appetite* (he *did* laugh) to further complicate his own very substantial *world*.

So let's eat, he said. Quickly accomplished with a minimum of talking. Full mouths make at best a rather sloppy, muffled response, and he had nothing much in mind that referred to their specific information. The meat was a little dry, not quite to his own taste, but to say that aloud to the other would only stir familiar disgruntlements, which, after a markedly long time of shared existence, were only of use when some larger counter of attack or coercion was factually at stake. He also disliked the faint experience of meanness, which tended to occur, a *je ne sais quoi* of uneasiness he had discovered to be depressing.

It was not really a bad life, he thought, again, not at all as *bad* as it might be. Certainly not for them, who had none of the real responsibility of their situation. Being a man, he wondered a little about that, what it might be like, to be thus an *object*. He couldn't finally think those who found alternatives had accomplished very much at all. At best they became somewhat card-board *people*, false *men* that no real one would ever be fooled by.

He recalled one's having told him that she was continually expected to look *feminine*, despite the fact that she was president of the small business involved. But surely that was her own problem, and her *meat* might surely have been sold without that complication. A handsome piece, in fact.

So the evening was as long as usual, nothing strange in that. He used time as now very sparingly at best. He found the least involvement with whatever the others might be occupied by, was best. He could speak to them, even warmly, with sufficient vagueness of understanding to divert their questions, if they had actually got that far, or, more likely, their somewhat insistent wish, it did seem, to tell him *things*. But what things? Well, he couldn't really remember even one of them because he did not really feel them close to his own centers of concern.

He shirked the question of the dog's feeding – he let that be governed by impulse, his own – and also participation in the washing of dishes. He felt that chores of the house, with the exception of those specifically involving his strength or knowledge of men's common interests and abilities, were rightly the labor of the others. One can't be given such things as he had been given, to take care of, and not come through with some strict codification of one sort or another. His parents had persistently told him of the need to *be a man*, in a great diversity of contexts, e.g., when in economic situation, when in social situation, when in sexual situation. Insofar as he too had wanted to *be a man*, there was no particular harshness, he felt, in what his parents had done. The whole society had conspired, so to speak, to so *create* him, after his initial birth – thanks to a *mother*, of course, who no doubt had been as passive in that role as in any other.

Life, he thought, is truly more than any one of its possible terms or persons. Thankfully. Appropriately. There could not be error in a circumstance which was, to begin with, so *natural* – men exist biologically without doubt, surely – and so *functional* – do they not have things to do? – and so explictly *social* – women really do love them *that way*. Such alternatives as he had ever chance to observe were almost without exception abhorrent – cocksuckers, weaklings, gigolos, babies. Not very happy prospects for the one about to be. Anything. So the world had literally saved him much time, and money, and self-respect.

Given Mabel, and her miniatures, their children, he had no very actual regrets. Possibly very few men ever really did have regrets, at least not for that part of their lives. It could not, given the circumstances, have been very markedly different. He supposed it was initially some *sexual* condition that insured the arrangement, brought them to men at all. He recalled some person he had read of, who had sexual *intercourse* early each morning with a prostitute so as to clear his head for the day's business. Good, if one could, to have that nagging enjoyment well satisfied before undertaking anything else at all. It was a persistent itch, somehow, not at all one he very clearly understood, and he had abjured masturbation early just that it left him somewhat weakly breathless and much confused, and was argued against as being *dirty* or even selfish. That is, he could not find a simple alternative that did so leave him *free* for other, more complicated responsibilities. He also at times enjoyed the quiet sense of power that the *meat's* response to him did engender.

The sun had sunk some time past, leaving the small house in a fixed tightness of glaring light bulbs and intensively emphasized *places*. Upstairs the lights now went off, to deactivate that area for the night. He could hear the mild snoring of the persons above, thankfully at rest. He had kissed each *good night*, as their father, and was grateful that that could be that. He imagined, very briefly, the unwieldy distortion of having some more insistent relation with any of them, something flooding the mind with confusions. It was not a pleasant consideration. Incest can never be a happy state, he thought, and continued with his initial *aperçu*.

Love comes riding in like a horse, like a pig in a waistcoat, like mama dancing at the Ritz. Fabulous show, so rich in its *appointments*. He catches the waitress' eye, whose clothes thus fall instantly from her voluptuous body, and her *tits* hit his plate with a jarring thud. He dozes in the brackish water, flops laconically in its mucky shallows. He scratches his proud balls with an *oof!* of contentment. He is uncommonly ready.

In bed, the *meat* beside him, he congratulates himself, as is said, on the provision he has managed. Nothing lacking, so to speak. The whole situation is wallowing in an apparent *hearsay* of Mabels, all of whom he has actually met at one time or another in their life together. What he has loved is this flashing, challenging *change* in the person, now this one, now that one. Fondling what he can unobtrusively reach, of it, he remembers the cutaway sections of the black gauzy nightgown, permitting the congested blood-red nipples to reveal themselves as *just for him.* Cozy. His own sex festers into a congealed erection. He gropes more particularly, one hand for light switch, one for dearly enduring Mabel's *meat.*

Give it to me, is what he is saying, but tries to think of other words. The meat rises. Severed from the body, a series of *steaks*, it considers him mutely. Thus he is fed.

•

WOMAN, THY NAME is *wife-man*, the word *man* being formerly applied to both sexes. This word became *wimman*, plural *wimmen*, in the tenth century, and this plural is still in use in spoken English. Your *womb* has *wombat won* and *wonder wondrous wonts* to *woo.* I see indeed, see *leman* is sweetheart, dear, "a man or woman."

Or *girl* – often used to mean boy, a *child.* 'And when the gaygirls were into the garden come, Fair flours they founde . . .' Circa 1350. Come by.

Oh *Gill*, a woman's name, a pitcher, ground ivy! Oh *Gillie!* my boy, my servant! Know that *wife* is a woman, neuter substantive, with plural *wif* (unchanged), and certainly *not* allied to *weave*, as the fable runs. It is *widow* and *wig* and *wigwams* in the *wild wilderness*, for all your wilful *wiles.* Madam.

My lady, *mea domina*, being femine of *dominus*, a lord. Or dear lady, perhaps *loaf kneader?* This is not right, lost in remote places, no doubt, as time has travelled and will. But that *lady* was specially used to mean the Virgin Mary, hence lady-bird, lady's-slipper, etc., I have little doubt. Thus a lass may well be loose, but most certain is the lack of a fixed abode, think you. Or *spinster*, or *lasch*, a woman (a term of contempt).

Dear adult female human. With allusion to qualities usually

attributable to female sex: mutability, capriciousness, proneness to tears. And also to position of inferiority or submission: "to make a woman of . . ." Shall we laugh in the seventeenth century, fond *woe-man*, dear *wee-men*? Ha.

But what then swells, muttering, behind us, *hysterical passion* – in English, Dutch, Icelandic, Danish, Swedish, German, Irish, and Gaelic, Russian, Lithuanian, Latin, Greek, Persian, and Sanskrit. With original sense uncertain. Be it mouth, or myth – the hole.

Into earth, out of earth.

> *O, how this mother swells up toward my heart!*
> *Hysterica passio, down, thou climbing sorrow;*
> *Thy element's below. Where is this daughter?*

This *mother, womb*, these *lees*, this *mouldiness*. We may even find in Greek *an old woman* used in the sense of mother or dregs. But the female parent is not only an apparatus for raising chickens artificially, nor that *scum* alone. *That* term may belong to the vocabulary of alchemy, earliest usage 1538.

Rather, *humours* – "tied to the mysterious physiology of fucking?" The womb is a *belly, wam*, belly of a fish. And mother England. "The rising of the mother in women, it cures . . ." Rising, swelling upward. Later superseded by *dam*, which was restricted to quadrupeds. All aspects of care, nourishment, source, etc.

Thoughtful, picks it from the fire, feels the warmth of its body, considers it. Is transformed.

•

As IF A translucent wall, an invisible shield, an implacable distance. As if time, space. As if.

Those gestures mimicking his own he realises without confusion, knows them easily. He catches the man's smile, feels his conforming. The kids he grew up with, the gang, the woods.

But one other he does not know at all. He seems to contain her, in thinking of her. He puts her in his head.

He remembers, at five, specific odors, somewhat sweet – cachets? Or has realized that for some reason the sweat, the perspiration, has a differentiating smell, or is it that he cannot smell his own, or that of the other boys, distinctly? Souring clothes, still wet in the overheated room, make a sweet stench. Gas. Wood smoke. Clean sheets.

She grunts, in her sleep, lying belly down, hair spread out on pillow. He stands by the bed, looking at her.

Before names, then, seeing, feeling her. Ride back from Boston, from Youth Concert, girl sitting jammed against him whose name he cannot now remember, simply the legs forced together, floods him with excitement so that his penis grows huge and ejaculates in floods of milky liquid. Like that. Late at night perhaps. Falls on her. Looking at the pictures.

First time seen truly, older quondam friend has brought them to his room to 'fuck', the 'prostitute' has been there, he says, for two days now, drunk. Taking turns. He is first and goes into bedroom, leaving the others in the room back of it, sees in faint light sprawled form of black woman, twenty-six, twenty-eight, large, body in vacant ease, asleep? Sees rounds of breasts, naked, legs stretched out, sheet off. Incredible. Sounds of her breathing, occasional shift or shrug of body. Eyes suddenly open, look, see him, she laughs and holds out her hands. He falls into them, helpless, holds to her sweating dark largeness. Sentimental. Long ago. Nothing at all ever happened.

What was it called – girl watching? With music? I'd like to put the boots to her. Flushed. Embarrassed. Apparently indelible photo in magazine found in France, extraordinarily small, fine-boned girl, very thin, in fact, breasts seeming shuddering immensities. Ahhh. Do it. Do it.

Let me hold that package for you while you open the door. It's time to feed the animals. I'll fix it tomorrow. One more shelf and all the books will be straight. Off the floor.

A man's place in the home. The garage? Out back? Come to bed, it's a big day tomorrow. I'm tired? Why questions.

Pilot program, to get it straight. You stand here and then look at me. A little higher. Can you please reach that plate off the shelf. The hook? Higher than I can. Bigger? Whatever you think, then. We're all so proud of you. Aunt Bernice and the birthday cake with the violets. Fuck me? Someone has to start it.

No idea whatsoever as to what else is the case. Other opinions. He simply likes the whole thing. He simply doesn't. Makes up his mind, or cannot. Why make trouble. One after another, all the same apparently. No one seems to mind.

He meets her on the dock as they leave the train to go to the cafe for the last time before they're back again. Over and over. Nowhere, he finds. The hair keeps growing, and being cut. The age is approximately thirty-six, seen from the angle of an inclined plane, having various pretensions. Things to do, that is. He raises a family in five minutes and then feels restless. What's the next thing. Another family in five minutes and then feels restless. Clock runs faster than he knew.

Who's her. What's. He sniffs persistently. He should blow his nose more often. No woman will like him, take to him, dripping all that effluvia. He sweats clinkers of unexpectedly black fat. He washes his face, then his hands, before going out.

He circles around coming again and again to himself. He crouches on the edge, silent, waits, then leaps. Himself. He is as close as he feels it possible to be, breathes in her mouth, sticks fingers in her actual body. Cannot get there. Returns to himself to consider.

I don't know why you even came. I certainly don't know what you want to do. Go away.

The pictures show a couple as two people, man and woman, with the frequent addition of children. A house, car out front. They put the bags into it. Will you help carry this? Sure.

He sees her sitting at a booth toward the back of the restaurant, talking to the friend, the other girl, who has arranged the meeting at his request. The first girl does not know that he is to be there. He gets up, walks toward the table, already practising gestures of greeting. Hi! He constructs love for her in his head, over and over. He is serious.

Eighty-six air conditioned rooms. Parties to five hundred. Possibly. But not yet.

When she sees him, she seems to scream, looks at the other girl, moves back against the booth. He sits down beside her. He wants her now.

If something's been planned for forty years, or minutes, and various real factors are in error, or else have been overlooked, who is to blame. Very possibly she is. Sitting, waiting. She hadn't expected to see him again ever. Still won't. They lived together for eight years. But where, when. His hand, in the air, feels nothing. She will not look at him directly.

Begin over again. At the very beginning. Note the points of differentiation. See if your hands, fingers, occupy the same apparent space. Feel the bed immediately after it has been vacated. Look for hairs. Put food out and see if it is gone in the morning.

2 · 3 · 1

Three
To Be

I THINK TO look in all directions, hopefully. Is there no other *one* in the world, who can tell me? What do I want to know. What it's like, in there.

Views, of people. Densities, from this window, looking down, at wet flat streets, trees, truck parked says "American", on top, on side, "Household Storage Co." and is orange. Flat. No one.

Don't let despair tell you what to do. But who? Faces on wall, of people, a woman, in grey, hair pulled back into bun, has one hand located across the swell of her belly, the other, elbow apparently resting on other hand, is bent and extended upward, so that chin rests on fist. Looks out past the person looking in, to her right, thoughtful. Bureau back of her is blue, then a large mirror, above it, reflects her back. And back. And all the *Marsh Wheeling*, and *Home Line*, and *September* in the world won't make a bit of difference now. Only *things*.

In the drug store, to get an extension cord, about six, come upon magazine looked at shows tall woman nude with arms back of head (remember?), breasts flattened in the pull of the skin. Upward. Where does she live now? Girl walks past as the store is left behind, hood of coat flopping back on brownish-green material. In place. Her brown hair also.

Mother? Hearing voice ". . . that that's a natural position that one would take, but you shouldn't really ever bring it up, or force one to make that decision . . . if I could just arrange it, so it might be a year or so before I could go. . ."

"And yes, that was all right, but when the time came, it was always a little hard. You know that she was always left behind, and I said, everybody would welcome you. And she said, well, on account of my condition, she said it really wouldn't be possible. And that's true, because we went just one time, to Mary Hoisington's, who lived in West Palm Beach, you know, and we had a miserable trip, you know, up all night long. She said, you see, I couldn't really visit anybody because just the fact I wasn't in my own home and might cause trouble, it would upset me. It went on that way . . ."

I remember that time we were talking, in Florida, you said you and Aunt Bernice and the whole family came from Deer Island, Deer Isle, Maine?

"Yes, that was our embarkation point, for Massachusetts. Yes, that was Little Dear Isle, now called Stonington. My father was born in Belfast, and my mother, in Winterport. I was born in Bucksport, Bernice was born in Bangor, and of course you were born in Arlington . . . I was thinking about *Hap*, was born in Brighton. He was the only one born in Massachusetts, of the family. And well, let's see now. We lived in various places in Maine, and I first went to school in a place called Head Tide, and Bernice, I think – she was a little older than I – I think she first went to school in Bangor – I think. We moved a great deal. Dad was not very good at finding work . . . Please? Yes, he never went to sea during my life time. When Will and Ernie were older, and Archie – she had three older boys, much older than we, I think – she had three boys, and then three girls, and she lost one between Bernice and I, I think. And then Hap. No, I never knew my father going to school *(sea?)*, he was a painter, to my recollection. His father was a painter who painted the drop curtains and things for the Bangor Opera House, it was his father. Getting back to *his* father, my story is, my father's, he came from Bordeaux, and that's wine country, I guess, and his people were engaged in that sort of business. As I remember, I guess they were very comfortable and there was compulsory military service, you know, in France. So to escape military service he came to Canada."

I remember meeting a woman, when we were living in France, the neighbor we had across the street. . . "Uhuh." *Was, uh, she had been born, she was then actually, she was an extraordinary lady, she was then a hundred years old. . .* "Yes." *She had been born when Napoleon the Third was the, uh, part of the late Napoleonic regime. She was born when Stendhal, the writer, the novelist, was still alive. . .* "Oh. Hmm." *And, uh, and so that it's very possible that grandfather's father would be of the same. . .* "The same." *When they were conscripting people in France for those. . .*

"Yes, he was, he was a young man and he was about to be conscripted, and so he left, and he came to Canada. Well, in Canada, he met my grandmother, her name was Poulet, P-O-U-L-E-T, her name was Clothilde Something Poulet. . ."

I'm curious, then, how did grandmother meet. . . "When he came back and had been in Canada?" *No, how did my grandmother meet, ah, meet, ah. . .* "My father?" *Right. . .*

"Well. . . I don't know when, he was born in Belfast. She met him somewhere in Maine. I don't know where they met but they were both Maine people. You see, Dad was born in Maine, Belfast, his mother, my grandmother, had seven children, all of whom were boys – my father was the oldest, Uncle George, Aunt Minnie's husband, was the youngest. And she was left a widow, you remember he was the one who in the course of his work got a septic infection. In those days, you know, there was nothing to do about it, so he died as a very young man. Grandmother was in her early twenties, married at fifteen, I suppose they had children rather fast, and she couldn't have been more than twenty four or five, and he couldn't have been more than that either. You see, he was gone, and she was widowed with seven children. Well, in the meantime, they came down from Canada into northern Maine, I don't know the area, and they were Catholics, and they were having these evangelistic meetings, and I guess they both got interested in the Protestant religion, and they were converts, to the Protestant religion, so when he died, they were Protestants. And I think after his death his people in France, wanted her to come on and bring the children. But there was a condition, that she would go back to the Catholic faith because they were naturally strong Catholics, and that she didn't do, didn't want to, didn't want to go anyway, but that she didn't do. And so she stayed on. And they must have gone on relief or had help somehow . . . And I know that Dad went to work when he was twelve. He finished what schooling he had and went to work when he was twelve, and he, uh, he was a painter, I suppose like his father was before him, and really, as I remember, he had some talent."

•

SEEN HER FIRST in friend's place of business, which was like an improvisation, presently a laundromat, but then an automobile business, both repair and sale, on main street of that city, going from east to west. About mid-afternoon, or possibly later. Sad desultory relation with other woman otherwise, student, working on Keats, wasn't what was good for her at all, emotional chaos and fragile expression of sexual need, like they say.

This one cut into space, vivid edges, package of matches going off in the hand. So that the forward movement in mind had a forward wake, so to speak, sailing through to purpose in this case to pick up car she'd purchased, or was to, on time, her own. Very handsome medium height person, sharp, aptly intent on business at hand, marked excitement but no dependence, was in and out of there, with car, in veritable moments.

Legend already known, she was ex-wife of diplomat lived in far off Asia friend in common had said already distorted by his ambition and bubble. Scene with him, sing in nightclub, make some possible money, and get off that hook. No way.

Weeks go by. Friends who sold her the car, man and wife, the wife specifically, say she is good news, *clear* is the adjective, gets it together and don't lean on counter for nobody. Watch her zap off down the street, gears grinding a little, as she gets it in motion, feeling it out for the first time her own time.

A grey car. Way people look in those VW's, thinking of the relative size of heads and shoulders, to those windows, driving the highways now, passing through. Lazy late summer fall days in New Mexico, high haze of blue sky, drifts of air and time.

Packed down from Taos for job teaching kids French was truly unknown language. Voulay vouz un per der this or that. No one the wiser. One kid, my mother don't say it that way and *she* lived there for four years. Later. Trying to dodge. Keep the job needed to get off friends' backs and drink a little less, save money, move again when able. Crashed, pull it back together piece by piece. Move out of friends' house into home of one's own, half of pseudo-seeming adobe house back of charming owners' authentic scene, two old ladies with great roses, years in the trade of *being there* keeps all the Anglos jumping.

Restless, winter coming. Manage to make bed each morning as it's got out of, have dishes washed as the food from them is eaten. Fear the process is becoming entirely internal and no trace left it seems of any thing otherwise at all. Complete loop at times. In bed again even as it's being gotten out of. Scared. Write like, *glancing bird's eye saw the sky it flew in.* No sense much available, just time.

Buy lumbering used '50 Mercury an indeterminate or unremembered color now. That *uuuh-rah, uuuh-rah, uuuh-rah,* trying to start it, weaker and weaker. All consciousness surfaces to check it out, the battery? Sure, no good. But it keeps moving, thudding, under the hood. Push it onwards, back up north on weekends, sit with old friend Max to hear what's happening. Trader's outpost as the first flakes fall.

Life in the forgotten suburbs, haunts of the so-called mind. Other side of wall is employer, drunk, ulcerated stomach, homosexual, yet all notwithstanding one to whom gratitude is well due. Is *dogs* a common interest? He raises small schizzy Chihuahuas, beetle dogs, popping eyes. Hear him crash about the room, getting ready to forget it for another day. So far so good.

Seeing friends local, from time to time. Always go round to back entered by anonymous side drive, then swing left through weathered high board fence, into grizzled sand dead tree area with the rusting barbecue trip among the junk elsewise. Knock on door, face looks through peephole in blanketed unexpected window. Ok.

Inside it's a maintain situation, shelves stocked with canned goods to point of no return. Always night. Always windows with shades drawn and then blankets nailed over. Always sit in the kitchen. Play the phonograph, Max Roach, Clifford Brown, L. A. days miles away. Turn on, grey smiles, shoot up. Hours pass.

In the backyard dusty Porsche, sometimes a Spider, next to VW sedan. Water the dying trees.

Christmas break can't face the situation and decide to take a trip, south, crash on friends there for a few days. They have a kid. Move by means of third class buses from El Paso to Durango, then turn right over mountains, ghost forgotten lumber camps at twenty thousand feet turn blue in the dust as driver, Indian, shifts into neutral for the descent into Mazatlan. Stone out, stagger into cheap hotel with no doors for night's sleep, onto bus again in some time of day or night, at stop get off and go in for drink and in patio have vision of the redeemer at sight of older man's great dignity at back table under tree with traditional white clothes on, in the moonlight. Approach respectfully for wisdom. Find he has passed out.

In Guadalajara, Christmas eve, high-ceilinged one room, hotel, fly circling old light bulb hanging from traditional center on frayed cord. Read Beckett's *Malone Dies* and get its message entirely. Feel confused about purposes and other aspects of being. Very physically close to people, as on bus, but seemingly no viable response. Continuing on bus, this time with roped-up madman, very vocal, and some chickens and small pigs, to coast, land mellows out as bus gets closer, banana trees, mud, lots of stuff growing with big splayed dark green leaves. Air wettish and hot. Blue ocean, lagoon, palm huts, easy food with the friends.

Back, back, back. Got to keep at it. After the holidays, to work. Room seems even more barren. Try to tell whomever what's been experienced. No takers. Get lost one night, drunk, trying to cross over distance, mesa, between two major arteries of the city, north. Lie on back on sand looking up at stars. Then slowly, desperately, locate, by tracking lights' flare from cars far away. Car waits, broken down, somewhere back there, find it the next day and get a push.

Movies, bars. The Chez Paree, etc. Not much happening. Write letters in endlessly available time to people elsewhere. Make up patterns. Can't eat every night with the local sponsors. Got to get it on, and get on with it. Masturbate to tired memory. Jump as friend's wife pulls out cord of TV was watching, just can't believe it's happened. Time to go home.

Events' conjunction to return *her* at literally crucial moment anticipated in back brain flash outs but no real hope. Pipe

dreams merely. Max comes down to dig the action, it's dull *up
there* apparently. Hit local bars till time to close ends that and
he has idea to visit local belle sits in all-night radio station, the
psycho shift, spinning the top forty for the paranoids still at
large. Friend of a friend of a friend. Tag along to keep awake and
away from dream home as long as possible. Big glass windows of
building station is in, he knocks on door, gets response, it's her.

Memory now, somewhere through transformed cells and other
apparatus of body, of what *that close to her* was like. Up close.
In booth with turn-table, records, paraphernalia of the trade.
Physically very real. She jumps an edged clear energy, black,
white, scale very articulate. Speaks, as in playing tennis, with
precise comprehension and address. All this in the roughly two
and a half minute intervals permitted by the space of the records
playing. Almost knees to knees. True waves of physical turn on,
closer and closer to the pin point. Vibrating.

Tell Max *go get coffee by yourself*, taken by him as some kind of
dicing or deal. He leaves. Sit there listening, talking, fine explicit
edges. *Love* the sound of *her* voice.

Old wise man of thirty. Years of practice. Max returns, drink
the coffee, then send him off again can't even remember where
to. Was he always just waiting for an errand? Those sad days.

Some guys show up later, co-workers, the chicken shuffle
number, banties. One with little Tyrolean hat particularly *in
there*. Going to set up his friend with the broad. Or show him
how to.

Proud of her knife. Proud of the way she cuts him to pieces and
he picks up shreds of person, himself, and backs out backwards.
So that's the way you want to *play*. Left, it's quiet and a little
empty. Soon, time to close, first light, the cars outside.

Ask to go home with her. Simple complex question. No *wrong
idea* hopefully. Can't think of letting go after literal months
between moments, that sight. Follow back of VW, north 4th,
left on Griegos, her place a one storey flat-square house on left,
after a mile or so.

Fed from Mexican cheese stew she keeps on the stove. Fridge
has a turret on top where the works are. Ample kitchen, central

light fixture overhead. Talk at table, late and early at the same time.

Don't want to push, to rush it, don't want mistakes, misassumptions, don't want to play it any way but right. Not a number, time, not a way through to something. Feel physical presence all the time, as in first seeing her in car salesroom passage past had made a *literal* wave. Want to talk and talk.

To sleep but can't make the move. As to crash. Casual guest of the household. Alone at last. She makes pallet on floor under standing lamp, fades back to her bedroom. Lie down, feel boards underneath, raise up to shut off the light. Day in the windows. Body shaking like with fever. Got to get up in an hour. Howsoever, *home* at last.

•

IT'S THE FIRST day of fall, markedly cold last night, below freezing, and this morning a great clarity, colors intensified, and drift of fluffy large clouds on the horizon. Across the street the chestnuts have begun to drop. The kids are delighted.

"Richard once said, "Women are only interested in power," or maybe he said, "Women want to control," and at the time I objected."

Seasons one recognizes each time, yet cannot ever anticipate somehow – even spring an instant surprise. Thinking of a vortex or whirlpool, and one's a little lower, or higher, each time that circumference is gone round. Two states, then, the experience, and the place.

"Women have the power. They do seem to have lost the necessary way of enforcing it or telling men when they have it. I do mean it is a power over men. The girl who won't use the contaminated [by men] telephone is right. The power has to be enforced and advertised because it is not there all the time. Think of the bitch in heat. The girl has to tell when the moments have come when she doesn't mind using the telephone, or rather when she must. She is right in her body, which she unfortunately confuses with her head, when she won't use the telephone, and wrong or just stupid dense blind not to feel the need to need to. When those moments come."

Think of "raise the great hem of the extended/World that nothing can leave. . ." Be here. Thinking, that those phases of the moon are not the sun's shining merely. Romanticisms.

"The lost power is to be able to inform men of the approach of the moment, over a period of days' fucks, when the time is of preparation. What then happens is totally satisfying, totally distasteful, totally more than enough, totally everything has been lost and everything taken and given and some men don't like it. But there is no mystery to it. The man can't physically willfully get his cock out till the woman's body lets it go, and her mind can't tell her cunt when to do this. Her cunt may in any case start them fucking again after awhile. She needs a cock in it and the subject of clitoris is by this time quite irrelevant."

Blue sky's very blue. Nostalgia's intensified in the moment's feeling of *goodbye*. If I had to think of something, I would think of you. But I truly want to let go of that aspect of will, possibly no longer capable of its energies. I certainly never liked the way all else had to yield. Was that a consequence of having been taught so, or the pull of a specific condition – like the wetness of water, the heat of fire. Musing, amusing.

Footnote: *No question of M's conceiving, unless something of this sort happens – and can tell when conception takes place. Where pages have no feet.*

$1 \cdot 2 \cdot 3$

Four
More

DOOR CLOSED, move back in to singular point of person, and hands, or feet, appear as strangers somehow hanging at the ends of unexpectedly meaty sticks. In there, bubble of head joggles in a heavily dense, odorous air. Not pleasant, specifically. Sickening, unavoidable apparently, fixed in place.

Door closed, shaft back to one, eyes locked on absent space now no one, sounds absent, listening, murmur of constant refrigerator, heater, something still outside.

Door closed, move back to bed, light, wall. Body angular, protrusions of fat here and there, belly, ass, parts previous to knees, sides of chest. Exploded veins in ankles. Expanding grey growths on back of each hand. Patches of mottled hair occurring in random pattern, also increased splotches on what can be seen of chest and stomach, moles. Upper head sick, constricted ability in breathing, dry phlegm residuum in upper throat back of nose hole. Cough, hurt. Dry insistent headache. Tightness in flexing fingers, toes.

Door closed, move to bed, sit, light low. Focus slowly of image in mind, naked. Body parts, fenders, breasts. Old days in warm weather. Bring to mind images, cards in the deck, jack, queen, king, ace. Fours. Animal patterns and abandon again. Panorama of indistinct people, slow motion, slow coercions, changes. One in turn becoming another, one after another. Use words as place, find people.

Days in mind, nights in mind. Not knowing you, had found

you. Arms crossed on chest held breasts tight, head forward, crossing floor. Didn't know you, body white absolute, thoughts climbing up the faints walls, lights low. Recall low small bed with square box phonograph adjacent, music, fucking, abstract success of pleasures. Paradoxically alone.

Heads and hearts, diamonds, clubs. Insistent dealing, arrangements. Whose turn again. Powdered sugar, white body, lips bloating, crusted, tongue thick, extended, breasts blubbery, protuberant, hot, cunt mud suck of boots. Odors.

Friend in restaurant jerked off at dinner. Movie star calls for screen to be put around table, makes it with waiter. Mules solicited for intraterrestial pleasure, lowered remotely on compliant expectations.

Hand holds, remote exactions, pieces of meat. Picture blurred at the edges, blue light memories. Young man at window looking in at sleeping blue white maiden, uncovered, sprawls climbing in his head.

Days doors shut, locked, bolted, gone away. Thump of fist on wood, metal, pounding. Nights rain poured, streets empty, far up faint light, fourth floor window, try to call, can't hear it. Names lost, faces, moved away, gone for good, got to keep walking, find someone new, keep it going.

Remote control closed door policy automatic fact first noted some Sunday edition 1938 left in pile with other papers by cellar door out back to be hauled off later. No human intervention necessary. Door closed.

•

THINK OF THE good times . . . Jo's commodious nature, sprawled amply at base of tree trunk wet extensive night somewhere in Wales. Being young, of course, room for it all possibly. Girls then to women, subtle but inevitable transfer. 'Thirty years on this case . . .'

And you wanted to be *good*, however you defined it for yourself, *fitting*, appropriate to the occasion. It's about all that's left of that way of thinking of it, 'shape up . . .'

Built up resentments inevitably also, also not to be avoided.

Bitterness. Anger. Frustration of being stuck with it, part now of the history. 'Fucking isn't everything . . .' Slapped face.

So you got stuck with it too, trying to please the ladies – and why weren't they pleased. Histories of shifting discontent, maladjustments, *try again*.

You put them where you thought they were, in your head, you saw them as a partial contest, of yourself, by some circumstance you had no information of otherwise. You considered them, possibly, to be the best judges, etc.

Again and again, 'it isn't really the point, that I come, that isn't what fucking's about, for me . . .' You thought. But could never really accept it as true, and how would you tell the others, if you thought to, and sometimes you did, that they didn't. Didn't what? They said.

Stuck with wanting to win, to prove it. Given world as destructive quicksand you had to find some purchase in, point of – struggling to get to mythic elsewhere was here all the time. Just lie down for once, simple enough.

The jungle's casual, good lord! Eighteen yet. In the middle or edge of the *second* world war. You'd heard enough about the first from your uncle, who lived unhappily next door. He even rode a motorcycle, in capacity of dispatch rider, through bombs busting in air to immaculate completion of his appointed rounds. Touch of chlorine gas, attractive occasional cough – ah, hero . . .

Whereas you hung on in the chaos to funked-out drunks and weirdos, the *men* – got hauled one night from water barrel you were sharing with several floating up-ended dead cats you were too stoned to realize were there too. Bothering the world again. But laughing.

Confusion, compulsion to stay in that company, freaked horror, minimal, at mode of coercion Murphy uses to 'get girls for us', friend King from San Diego riding shotgun, you in back seat of truly careening jeep. Take the boss man of this charming village for a ride! Trees so huge, so steamy, they look like parboiled fingers coming out of the earth. 'This is Burma, buddy. I see you're back. . .'

Give the head man a drink, friend. Sits in unconfident dignity as jeep plows on and on, bullock tracks, miles from home now, gentle man in some consternation as to how return shall be accomplished. Explains that the kind of women you have in mind are not persons of the town. Another five miles, he's reconsidered. So three, for you three, are presented once you have given him back to his people. Three relaxed maidens, hopefully, yours the small sort of vigorous one, giggles. In jeep, as you drive back to base, her hands are busy about your proud young body, much to your thoughtful dismay, you think. In camp you separate from the friends, crawl into back of your ambulance with newly acquired companion, let back flap fall.

The world's smallest room. Or vice versa. You don't share a language, like they say. Few cultural pursuits in common. Just one of each. Amazing how factually and persistently it works out. Thuds, shudders, grunts of body's delight. She is *pleased*, she is *happy*, she is *laughing!* No joke. Later, leaving, you give her carton of cigarettes *in memoriam*. She breaks up!

Fumbling around world in subsequent years, head full of plans and patterns, you remember wistfully that clandestine affair. If you could just get it together again, of course no gun at the temple this time, no flooring the car just to prove the point. These are more thoughtful people presently your company. They tell you a lot about yourself that otherwise you would never have known.

Animal body with wired up head. Back tracking through maze of knotted kite strings. If you could just get it clear of that one branch up there, it might come down. Elsewise whiff of pleasing sweat stench, gutsy chuckles. Won't they let you out anymore to play?

Sadly they don't dig you anymore. Got to face up to that. You land too much on their heads, breaks the rhythm. Who wants to hear about the dead and dying or the terms of the new job, with their hands in yours, put it. Can't you shut up and let them go to sleep? How many have you got in there?

Fantasies of past present improvements possible. Remember the lady who used to change you into Dostoyevsky? You spent a lot of time with that one, flattered no doubt. But she finally switched authors.

So a few times you dance in the rain, telling the neighbors for days after what a great place you live in because you can be naked in your own backyard. Gee whiz. Next time you should have a party. You come so close, as it is.

Possibly it's over, hairy greying old person. Pull up a chair and get that load off. Your feet. Surely life had its moments in spite of you. And you saw the point – dazzling, clear, *open* – even as you missed it. Closer than most. And next time you'll know better.

When that head gives up, and that skin's finally gone, and the old bones have been kicked around, and it's moldy and natural and quiet, you'll have done well enough. There'll be another Jo's broad bottom, flat on that moist luxurious earth, and the humming generous darkness, you old tree, you. And for once you won't care she isn't listening.

•

As a kid in school, I can remember that one of the stories that got to me concerned the wife of a farmer with the usual large family. It seemed that they were getting along reasonably well, but there wasn't sense of any very large provision. I could fit that comfortably in mind because the town we lived in was small and the predominant activity was farming. I could recognize that some of my friends were poor, and some less so, some even comfortably off. But it was all a scale, so to speak, that kept an easily apparent relationship between its upper and lower limits. You didn't have to dream of the rich, you could see them daily, and what their being rich seemed to involve was having more of what others had also in some degree, that is, land, or tractors, hired help, new cars and all.

In any case, this woman had been patient with the fact that life was difficult, and there were many mouths to feed, clothes to mend, chores in that way one had to get to daily. Her husband was a thrifty, provident man, and the farm was doing well enough, but again, there was not much leeway that they could count on. The point was that he needed a new barn, which constituted a large expense, but he felt it would make the farm more productive and his stock really needed the extra room. I guess he was a dairy farmer, although I can't now recall that detail very clearly.

His wife, in the meantime, had felt that what they really needed even more, as a family, was a larger house. Her husband could hear that, but his argument was that first of all the productivity of the farm had to be respected, and a barn was the first thing required. So the barn begins to be built.

At this point, I remember there is almost a physical sense of its roominess. You can look up and see the great spread of the hay loft, and the heavy cross timbers and stanchions, a very solid sense of a four-square and well-fitted piece of work. Here's the place where the cows will go, and there are the stalls for the horses, and other rooms for machinery and harness, piping and faucets for water, and so on. There is also the sense of freshly cut and nailed wood, a strong clear smell, pleasantly sharp to the nose.

The woman watches it all going up, and you don't have the feeling that she is mad about it. What she really seems is patient, and thoughtful, and the kids intuitively know that she's got something in mind. The husband is in good spirits because the work is going well, and he's seeing something he'd long hoped for now becoming a real thing. At supper he talks of how his own work will now be simpler, and of how they can hope to get a few more cows, store more hay against the winter, and, generally, make the farm more profitable. His wife doesn't seem to sit there sullenly or anything, but again you know she has something up her sleeve.

So the day comes when the barn is just about done, and all the stock and machinery will be moved into it. Just a few odds and ends to attend to, and he'll have it together. That night, however, the woman alerts the children that she wants them all to be ready to help her with a plan she has in mind very early the next morning. I can't now remember what happens to occupy the husband during the crucial hours, possibly he goes to town for something, although that doesn't quite make sense. In any case, he's gone for awhile, and during that time, to make a long story short, the wife and the children move all of the household situation into the barn, shifting stalls into bedrooms, improvising a kitchen and place to eat, and so on. So that when he comes back, he finds them all comfortably and completely settled in. I think at that point he recognises just how much she wanted and even needed the new house, and he accepts what she's done in good spirits.

Possibly the story had a title that in some way signalled what was to happen, but that I can't now remember either. What most impressed me was that she had, first of all, acted against the husband's and/or father's wishes – revealing a disposition of her own. And then, somehow, that what she'd done is not only right, if that's the word for it, but also far more useful to the family's life than what he had, reasonably and logically, felt was the immediate need. Too, there was the underlying sense that women did somehow know about these things, and that men would always have to know that, and trust them, no matter how many barns got turned into houses in the process. It made me a little uneasy, even then, but there was curious, unexpected joy in the fact that she made it and that it worked out.

Somehow it all reminds me of an old friend in New Hampshire I haven't thought of for some time, Calvin Eastman, Uncle Cad as he was known. He lived with our neighbours, the Ainsworths, in a house through the woods about a quarter of a mile from ours. He had a small amount of money from a pension, and so contributed that to their modest provision as a family. He also helped with the kids, very much as the traditional grandfather, and in the family confusions and dismays he was often a wry and resourceful judge. He paid us frequent visits, possibly just to get out of the small house they all lived in, but he had also an interest in reading that the family did not share, and I remember he read through all the books of Faulkner that I had one winter, and we would talk about them very specifically. I respected him and liked him very much.

He told us that he'd grown up in the south of New Hampshire, close to the Massachusetts' line. Times had been hard, his real father had either died or gone off, and he was the eldest boy. The man who came to be his stepfather seems to have been particularly harsh. For example, Cad told us that when he had done something against the man's will, his punishment would be to run a certain distance, naked, through heavy snow, or else he was forced to stay outside until he agreed to the man's wishes. He loved his mother, he said, but he could never understand how this man had been acceptable to her, even acknowledging the fact that a man was possibly necessary to her, given the place and time of her life.

He was about twelve or so when he contrived to get himself hired out to a local farmer, for board and room and twelve dollars, for a year's employment. The farmer would also buy him shoes and other necessary clothing during the same period, and would arrange for him going to school. He liked the man and felt successful in what he had managed to arrange with him. He needed his stepfather's consent, being a minor, but he assumed it since the money involved was more than was usual in those days, and he felt the man would be pleased that Cad had worked it all out by himself. However, when he told him, it turned out that the stepfather had already sold him, for eight dollars, to another farmer, and had got the money in advance, and had spent it, so that there was no way out. Cad went to work and during the year his stepfather moved away with his mother, and he never heard from them again.

Hard to imagine either the man or the woman. Or he's possibly simple enough, shiftless, selfish, fearful the kid will be a problem. The woman may just have been without any resources left at all. Cad said he hated the man for years after, and that one time, finishing a job at a saw mill, he took the accumulated money and spent it trying to track them down. From time to time he'd locate some small town they had been in, but always years previous, and any possibility of catching up with them seemed pretty hopeless. Yet he kept on, for some time, just that he savored the sense of confronting the man, saying, I'm Calvin Eastman, and then letting him have it with an axe. It would be worth it, he felt, just to kill him once and for all.

But he finally gave it up, went on with his own life, slowly trusted things again, and then he met a woman and married. He was still pretty young, had little money, and what they did have they put into buying a small tract of land which they hoped to make into a farm. The first year was very hard, he had to do something to make money for the payment coming due on the property, and the only job he could find was in Boston, working for the railroad. He got up a cabin of sorts, to house them, had broken some ground for planting, had a horse and some chickens, yet it was pretty little for a beginning. He left his wife there, to take care of it, went down to Boston, found a cheap room, went to work and saved his money. A year later he went home, with the money for the payment in hand, and found, to his surprise, that not only had his wife kept the place together, but that she'd managed to break more ground, had got a cow, and had somehow made it all a true home for them. He spoke of it all with proud shy tears in his eyes. She was dead now, but she'd been the proverbial joy and measure of his life.

One time I'd driven him into town for something, and he asked me to take a certain road that went by the house in which they'd lived before her death. He'd thought for a while to stay on there, but it proved too lonely and his own age made it hard to keep up. Still he liked to see the old place, now and then, just to remember. The house itself was not very much, on a small knoll, with various shrubs and rose bushes planted about. He was pleased to see that they were still there, she had planted them. He said that flowers were the things most like her. Her name was Alice and they lived together about forty years.

3 · 1 · 2

Five
Enough

ALREADY LATE, as back here last night, in bed, have sudden in bones, bed-rock feeling, *no one*. No one at all. Sliding days, but ways not so easy, any more. Was it all some so-called social need, some company, warms the bed. Life, with its streaming, cell-dense, genetic tracers, elsewise no respecter of persons. Lone days now falling forward, pages blown from calendar like in old movie, down on all sad fours to make a stand. *Here I am*. So?

Company. In house scantily insulated, at woods' edge, being young couple of that moment, dreaming forward into time, the warmth, the kids, the Christmas morning it was ten above in the kitchen, with tiny son's chattering teeth and freezing hands, trying to open the hopeful presents. Later, she took muzzle of twenty-two, swinging it, hysterical in outrage, wanting to hurt. Long ago now walked off into another life. Another and another.

Somewhere reading, Picasso's mother would only remember that she was the age of that fact, when she looked in a mirror. What otherwise see? The *what did I look like*, backwards, turned into time as ripples of water, fractured persisting surface.

I guess I want one story, seemingly to be forever like they say, circular and containing and centered. "What was I like?" "You were beautiful" – once, truly, upon a time.

Never touched her, like they say, and can't now really remember just when we met, but it wasn't too long after having come to rest in New Mexico, exhausted and sans any sense of the next move. She was a classic tall tough blonde, from someplace like

Cleveland, but she'd come to New Mexico via Denver where she still had friends. Her daughter was a fey little kid, about four, whose blackness was literal enough, the father being, she said, a musician from someplace to the north. Sometime back in the east, while still in highschool, she'd moved off white men entirely, possibly identifying the black scene with her own ripped-off derelict homelife as a kid.

I felt very easy and at home with her, and hung out at her place when I couldn't face my own emptiness. I felt such screwed-up distinctions and senses of people, couldn't sort out the habits I had just by being raised in a pattern fixed with hierarchies and preferments. Her bigger-than-lifesize quality and indifference to such schemas were really good news. Going to the supermarket with her sometimes, some guy would start to come on to her blonde bomber aspect, and she'd draw up foursquare smack in front of them, and just wipe them out with an icy, relentless grey-hazel stare. Then she'd call her daughter over from wherever she was playing, and the kid's fact would really wipe them out in that play-pen of Anglo-greaser relationships. It was just too goddamn real.

Meantime I was in love with somebody else, as usual, or thought I was. There was little else to do, in a way, having recently been x'd in one marriage, then again in a subsequent relationship, and hence was victim to many doubts, como se dice. Pleasure therefore in carrying Laverne's groceries to her battered car, and taking place in same like true old buddy. I'd look back on the battlefield with considerable satisfaction and split the scene with as cool a tone as car's coughing would permit. She never looked back in any case.

Friends dug her, but she didn't ever talk much. When there were more than a couple of people around, she tended to do some physical job or other, or else just wander off, outside or into another room. The kind of jabber common to people lushing it up and wanting to make the world their oyster seemingly had little interest for her.

People at times rather generously figured I probably had a scene with her, and her stand-offishness was fact of that. But I was never more than buddy, and she also liked it that I played with her daughter and gave her some sort of meager *daddy* sense of

things. Still she didn't have much concern with that part
although she was bugged that the kid's actual father was so
busy laying low from possible non-support claims he couldn't
make any move, apparently, to spend some time with her. She
felt men, in that respect, were really a drag – weak, dumb,
pompous and self-concerned beyond belief. White men
especially she found really ridiculous. The very few she said
she'd ever made it with were worse than useless. The black ones
at least she could play with in her head.

There was some guy named Frank, or Larry, she considered
herself still involved with, some Indian from Denver that she'd
lived with for a time, until he split and she drifted south to Taos
where she thought the artsy-craftsy scene might give her some
dollars for the ceramics she did from time to time. These were
classically generalized African figurines, big lips and all. I used
to have a hard time putting them together with the lord of the
jungle numbers she otherwise seemed to be fantasizing. It was
hard to tell if they were some kind of trip she was running on
the white man's head, just to see how much he'd take before
screaming *no*. They sold, surprisingly enough, though how they
did in that place so stuffed with Big Chief's very own wampum
and Mexicali Rose's last stand, etc., is hard now to figure. Since
she wasn't selling them in person, that couldn't have been it.
Anyhow she always had a few dollars.

I was getting restless to go back to S.F., just to see what could
be salvaged of that disaster, which sadly had involved an older
man's wife. Laverne had heard all about it, without the least
interest, but the idea of going to San Francisco was markedly
more attractive since winter was coming on, work was scarce,
and the tourists long gone. Vague word also placed Frank quite
possibly in the area. So we figured to use her car, and I would
drive, and we would split whatever expenses. She could also
stop in Denver long enough to see if there was any money
accumulated from sale of her stuff she'd left with people there.
So we got our divers shit together, and into the car, and one
morning at a reasonable hour we headed out.
   The car's condition was familiar enough to us both, heavy
sort of thudding sound signalling somewhat hopeless state of
pistons, but I figured if I didn't push it much over fifty, kept it
loaded with oil, and avoided direct ascent of the Rockies by

going around them to the north through Fort Collins, we just might do it. We got to Denver fair enough, checked out her friends, and she got increasingly relaxed and talkative with the memories of having lived there. We drove past all her old haunts as she gave me the run-down on each one, and then we headed north again.

It was some time around the middle of the day, and we were about fifty miles south of Fort Collins, with the Rockies clear a few miles away on our left. Car was doing ok, not over-heating particularly, and then there was just a very loud thumping and momently it stopped dead. Lifting hood, I got a lot of smoke in my face and knew that was that. Laverne asked if I thought it could be fixed, and I told her I didn't. We hitch-hiked into Fort Collins, and got off at the first garage we came to, happily an old one, with straight owner, who went off to haul in the car while we crossed the street to a semi-derelict boarding house we managed to get use of a room in, for the afteroon and/or until the car situation was clarified. Lady was a little bemused by our group, but dug we were almost broke and had the kid to consider. So she gave us a break on the price and up we went.

No doubt on the stairs I must have had subliminal flash of old time possibility. *Get up them stairs*, like. Once in the room we dug there was one large bed only, and that was where the three of us would have to crash. It was a very hot afternoon, and the lady downstairs called up to offer us a pitcher of ice water, which I went down to get. When I came back up, Laverne had stripped down to bra and pants and was lying on one side of the bed with daughter tucked in alongside already asleep. She took a couple of glasses of the ice water, then stretched out again, saying something about waking her up when car scene was resolved. She also made explicit gesture to side of bed I could make use of. Then she was gone.

I took off my own clothes, leaving shorts on. Funny how real all those things seemed then, areas of body, what you put on them, what you didn't. Out the window it was just another dusty day in a nowhere western town. How did we ever end up there? Lying down, I could feel Laverne's long wet body sending out that crazy dear human *heat*. Already there was sound of her breathing, shifting to slower, deeper snoozing. I tried to let myself fall away from her, I was certainly tired enough to sleep too, but couldn't make it. Instead I raised up again and took a long, true look.

I never had, somehow. Something about someone's sleeping makes the body so real. So heart-breakingly human and tender. All that length of her, all so fragile despite its strength. But with the head sleeping, no eyes and tongue to keep world off her back, she was *lovely* with an intensity I hope some damn man or woman or thing did give her finally sense of. Not just an idiot compliment or scratch-me-back. I'm so tired of those arrange-ments, and anyhow she never would have even heard them. Then she shifted, probably sensing me watching, looked at me with those wild eyes, and said, *no funny stuff*. Then, a moment later, was gone again.

The old guy at the garage gave us $50 for the car and we got a bus to Cheyenne, and from there another to S.F., riding all night and much of the next day. When people looked at us funny, Laverne would just stare them down. Terrific. Once in the city we split up, getting together just once after, to go hear some music. Then I never saw her again, nor heard from her either, except for one card, about two years later, from Haiti no less, where she said they'd made her some kind of honorary princess and she was having a great time. I can dig it, like they say.

•

HER HAIR *is long and soft*
and dancing
wildly in the breeze of his
gentle whispers. They whisper
together the soft "I love you" 's
of the night. She sighs;
he heaves.
The air is gently still and smelling
    the sweetness of her body. Her eyes
reveal the deepness of her thought;
her breasts full with impatience;
        thighs wet
with the stickiness like honey
    sweet smooth delectable

She thinks of when her legs were closed;
when her breasts were covered to the neck;
her eyes looking to the ground when
   uninvited hands crept from seclusion.
She was a woman
  a virgin woman
    a white and blue woman virgin
She was a virgin long ago
when days were bright with golden sun. . .
She'd crawl
on hands and knees to the feet
  of master men – going no farther
      than the feet
and
not looking up or ahead but
down
as if pleading with Satan to forgive
      her
for being a
  woman.
     But yes
a woman she was
  is will be
and now the sky is bright with golden sun
and she
is flowing in silken white
  walking hand
in hand with one she loves
She looks –
  his eyes are a beautiful brown
her breasts are full;
  the honey is sweet and
she sees that he is ready
to taste the sweetness of the
      woman.

           –M.M.

•

THE WATER will not yield it. Shifting, wavering surfaces of itself.

The pool of memory. Days, weeks, months. Time is an echo. The only years are your own.

No wiseness, nothing at last to come to. *Hold me!* Shattered glass. Now hands turn physically to age, face falls to flaccid skin, etc. Unexpectedly cheerful, getting the joke at last.

So and so off to Kansas City, having gone previously to Alaska, *to get herself a man.* That old fool! Wasting time, wasting money.

But to have had nothing, so to speak. Or to have had it, and lost it. Why not? Seeing that beauty in its instant, met at the crossroads which are three. Young man, with trivia, which he loves as his life. His wife.

'Dear Robert:
              I mean dear Bob:
                               What a funny slip of the pen: because I am never called Bob and never called you Robert, but probably it means that I feel friendly to you.

"Teaching boys in the desert? I wonder what? How to behead rattlesnakes and snare mirages? We are turned school mistress and master with Betsy and John who no longer go to Spanish schools, and it's rather fun in a way – we get to know them better at least.

"Ann looked very well and confident when we met last just before she went – but how dismally shy those children of yours are! I hope they can face the great extrovert American child. They are sweet children. . ."

Sweet? Men and women, two having married. And time, and time again. It's under the ground one should look, dig a hole. First thing in the morning, while the earth's still damp, makes it easier.

Marries maiden for mother. *Mother.* Can't help now. Had to let go, had other things to do finally, had to die. Turned into herself, little girl, chuckling with relief she had the time at last.

But. Alone in *this* world? To have come for no reason, pushed out? You? *She who brings destruction.* The cat forever on the windowsill, outside, looking into that room. Sweep it and sweep it and sweep it and sweep it. Broom's worn with use and still the dirt and the dust and the mess and the scars and the wear and the tear.

Check notes, so to speak. *Anima.* The reflective partner. Distinction between eros and psyche – psyche without eros. Anima as relationship mediates between *personal* and *collective* – "non-human", "half-human creature".

"The most striking feature about the anima-type is that the maternal element is lacking. . ." Makes possible "purely human relationship" sans "nature" – "growth away from nature. . ." bending back and turning inwards: reflective. Brooding, uncertain.

Why *you* never talk to me, why I can never make anything out of *you*, why *you* are never there when I want *you*, why I look for *you* and never find *you*, why I can never understand *you*, why it all goes wrong. . .

Roars of laughter. Crones. A new arrival. As older to younger, that sweet youth.

As years ago, again, in love, and would not lead the men but rather contested them, turning to women for response. There is a ring round my head, that crushes it. I am fearful, seeing another man met randomly. My exercise is singularly committed to the goddess, whom I do not know and have heard but tales of, as others talked; I sat always at the outer edge of the circle, and could not hear much of what they said. Their laughter was strange to me, sometimes frightening. I felt the presence of the woods all around. There was a fire burning at the center of the clearing. The flames gave strange, dancing shadows to their bodies. These were the men.

Under the rocks, back of the trees, in the dampness of the moss, I felt the women. I was no leader. My feet grew into the ground, I could not fly.

Why must it be so? I watch the other men now going off to hunt, I see the women left, cooking, sewing, minding the children. I find myself on all fours, crouched as an animal. A child, still rooted there. The earth is all I have.

She would laugh, could she hear me, still muttering, *mothering* myself. And why, and why not. Either hand. Take your choice, in this timeless existence, and begin the world again.

So, having got that far, and got her away from previous man she was involved with, we drove all that day to her family's summer house in New Hampshire, where we got a fire going in the old cook stove and ate, and then settled down for the night in one of the upstairs bedrooms. Next morning we had visitors, all the old local boyfriends from her past. I got on ok with them, even went out on the lake fishing. I guess they were checking me out. One, however, was a sneaky son-of-a-bitch, and while the rest of them and myself were still drinking he apparently went upstairs where she'd now passed out and tried to make it with her. One of the gang with me was wise to what this other was doing, and put it to me to do something about it – if I could. So I went upstairs, got the other guy down, then started sharpening a knife I always carried, talking about street fights, etc., and bluffed him down and finally out of the house entirely. Then the rest left not long after, and I went back upstairs, hauled her down, and we had a talk. I couldn't figure her out at all.

So I got drunk, and ended way the hell and gone up a dirt road into the woods, in a car I'd managed to get in there, but couldn't now turn around and get out. I was staggering about, also shitting from all the beer we'd drunk, when this wild deer appears, doing those crazy leaps, just in front of me in the field. *Follow me!*

THE END

Air's way,
fire's home,
water's
won again.

Ma belle,

heart's
peace
passes
into earth.

THE END

CODA

La Cabeza

For Ramon Sender

THERE WAS a news item in the paper a few days ago about a man discovered in his backyard murdered, with the head cut completely from the body. He was a paraplegic who had won a substantial award from the court in some suit presumably having to do with his physical state. Otherwise no one seemed to know much about him at all. TV reports that night showed a usual small yard, the wrapped torso, stains of blood and a common butcher knife with which, apparently, the head had been taken off. Curiously, the woman spoke of the "severed body" in her report. Someone like a brother-in-law had found him.

Not long after there was further information that he had been dead before the actual dismemberment. It was some relief to know he had not been killed by the act. It would have been a terrifying prospect, at least thinking of it is very fearful. To get through the actual neck with something like a knife of that kind is very difficult. There is obvious bone but also a lot of muscle, cartilage, much that would hamper the action of the knife. Too, such a knife as it seems to have been is not often either sharp enough or hefty enough to allow a clean hack or slicing action. The blade would tend to bend or stick with whatever worked against it.

In the meantime the police say they have a suspect but who knows. They must feel people are sufficiently horrified by what happened to want to feel the police will take care of it. What would most reassure them is the actual arrest of the culprit himself. Presumably it is a man since one cannot think of a woman's having the strength sufficient to remove the head. The people know of the man not only because he has been killed but also because he did win that large amount of money. It must have been close to a million dollars. One doesn't even know yet what he had done or been doing with it. It seems he was still in the same house just like so many others.

There must be a lot of people thinking about it and trying to figure it out. If he was dead already, it is odd that whoever did it went to such labor to get the head off like that. Then it was some distance from the body on the grass. The body was sitting still in the chair. The police think he could even have died of natural causes, not been killed at all. Maybe someone was really mad at him and finding him there, got even, so to speak. Still what a job it must have been. There was a crudely drawn picture of a saint, like a saint, the police said, near the neck. It's like the story of some men in Mexico years ago coming home from work and arguing as to how much a certain movie star got. One said three thousand, another said no, much more than that, five thousand, and a third, the other one of the company, said no to both of them. No one could make that much money in one week.

They couldn't resolve it so their argument grew until at last they were really yelling at each other, there in the street, and suddenly one pulled a knife and stabbed the one who wouldn't believe the star could make as much as five thousand a week. She was a woman everyone knew at the time, like Marilyn Monroe. The man was dead in instants. The two left ran off. But when the police came they found them back again, now kneeling by their friend's body, praying for the rest of his soul. They were taken away without problem.

They used to say, in fact, there were many situations like that, not just family crimes but cases where once the thing was done, somehow it was finished and the person who had done it would go without protest. Or even more to the point, there was a small town way out in the country where these two friends were driving, and as they came into it, the one who was a lawyer was stopped by the town's policeman. The other, strange to this part of the country, listened closely to their conversation which at first had to do with local affairs, who had done what, and not knowing any of what they were talking about, it got expectably boring. Then the policeman asked how his case was going, meaning, it seemed, his own. Well enough, the lawyer said. I'll have some report on the appeal within the month. The policeman thanked him for the information and went off about his business, and the two friends drove on.

Later, in a cafe, the friend who'd been listening asked the lawyer about the case the policeman was involved with. The question, of course, had to do with how could a policeman be involved with a lawsuit and still be walking around with his gun on. The lawyer answered that it was much more than that. The man was a convicted murderer and the case was his appeal against the judgment he'd received. Why then make him a policeman in this small town? Because he's beyond appeal himself; he's waiting to be executed. So no one can bribe him or persuade him with such favors. If he doesn't win his case, then off comes his head and that's that.

Homage to Turgenev

However, I think I have said enough;
and when it comes down to it, all this is nothing but words.
TURGENEV, LETTER TO M. A. MILYUTINA

PARIS, 6 MARCH 1875

THE WANDERING STORY begins in the mid-1800s in Russia with a gathering of young men, nobles of some sort, at a comfortable club of their provision in a provincial town miles from the social authority of Moscow. One senses the author's habitual questioning of the entrenched habits of power or of what passes for it in such centers as Moscow, and there seems, tacitly, the thought that such concentrations are even more closed in upon themselves than are the smaller societies of those cities and towns more remote from such confident hubs. There is also the wondering disposition of an author on the edge of the late nineteenth century in Europe, hardly a moment of significant stability even if peculiarly hushed, muted by a curious containment of impulse, a waiting for a *je ne sais quoi* of whatever fact.

I had told the story any number of times, wondering how it had been so poised, first of all, how he'd thought of it. These reflective, reflexive moments would seem to constitute nine-tenths of all one ever gets to think of. How come it's that way, etc. Dazzling.

But on this evening, which memory does not now describe except that it feels cold, fragile, one of the company has discovered himself as destitute, having lost at cards or some similar adventure all of his land and money. Why he has come to the club at

all one may wonder, because he now becomes the butt of his
fellows, who face him with increasingly sneering contempt and
dismissal. All but one, that is, for the unfortunate bankrupt has
not merely a champion but a stalwart friend, who steps forward
to defend his vulnerable fellow and abruptly offers him the
resources of his own estate, proposing they leave the surly
company and go there at once.

*This time he had contrived to gather us in a usefully unfamiliar place,
the small town ambience of clustered nobility, or at least money. Yet one
in the company was broke and all the others picked on him mercilessly,
no doubt to break the tedium. I feel a press, almost as if one would have
to break a way through, just to get into the building.*

What is time in such worlds? Only the next moment, or else a
vast plain of almost undifferentiated accumulation, days, years,
centuries, until all moves with an oozing solidity. It is the place
of cause and effect but of such scale that an eyeblink resonates
for endless hours and effects such a plethora of absolutely
unthinkable results. "For want of a nail, a shoe was lost. . . ." Is it
truly just the mind which thinks of things? Nonetheless our story
continues.

*At this moment, then, another young man there, much as all, stands up
and abruptly defends the indigent person, the bankrupt, saying that he
now constitutes the erstwhile victim's support. What does he say exactly?
Something like, come home with me, your troubles are over.*

One thing settled, another soon begins. So the friend brought
home and given a securing place quickly became a part of that
backdrop for the hero's own drama, which, one soon learns, is a
complex but painfully vivid rapprochement with one of the
household's maids. This forthright person is an exceptionally
handsome young woman who has but lately come into service
and so feels no limiting habit of wary self-abasement. She is, in
that sense, naive, yet not in the least unintelligent. The young
man feels her equal to himself in every way, if not beyond him,
in fact, in the capability of her independent manner of thinking.

*But "there" there is no one one knows, no locating warmth or answer.
She speaks from quite elsewhere, this familiar and final friend. She is
not ever one or two or three. She does not divide by evens and odds. The*

*kaleidoscopic manifestations might just as well be the fingers of one's
hands. What does one feel?*

No doubt there was a time when all of us, perhaps, were poised
upon our own capabilities with just such a freshness, speaking
out of head and heart simultaneously, without caring, or thinking
to, how we might be heard. Then we were truly *lovely*, endearing,
utterly human in our unintentional pretensions of a world of
such openness. Even the clouds might speak clearly.

*Impatient with all conversions of love, indifferent to whatever they have
been implicated to mean, he will not see beyond the enclosing tunnels of
his own various intentions, his plans for immediate action. He surveys
his rested body as if it were a machine, well-oiled, well-designed, well-
equipped for the tasks he has in mind to give it.*

Now, however, complications occur which have not been
anticipated. There is much discussion with the ensconced friend,
who has become the ear for all such ruminations, but neither
can quite understand what has happened. The love was fierce,
direct and passionate. The two had met whenever able to, fell
directly upon each other as massive stones weighted by an irre-
vocable destiny. They both were seemingly in a state of profound
and absolute love.

*Trust the world to provide answers! That would be, in fact, its definition,
that it was finally, if uncomfortably, everywhere one was. No high roads
or low roads to lead elsewhere. He has followed the wrong career, so to
speak. He might have been a highly proficient opera star or a bowler,
taken in the washing or counted sheep. He looked only to the other for
resolutions. Where was he?*

Yet what had so attracted him to her — her remarkable clarity,
her determined integrity of feeling — now rebuffs him. She has
thought of all that living which her love for him must necessarily
preclude, all that might otherwise happen which she will never
know now, because of him. Many persons have experienced the
consternation of love's obstinate enclosure, yet few have turned
away because they would not accept such transforming delight
as sufficient. So she is humble in such questioning, but she knows
that a life simply with him must argue against the vast potential

she senses it might otherwise prove. She turns from him with great care and compassion, but leaves him nonetheless. Instantly all his life becomes a vapid emptiness.

It seems much like crying in a graveyard, for the loss of a loved one. The very magnitude of grief, the densities of despair, the profoundly grounded shock of absences noted so repetitively must mean that one is one of many, as was the one now gone also. I cannot believe you call me back just to tell me that, so often, so expectedly, with nothing ever added.

You must enter this moment as closely as possible in that no time will now separate you, no other place be so far from you, that this heartbreaking confusion, this insistently destructive turn of events, will not prove familiar. When one leaves, one leaves forever, be it by fact of death, or love's absence, or a simple mis-understanding one only recognizes as such too late. With love so lost, one's self is no more than a painful reflection, an abhorrent survival of that which no longer matters.

Pause for revelation, no doubt. "If she be not fair for me, what care I how fair she be. . . ." There are certainly other dispositions in this matter. Yet they are not ours particularly, not after such a long life with so many habits in it. Triangulation sometimes sounds at least like strangulation. What a sight to see she was. You too.

He himself wanders, almost; crazed, from tavern to tavern, village to village, and soon becomes a peculiar presence of that vast tapestry of small towns and rivers, those echoing hills and valleys, the tenacious, small presences of the local, the enduring provincial fabric of place. One day he comes upon a horse fair and watches, half distracted by his manic preoccupation, while an old horse dealer, a Jew, is set upon by irate yokels who think he has cheated them with his close dealing. Defensively the trader prepares for their attack, which is, unfortunately, soon coming. The frustrated crowd now batters against him with fists and sticks.

What happened to the friend? He grew old and died, literally. It is the simple reality of the story that engages one's attention. Coming into the house, one knows where things are. One follows after, concerned that our friend may do himself some real harm, now that the old companion he had rescued earlier has gone, and also the vivid love who had burned his heart so deeply. I like the looks of the old horse trader, come in from some other tale no doubt, a familiar figure in these times. He knows far more than he finds reason to speak of. Trust him.

A complex sense of fairness and the same unthinking ability to respond again prompt the young man to act. Instantly he has thrust himself forward, into the surly crowd's most volatile numbers, and here he pushes one, then another, calling upon them to stand back and stop their harassing of this innocent old man. Possibly it is his own fierceness now persuades them for they hesitate, confused by his presumptive and immediate contest of their collective judgment. They begin to slink off as he continues to shout at them, the trader at his side.

All the meannesses, the meagernesses, the pinched, small avoidances I had thought swept behind me here recollect. "Do I have perchance a debt to a man named. . . ." Most echoing the gray morning we awoke to find ourselves entangled against affection or loyalty, struck again by the world's defensive patterns. Do you remember how the boys feed bread with a fishhook in it to that old dog who waits each day for them as they pass on their way to and from school? I think of you across the long years still waiting, etc.

Expectably, the one he has rescued is grateful indeed. Who can say what his actual conduct has been? In this close world such an outsider must of necessity be suspect and that generality itself no doubt serves to prompt a behavior unlike the common. Shrewdly he considers his benefactor even as isolated as himself. He must sense that for this man there is never a rescuer, a respite from the singularity of his own life. Almost with foresight the trader thanks the younger man with the gift of one of his horses, a magnificent grey stallion, a dream of compact energies and astute breeding. It is his prophetic thanks for the wonder of their meeting, just in time.

There are no parallels, there are only repetitions. Off I ride on my cousin's half-horselike gray pony across the farmer's fields where the cows feed under the apple trees. They startle to see us come at them and begin themselves to run, some dragging tether ropes and chains. Vive le peuple! There are so many stories still to tell.

So a new chapter begins, so to speak, and our hero is utterly possessed by his miraculous steed. Noble visitors to that remote landscape, themselves out riding to dispel the tedium, confront an unexpected arc of speed across their prospect, a rush of thundering hooves which carry the concentrated owner past them in a blur. All attempts to make an attractive offer, thus to purchase this paragon of horseflesh, fail. It is adamantly not for sale. Days now pass in the rigorous routine of the horse's care and exercise. The obsessed owner all but lives in the stable except for those hours he spends in the saddle, pounding over the expansive wastes of valley and hill.

Yet when he had finally bought the stupid car and managed to get it back to his house without incident, he then tried to secure it within the far too small garage only to mistake controls in the process and so lumbered on through the rear end of the flimsy building out into the backyard where his vague companion stood hanging sheets, amazed. Together they watched an angel descend with gauzy wings and a severely sunburned forehead, impatient that their faith required its attendance when all else in the universe was so markedly more attractive. The dogs, meantime, sat on the sidewalk and laughed.

But then, one morning, he goes in usual fashion to attend his magnificent steed only to find it gone. Can a servant perhaps have taken it out to pasture? Surely there must be a comforting explanation. Slowly, despairingly, he recognizes that the horse has been stolen, which has for many days been even unthinkable, yet nonetheless present in the back of his mind because of the intense and persistent interest in acquiring the horse all had shown. He tears at his body and clothing in anger. He confronts with rage all his staff. How has the horse been so let loose, in care and now in fact? His despair becomes absolute as he ranges far and wide, asking questions of all he meets but never finding even a wisp of evidence as to the horse's whereabouts. He applies to the old trader for advice but the man can only say that he will put out the word and report such findings as come of it.

No one ever said it could work out. You pay your money and you take your choice. Would it be better never to step outside the house. There are people who live whole lifetimes together, people who have married one another, who then never speak, just write little notes like, "I am going to

*the doctor's," or "The upstairs toilet has backed up." The small voice
hardly of conscience says silently I love your big fat tits, your huge penis,
but then I have little say in these matters. Those are unseemly thoughts
at best. Think of the one that got away.*

If the end of things were as expected, then the story would
itself wander off, past the interval of initial friendship, the transforming of love then following to lead him elsewhere, the sudden
truncation of all he had thus come to look to, and then an old
and vulnerable horse trader and the gift of the wondrous horse,
then its loss, and thus the end. Many years have passed and that
friend first met in all his vulnerability has long since died. The
woman too may well be a grandmother. But this is quite another
tale and so one day the old trader comes to the man's house
with a horse, the very horse he had lost. By means of his extensive fellows in the trade, the gray horse had been recovered and
now all might be as before.

*Maybe Lazarus would have preferred to let things be, however grateful
he was reported as being. The stories of that book are finally buried
under the apparent doctrine, which is, as all such, there to make a point.
If it were the keys to the car, then welcome always their recovery. Yet if
blame were to follow? I have nothing more to say on the grounds that it
may tend to incriminate me. What sort of writer could that be.*

The routine again begins, the procedures of the stable, the
long rides over the adjoining estates and woods, and life returns
almost as if the blood came back into a body. Daily he feels himself blessed by a bounty no human can ever feel deserved. Then
a simple question comes, almost as if it too were a wanderer, a
traveler from some distant place prompted by no clarifying
intent more than that it had simply arrived. A neighbor, well-
meaning, one morning had asked him if he were finally certain
that this was the horse which had been stolen from him. Of
course, he said, how could it be otherwise? The horse so performed, the color of its coat was just the right shade of gray —
what could be suspected as different? But, said the man, it is a
well-known fact that a young gray will show a distinct change of
shading in that color after its yearly shedding. Is that so, he felt,
and how could it be that he had not thought of it, having thought
of everything else imaginable? So, the reasoning went, if this

horse is just that gray you remember, then it cannot be your horse since that gray would now be not the same. But it was, of course, his horse. Who should know better? No one, at last he had to realize. Now no one will ever know at all.

So I sat then reading. The story had been told through the words of another person, an Englishwoman whose son then came to live in the house of one of my wife's elder relatives, wherein both were eventually to die without the reminiscences one might well have hoped to have heard. Possibly the son's being a writer argued the necessity of some other thing to say, some requisite distance. Our author speaks of none of them. But the mother's sensitive listening had made his initiating words carry a formidable distance, like the faded country squire upon the great gray horse's back. I may wonder why she thought to break it into two halves, like a cookie, but what after all do I know of her, except that she too cares? The green trees grow more slowly. The river winds on.

LANNAN SELECTIONS

The Lannan Foundation, located in Santa Fe, New Mexico, is a family foundation whose funding focuses on special cultural projects and ideas which promote and protect cultural freedom, diversity, and creativity.

The literary aspect of Lannan's cultural program supports the creation and presentation of exceptional English-language literature and develops a wider audience for poetry, fiction, and nonfiction.

Since 1990, the Lannan Foundation has supported Dalkey Archive Press projects in a variety of ways, including monetary support for authors, audience development programs, and direct funding for the publication of the Press's books.

In the year 2000, the Lannan Selections Series was established to promote both organizations' commitment to the highest expressions of literary creativity. The Foundation supports the publication of this series of books each year, and works closely with the Press to ensure that these books will reach as many readers as possible and achieve a permanent place in literature. Authors whose works have been published as Lannan Selections include: Ishmael Reed, Stanley Elkin, Ann Quin, Nicholas Mosley, William Eastlake, and David Antin, among others.

SELECTED DALKEY ARCHIVE PAPERBACKS

FOR A FULL LIST OF PUBLICATIONS, VISIT:
www.dalkeyarchive.com

SELECTED DALKEY ARCHIVE PAPERBACKS

FOR A FULL LIST OF PUBLICATIONS, VISIT:
www.dalkeyarchive.com